GATHERED FOR THE JOURNEY

Gathered for the Journey

Moral Theology in Catholic Perspective

Edited by

David Matzko McCarthy & M. Therese Lysaught

WILLIAM B. EERDMANS PUBLISHING COMPANY

GRAND RAPIDS, MICHIGAN / CAMBRIDGE, U.K.

Published 2007 by
Wm. B. Eerdmans Publishing Co.
2140 Oak Industrial Drive N.E., Grand Rapids, Michigan 49505 /
P.O. Box 163, Cambridge CB3 9PU U.K.

Printed in the United States of America

12 11 10 09 08 07   7 6 5 4 3 2 1

Library of Congress Cataloging-in-Publication Data

Gathered for the journey : moral theology in Catholic perspective /
    edited by David Matzko McCarthy & M. Therese Lysaught.
        p.   cm.
    Includes bibliographical references.
    ISBN 978-0-8028-2595-7 (pbk.: alk. paper)
    1. Christian ethics — Catholic authors. 2. Catholic Church — Theology.
    I. McCarthy, David Matzko. II. Lysaught, M. Therese.

    BJ1249.G345 2007
    241′.042 — dc22

                                                        2007019920

www.eerdmans.com

Contents

Contributors

Frederick Christian Bauerschmidt is Associate Professor of Theology at Loyola College in Maryland and a Deacon of the Archdiocese of Baltimore. His publications include *Why the Mystics Matter Now* and *Holy Teaching: Introducing the "Summa Theologiae" of St. Thomas Aquinas*.

William T. Cavanaugh is Associate Professor in the Department of Theology at the University of St. Thomas in St. Paul, Minnesota. He is the author of *Theopolitical Imagination: Discovering the Liturgy as a Political Act in an Age of Global Consumerism* and *Torture and Eucharist: Theology, Politics, and the Body of Christ*.

David Cloutier is Assistant Professor of Theology at Mount St. Mary's University, in Emmitsburg, Maryland. His publications include "Moral Theology for Real People: Agency, Practical Reason, and the Task of the Moral Theologian," in *New Wine, New Wineskins: A Next Generation Reflects on Key Issues in Catholic Moral Theology* and a forthcoming textbook on sexual ethics from Saint Mary's Press.

Dana L. Dillon is on the theology faculty at Providence College in Providence, Rhode Island, where she teaches courses in moral theology and Catholic social thought. She is completing a study of the relationship between interior and exterior acts in Aquinas with a view to enhance current understandings of subjectivity and objectivity in human action.

James M. Donohue, C.R., is a Resurrectionist priest who teaches Christology, Sacraments, and Pastoral Ministry. His published articles and essays are in the areas of liturgy and ministry. He is the Chair of the Theology Department and the Director of Pastoral Education at Mount St. Mary's University in Emmitsburg, Maryland.

Kelly S. Johnson is an Assistant Professor in the Department of Religious Studies at the University of Dayton. Her first book, *The Fear of Beggars: Stewardship and Poverty in Christian Ethics* (Eerdmans, 2007), examines how anxieties about begging shape both classical economics and the modern ethics of Christian stewardship.

M. Therese Lysaught is an Associate Professor in the Department of Theology at Marquette University, where she teaches moral theology, specializing in health care and social ethics. In addition to *Gathered for the Journey,* she is co-editor of the forthcoming third edition of *On Moral Medicine: Theological Perspectives in Medical Ethics* (Eerdmans, 2008).

William C. Mattison III teaches moral theology at the Catholic University of America. He is the co-founder of a symposium for pre-tenure Catholic moral theologians called "New Wine, New Wineskins." He has edited *New Wine, New Wineskins: A Next Generation Reflects on Key Issues in Catholic Moral Theology,* and is also completing an introductory textbook on moral theology with Brazos Press.

David Matzko McCarthy is the Father James M. Forker Professor of Catholic Social Teaching at Mount St. Mary's University in Emmitsburg, Maryland. He is the author of *The Good Life: Genuine Christianity for the Middle Class.*

Michael R. Miller teaches philosophy at Mount St. Mary's University in Emmitsburg, Maryland, and his expertise is in medieval and Islamic thought. He is the editor of *Doing More with Life* (Baylor University Press), a volume exploring the meaning of vocation and a life of service.

Julie Hanlon Rubio is Associate Professor of Christian Ethics at Saint Louis University in St. Louis, Missouri. She is the author of *A Christian Theology of Marriage and Family* (Paulist, 2003).

Jeanne Heffernan Schindler teaches in the Department of Humanities and Augustinian Traditions at Villanova University and is an affiliate professor at the university's School of Law. She has published articles in the areas of Christian political thought, virtue ethics, democratic theory, and the philosophy of law, and she is the editor of a forthcoming book on Christianity and civil society.

Tobias Winright teaches moral theology and Catholic social teaching at Saint Louis University in St. Louis, Missouri. A former law enforcement officer, with experience in both corrections and policing, he has written articles pertaining to pacifism, just war, capital punishment, and policing.

The Course of Moral Thinking

Studying Moral Theology:
What Can a Book on Moral Theology Do?

This study of the Christian life is not unlike a book on golf. Many of us, including most of the contributors, do not play the sport. If we novices were to study a book on golf, we would very likely find the book to be uninteresting, confusing, and nearly meaningless. For the book to be more useful, we would need to at least watch and analyze the actions of others as they play (perhaps on television). Better, of course, would be to rent or borrow some clubs and actually play. The book on golf would give us terms and concepts to understand what is happening on a golf course, such as the purposes and goals of the game, the key elements of an exemplary swing, and the bad and good habits that hurt and help a player's progress. After reading the book we would be able to develop a perspective, a way to see what is going on, and thereby learn the game. Through this ongoing combination of study and practice, we might actually become better golfers. We might even come to love the game.

In this sense *Gathered for the Journey* is like a book on golf. If read in isolation from the actual practice of the Christian life, this book most likely will be uninteresting, nearly meaningless, and no doubt confusing. But if we (both authors and readers) use it to ask questions about the course of our lives, to try to live better as Christians, then this book may not only prove to be useful but may even change our lives! The book offers readers a way to name, and therefore to analyze, key elements of the moral life. It offers terms, concepts, principles, and analogies. Our hope is that *Gathered for the Journey*'s exercise in understanding and analysis will assist you in seeing the significance and adventure of day-to-day life, particularly the life and calling of a Christian.

While books on moral theology and golf might help one understand purposes, offer a way to recognize excellence, and even generate an interest in the game, there is no substitute for actually playing. Most people who learn to play golf do not read a book first. Long before they show interest in reading a book or article about the sport, they join with others who play, and they learn as they go. The sport is a practical and shared endeavor. So it is with the moral life. All of us, as we begin to be able to communicate and respond, are invited into a life with others and to share goals, purposes, habits, and ways of doing things. A book on the Christian life, like a book on golf, does not give us a start or the goal, but an opportunity to reflect on what life is about, to ask probing questions about what we do, and to see what we are doing in a new light.

Just as one will never become a golfer by simply reading a book, so also will one never become a "good" golfer overnight. One will never wake up one morning and — voila! — be an excellent golfer. Such excellence takes time. It is a matter of formation, a matter of engaging in the practices necessary to train one's body and one's sensibilities. Only by hitting bucket after bucket of balls does one's body begin to intuitively know how to stand and swing to avoid hitting the ball out of bounds or sailing it over the green. Only through such ongoing practice does one develop the ability to assess distances, slope, and the like, without having to arduously measure, and to know which club will work best for which shot. Such practice will not necessarily be fun or enjoyable; much of it will be boring and frustrating; we will fail or do poorly; but we will keep at it. Because if one stops practicing and playing, one loses one's skills; one becomes rusty.

So it is with the moral life. One will not become moral by reading a book, nor will one wake up one morning and — voila! — be a thoroughly moral person, or a Christian for that matter. Excellence in Christian moral living is a skill that can be acquired only over time, through ongoing practice (and with much grace). Not unlike the practices it takes to become a good golfer, the practices of the Christian life — praying, attending Mass, confessing, loving one's enemy, eating with the poor — shape our bodies to act and respond "intuitively" in particular sorts of ways. By engaging in such practice, we likewise become trained to see aspects of "the course" (the world) others might not see, to more "instinctively" render the judgments necessary to live life well.

Finally, this process of formation, of learning the game, is difficult — if not impossible — to do on one's own. If one is going to learn to play golf or engage in Christian living, one will almost certainly learn from someone who knows how to "play the game" well. We will "apprentice" ourselves to that person, watch how the person plays, listen to his or her advice, do what the person says, do what he or she does. And in doing so, over time, with practice, we will not only "learn how to play golf" or "learn about Christian ethics," we will also gain an identity — we will *become* "a golfer" or "a Christian."

The structure of *Gathered for the Journey* reflects this analogy. If we are right that this sort of study and reflection best and truly follows upon experience of playing the game, then this is where we must start. While most readers will not be familiar with the technical language of natural law or infused virtues found in the tradition of Catholic moral thought, we trust (and hope) that most readers will have some experience with the practical and shared endeavor of the Christian life. Therefore, we begin the book in part 1, entitled "Life Together: Moral Reasoning in Theological Context," by reflecting on those key sources of Christian living — liturgy, Scripture, Jesus, Trinity, church. We also take up questions of personal, social formation here.

Moreover, part 1 begins (chapter 1: "Love and Liturgy") and ends (chapter 4: "Pilgrim People") with the gathering of people to worship. This framework suggests the obvious, that God is the source of life, but it also indicates that Christians are called into community to worship and to follow the way of the God we call on in the name of Jesus Christ. M. Therese Lysaught, in chapter 1, and William Cavanaugh, in chapter 4, make clear that our relationship to God is ultimately not a simple transaction between an individual and God, but a role to play (our participation) in God's love for the world and our membership in a people God has gathered to be salt and light for the world (Matt. 5:13-14). In this vein David McCarthy's treatment of Jesus, Scripture, and ethics (in chapter 2) and Frederick Bauerschmidt's discussion of the Trinity (chapter 3) are concerned with who God is (what kind of God) and what it means to be a disciple. Worship, like many basic activities of life, is a practice that we may do often but reflect upon infrequently. The first chapter of part 1 on love and the liturgy and the chapters that follow intend to open up a way of thinking that helps the reader connect faith with day-to-day life.

Part 2, "Pilgrim's Progress: Virtues and the End of the Journey," moves to the more "technical" material — taking up topics and methods of analysis that are common in the tradition of Catholic moral theology and basic to the journey of discipleship. This second part offers terms and concepts that help us describe and examine our lives more deeply. It draws on key terms and categories of analysis offered by Catholic theology to understand not only the Christian life but also the aspirations and purposes of human life in general. The first chapter of this part, chapter 5, "Baptism, Mission, and Ministry," provides a natural connection with chapter 4 on the church and the whole of part 1. Here James Donohue sets our lives within the framework of our role and place as members of the body of Christ, and he does so by drawing on sources and themes of the first part (e.g., our baptism, living out Scripture, the gifts of the Spirit, and the mission of the church).

Chapters 6 through 9 treat questions of human life within a framework that draws directly from the discipline of Catholic moral theology. David Cloutier entitles chapter 6 "Human Fulfillment," and provides a philosophical analysis of the purposes of life under the Aristotelian heading of *eudaimonia*, or "happiness." Cloutier's chapter, like the three that follow, relies a great deal upon Thomas Aquinas (d. 1274) and the present-day work in the Thomist tradition. Cloutier expands Donohue's treatment of our "life-call" by asking questions about the purpose of life, personal identity, desire, and love. Chapter 7, by David McCarthy and Dana Dillon, follows the chapter on human fulfillment with an outline of natural law within Catholic thought. It deals with basic questions about human nature, and like the previous chapter, it sets this inquiry in the framework of human goods, purposes, and ends. It also discusses human reason, freedom, and the function of law and conscience in the moral life.

Chapter 8, by Michael Miller, takes up the puzzling issue of the relationship between God's plan for us and human freedom, as well as an account of God's grace as the animating gift of the Christian life. It treats these topics under the title "Freedom and Grace." The following chapter, "Moral Virtue, the Grace of God, and Discipleship," presents what are traditionally known as the cardinal or "hinge" moral virtues: prudence, justice, fortitude, and temperance. In this chapter William Mattison points us back to the beginning of part 2, where Donohue and Cloutier ask questions about human purposes and fulfillment. Mattison concludes with the time-honored proposal that God's grace brings the fulfillment of our natures.

It is a common criticism by our students that Christians do fine with Sunday but not so well living out their faith during the rest of the week. While this concern will be dealt with directly in chapter 1, it is also directly pertinent to part 3, "The Imitation of Christ: Issues along the Way." This third part of the book fleshes out what it means to "go forth" from Mass to be in service of the world. It deals with issues like labor practices, the global economy, consumerism, law and order, parenting, medical care, and our care for the earth. These issues are approached in a manner that makes con-

nections with the sources of the Christian life and the questions of formation that are prominent in part 1 and equally draws on the language of virtues, nature, and ends elaborated in part 2.

This interconnection between the three parts of the book, we believe, is
one of its key features. Ideally, readers will follow the format of the book as it
stands. If they do, we hope they will see that the structure of the book itself
makes an argument; it proposes a method for the study of moral theology
and the practice of Christian living. The chapters in parts 1 and 2 are meant
to build on each other, moving the reader step-by-step through the practice
of moral theology. The chapters in part 3, then, draw on this wealth of earlier
resources, combining them in different ways as tools for thinking about
Christian engagement in the world. Thus, we hope that as students work
through the chapters, they will refer back to material in previous chapters, in
a process that should mutually illuminate the different parts of the book.

The sequence of chapters within part 1 and part 2 has been organized
carefully. We do not recommend reading the chapters in these parts out of
order. At the same time, reading straight through is not the only way to approach this text. One might, alternatively, read chapters from part 3 side by
side with those from parts 1 and 2. For example, Julie Hanlon Rubio's essay
on parenting (chapter 12) describes a set of social practices in theological
terms and poses questions that draw upon questions of social formation
(chapter 1) and the call of discipleship (chapter 5). One might turn to
Cavanaugh's chapter on consumer culture (chapter 11) to see further implications of his chapter on the church (chapter 4). Likewise, Lysaught's chap-
ter on bioethics (chapter 14) complements "Love and Liturgy" (chapter 1),
especially where she puts moral formation in the context of Christian worship. Kelly Johnson's chapter, "Catholic Social Teaching" (chapter 10),
might be matched with McCarthy's chapter 2, "Jesus Christ, Scripture, and
Ethics," or might be read profitably between "Natural Law, Law, and Freedom" (chapter 7) and "Freedom and Grace" (chapter 8). Bauerschmidt's
chapter, "The Trinity" (chapter 3), might be paired with Jeanne Heffernan
Schindler's account of the sacramentality of creation (chapter 15). Finally,
one might read Tobias Winright's chapter on war and peace (chapter 13) in
relationship to the chapters on natural law and the cardinal virtues (chapters 7 and 9). This set of chapters offers an occasion to think through issues
of law and justice in terms of human fulfillment, natural law claims, and
virtue. In short, the topics of the chapters in parts 1 and 2 are extended in
the treatment of issues in the third part, and reading one chapter in relationship to another will be fruitful.

Our goal, then, is to bring the tools of description and analysis, from the Catholic tradition, to bear upon basic questions of life, and to show that these tools and resources come from a particular way of life — of Christian worship and discipleship. This point is highlighted in the title of the book: the starting point is being *gathered for a common journey*. Here we can return to our analogy of a book on golf. The perspective and resources for understanding and playing the game better depend on those who set their lives to the purposes of playing the game well — to living it. From living it come ways to think about it better, which then will bear on our performance.

Modern Moral Theories and Practical Reasoning

The subtitle of the book, *Moral Theology in Catholic Perspective*, indicates that our project is set within a particular place within a broad field of contemporary ethics — the discipline of Catholic theology. This distinction as Catholic does not mean that our efforts will be inaccessible to non-Catholics. For those unfamiliar with the Catholic tradition, we recommend what John Dunne calls a practice of "passing over and coming back."[1] According to this approach, "one takes stock of one's own standpoint, then 'passes over' through sympathetic understanding to the standpoint of another person, culture, or religion, searching for resonances or conflicts with one's own experience, then 'comes back' to one's own life with an enriched understanding."[2] In this way we intend our Catholic perspective to specify not an exclusive audience, but a way of life and common goals among Christians, especially Roman Catholics. We recognize that thinking about moral matters is a rational (objective) activity that involves thinking, not just "about," but also "within" a community of shared goods and purposes.[3]

In our day the task of thinking through practical, moral matters — thinking substantively and reasonably — requires that one speak within a community that extends (and does not merely repeat) an ongoing tradition of shared ways of acting and reflecting upon the purposes of life. By begin-

---

1. John S. Dunne, *The Way of All the Earth: Experiments in Truth and Religion* (New York: Macmillan, 1972), pp. ix, 53. Dunne's way of describing this approach was recommended to us by William Collinge, Knott Professor of Theology, Mount St. Mary's University.

2. The quotation is Collinge's encapsulation of Dunne's approach, January 30, 2006.

3. A concise development of this idea can be found in Nancey Murphy, "Using MacIntyre's Method in Christian Ethics," in *Virtues and Practices in the Christian Tradition*, ed. Nancey Murphy, Brad J. Kallenberg, and Mark Thiessen Nation (Harrisburg, Pa.: Trinity, 1997), pp. 30-34; also, see Murphy's *Theology in the Age of Scientific Reasoning* (Ithaca, N.Y.: Cornell University Press, 1990), pp. 51-87.

ning within a tradition of thought, our text on moral theology is situated in a context where good arguments can be made. By "good arguments" we mean what people usually imply when they are figuring out how to do the right thing. From day to day we think through our actions in terms of specific and wide-ranging purposes. We reason within a "life setting" where our purposes of life dwell within our actions and relationships. In other words, reasons for good decision making on the golf course are "embedded" in the game of golf. Through a consideration of reasons for doing things (the course and the game), we find good arguments.

For example, mothers and fathers approach questions of how to discipline their children in terms of the purposes of parenting, which develop from the very purposes of life. "What requires more stringent correction, spilling milk or ridiculing a sibling?" The answer may be obvious, but only because it entails deeper (and equally obvious) questions about what is important in life. We do not invent the purposes of parenting from thin air. We are part of a lineage of parenting. We think through issues of parenting in a "thick" environment of shared experiences and sets of arguments about reasonable and effective discipline. We are part of an ongoing conversation — with parenting books (which might give us a short history of parenting as well as advice), our own parents, our experiences as children, our brothers and sisters, our friends who are parents, and so on. Only within such a context — within this sort of "thick environment" — is one able to reason coherently, reasonably, and convincingly about how to raise children.

Thinking within the context of a community and its conceptions of life purposes, duties, roles, fulfillment, and happiness is vital to coherent and effective moral reasoning. A contemporary problem in the industrialized West is that a shared sense of social life has become "thin." One of the goals of *Gathered for the Journey* is to introduce the rich sources of the Christian tradition. We hope to offer a substantive context for thinking, a place to stand.

This "contextual" view of moral reasoning is not, however, shared by all ethicists. Popular theories of moral development often espouse a contrary idea, that we become mature in matters of moral decision making when we detach ourselves from the very fabric of social life through which we undergo our moral formation.[4] According to this view, only by detach-

4. In the field of psychology, this point is expressed by Lawrence Kohlberg, *The Philosophy of Moral Development* (San Francisco: Harper and Row, 1981); in political theory, by John Rawls, *A Theory of Justice* (Cambridge: Harvard University Press, Belknap Press, 1971); in sociology, by Robert Bellah et al., *Habits of the Heart: Individualism and Commitment in American Life,* updated ed. (Berkeley: University of California Press, 1996).

ment does a person become self-ruled.[5] Moral thinking likewise requires a kind of mental separation from who we are and how we have come to be who we are.[6] On a recent exam (at Mount St. Mary's University), a student proposed that to study morality we must first divorce ourselves from any vestige of our own morality. We would not say the same about golf or medicine or parenting or any other practical endeavor. Nevertheless, students are likely to encounter this presumption of separation if they begin a course in moral philosophy that attempts to offer a "neutral" point of view.[7]

By and large, modern moral theory ("modern" in a philosophical, not chronological, sense) has attempted to establish its rational basis by rejecting appeals to the purposes of life and our formation in community. By bracketing purposes and the specifics of a person's roles and duties in everyday life, the moral philosopher can enter a classroom and allow each individual student to determine his or her own good. At first glance, this approach seems inviting and quintessentially moral because no point of view is imposed. However, there are critical drawbacks to this disengaged approach, the most important being that it undermines the very nature of moral inquiry: to communicate a shared vision of life. We, the writers of *Gathered for the Journey,* do not intend to force our vision upon the reader, but we do hope to offer a compelling invitation to enter more deeply into a common life that is opened to us by God's revelation in Jesus Christ. While our approach will be developed in more detail below, at this juncture let us turn to the basic framework and options in modern moral theory.

As a guide to understanding popular approaches in moral theory we will use the textbook *Social and Personal Ethics,* by William H. Shaw (San Jose State University). It is one of the standard texts in moral philosophy; in 2004 it went into its fifth edition.[8] As Shaw attempts to represent the field in ethics, he begins his introduction on moral theories by discussing what he calls "the normative perspectives and rival ethical principles that are our

5. Charles Taylor, *Sources of the Self: The Making of the Modern Identity* (Cambridge: Harvard University Press, 1989), pp. 159-76.

6. Alasdair MacIntyre, *After Virtue,* 2nd ed. (Notre Dame, Ind.: University of Notre Dame Press, 1984), pp. 204-25.

7. Although this approach is often characterized as offering a "neutral" point of view, it clearly privileges certain substantive norms, such as autonomy, individuality, and so forth, as well as making substantive claims about the world — e.g., that there is no "common good" or good(s) that we all hold in common.

8. The edition cited here is William H. Shaw, *Social and Personal Ethics,* 4th ed. (Belmont, Calif.: Wadsworth/Thomson Learning, 2002).

heritage."[9] This distinctively modern heritage is represented by two dominant theories: utilitarianism, which has its roots in the writings of nineteenth-century philosophers Jeremy Bentham and John Stuart Mill, and nonconsequentialism or deontological ethics, which has its modern beginning in the philosophy of Immanuel Kant (1724-1804). The first thing to note about these theories is that they offer (and in a sense define) what is needed for a proposal about morality to be considered a viable modern theory. Each provides a single set of principles. According to Shaw, *"normative theories* propose some principle or principles for distinguishing right action from wrong actions."[10]

This definition of a normative theory seems obvious, but in a moment we will point out how *Gathered for the Journey* will diverge from this popular way of understanding the task of moral inquiry. At this point it is important to state the basic utilitarian and Kantian principles. Each theory states a rule that can be applied to an action. "Utilitarianism is the moral doctrine that we should always act to produce the greatest possible balance of good over bad for everyone affected by our actions," and "Kant's categorical imperative says that we should always act in such a way that we can will the maxim of our action to become universal law."[11] We should avoid simplifying these principles (as is done too often). With this caveat, let it suffice to say that the utilitarian doctrine determines the morality or immorality of an act according to a calculation of its consequences. In utilitarianism, acts in themselves are considered neutral. Kantianism, in contrast, sets out to determine the morality of the act-in-itself by reference, not to results or any prior conception of what is good, but to the rational will of the acting person. The rationality of the will is determined by a person's self-determination to act in accord with what is believed to be the moral law for all humanity.

These two theories are defined in opposition to one another, but at first glance, it seems that their central concerns need not conflict. A concern for the effects of one's actions need not exclude a concern for the goodness of the act-in-itself, and vice versa. Indeed, people generally keep both in view. We want to act in good ways that have a good effect. The problem with utilitarian and Kantian theories is that they are purported to be freestanding formulae like steps in a mathematical proof or lab experiment. By inserting data and processing it, the theories attempt to construct what is good. The two theories are alike in their attempt to be freestanding, but

9. Shaw, *Social and Personal Ethics*, p. 15.
10. Shaw, *Social and Personal Ethics*, p. 15.
11. Shaw, *Social and Personal Ethics*, pp. 19, 24.

they are completely opposed in the kind of reasoning that their formulae require. Utilitarianism includes a wide array of theories about what counts as important consequences, but its practitioners agree that morality hinges entirely on consequences. Kantianism and nonconsequentialism also represent a wide breadth of development, but all these theories exclude consequences and seek a way to judge the "willed-act-in-itself." Each theory intends to filter all of what is right and good through a single formula.[12]

Shaw's review of these theories includes what have become standard criticisms. Utilitarianism is based on the calculation of consequences that produce the greatest good. But the theory offers no way to determine what "good" is better than other "goods" or whose opinion of what is good counts most. Further, "in hard cases, we may be very uncertain about the likely results of the alternative courses of action open to us."[13] We will have trouble deciding whom and what to include in our calculation of good. Who counts or counts most in my considerations? My family, other families, a nation, a continent, the world, future generations, or the environment? Utilitarian reasoning falters on the difficulty of managing its own categories: calculation and consequences. This is a decisive criticism. If the very categories are used inconsistently, how can the theory claim to be rational?

While the criticisms just cited apply to the theory itself, Shaw also outlines important criticisms concerning what utilitarianism excludes. Because moral judgments hinge on consequences, utilitarianism may recommend actions that undermine basic moral intuitions and standards of justice, such as breaking promises or falsely accusing the innocent. Peter Singer, one of the world's most prominent utilitarians, has argued for the morality of killing handicapped infants if the parents will have a second infant who has the prospects for a happier life.[14] Singer's example of a handicap is an infant with hemophilia. Here we see a great flaw in utilitarianism, that its basic concepts of happy and good are very elusive. Does hemophilia by definition lessen the joy and goodness of a life? Can we even dare to calculate the right for a human being to exist?

Most utilitarians will not go as far as Singer, but their logic will be similar. Moral judgments hinge on a calculation of outcomes (however imprecise) rather than on our character, our roles and duties (such as parenting), and our basic moral inclinations. In the example from Singer,

12. See the critique of "ethical principle monism" offered by Charles R. Pinches, *Theology and Action: After Theory in Christian Ethics* (Grand Rapids: Eerdmans, 2002), pp. 34-58.

13. Shaw, *Social and Personal Ethics,* p. 21.

14. Peter Singer, *Practical Ethics,* 2nd ed. (Cambridge: Cambridge University Press, 1993), pp. 181-91.

we are supposed to calculate whether some future child of ours will have a happier life than our newborn infant. We are instructed to overlook questions about the purposes of shared life with our child, about the essential good of human life, and about our duties to care for the vulnerable. In Singer's view, we are obliged to resist the basic moral orientation of a parent toward his or her child.

On matters such as this, Kantian ethics is usually considered the best counter to utilitarianism. But like utilitarianism, it will attempt to avoid specific questions about one's role and duties in relationship to others and questions (both particular and general) about the purposes of life. Immanuel Kant argues that moral deliberations should bracket out concerns for both the effects and goals of our actions. He calls these effects and goals "hypothetical imperatives" or qualifications on what one ought to do. An example would be, "if you want be seen as an honest retailer, charge a fair price."[15] According to Kant, the moral "ought" should have no qualifications; it should stand as a "categorical imperative," simply, "charge a fair price." Kant's view seems to be obvious, that we should act well regardless of personal interests. We should charge a fair price regardless of the effect on our reputation.

However, there is a problem with the distinction between the "hypothetical" and the "categorical." Kant sets the purposes of an action over against the imperative to act. He assumes that all our purposes are self-serving, that one would want to be seen as an honest retailer only for self-interested or manipulative reasons. In the process, he excludes our most basic purposes for acting well. Kant rejects the moral worth of the following motivation, "If you want to live well, be good, and do right by others, charge a fair price."[16] Shaw indicates that Kantianism diminishes the moral worth of wanting to do the right thing. If I give money to famine relief because I am emotionally moved to do so, my actions (in Kant's view) have less moral worth than if I, in a disinterested way, simply judged that I should give money (even though I don't feel like it).[17] Like the utilitarians, Kantians set us apart from our basic moral inclinations. We are at odds with ourselves.

An additional criticism can be applied to both theories. Both utilitarianism and Kantianism have difficulty controlling or accounting for the basic elements that are inserted into the formula for moral deliberation.

15. Immanuel Kant, *Foundations of the Metaphysics of Morals,* trans. Lewis White Beck (New York: Macmillan, 1959), pp. 31-32.

16. David M. McCarthy, "Foot's Natural Goodness and the Good of Nature," *New Blackfriars* 83, no. 972 (March 2002): 112; Philippa Foot, "Morality as a System of Hypothetical Imperatives," *Philosophical Review* 81, no. 3 (July 1972): 305-16.

17. Shaw, *Social and Personal Ethics,* p. 27.

Utilitarianism, it has already been noted, has difficulty defining good consequences and happiness. Generally speaking, Kantians and other non-consequentialists resist judging actions by their consequences. Kantians reject the possibility of falsely accusing an innocent person regardless of the good results. Nevertheless, Shaw points out that Kant's categorical imperative could be used consistently to argue that all people ought not to lie "unless necessary to avoid the suffering of innocent people."[18]

Kantians are likely to resist this formulation; however, it fits the Kantian rules of moral reasoning. In the now classic example, we can, in a Kantian fashion, reason that all people should lie to Nazis who are seeking to root out and send Jews to concentration camps. "Lie to the Nazis regardless of the effects of your actions or your own interests in the matter." That rule can be universalized in the way Kant proposes. Here the Kantian framework appears inconsistent with Kantian intuitions: Can lying be recommended for all? Likewise, suicide is one of Kant's key examples in his *Foundation of the Metaphysics of Morals*.[19] Kant is convinced that "do not commit suicide" is a categorical imperative; yet the imperative to end one's life can be construed as a universal claim. Consider this argument: because a person is an "end" and never to be used as a "means" to an end, individuals ought to end their lives when they see fit. The categorical imperative also might demand more: "those who are a burden on others and are terminally ill ought to end their own lives." Here, Kant's method is used to propose the opposite of one of Kant's own key examples.

The overall point of these criticisms is that a utilitarian or Kantian decision-making theory can be used correctly and consistently and, at the same time, be used to justify contradictory conclusions. One Kantian can argue for suicide and another against it, and both can do so by using the theory consistently. This situation makes clear that the theories are not doing a good job accounting for what actually shapes moral judgments. Utilitarians will not necessarily agree among themselves on falsely accusing the innocent or euthanizing an infant with hemophilia or Down syndrome. Kantians do not agree with each other on how to deal with exceptions to the rule against lying or the rules that protect human dignity. Each theory attempts to provide rationally compelling conclusions, but they are unable to come to an agreement even with those who hold the same theory.

Whence such intractable disagreement? Those who have contributed to *Gathered for the Journey* recognize that something more fundamental is

18. Shaw, *Social and Personal Ethics*, p. 27.
19. Kant, *Foundations*, pp. 39-40.

operative: convictions about the purpose of life, human community, the place of suffering, the nature of true happiness — the very way we see issues, encounter suffering and tragedy, and understand the meaning of life's trials and find our place in a life well lived. By attending to these fundamental convictions, *Gathered for the Journey* does not set out to provide a typically modern theory as defined by William Shaw. It will not focus solely on the task of providing a "principle or principles for distinguishing right action from wrong actions."[20] Morality is not simply about a method or model of decision making. Rather, it is about how we tell the story of our lives, how we see continuity between how we live and the big picture of "how things are" and "what life is about."

This understanding of moral inquiry corresponds to the format of our volume. Every moral theory presupposes a view of social life.[21] Contemporary utilitarian and Kantian methods tend to presuppose an individualist world of competing interests. *Gathered for the Journey* sees the world differently. Part 1 — "Life Together: Moral Reasoning in Theological Context" — attends to questions about the order of our lives in relationship to God and God's relationship to the world. The chapters on worship, Scripture, Trinity, and the church give account of our role and place, as Christians, from which we are able to approach the moral life — to understand who we are, where we are, and the direction in life that we need to go.

Part 2 — "Pilgrim's Progress: Virtues and the Goal of the Journey" — moves from our place and orientation in the first part to an account of the moral life as a pathway. By framing life as a journey, this section orders the moral life according to the goal of human fulfillment and the virtues (the forms of action and excellences) that will guide us in seeking a happy life. There is a symmetry to part 2 (a going out and coming back), as it begins with our callings in the world and ends with the infused moral virtues, which give us the capacity to direct "this-worldly goods" to the good of God.

By attending to our common good, to basic claims about God, the world in relation to God, and the goods of human life, moral theology explores ways of living that form an environment for principles to be set into action and consistent moral judgments to be made. Essential to objective moral judgments is an understanding of one's role in a structure of life and of the purposes of life that give intelligibility to that role and structure. Recall the example used above pertaining to parenting and judgments about punishments and discipline. This model of moral judgment, set within a

20. Shaw, *Social and Personal Ethics,* p. 15.
21. MacIntyre, *After Virtue,* p. 36.

"thick" environment of duties, goods, and purposes, can be extended to a wide array of issues. This is done in part 3 — "The Imitation of Christ: Issues along the Way." Here the book takes up several practical matters — setting personal, economic, and political issues within the context of Christian formation and witness in the world. In doing so, it displays in rich detail the primary role that we will describe in *Gathered for the Journey* — the shared role of Christians in seeking to love God, follow Jesus, participate in God's love for the world, live as a people of forgiveness and hope, and in being gathered by God despite our faults and frailty as an embodiment of God's offer of hospitality to the world.

Hospitality, Pluralism, and Community

Hospitality is a mode of life for Christians amid a world of conflict and moral pluralism. By hospitality we mean sharing a way of life with others in such a way that God's offer of grace in Jesus Christ is visible and God's love for the world is acted out. This idea of hospitality includes witness to our faith and preaching the word, but it works on the presumption that words need a practical context, an environment where the meaning of words can be discovered in their use. In his primitive rule, for example, Saint Francis instructs his brothers to "preach by their deeds."[22] In this way faith is a practical endeavor. It does not require perfection or moral heroics to be effective. On the contrary, we Christians are first of all called to recognize our sins, to be open to God's hospitality, and to become part of God's offer of love to the world. We are called to seek the good for our neighbors, to love one another amid the basic struggles of life, to face up to our shortcomings, and to live in faith and hope that God's love is what we need, is what will fulfill our desires and give us a home.

To claim that Christians can enact or embody God's offer of hospitality to the world, or that there is any connection between our actions and God's actions, may seem a bit presumptuous. Yet such a claim has long been central to the tradition of Catholic moral reasoning. And not only have generations of Christians claimed this as possible, they have also believed it was the essence of human fulfillment and therefore of the moral endeavor. *Gathered for the Journey* is based on the faith that what fulfills human beings are our lives — our "end" — in Jesus Christ.

22. *Francis and Claire: The Complete Works,* trans. Regis J. Armstrong, O.F.M. Cap., and Ignatius C. Brady, O.F.M. (New York: Paulist, 1982), p. 122.

This claim requires a brief explanation. In moral theology the "end" of an action or our "end" as human beings is not simply how something concludes but rather a purpose and function. Human beings and our actions are defined, first of all and ultimately, by the end (purpose, function) for which we have been made or the end for which an action has been performed. To reach one's end, to achieve one's purpose or function, is to attain fulfillment in what is good. Such fulfillment defines happiness. To have an "end" implies that we have the capacity to act on and toward this purpose and experience of fulfillment — that it is within our own power. As created by God, we have a natural end: as creatures we have certain capacities for good, which can be fulfilled in this life. Essential to this human fulfillment is our capacity to act intelligently and freely. Moreover, when we do so and thereby attain the good that we desire, we become good in the process. We become the good that suits us as human beings.

The concept of "ends" gives a mental picture of a journey and helps us to see the walk of the moral life as a way of realizing — making real and actual — the potential that is ours to be. But just as one can reach one's destination, one can also fail to do so. For along with the capacity to act on what fulfills us comes, as well, the possibility of misdirection and the misuse of our potential. Moral theology focuses not only on our end as our fulfillment in what is good, but also on the barriers and roadblocks to our realization of the good — obstacles that frustrate our deepest desires for wholeness. Moral theology, in other words, focuses on sin. Along the line of the life-as-journey analogy, sin constitutes a devastating or debilitating ailment, a moral unsteadiness, a faulty sense of direction. When we human beings are in the grip of sin, it is very difficult, if not completely impossible, for us to acquire the virtues required to reach the goods of the journey. Our lives would appear to us to be aimless. Indeed, we may claim that life itself has no purpose, except what we as particular individuals can contrive for ourselves. According to the *The Pastoral Constitution on the Church in the Modern World (Gaudium et Spes)*, sin undermines our good. "[M]an finds that by himself he is incapable of battling evil successfully, so that everyone feels as though he is bound by chains. . . . For sin has diminished man, blocking his path to fulfillment."[23] Likewise, Saint Paul explains the puzzlement of sin, that "I do not do the good I want" and "I do what I do not want" (Rom. 7:19-20).

---

23. *The Pastoral Constitution on the Church in the Modern World (Gaudium et Spes)*, in *Catholic Social Thought: A Documentary Heritage*, ed. David J. O'Brien and Thomas A. Shannon (Maryknoll, N.Y.: Orbis, 1992), §13.

But we have faith that sin does not win the race. Rather, the biblical narrative of sin and salvation (the narrative of God's journey with humanity) tells the story of how God's grace in Jesus Christ overcomes our self-imposed disorder and gives us a second nature, a new capacity, a share in God's nature so that we might respond to God in love. This same grace restores our created human capacities for life in this world. God's love — or grace — frees us to act effectively toward our natural end and enables us to be fulfilled in God as our ultimate good. Grace restores the order of our natural capacities and gives a second nature, which elevates us to sharing life with God.

In this way, our natural end as human beings is linked to our supernatural end of communion with God, as our journey with God expands beyond our natural life and our attainment of natural goods. The Catholic tradition holds that, in principle, natural fulfillment can be attained without redemption in Jesus Christ. We find just and honorable nonbelievers among us. We are reminded of important truths by adherents of the world's religions. We celebrate exemplary lives from communities across the globe. Human beings have a created integrity, a suitability to the natural goods to which we are directed. Our created nature, precisely as created by God, has a good (which is undermined by sin) for which we are destined. We ought not to think about our natural activities (e.g., eating, raising children, studying physics) and our supernatural end (shared life with God) as merely a two-stage journey, as if our life with God as an end is more distant and futuristic than our attainment of "this-worldly goods." To do so risks losing sight of God's ever-active presence in the world.

Grace — God's ongoing presence in the world — is a gift that gives freedom to love and makes our efforts fruitful. This account of grace is encapsulated in the common Catholic aphorism "Grace perfects nature." It is not that grace is the supernatural "icing" on the natural "cake." It is not an add-on. Rather, to switch cooking metaphors, grace is the leaven that gives rise to the fulfillment of our human nature. Faith, hope, and love do not lift us out of this world, but give us the capacity to bring the ordinary things of life to a deep and abiding, day-to-day fulfillment. Most saints have lived ordinary lives, but they have been extraordinarily alive to the depths of the everyday.

Saints (those through whom God's love shines) are the necessary verification that, through the working of the Holy Spirit, we human beings can really share in God's life.[24] We can share the fullness of God's love in this

---

24. Patrick Sherry, *Spirit, Saints, and Immortality* (Albany: State University of New York Press, 1984).

life. Yet grace is the gift of really sharing life with God so that we will have to *participate* with God for grace to flourish within us. Grace will not magically make a person free to never sin again or magically become the best person he or she could possibly be. Instant or magical perfection would undermine the gift of joining with God. God's grace gives us the capacity to be truly good, but we all start in a different place, and some of us have a very long way to go.[25] Grace gives us the desire and capacity to move forward.

Thus, although natural and supernatural destinations are different, they are not separable paths in our walk-of-life. Just as we cannot divide ourselves in two, we cannot divide our relationship with God from our love of neighbor and our fulfillment as human beings. The faith that draws us nearer to God will draw us to our natural good. The gifts of grace will facilitate our acquisition of the virtues for our sojourn with family, friends, co-workers, and enemies. The good that is God opens us to acting well in relationship to this-worldly goods.

In face of our many limitations, we are restored by God's grace and given the form of a renewed self — in faith, hope, and love. In this way the grace that expands our capacity for life with God (the supernatural end) is the same grace that restores the purposes and facility of our this-worldly path.[26] Grace does not free us from doing what is good; faith does not make works unnecessary. The love of God in us cultivates justice in day-to-day life, as well as good judgment, perseverance in doing what is right, and solidarity with our neighbors.

If God's grace in Jesus Christ welcomes us into life with God, our way in the world is to become part of this hospitality. We believe that a Catholic theological approach to understanding human life has much to offer non-Catholic and non-Christian people and perspectives. We assume that our readers, like us, live in a context of moral pluralism, where we cannot assume agreement with our neighbors on some elemental convictions about the purposes and meaning of life. We can and do cooperate with very different people on civic matters like school bus safety, snow removal, making and selling good products, and so on. But usually we manage such cooperation by "keeping it shallow," by allowing a certain kind of social fragmentation to create a workable cease-fire on the tough issues. Pluralism can be defined as a situation where there are "conflicting comprehen-

---

25. See the chapter titled "Nice People or New Men," in C. S. Lewis, *Mere Christianity* (New York: HarperCollins, 2001), pp. 207-17.

26. Thomas Aquinas, *Summa Theologiae,* trans. Fathers of the English Dominican Province (New York: Benziger Brothers, 1948), I.II.109-114.

sive doctrines."[27] In such a context we Christians are called neither to impose our convictions by force nor to withdraw and be indifferent to matters of our common good as human beings.[28] We are called to live out God's hospitality and witness to our convictions, to bring depth and richness to common life of human societies.

We assume that *Gathered for the Journey* will be read in a context of "conflicting comprehensive doctrines," and it is our hope that we can explain how the sources of the Christian faith shed light on the issues of our time. To non-Catholic and non-Christian readers, we offer an invitation to become part of our conversation. To Catholics and Christians, we share a call to participate more fully in God's love for the world. We offer an additional invitation to Christian readers: to gather for the journey of the Christian life. Pluralism can be defined not only in terms of competing views of life but also in terms of a common view of life that facilitates intractable differences.[29] Our culture in the United States (and increasingly in Europe) is dominated by this second kind of pluralism, by an individualism that undermines common endeavors and encourages the notion that we flourish as individuals only in opposition to the contrasts of community and society.

Sociologist Robert Bellah and his team of researchers call individualism the "first language" of American life.[30] As a language, it shapes how we see the world and basic matters of human life like freedom, happiness, and fulfillment. In individualist terms, our lives with others are defined by a cost-benefit analysis of relationships, our market preferences, and a desire to express ourselves by creating differences and a great degree of separation from others.[31] The individual, in the context of individualism, is defined by his or her ability to be free from community. When explaining the loss of community in modern culture, Bellah and his collaborators refer to the results of Robert Wuthnow's study of the proliferation of support groups. For Wuthnow, the support group is emblematic of a wider trend. He concludes that the contemporary quest for community is being sought through groups that "make minimal demands on their members and are oriented primarily to the needs of individuals." This kind of community is

---

27. John Rawls, *Political Liberalism* (New York: Columbia University Press, 1993), p. 36; Phillip Montague, "Religious Reasons and Political Debate," *Social Theory and Practice* 30, no. 3 (July 2004): 339.

28. Benedict XVI, *Deus Caritas Est* (2006), §28.

29. Montague, "Religious Reasons," p. 339.

30. Bellah et al., *Habits of the Heart*, p. viii.

31. Bellah et al., *Habits of the Heart*, pp. 75-84.

constituted by "individuals who 'focus on themselves in the presence of others,' what we might call being alone together."[32]

Gathered for the Journey attempts to understand God's call for us to share our lives in an entirely different kind of way. For the purposes of this introduction, we have used the term "hospitality" and the idea of our call to be a people of hospitality, but we could have easily said that the task for us in this volume is to make the language of discipleship, the language of redemption in Jesus Christ, our first language. Individualism fails as a first language, according to Bellah and his fellow sociologists, because it cannot sufficiently account for how we live and the meaning and purposes of our lives. The authors of *Habits of the Heart* include many stories of people who fumble around with their individualistic words in trying to explain the meaning of their lives with others. While we may at times fumble with our terminology in *Gathered for the Journey,* we hope that the multiplicity of ways of expressing things (among the thirteen authors) points to the unfathomable mystery that is the God with whom we journey and to the ever-creative richness of the Christian life. In any case, we introduce the language of the Christian moral life, not as a language of separation and division, but as the terms through which we begin to see and respond to our unity in God and the common good of human life.

---

32. Robert Wuthnow, *Sharing the Journey: Support Groups and America's New Quest for Community* (New York: Free Press, 1994), p. 3, cited in Bellah et al., *Habits of the Heart,* p. xvii.

Life Together:
Moral Reasoning in Theological Context

All reasoning proceeds from a context. A person is able to do advanced thinking about the physical or biological elements of our world after being trained by the scientific community. An employee may spend her days making judgments about sophisticated computations as a member of the American Institute of Certified Public Accountants. A student may spend years following the guidance of doctors and nurses as he is initiated into the medical community. The common sense of a community is developed through common practices and methods of analysis. Life amid these and other communities (neighborhood, church, and family) will facilitate practical reasoning and ways of thinking about living well. Likewise, discernment about how to live as a Christian proceeds from the complex context that is the Christian life, the life of the church as it journeys through history. We might say, if one is going to "do" moral theology, one must begin with theology, with disciplined reflection on the Christian life and its ways of seeing and understanding the world — its practices, its texts, its ideas, its history, and its place in common life.

In part i we attempt to give the broad outlines of this context — worship, Scripture, doctrine, and the church. As we hope will become clear, these pieces all fit together. It is not possible to give an adequate account of one without talking about the others as well. For example, Scripture is shaped by and continues to shape the worship of the church, and the doctrine of the Trinity is not some abstruse mind-bender but is always in the background as the "grammar" for how Christians read Scripture and understand God's ever-present activity in the world. Moreover, the Christian life provides the "place" from which Christian moral reasoning proceeds. As far back as ancient Greece, it has been understood that an essential component of the moral life is a person's social formation. We are always formed to be particular kinds of people (whether Christian or not), and that formation, that identity, shapes how we act in the world. Part 1, then, points to the various ways that the Christian life forms us — our bodies, our vision (the very way we "see" the world), our knowledge, and our hearts.

M. Therese Lysaught begins in chapter 1 with a consideration of love and liturgy. Central to the book as a whole are claims about God's relation to the world. Christian convictions about God's relation to the world are not principally philosophical claims. They are not convictions that can be reached primarily through rational deduction. They are, rather, claims that have been revealed to us through God's journey with the people of Israel and, most fully, through the person and work of Jesus the Christ. Through this journey we come to know that God's relation to the world is primarily one of love. We come to realize that our response to this love (our lives in relation to this love) can be nothing other than worship. In chapter 1 Lysaught presents a unifying premise of the book, that liturgy is the paradigmatic context where God's relationship to the world is expressed (in Word and Eucharist) and where we, as a community and as persons, are formed — for here we learn to see and do nothing less than *participate in* God's love for the world. We hope the first chapter will enable readers to see their ordinary (even tedious) acts of worship in a new light.

One of the perennial quandaries for Christian ethics is how one "relates" Scripture and ethics. Chapter 2, "Jesus Christ, Scripture, and Ethics," is set within this methodological locus. Relocating Scripture firmly within its liturgical home, David McCarthy situates the connection between Scripture and ethics within the overarching narrative of salvation history, a narrative that begins with creation, takes a decisive turn in the call to Abraham, and culminates in Jesus' life. The chapter connects this story of salvation with moral reasoning, especially as the two are linked to theological convictions concerning the resurrection (atonement, reconciliation, and new life) and the church as the continuing history of Christ's body, of Christ's Spirit in the world. McCarthy argues for an "incarnational" model of reading Scripture, one that aims at forming us as "fit interpreters" of Scripture — those who can recognize their failures and be open to forgiveness, and in the process embody the gospel in our world.

The great danger of thinking about "embodiment" is that we may cast a reflection of ourselves upon the face of God, rather than vice versa. Chapter 3, "The Trinity," takes up the question of the nature and identity of God, whom we — as church and as Christians — are called to incarnate in the world. How might the "mysterious" doctrine of the Trinity shape the "being-in-the-world" of Christians? What difference does it make that week after week at Mass we pray the creed, in which we affirm that we believe in the Father, Son, and Holy Spirit? Frederick Bauerschmidt argues that the doctrine of the Trinity is relevant to the moral life by giving us a "grammar of imitation and reflection," a structure for thinking about and acting on our faith in God.

Part I closes with "Pilgrim People," a chapter on the church. William Cavanaugh draws his title from the *Dogmatic Constitution of the Church: Lumen Gentium* (Vatican II). The term identifies an ecclesiology that extends the treatment of salvation history that will be introduced in chapter 2. The church is called to a way (a pilgrimage) of embodying the gospel. The metaphor of a pilgrim people also reflects an image that will be continued in part 2 of the book ("Pilgrim's Progress: Virtues and the Goal of the Journey"). Like the previous chapters, this chapter on the church points to the relationship between theological claims and the church's context of practical reason. Critical for how Christians are called to think about the moral life is the conviction that Christians live and act, not solely or primarily as individuals, but as members of a body, Christ's body — with a shared mission and ministry. We have a role to play in nothing less than the cosmic drama of salvation, for the church is a gathered people charged with the task (to which we do not always live up) of making God's reconciliation visible in the world. It is to this adventure that God lovingly invites us, for it is a boundless love that is God's relationship with the world.

Love and Liturgy

M. Therese Lysaught

Love

Imagine, for a moment, that you are in love. Imagine with me the shape love takes in our lives.

What sorts of things do we do when we are in love? We want to see the person we love as much as possible. We want to talk to him or to just listen to him, hanging swooningly on every word. We find out everything we can about him — where he is from, the story of his life, what he likes and dislikes, the activities about which he is passionate. We want to do everything we can to please her — look our best, say the right things, be hip in whatever mode she is. Her friends become our friends. Sometimes this is easier to see in other people. They mention the name of their love interest every three sentences. They begin to rearrange their life, learning about things their beloved finds interesting, perhaps taking up an entirely new set of activities. Carnivores become vegetarian. We never see them because they are spending all their time with their darling and his or her friends.

These habits of love are not of course limited to romance. Think about the pop idols we have all "worshiped" — be it Bono or Britney, Michael Jordan or Dale Earnhardt — or sports teams we follow "fan"-atically. We buy everything that has their name on it and spend serious amounts of money to see them at a concert or sporting event. Some of us strive to look as much like them as possible, copying their hairstyles or fashion innovations; others of us deck ourselves out in clothes brandishing our team's name. What we wouldn't give to really get to know them, to become part of their world, their inner circle. We become friends with others who share our passion.

When we are in love, then, when we have a passion, it is obvious to everyone. It becomes a part of who we are. It becomes the center of our life. We take on an "identity." We yearn to be with the objects of our passion. We yearn to be like them. We give them our money (via the purchase of products or tickets or gifts). We spend as much time as we can with them. They shape our lives.

Equally, we could say that by looking at the shape of a person's life, we can tell who or what the person loves. By looking at how we spend our time and our money, by listening to the stories we tell and the language we use, by watching what identity we present in the world, one can tell a lot about who or what we love.

Who or what we love, then, plays a significant role in how we live, in how we act, in what we do. And what we do, how we practice our lives, our everyday activity — these are the questions of morality. Love, we could say, shapes the moral life. An exploration of Christian ethics or Catholic moral theology, then, requires first that we be clear on who or what we love.

To be a Christian is to be in love. It is to be in love with the God of Jesus Christ. Saint Augustine, in the fourth century, recognized that the Christian life is precisely about love. "Love God, and do as you please," counseled Augustine. Rather than opening the door to moral anarchy, Augustine was instead making a radical claim. If we truly love God, if God is truly the center of our lives in all the ways described above, what we desire — what "we please" — will be deeply transformed. If I love the Chicago Cubs, it will "please" me to do as many things as possible to satisfy that love. If I love another person, I would despair at the thought of "displeasing" her or him. If I truly love God, then it will please me to act in ways equally pleasing to God.

If we are Christians, then, if we love God, it should be obvious. In becoming a Christian, we have taken on a particular identity. The trinitarian God known through Jesus Christ becomes a part of who we are, the center of our lives. We yearn to be with God; we yearn, over the course of our lives, to become more and more like God.

To explore the Christian moral life, then, is to explore what it means to love God. Clearly, to love God is not necessarily easy. As even our brief meditation on love suggests, too many aspects of God's good creation compete for our love. From the time Genesis was written, Jews and Christians have recognized how easy it is to fall in love with and thus center our lives around some object that is both not God and not worthy of our adoration.

For this is what it comes down to: adoration — or better, worship.[1]

---

1. Not accidentally, the marriage rite in the Anglican *Book of Common Prayer* long included the words between the bride and groom: "with my body, I thee worship," indicating

Thus we might say: worship is the beginning of the Christian moral life. The first question, then, in our study of Christian ethics is: Who or what do we worship?[2]

"Love the Lord Your God with All Your Heart, with All Your Soul, and with All Your Mind . . ."

For many, worship — or the liturgy, or the Mass — seems an odd place to start in thinking about the Christian moral life, in thinking about Christian "ethics."[3] "Morality," it seems, is rather about obligations or rights or freedom or rules. Apart from the obligation incumbent upon Catholics to go to Mass and observe all those rubrics and rules for sitting, standing, and what to say when, worship seems about as far as one can get from Christian ethics.

Augustine, though, in the passage cited above, is riffing off the Great Commandment: "Hear, O Israel: the Lord our God, the Lord is one; you shall love the Lord your God with all your heart, and with all your soul, and with

---

not only the sacramental nature of marriage but also that even in the realm of human love we make a deep — even material — connection between love and worship.

2. Equally, one might claim that who or what we fear shapes our lives. It is not accidental that not infrequently in the Christian scriptures, God and God's agents counsel: "Be not afraid." Similarly, when those in Scripture stand in fear, God's word to them is "Peace be with you." Fear stands as the primary antithesis to love whose shape is peace, to the trinitarian kenotic love displayed throughout Scripture. And love stands as the antidote to fear, as 1 John 4:18 notes: "There is no fear in love, for perfect love casts out fear." Fear, as John continues, has to do with punishment; it is a sign of bondage, of enslavement; it is a characteristic of idolatry, that "imperfect" love that is misdirected at God's creatures. It is also for this reason that central to the Gospels, to the work of Christ in the world, is the call to overcome idolatry and to worship rightly — the call to worship God as the one true God, the God above all other gods. A first step in the practice of Christian ethics, then, is to consider both what we love and what we fear.

3. In this chapter I use the words "worship," "liturgy," "Mass," and "Eucharist" interchangeably, and I do so intentionally for a number of reasons. First, I wish to indicate that what is at stake here is not some automatic, robotic formative function of "the liturgy." One can certainly attend Mass and simply go through the motions without actually "worshiping." In this chapter, when I speak of "liturgy," I am presuming that those engaged in the liturgy are equally engaged in worship. Second, the context of this chapter is Catholic moral theology; thus, the paradigmatic liturgical worship is the eucharistic Mass. Certainly the Mass is not the only venue within which God can be worshiped. God can be found in all places, and personal prayer-lives are equally critical. Sacramental practices carry us from liturgy to liturgy. But theologically, for a number of reasons outlined below, it is the Eucharist that norms personal or other corporate forms of prayer outside of the Mass. This priority of the Eucharist is crucial to maintain.

all your mind, and with all your strength" (Mark 12:29-30). "This," Jesus said, "is the greatest and first commandment" (Matt. 22:37-38; see also Deut. 6:5).[4]

Why ought we to love the Lord? Because God loved us first and longs for our love. Augustine, in counseling Christians to "love God, and do as you please," is on good scriptural grounds. From Genesis through Hosea, through the Gospels and the Epistles and clear through to Revelation, one theme rings out resoundingly: God loves us, seeks us out, desires to be with us, waits for us to love in return. God loved us first, and, as banners at so many sporting events remind us, so loved us in fact that he gave his very self, his only Son.

And that Son invites us to become his friends. "No longer," Jesus tells his disciples, "do I call you servants, for the servant does not know what his master is doing; but I have called you friends *(philos)*" (John 15:15 RSV). Friendship — *philia* — in the Greco-Roman context was a much richer practice than it often is today. To be friends meant above all to have the same mind, the same outlook, the same view of reality. Moreover, friendship was one of three senses of love (along with *eros* and *agape*).

Thus, God longs for our love and invites us to become his friends. God does so, the Christian tradition holds, because to love God and be friends with God is the fulfillment of who we are, of what it means to be human. One of the giants of Catholic moral theology is the thirteenth-century master of theology, Saint Thomas Aquinas. For Aquinas, one of the most fundamental Christian claims is that God created us. But why would God do this, and what for? God, Aquinas maintains, created human beings for happiness, for flourishing, for a good, full, human life. But importantly this "happiness" has a very specific shape and content. For we, being who we are, and God being who God is, real, true, ultimate, complete human happiness consists in one thing: enjoying union with God. (Thomas calls this "the beatific vision.")

Augustine echoes this claim: "Lord, you made us for yourself, and our hearts find no peace until they rest in you."[5] God has made us for God's very self, to enjoy and celebrate in God's presence, to be nothing less than friends of God.[6] This, then, is our "end" — the purpose for which we were made. If we are to be in sync with reality, if we are to fulfill the deepest pos-

---

4. In light of some of the chapters to follow, it is worth noting that Mark's version of this Gospel story has Jesus preface the statement of the Great Commandment with the Shema.

5. Augustine, *Confessions,* translated and with an introduction by R. S. Pine-Coffin (London: Penguin Books, 1961), 1.1.

6. Thomas Aquinas, *Summa Theologiae* II-II.23.1.

sibilities of our selves, this is the goal toward which all of our life — in each moment and its wholeness — should move.

But for Christians this goal is not simply something that will be attained "in eternity," after death. Too often we act as if God waits somewhere outside of time and geography, that the Christian life is just about following certain rules to ensure that one "goes to heaven." But from the beginning, the church has recognized the much more awesome truth: Christ is risen. Christ — the incarnate Son of the living God, the God who broke into history in the greatest act of love — is here with us now. Therefore, Christ has made it possible for us to begin enjoying union with God, friendship with God, God's living presence, now. God has made us for God's very self and longs for us to rejoice in God's presence — now, today, tomorrow, and every day of our life. As Saint Catherine of Siena rejoiced: "All the way to Heaven is heaven, because He said 'I am the Way.'"

To be in God's presence and to rejoice in it is nothing other than . . . worship! Worship — or liturgy — is the beginning of the Christian moral life because here we fulfill in a paradigmatic way the Great Commandment. It is here, in the Scriptures and the Eucharist, that we meet again and again God's ultimate act of love for us — his laying down his life for his friends and his enemies. And what can we do but respond to the amazing gift of God's love by loving God in return, praising God with our whole heart, soul, mind, and body? What can we do but worship?

Liturgy Is Not . . .

Admittedly, one problem immediately presents itself. Truth be told, all too often Mass is boring, irrelevant, just plain aggravating . . . or worse![7] It's the same thing, week after week. People with no obvious skill lead the singing. We stand, we sit, we stand, we sit. The homilies exasperate congregants for different and contradictory reasons. Too many churchgoers are quite possibly the worst advertisements for Christianity there can be. And all too often we leave thinking, "I didn't get anything out of that."

Granted, too often liturgy is just badly done, and having people trained to do liturgy better would solve a myriad of problems. Yet, might the source of the problem lie elsewhere? Might it have something to do with how we have been trained to think about liturgy?

---

7. Elizabeth Newman provides a far better discussion of the problems that can plague worship than I offer here, in the second chapter of her book *Untamed Hospitality: Welcoming God and Other Strangers* (Grand Rapids: Brazos, 2007).

Let us return for a moment to our reflections on love and friendship. If we think about the time we spend with our friends, we have to admit: most of the time we spend together is rather ordinary, not particularly exciting, sometimes actually aggravating . . . or worse! We do the same mundane things over and over — "hang out," go to the mall, listen to music. Likewise with love — those whose romantic relationships have lasted beyond the rush of infatuation know that most of what goes on in a relationship becomes quite commonplace: candlelight dinners give way to leftovers; special dates give way to doing homework together or trips to Home Depot. A friend once told me that when she and her boyfriend lived three thousand miles apart, every time they got together was full of *passion,* but when they finally lived in the same city, were engaged, and got caught up in their studies, they realized that they had not passionately kissed for months!

As with friendship, so with the liturgy. Every Mass cannot be a "peak experience." In fact, the church has even designated a large portion of the year as "ordinary time." What matters is not that every single liturgy be absolutely transporting. Rather, as with friendship and love, what matters is the sum total of a life together. What matters is that we spend our life with God, knowing that many of the days will be ordinary, boring, aggravating (just think about those forty years that the people of Israel traveled with God in the desert). Equally, however, we trust that there will be moments of intimacy, joy, transcendence, delight.

If we continue to tease out the analogy between liturgy, friendship, and love, we might ask the question: What is the liturgy for? Too often people speak about the Mass as if it were about us. Liturgy, it is often remarked, has the job of "fueling us up spiritually for the week," and if it does not fulfill that purpose, it has failed. Others speak of it as an entitlement, as something we have a "right" to participate in.

But like friendship and love, liturgy is not primarily about us! Love is ecstatic — it draws us outside of ourselves. Like all aspects of the Christian life, liturgy is designed to point away from us, to point to God. Liturgy, like authentic love, is supremely an end-in-itself. We do not love another person or befriend others *in order to* obtain certain ends beyond the relationship itself (though certainly other ends, like shared interests, community, children, and so on, often follow). Similarly, we ought not understand liturgy as a "means to an end." We worship not *in order to* get something out of it.[8] We

8. Robert Taft, longtime professor of liturgy at the University of Notre Dame, was known to remark: "What you get out of liturgy is the inestimable privilege of giving glory to the Almighty God."

go to Mass simply to worship and love God. Aquinas, again, makes this point, noting that "we love God not for anything else, but for Himself."[9] God and our love for God that is worship of God are the ends for which we were made and must be ends in themselves.[10]

Clearly, of course, if we do this we cannot help but "get something out of it," for one cannot worship and remain unchanged. In worship we stand in the presence of God, we stand before grace. And as grace, it will not change us by force. God is persuasive, not coercive. As the story of Scripture shows, grace waits with, at times, unbearable patience. Our task is to be open to it, like the seed that does not get choked out because it lands on rock, soil, or among weeds. Our task is to be ready for it.

Are we? Do we come to Mass excited to rendezvous with our friend and beloved? Do we look forward to Sunday, counting the days until we can "meet" our beloved? Do we, in fact, think of being Christian as being in a relationship, necessarily sustained by faithfulness between meetings? Most of us know what it is like to be in a relationship with someone who does not call us all week. What would it be like to get together, knowing that during the week our beloved or even our friends had been acting in ways inconsiderate of us, betraying our affection, disregarding those things that are important to us? Could the relationship last?

Analogously we can ask: Have we, as Christians, spent the week in a way that builds up our friendship with God, this relationship of love? Or do we too often betray the relationship — fail to acknowledge that we are even *in* this relationship, disregarding those things that are important to God? If you are like me, the answer here is, too often, "yes."

This is why Catholics used to faithfully make their confession before going to Mass, and why the Mass still opens with an act of confession. Certainly confession as practiced prior to the Second Vatican Council presented its own set of issues. But the practice captures a fundamental question: Who do *we* have to *be* to participate in liturgy?[11] Do we live our lives

---

9. Aquinas, *Summa Theologiae* II-II.27.

10. Or to state it slightly differently, liturgy is not functional, utilitarian, a means toward some other end. The purpose of liturgy is not "to make us moral."

11. That Catholics used to practice the sacrament of confession much more faithfully than we do now points toward the fundamental claim of this chapter, that worship is the beginning of the Christian moral life. For as is widely recognized, the sacrament of confession was also the primary context of the theological discipline of "Catholic moral theology" — a theological discipline that emerged after the Council of Trent and maintained a very particular shape up until the Second Vatican Council. Catholic moral theology as a discipline was integrated within an infrastructure of practices that presumed the centrality

during the week in such a way that we come prepared to rejoice in God's presence on Sunday, celebrating who God is and the amazing things God has done? Do we come to Mass prepared to meet our beloved? It is not that God will reject us if we are somehow not prepared (although that parable about the wrongly dressed wedding guest does always give one pause). Rather, if we have not prepared our lives, we will not be able to accept the invitation, hospitality, and love God offers when we meet. If we come with hardened hearts, will we not more likely refuse God's grace? The question when we come to worship is: Are we ready to respond to God's love?

"All the Way to Heaven Is Heaven"

In the early church, Christians gathered to celebrate *agape* meals, or "love" feasts. For they understood that when "two or three gathered," Christ had promised to be present, and thus where two or three or more had gathered, they were in the presence of God's love. And it is here, in our gathering, that Christians make clear who it is that loves us and who is the object of our passion.

For one thing, going to Mass makes it obvious. To worship is to make a public statement. It is a public act. In the New Testament the word for the church, for the gathering of Christians for their distinctive time of worship, is *ekklesia*. The word comes from a root that means "called out" and referred originally to an assembly of citizens who were called out of the affairs of their everyday work and lives because they had a particular identity or status. And so it is with liturgy. Here Christians are "called out" of the world. We assemble together as "church," as the body of Christ, as citizens of the kingdom of God.[12]

When we worship, then, we state plainly through our actions that we are Christians, those claimed by God's love. Because God so loves us, God becomes the one with whom we long to spend time, the one we yearn to be

---

of eucharistic liturgy for the Christian life. In many ways this connection between Catholic moral theology and the liturgy was lost after the Second Vatican Council. For our purposes, the practices of confession/reconciliation highlight two additional points that must be made in the context of this chapter and book — that the church is not a group of perfect people, and that the Mass does not magically make people better Christians.

12. Importantly, Christians do not worship alone — the liturgy is a gathering of the people of God, of the body of Christ. As much as people wish to construe faith and religion as "private," worship is a public activity. Whether done with "two or three" or a typical Catholic Mass of many hundreds, worship is a "public" act.

with. The traditional day that Christians gather for worship is an extension of the Jewish practice of the Sabbath. The Sabbath, as Genesis notes, is the day of God's rest, a day when all of humanity — and indeed, all living creatures — are called to rest as well, to simply spend time celebrating God and one another. Rabbi Abraham Heschel, in his splendid reflection *The Sabbath*, notes that the first thing God names as holy in the creation of the world is the Sabbath, the seventh day.[13] This day, and not some sacred place, is the "space" where God and (later) God's holy people dwell together. And so it must be, for love is practiced not primarily through shared spaces but through spending time together.

This is why Josef Pieper, a twentieth-century Catholic philosopher, attempts to invert how we too often think about Sunday. Too often we see it as a day of rest from work, from our lives, a vacation, a respite that allows us to rejuvenate for the toil of our lives. Pieper, however, sees it the other way around. It is not, he maintains, that Sunday exists for the sake of the week, as a means to an end. To see it this way is to get it backward. Rather, echoing Aquinas, Pieper reminds us that Sunday, the Sabbath, is our proper end, that for which we were made. All else — our work, our weeks, our lives — should move us toward that end.[14] As Jesus rebuked the Pharisees: "The sabbath was made for humankind, and not humankind for the sabbath" (Mark 2:27).

While Christian worship is rooted in Jewish Sabbath practices, the early church moved its Sabbath from Friday to Sunday, to the "eighth day." Christians dwell with God no longer in the last day of creation but in the first day of the new creation, in the eschatological time of the resurrection. As the Orthodox theologian Alexander Schmemann claims, the liturgy is a moment where the eschaton breaks into time. The Orthodox refer to the Mass as "The Divine Liturgy," for they maintain that in the liturgy we are, already, at the gates of heaven! In Mass we stand together with the saints in God's kingdom "already." Here we learn to see not only that God created the world and all that is in it. We learn to see that God has acted to redeem that same creation, to make all of creation new.

Thus, one of the things that happens when we spend time with God is that we begin to see the world, to see "reality," in a new way. We begin to see that we live in a world not of scarce resources but of abundant gifts. We begin to see that justice means not strictly "to each person her due" but rather

13. Abraham Heschel, *The Sabbath* (New York: Farrar, Straus and Giroux, 2005), p. 9.

14. Josef Pieper, *Leisure: The Basis of Culture,* introduction by Roger Scruton, new translation by Gerald Malsbary (South Bend, Ind.: St. Augustine's Press, 1998), pp. 34, 54.

a "preferential option for the poor." We begin to see that the victorious story of the world is not conflict and violence, but that true power is manifest through peace and reconciliation. And so on. And we learn this in a number of ways.

First, in liturgy we listen to God's stories. We hang on God's every word. We enter into the world of the Scriptures, the world of God's Word, where we learn the story of God's constant love for God's people, and how that love opens up to the entire world through the mission to the Gentiles and the redemption of all creation. We learn what it means to be God, what it means to love, to be merciful, kind, faithful, and so on.

To really learn and understand these stories takes time. We are deeply shaped by a world of stories that are very different — stories of "nature red in tooth and claw," the survival of the fittest, life as a zero-sum game, an eye for an eye. The Christian tradition, however, maintains that God's story, that found in Scripture, is the truest version of reality, no matter how different the world might look day to day. People often say ethics need to be "realistic" — that Christians have to navigate in the "real" world and therefore make all sorts of compromises. But Christians proclaim that the world described in Scripture *is* the "real" world — that through Jesus' incarnation, cross, and resurrection God initiated a new reality. As Saint Paul says, "If any one is in Christ, he is a new creation" (2 Cor. 5:17 RSV). By hearing this story in worship, we come to see differently — to see all the world differently, to see the world truthfully.

The stories that shape us are critical for ethics, for we can only act and live in a world that we can see. If I believe the story of "an eye for an eye," that will shape how I act. Until I hear the story of "love one's enemies," that cannot become an option for how I live.[15] Moreover, it cannot become an option for how I live unless I practice it. Liturgy is one place where we practice how to do these things, where we learn what it means to live within this new creation. For clearly, God's new creation operates according to different rules than "business as usual." In worship we enter a space where by learning to see the world in a new way we are trained to act in a new way. Here we learn to "meet people, acknowledge our faults and failures, celebrate, thank, read, speak with authority, reflect on wisdom,

---

15. Returning to the practice of the Sabbath — that day when God rested from the work of creating and rejoiced in the goodness of creation — Rabbi Heschel reminds us that the Sabbath is equally a way of learning to see. In it we learn to see ourselves differently, as human beings, not as "beasts of burden," that we were not created to be tethered to work, to be slaves, but rather were created by God to be free. Pieper makes this same point.

name truth, register need, bring about reconciliation, share food and our goods, week in and week out."[16]

As we learn new ways of acting, these practices of liturgy help to train us out of the habits of our dominant culture. Take, for example, the practice of silence. In our culture silence is hard to find. Silence is uncomfortable, "dead air." Silence is so foreign to our everyday lives that it can be used as an effective advertising tool — "silent" commercials function by playing off the noise that surrounds us.[17] But silence in Christian and liturgical contexts has different shapes, different purposes. By practicing silence regularly — as a community of people being silent together — those who worship can come to appreciate the internal goods of silence. We become people who can practice silence beyond the time and space of Sunday morning, as we become increasingly sensitized to the function of noise in our culture.

It is for these sorts of reasons that the late Pope John Paul II called the liturgy "the school of holiness." In the liturgy we dwell in God's presence, we are given the opportunity to be schooled by grace, to become — through grace — holy, to become who we were made to be, the image of God. Too often Christians mistakenly identify some human character trait as the "image" of God in us — for example, our reason or free will or creativity. The early church theologian and bishop Athanasius, however, gets it right when he reminds us that the true "image of God" is Jesus Christ.[18] To be the "image" of God is to be like Christ, he who "suffered death on the cross." Thus it is in the liturgy that we learn who we are meant to be.

This is why the centerpoint of Christian worship is the Eucharist. Each time we come together for worship, we not only listen to God's stories and practice living in the new creation. We equally stand again and again at the foot of the cross. We stand again and again in the presence of God's greatest act of love, learning the extraordinarily difficult lesson of what *agape* looks like.[19] Indeed, the Eucharist embodies the eschatological tension that characterizes the Christian life — placing us equally at the gates of heaven yet also, once again, at the original event of the crucifixion.

16. Stanley Hauerwas and Samuel Wells, eds., *The Blackwell Companion to Christian Ethics* (Malden, Mass.: Blackwell, 2004), p. 7.

17. For a similar analysis see Michael Budde, *The (Magic) Kingdom of God: Christianity and Global Culture Industries* (Boulder, Colo.: Westview, 1998), pp. 73-82.

18. Athanasius, *First Oration against the Arians,* in *A Select Library of Nicene and Post-Nicene Fathers,* 2nd ser., vol. 4 (Peabody, Mass.: Hendrickson, 1994).

19. Reminding us that the Eucharist is centrally about love, Saint Thérèse of Lisieux describes her first communion as "the first kiss of Jesus" (*Story of a Soul,* trans. John Beevers [New York: Image Books, 1957], p. 52).

This person, this Jesus crucified, is the one whose name we bear, the one whose identity we have taken on. In bearing the name Christian we claim that he is the one we yearn to be like — in his living as depicted in the Gospels and in his dying, refusing to the end to allow hatred to determine his life, faithfully pursuing the course of loving his enemies in faithful obedience to God. Paul Wadell reminds us that although we have learned to approach the liturgy as something safe and comfortable and constantly reassuring, we ought rather to understand it as something terribly dangerous.[20] We risk becoming the bread of life whom we eat — we risk becoming the body of this Christ who died for us. For in partaking of Christ's broken body and poured-out blood, we are changed — as Augustine and Aquinas held — into Christ.[21] We become a new creature.

Of course, grace works over time, our participation in the Eucharist being but an ongoing manifestation of our baptism. In baptism we are grafted into the church, which is the body of Christ.[22] In that moment our fundamental identity is changed — we have *become* members of the body of Christ. This is part of *who* we are. We become Christ-ian. We might compare it to a national identity. Those born in Italy are, by birth, Ital-ian; they are of Italy; it is and will always be part of who they are. Through baptism, though, God takes us up into an identity that transcends all nations, into the body of his Son. And it is not simply that we become part of Christ (Christ-ian); rather, Christ becomes part of us. Or, in Saint Paul's even stronger terms, in baptism we "have been crucified with Christ; and it is no longer I who live, but it is Christ who lives in me" (Gal. 2:19-20).

But unlike national identities, Christians are, in the words of the early church theologian Tertullian, "made not born." Christian identity is given by grace at baptism. But like the disciples in the Gospels, who signed on early to follow Jesus, learning what that means and becoming capable of doing it takes time — takes, in fact, a lifetime. For the disciples it required

20. Paul Wadell, *Becoming Friends: Worship, Justice, and the Practices of the Christian Life* (Grand Rapids: Brazos, 2002), p. 16.

21. Wadell, "What Do All Those Masses Do for Us? Reflections on the Christian Moral Life and the Eucharist," in *Living No Longer for Ourselves: Liturgy and Justice in the Nineties,* ed. Kathleen Hughes and Mark R. Francis (Collegeville, Minn.: Liturgical Press, 1991), p. 167. See also Aquinas, *Summa Theologiae* III.79.3.

22. Some people think that it is better to wait and let their children decide what religion they want to be, that it's wrong for parents to "push" their religion on their children, to "force" kids to go to church. But as David McCarthy says: "Why? We force kids to take math because we think it's good for them. Why wouldn't we make them go to church?" To maintain that one ought not to "force" religion on one's children is to imply that religion is not about truth.

dwelling with him, learning the Scriptures anew through his telling of them, submitting to his reproof and correction, learning new ways of acting and living, eating with him, and standing with him at the cross. It requires no less of us.

Thus, in the liturgy we gather as the church, the body of Christ, to dwell with the one whose identity we have taken. God — as God always does — takes the initiative, becomes present to us, reaches out to us again and again. We listen to his Word in the Scripture, learning again and again to see our lives and the world within his story, learning to see and judge the world as God does — which is most often the opposite of how we are inclined to see it. We train our bodies to live as he lived — to pass peace, to keep silence and listen attentively to God, to give abundantly of our gifts. We are formed in the habit of being receptive to God's action in the world. We come to know the fullest vision of "the good life," or God's life with us, standing at the gates of heaven, never forgetting that the shape of the Christian life this side of the gate is the cross — that this, as the Way, is yet heaven.

It means being schooled by grace. Grace, as Aquinas reminds us, transforms nature — it works on who we are to help us become who we were made to be. Think, perhaps, of Zacchaeus (Luke 19:1-10). He, who wanted but a glimpse of the Lord from a safe distance, got a lot more than he bargained for. Jesus espies him, invites himself to Zacchaeus's house; grace abounds and he is taken into it — and his life is transformed. Invited by grace, Zacchaeus becomes a disciple; he turns to follow Jesus.

"Go in Peace to Love and Serve the Lord"

Like Zacchaeus, we get more than we bargain for in liturgy. God reaches out to us through the Word, reaches down to us through the Eucharist, and calls us to follow. If we truly worship, we cannot remain unchanged. The liturgy calls us, challenges us, confronts us with the need to change how we live, to follow Jesus. Liturgy threatens to change us, to unsettle our safe, comfortable, and constantly reassuring lives. If not, something has gone wrong.

Worship, in other words, is the beginning of Christian ethics. In his first encyclical, *God Is Love (Deus Caritas Est),* Pope Benedict XVI states this pointedly:

> Faith, worship, and ethos are interwoven as a single reality which takes shape in our encounter with God's *agape.* Here the usual contraposition between worship and ethics simply falls apart. "Worship" itself,

Eucharistic communion, includes the reality both of being loved and of loving others in turn. A Eucharist which does not pass over into the concrete practice of love is intrinsically fragmented. Conversely . . . the "commandment" of love is only possible because it is more than a requirement. Love can be "commanded" because it has first been given.[23]

Worship, in other words, is only the beginning. Worship is but that joyful response to being loved first, the celebration of what God has done for us, for God's gracious gift of God's self to us. In worship we comply with the "command" that we are happy to follow — to love God with all our heart, mind, and soul.

But that is not the end of the commandment. Jesus does not stop there. He continues: "And the second is like it: 'You shall love your neighbor as yourself'" (Matt. 22:39). The love celebrated in worship spills out beyond the time and space of Mass itself. Receiving the gift of God's love, we carry it into the world, into our everyday lives.[24] If not, something has gone wrong. As Benedict notes: "A Eucharist which does not pass over into the concrete practice of love is intrinsically fragmented."

Benedict's claim returns us to Aquinas. For Aquinas held that the *shape* of the Christian life was "charity." Charity, he noted, is the *form* of the virtues.[25] Charity is an ancient theological concept whose richness has mostly been lost. Too often when used in our contemporary context, the word "charity" is understood as referring to donations of money or clothes we no longer want. It has connotations of "taking care of" the poor.

But for Aquinas and the Christian tradition, the word means far more. The Latin word for charity is *caritas,* "love." So first and foremost to speak of charity is to speak of love. To be a person of charity is to be a person who loves. But just as happiness for Thomas and the Christian tradition had a particular content, so does love. For the love of charity is the kind of love manifested by God — not just a love that gives but a love that gives all, that creates *ex nihilo* (out of nothing), that gives abundantly, a love that by giving the self "empties" one of one's self. This is the love we see displayed in the life of Christ. In theological language, this love is called *kenotic.*

---

23. Benedict XVI, *Deus Caritas Est (God Is Love),* §14. The encyclical can be accessed online at: http://www.vatican.va/holy_father/benedict_xvi/encyclicals/documents/hf_ben-xvi_enc_20051225_deus-caritas-est_en.html.

24. The Orthodox refer to this as "the liturgy after the liturgy," to signal that worship does not end (nor do we cease being church) when we leave the building. I am grateful to Elizabeth Newman for bringing this to my attention.

25. Aquinas, *Summa Theologiae* II-II.23.8.

The shape of the Christian life, then, for Aquinas, is given in the life of Christ. Christ, who was divine, "did not regard equality with God as something to be exploited" (Phil. 2:6). Rather than insisting on his rights, Christ took "the form of a slave" and became one of us. Out of love, God in Christ gave up the comfort and safety of divine existence to enter into the painful, scary, messy, and complicated world of human existence. And he refused to abandon this course of love, this love of God for humanity, even when faced with death, continuing to love even when that love was not returned.

This, of course, is the love we meet in the Eucharist. And it is this love that is to pass over into concrete practice in the world, the love we are commanded to bring to our neighbors. As we meet this love in the Eucharist, so we are — by grace — to incarnate that kenotic love in the world. God's love — *caritas,* charity — is to become the shape of our lives. This is a love that does not give money or things, but is exemplified in solidarity, in face-to-face personal interaction. Thus, Christian charity is less about giving money than about *being with* others, spending time with them, especially the poor. As has been noted, "Christian witness will continue to be identified not by those to whom Christians give money but by those with whom Christians take time to eat."[26]

More specifically, charity becomes the "form" or "shape" of all the Christian virtues. Each virtue, from a Christian perspective, becomes redefined in light of kenotic *caritas.* Or, in more traditional Catholic terms, grace transforms nature (as will be discussed further in part 2). Thus, through the grace that we meet in the Eucharist, we are formed not only to practice, say, the virtue of justice, a natural virtue extolled even by the Greco-Roman philosophers. For Christians, justice looks different — for God's ways are not our ways. Justice (trans)formed by charity not only renders "each his due," but also knows that the last will be first. Justice is not simply "being fair"; it is also the preferential option for the poor. Likewise, charity (trans)forms what counts as virtue. No longer do the central virtues of Christians include pride, dominance, and self-reliance, as they did for the Greco-Romans, but now the spectrum of Christian virtues includes humility, patient endurance, and mutual interdependence.

Thus, theologically, the overall defining shape of the Christian moral life is *caritas,* self-emptying love, a love that seeks not its own interests but pours itself out in love for the other. But insofar as we meet this love first and foremost in the Eucharist, we might equally say that worship is the

26. Hauerwas and Wells, *The Blackwell Companion,* p. 42.

"form" of the Christian life.[27] Worship — worship that is really worship! — embraces a Christian's life in its entirety; it cannot be compartmentalized into one hour a week. At the same time, it provides the overriding shape or character of the Christian life: the love at the heart of worship carries over in our minds, hearts, souls, and bodies and into the way we navigate in our day-to-day lives in the world. Worship changes us; so changed, we cannot help but live differently in the world.[28]

Paul Wadell sums this up well:

> What do all those Masses do for us? They should make us a new creation. They should help us live a paschal life. No one should be able to celebrate the Eucharist and remain the same. If that happens, something is wrong, the power of the Eucharist is being thwarted. What should happen is that through the Eucharist all of us are freed from sin for God. And that means we are free for life, free for peace, free for a happiness and joy we have never tasted before. It is the joy of God fully alive in us. When that happens, everything we are is worship, everything we do is good.[29]

Christians, of course, live as these "new creations" not for their own sake, but — following Christ — for the sake of the world. We carry this *caritas* into the

---

27. Paul Wadell fleshes out this notion of worship as a "form" of life in more explicitly Wittgensteinian terms. He compares the journey of the Christian life to going to a foreign country. When we do so, we have to learn a new language, and as we do so, we cannot help but become at least somewhat different. Moreover, the point of becoming fluent is to become fluent. Languages are ends in themselves. As he notes: "Learning to be moral is something like learning a language. . . . The Christian moral life is nothing more than the ongoing endeavor to live from the good we call Jesus, a good that bonds us together and reminds us of who we want to be. This is why we can speak of Christian morality as a community's conversation about the purpose and goal of its life. To have a language is to have a common way of life. To be a Christian is to be given the language of God that comes to us in Jesus and to embrace a way of life we call discipleship. As we speak this language of God we are formed in it, and as we live it we become one with it. In this respect, the goal of the Christian moral life is to become articulate in the Word we call Jesus; in fact, so eloquently that we are his presence in the world" (Wadell, "What?" p. 154). Citing Herbert McCabe, Wadell further notes that "to enter the Christian moral life is to allow the Word we call Jesus to become the grammar of our lives" (p. 155).

28. Here let me briefly note the importance of prayer, sacraments, and worship for the traditional Catholic notion of conscience. Conscience, a critical faculty in moral discernment, must for Catholics be shaped by worship (*Catechism of the Catholic Church*, §1785; the *Catechism* can be accessed online at: http://www.vatican.va/archive/ccc_css/archive/catechism/ccc_toc.htm). For in our consciences we meet God, which can be nothing other than worship (*Catechism*, §1776).

29. Wadell, "What?" p. 169.

world because we believe that God's redemption is real, that it is possible for God's reality — met in the liturgy — to become just as tangible, obvious, incarnate, and experienced in our day-to-day lives. God has made not only *us* for God's self but also all of reality. God longs for all of the world to rest in him. Christians affirm that God has created all of reality and that, therefore, the end, goal, purpose of all reality is to move toward union with God.

Will the world be open to the incarnation of God's reality? Most often not. The cross of Christ testifies to that. Nonetheless, as followers of Christ, we are called to witness to God's gracious love and way of being. As Stanley Hauerwas and Sam Wells note: "Witness names the Christian hope that every action — whether for peace, for justice, for stability, for alleviating distress, for empowering the young and weak, for comforting the lonely, for showing mercy to the outcast, for offering hospitality, for making friends, or for earning a living — points to God, and invites an inquiry into the joy that inspires such actions."[30] Following Christ, those of us formed in worship are called to make a persuasive case for God's love to the world through the shape of our lives. On this journey we have, for companions, the saints — those whose lives have been shaped in diverse and phenomenal ways by an all-consuming love of God. From Augustine's *Confessions* to Saint Thérèse's *Story of a Soul,* the stories of the saints are stories of God's love for them and their burning love for God. Saint Thérèse tells the story of finding her vocation:

> Charity gave me the key to *my vocation.* I realized that if the Church was a body made up of different members, she would not be without the greatest and most essential of them all. I realized that love includes all vocations, that love is all things, and that, because it is eternal, it embraces every time and place.
>
> Swept up by an ecstatic joy, I cried: "Jesus, my love! At last I have found my vocation. My vocation is love! I have found my place in the bosom of the Church and it is You, Lord, who has given it to me. In the heart of the Church, who is my Mother, *I will be love.*"[31]

Love God and do as you please. God's love for us and our passionate return, worship, is the beginning of Christian ethics, of the Christian moral life. Worship — where we meet and are given the gift of this *caritas* by God — becomes the place and time from which God works to transform the world. Through worship, then, the church lives not for its own sake but for the

---

30. Hauerwas and Wells, *The Blackwell Companion,* p. 19.

31. Thérèse of Lisieux, *Story of a Soul,* p. 155.

sake of the world.[32] Just as through Jesus Christ God acted to bless all of creation, to redeem it, to call it to worship, rejoice, and live in God's new reality, so the church — the body of Christ risen and in the world — continues this work. And the work of Christ is, in the end, the Christian life.

Concurrent Readings

Aquinas, Thomas. *Summa Theologiae* II-II.1-46. Here he discusses the theological virtues of faith, hope, and charity.

Augustine. *Confessions*. Translated and with an introduction by R. S. Pine-Coffin. New York: Penguin Books, 1961. The *Confessions* might also be called a love story, for in it Augustine waxes eloquent about his love for God and God's love for us and the world.

Hauerwas, Stanley, and Samuel Wells, eds. *The Blackwell Companion to Christian Ethics*. Malden, Mass.: Blackwell, 2004. Hauerwas and Wells provide a further introduction to seeing worship as the beginning of Christian ethics. The anthology includes a number of essays on particular topics, each seeking to think differently (and theologically) about the assigned topic out of the rich context of worship.

Heschel, Abraham Joshua. *The Sabbath: Its Meaning for Modern Man*. New York: Farrar, Straus and Giroux, 1951. Heschel's book is valuable not only because it highlights the continuities between the Christian and Jewish traditions on the question of Sabbath worship, but also because it reorients how we think about worship.

Newman, Elizabeth. *Untamed Hospitality: Welcoming God and Other Strangers*. Grand Rapids: Brazos, 2007. Newman masterfully provides a thoroughgoing theological analysis of Christian hospitality and its implication for the life of the church. Of particular interest here is her second chapter, "The Strange Hospitality of Christian Worship," which argues for understanding worship itself as hospitality insofar as it is our participation in God's own triune life, which is God's hospitality.

Pieper, Josef. *Leisure: The Basis of Culture*. Introduction by Roger Scruton. New translation by Gerald Malsbary. South Bend, Ind.: St. Augustine's Press, 1998. Pieper offers a Catholic version of Heschel's commentary on the Sabbath, although Pieper includes a more scathing critique of how the structures of the world work to undercut worship as our true end.

---

32. *The Pastoral Constitution on the Church in the Modern World (Gaudium et Spes)*, in *The Documents of Vatican II*, ed. Walter M. Abbott, S.J. (New York: America Press, 1966).

Thérèse of Lisieux. *The Story of a Soul.* Translated by John Beevers. New York: Doubleday, 1957. Like Augustine, Thérèse's story of her journey with God is a love story. The stories of the saints are nothing if not love stories; for that reason they are fun and fruitful to read.

Wadell, Paul. *Becoming Friends: Worship, Justice, and the Practice of Christian Friendship.* Grand Rapids: Brazos, 2002. Wadell's book expands on the fundamental premise of this chapter and does so in thick dialogue with Thomas Aquinas.

Chapter 2

Jesus Christ, Scripture, and Ethics

David M. McCarthy

The books of the New Testament emerge out of an organic, grassroots process (a few centuries long) where an oral tradition of the apostolic faith comes to bear on what writings (letters and gospels) are integrated into Christian worship and teaching.[1] This grassroots process of canonization indicates that the authority of Scripture comes from within the life of worshiping communities. Before the New Testament was written, early Christians "identified God by narrating key events recorded in the [Old Testament] Scriptures, the creation of the world, the inspiration of the prophets, the coming of Christ in the flesh, his death and resurrection, the outpouring of the Holy Spirit."[2] The New Testament attests to the conviction that Jesus Christ is the fulfillment of the Jewish scriptures, and the Old Testament is understood to be authoritative precisely in this framework, that Christ can be seen as one with God from the beginning (John 1:1-18).

The experience of salvation in Jesus Christ and the proclamation of this salvation are the basis of biblical authority. Scriptural authority for Christians draws from the transforming power of new life that is experienced by Christians through Christ's death and resurrection. In the moral life, therefore, biblical authority is not imposed from the outside, but comes from within the lives of people of faith. The commands in Scripture (e.g., "love your enemies," in Matt. 5:44) show the contours of a way of life that calls for personal transformation and the "renewal" of our minds

---

1. Luke Timothy Johnson, *The Writings of the New Testament* (Minneapolis: Fortress, 1999), pp. 603-6.

2. Robert Louis Wilken, "Interpreting the New Testament," *Pro Ecclesia* 14, no. 1 (Winter 2005): 18.

(Rom. 12:2). Likewise, the biblical tradition is best expressed in the lives and practical reason of saintly people.[3] Biblical authority comes not through the enforcement of commands, but from its fruitfulness as a medium of new life in Christ. The function of Scripture in the moral life is to open us to an encounter with God.

The meaning of our lives in light of the life, death, and resurrection of Jesus Christ is the focus of this chapter. The first section of the chapter explains that the New Testament develops within the process of proclaiming that Jesus has risen, and the following sections give account of Jesus' ministry, death, and resurrection. The last section of the chapter deals with a much-debated issue in moral theology: the relationship of Scripture and ethics. The main point of the final section is that Scripture has its life as we are enlivened by the Spirit of God. In the Bible we hear the call to follow: to respond to "God with us" in Jesus Christ and his Spirit. Scripture and morality are connected, not by certain methods of biblical interpretation or moral theory, but by the Spirit in our lives today. The primary role of Scripture in moral discernment is to open our lives to seeing and experiencing God's presence in the world, to understanding our identity as part of a community of faith, and to living our role as Christians in our time.

Scripture and the Church

The Bible itself is a very human book to the degree that it is full of imperfections and imperfect people (think of Abraham or Peter). An accusation often levied against Scripture is that it is all too human. It is too bound up with human history, not only in its composition over a thousand-year period, but also in the vicissitudes of its oral transmission, written formation, transcription, and translation — all subject to human hands and interests. Many Christians unwittingly support this accusation by claiming that every word of the Bible is the literal truth and that no interpretation is required. The Bible, they claim, is free from human involvement. In making these claims, especially that the Bible speaks for itself and needs no interpretation, they give a false idea about our role in Scripture and set up an easy target for skeptics. Even worse, such a claim encourages the idea that the exact

---

3. Hans-Georg Gadamer, *Truth and Method* (New York: Crossroad, 1988), pp. 245-53. According to Gadamer, authority is not an arbitrary exertion of will over against reason, but it is based in reasoning and mastery of reasoning. Here the saints or holy ones are those who gain mastery in the reasoning of faith.

words of the Bible themselves (even in their English translation) are God's Word rather than an instrument of the Word, of God's presence in Jesus Christ.

It should cause no crisis of faith to admit that the imprint of human life (with its imperfections) is clearly upon Scripture. Modern historical-critical methods have attempted to reconstruct the diverse sources from which the biblical writers and communities drew their understanding of Jesus, to trace how the words and actions of Jesus were passed on in oral and written form, to construct a picture of the cultural settings in which the writings emerged, and to clarify the specific social and theological concerns of biblical authors. When modern historical-critical methods are put to the task, we find, for instance, that the Gospel writers were themselves not eyewitnesses, that they drew on various sources about Jesus, that each arranged his sources according to his own rhetorical and evangelical plan, and that the actual words of Jesus, his actions, and the chronology of his actions cannot be disentangled from this process of the church's proclamation and reception. All these points are likely to be familiar, but if not, they can be found in reading guides and notes of *The Catholic Study Bible*.[4]

The modern methods of interpretation are affirmed in *Dei Verbum,* the *Dogmatic Constitution on Divine Revelation* of Vatican Council II (1965).[5] In the document, modern historical methods are set within the history of proclamation, worship, and discipleship, so that, in the words of Sandra Schneiders, "the real Jesus is not the earthly Jesus stripped of transhistorical dimensions and uninterpreted by faith informed by the paschal mystery. . . . [J]ust as there is no such thing as a human Jesus who is not divine or a divine Jesus who is not human, so there is no historical Jesus who is not the proclaimed Jesus or vice versa."[6] Schneiders here puts the very human nature of the Bible in an "incarnational" framework: in Christ God takes human flesh, and faith in the incarnation shapes how we understand God's presence in the frailties of human life. As *Dei Verbum* explains, "the words of God, expressed in human language, have been made like human discourse, just as of old the Word of the eternal Father, when he took to Himself the weak flesh of humanity, became like other men."[7]

---

4. Donald Senior, ed., *The Catholic Study Bible* (New York: Oxford University Press, 1990).

5. *Dogmatic Constitution on Divine Revelation (Dei Verbum)*, §12, in *The Documents of Vatican II,* ed. Walter M. Abbott, S.J. (New York: America Press, 1966), pp. 111-28.

6. Sandra M. Schneiders, I.H.M., *The Revelatory Text: Interpreting the New Testament as Sacred Scripture* (Collegeville, Minn.: Liturgical Press, 1999), pp. 107-8.

7. *Dogmatic Constitution on Divine Revelation (Dei Verbum)*, §13.

Although the Bible is full of human flaws and frailties, these frailties become part of a larger story. The limitations of human history in passing on the word of God are the very medium through which the Word of God is made present to us. This is the meaning of the incarnation, and in this sense God is the author of Scripture through the vulnerability of human authorship. The very human, social, and historical processes from which the Scriptures emerge are the material, the earthly stuff, that conveys the reality of God's salvation for the world. In the context of faith in the incarnation, the *Dogmatic Constitution on Divine Revelation* makes a bold claim. "Since everything asserted by the inspired authors or sacred writers must be held to be asserted by the Holy Spirit, it follows that the books of Scripture must be acknowledged as teaching firmly, faithfully, and without error that truth which God wanted put into the sacred writings for the sake of our salvation."[8] In this way the biblical word of salvation, precisely through the limitations of human words, reveals God's full self-communication to us in Jesus Christ. Our human *words* are the medium of the divine *message*. Essential to the message of salvation is that our frail humanity becomes part of the proclamation of the kingdom of God.

Salvation History

The claim that we encounter God in Scripture raises questions about how we conceive of God's relationship to the world. Too often we slip into an unsophisticated notion (often influenced by the natural sciences) that God's activity amounts to an intervention into the processes of a closed system of the world. I have been searching for a short quotation that would suggest an alternative and also avoid a long explanation. Here it is. When discussing the nature of human freedom in relationship to God, Herbert McCabe explains that our freedom does not compete with God, but depends upon God as its source. "The creative causal power of God does not operate on me from outside, as an alternative to me; it is the creative causal power of God that makes me *me*."[9] If we insert "creation" in the place of "me," we might begin to understand God's relationship to the world. God's presence to the world makes creation *creation*. We often fall into the mistaken idea that God is like any cause or power in the world, only more powerful. McCabe suggests that we have to think about God's activity in the world as

---

8. *Dogmatic Constitution on Divine Revelation (Dei Verbum)*, §11.
9. Herbert McCabe, *God Matters* (Springfield, Ill.: Templegate, 1991), p. 13.

different in kind, as different than we are inclined (as creatures) to think and not entirely graspable (as we cannot put our minds around the very source of all life itself).

The knowledge that God's activity is not entirely within our reach helps explain the biblical story as salvation history. Consider that we, represented by Adam and Eve in Paradise, are quick to listen to the serpent who tells us that we are in competition with God, that God is keeping divine knowledge from us (Gen. 3:5), and that we need only to grasp it surreptitiously and take possession of it on our own. In a real sense, our primordial sin is to grasp at God's creation itself to call it ours rather than God's. We want to make ourselves. We want to be our own lords. For Christians, the irony of this grasping is that we desire to grab for ourselves something that will be given to us as a gift, a sharing in God's nature.[10] One outcome of continuing to reject the gift, and of failing even to see it as a gift, is to project upon the nature of God our view of how we would like gods to be (e.g., divine power should be on our country's side and against our enemies, or God should accept our personal lifestyles). We like to talk about the unconditional love of God, but are quick to love God according to our own conditions.

The biblical story of salvation sets out a course of events that most of us could not have imagined or developed in theory. At the decisive moment of victory and the inauguration of God's new day, the anointed one, the Lord, is executed by his antagonists with at least verbal approval of just about everyone (Mark 15:13-14). For Christians, the crucifixion and resurrection form the climax of a long covenant history, and we have learned to look back and see what we could not have seen before, that Jesus' life and death are consistent with the story of salvation from the beginning. One point has already been noted: the primordial sin, which we humans share, is to think that we are in competition with God, and a powerful aspect of God's answer to our sin is that Jesus refuses to play the rival. No army of angels is sent to stop his enemies (Matt. 4:6-7). He overcomes sin through what, in terms of worldly power, we are more likely to call losing than winning. In worldly terms, we like to name winners and losers, but in the cross there is reconciliation.

Another key aspect of salvation history is God's calling out and setting apart a people. This "setting apart" shapes Israel's identity and constitutes the context in which Jesus proclaims the coming kingdom of God,

---

10. Robert Barron, *The Strangest Way: Walking the Christian Path* (Maryknoll, N.Y.: Orbis, 2002), p. 33.

gathers disciples and sends them out to the "lost sheep of Israel" (Matt. 10:1-15).[11] Jesus' healing power, his eating with sinners, and his good news to the poor are also connected to the gathering and restoration of Israel, as a sign that God's reign is at hand.[12] In our time, this special attention to gathering a "people of God" may appear to be exclusivist.[13] One might ask, "Doesn't each individual have a relationship to God?" Yes, this is true; but the question misses the point. In the Bible, God's redemption for the world hinges on the "setting apart" of a people to share in God's holiness (Exod. 19:3-6; Lev. 19:1-3). And when this holiness shines, God's people will be like salt and light for the world (Matt. 5:16).

The people Jesus gathers are called to the task of living out God's offer of salvation.[14] The logic of this task makes sense in view of Scripture as a whole. First, salvation is social (it is certainly personal, but not the possession of individuals per se). Second, grace is not coercive, but an offer of liberty. Essential to the freedom of redemption is freedom from self-centeredness — from the idea that life (not to mention salvation) is about me (or about me and God).[15] God's love is for all creation; therefore a "gathered people" is needed — a people called as one in Christ. Sin is a deliberate rejection of God's will for us, and in salvation we are saved from our turning away from God.

Our reconciliation is becoming part of God's love for the world. Love, then, cannot be imposed. If we are forced to turn to God, then we will not be given the grace of being active in God's love. God's love will have to be embodied in the world as an offer. Indeed, the crucified and risen Lord enacts a strange but beautiful offer, and Christians accept the task (patterned after God's covenant with Israel) to embody the offer of the incarnate Son of God. This task sets the church up for constant failure. By voluntarily taking on the task of God's love, we make every slip into ungodly thinking and action all the more sinful.

It would make more sense (it may seem) for God to make a people perfect before offering a job requiring holiness. God could certainly improve the certification process and quality control before issuing a call. However, this seemingly sensible plan (to make people perfect for the job) would serve better to show our own inclinations of love rather than to communi-

---

11. Gerhard Lohfink, *Jesus and Community: The Social Dimension of Christian Faith,* trans. John P. Galvin (Philadelphia: Fortress, 1984), pp. 9-12.

12. Lohfink, *Jesus and Community,* pp. 12-14.

13. Lohfink, *Jesus and Community,* p. 17.

14. Lohfink, *Jesus and Community,* pp. 17-20.

15. Barron, *The Strangest Way,* pp. 113-23.

cate and make present the self-giving that is God's love. We tend to love those who are already most like us, and I suspect that many of us (like me) prefer to be loved because of the goodness and nobility that we already possess. Few of us want to be pitied as a charity case. In contrast, God's love is an invitation of friendship through God's self-giving — giving us what we cannot achieve on our own, a share in God's own life. The continuing foundation of God's love and the life of the church is forgiveness. The biblical history of salvation is the story of our God who is just, steadfast, and faithful, and always calling us back with a continual offer of reconciliation.

The Good News of Easter

The previous section introduced the biblical story of salvation history. This section will continue on the topic of salvation by focusing on the liturgy of the Word during the Easter Vigil. Easter is the inauguration of the biblical proclamation "He is risen." The Easter Vigil begins during the night of Holy Saturday, when Jesus has descended to the dead, and looks forward to the dawn of Easter morning. It is central to the Christian moral life. It is the time of our baptism. Even if we were baptized on another day, the vigil is the theological context where our baptism is best understood. It sets our lives within God's salvation history. We die and rise with Christ.

The vigil remembers salvation history by incorporating several readings in the liturgy of the Word: the account of creation in Genesis 1; Abraham's near sacrifice of his son Isaac (Gen. 22:1-18); Israel's passage through the Red Sea (Exod. 14:15–15:1); readings from the prophetic books of Isaiah, Baruch, and Ezekiel; the apostle Paul's call to die and rise with Christ (Rom. 6:3-11); and Matthew 28:1-10, where Mary Magdalene and Mary the mother of James and Joseph witness the empty tomb and encounter the risen Jesus.[16] The Easter Vigil encapsulates the Christian proclamation of salvation from biblical times until today.

Some of the connections between Easter and the moral life can be understood through the formative and expressive functions of language in our lives. "A language is a system of communication that grows up around a common life."[17] It forms how we think about the world and expresses who

16. Matt. 28:1-10 is read during Year A of the liturgical calendar.
17. Paul J. Wadell, "What Do All Those Masses Do for Us? Reflections on the Christian Moral Life and the Eucharist," in *Living No Longer for Ourselves: Liturgy and Justice in the Nineties,* ed. Kathleen Hughes and Mark R. Francis (Collegeville, Minn.: Liturgical Press, 1991), p. 154.

we are. In worship we encounter the Word, the expression of God's "Easter" in the world, and we are invited into common life with God. "The Christian moral life is the steadfast commitment to learn the language of God that comes to us in Christ, to embody it, and to witness it to the world."[18] During the Easter Vigil (Matt. 28), we remember that Jesus calls his disciples "forward into a mission to Galilee and to the whole world, calling them to meet him in the continuing task of redemption and reconciliation. . . . We are called to be where Christ is."[19]

In the Easter liturgy, the focal point of the first reading is Genesis 1:27, "God created humankind in his image." The destiny of "the image" tells a story of our redemption. The image of God is given, yet is distorted by our sins, which direct us away from God and undermine our fulfillment in God and as human beings. On our behalf the Son of God — the Word that is God (John 1:1) — "emptied himself, / taking the form of a slave, / being born in human likeness" (Phil. 2:7), so that our humanity as God's image could be restored and transformed. During the vigil the readings from the prophets Isaiah and Ezekiel as well as from Baruch put the theme of restoration in terms of God's reign and the mission of the people of God.

The readings from the prophets awaken hope for the restoration of God's people and, through God's people, all nations and peoples. This is the biblical logic of salvation history. Reconciliation comes as an offer through the gathering of a people. In this way Isaiah proclaims Israel's exoneration:

> My steadfast love shall not depart from you,
> > and my covenant of peace shall not be removed,
> > says the LORD, who has compassion on you.
>
> > > > > > (Isa. 54:10)

Comments James Donohue, "Isaiah 54:5-14 evokes the new Jerusalem where humanity will be transformed and a new kingdom will be established, a dominion of life and grace."[20] Isaiah 55 develops the wider implications of God's covenant renewal. Peoples throughout the world ("nations that do

---

18. Wadell, "What?" p. 155.

19. Monika K. Hellwig, *Gladness Their Escort: Homiletic Reflections for Sundays and Feastdays* (Wilmington, Del.: Michael Glazier, 1987), p. 50.

20. James Donohue, C.R., "The Concepts of Redemption Found in the Liturgies of Good Friday and the Easter Vigil," in *Proceedings of the North American Academy of Liturgy: Annual Meeting, Charleston, SC, 2-5 January 1994*, ed. David G. Truemper (Valparaiso, Ind.: North American Academy of Liturgy, 1994), pp. 105-6.

not know you") will see God's glory shine in Israel and will be attracted to it and saved. The reading from Baruch shows that "the way of salvation is to hear the precepts of the Lord and to follow them in our lives."[21] Finally, Ezekiel 36:16-28 "speaks of salvation in terms of forgiveness of sins," and "when interpreted in light of the Easter Vigil, the concluding verse, 'You shall be my people and I will be your God,' gives rise to a certain confidence in God's fidelity."[22]

The two remaining readings from the Old Testament (Gen. 22:1-18 and Exod. 14:15–15:1) put Jesus' crucifixion in context of covenant and sacrifice. Before discussing these passages, it will be helpful to attend to the meaning of sacrifice in biblical times. Frances Young, in her historical study *Sacrifice and the Death of Christ*, points out that "the most consistent misunderstanding in modern studies is that sacrifice can be defined in only one sense, or given only one kind of meaning or rationale."[23] Sacrifice was a practice set within relationships (with God and others) that provided a context of meaning. By analogy, I might invite a friend to dinner to talk about a serious matter, but it is wrong to define the common meal as a means for broaching difficult issues. Rather, the serious talk is possible because the common meal is already a regular practice of shared life. Likewise, Young explains that sacrifice in the ancient world was universal, and that "it never occurred to anyone that it needed explanation or definition."[24] The implication of Young's point is that a definition of sacrifice — as payment for sin, for example — does not precede or determine the need for Christ to be sacrificed. Rather, the practices of sacrifice form a complex matrix of an ongoing relationship between the people and God. For Christians, the death of Christ, along with the very incarnation of God in Christ, becomes the whole of this matrix. The crucifixion is the end of all sacrifice. Jesus Christ's life and death are the practical and concrete matrix (or location) of God's relationship to the world.

Young shows that ancient uses of sacrifice are central for how Christians come to understand the redemptive nature of the crucifixion. She explains, for instance, that sacrifices within "the Old Testament sacrificial system" are occasions for praise, thanksgiving, and communion.[25] First of all, however, Christ's sacrifice is understood within the frame of a sacrifice for sin, as a "sin offering." Young argues that a sacrificial offering makes

---

21. Donohue, "The Concepts of Redemption," p. 106.
22. Donohue, "The Concepts of Redemption," p. 106.
23. Frances M. Young, *Sacrifice and the Death of Christ* (London: SPCK, 1975), p. 21.
24. Young, *Sacrifice*, p. 21.
25. Young, *Sacrifice*, pp. 80-81.

sense, for the early church, only within a wider context of Christ's sacrifice as fulfillment of the Old Testament law.[26] Within the context of Israel's history and religious practice, a sacrifice — specifically the sacrificial blood (Lev. 17:11) — is a gift from God for the purification of the people.[27] In other words, among Christians of the New Testament and Jews of the Old, a sin offering does not function to appease or pay off a wrathful God.[28] "Sin-offerings were not human attempts to buy off the anger of a righteous and vindictive God; they were not propitiatory, in the sense that they were an attempt to change God. Rather they were a means given by God himself for wiping away the sins which prevented his chosen people from fulfilling the obligations of the covenant-relationship and offering him fitting worship."[29] Further, Young notes that, in the rituals of the Old Testament, the connection between sacrificial blood and forgiveness was simply a given that "required no further rationale or explanation." The early church "accepted this from the Old Testament Scriptures, and saw the blood of Christ as the new God-given means of expiation, God's way of dealing with sin."[30]

This biblical idea of the gift (not the penalty) of purifying sacrifice gives us a perspective from which to consider the reading of Genesis 22:1-18 and Exodus 14:15–15:1 at the Easter Vigil. Genesis 22:1-18 tells of "the binding of Isaac," when Abraham obeys God's call to take Isaac, his son, to the mountainside and offer him up as a sacrifice of worship. Exodus 14 recounts God's deliverance of Israel from Egypt, as the Israelites cross the sea and the Egyptian army is vanquished. Jews remember these events of the exodus in the annual celebration of Passover. In Jewish and Christian traditions, there is a connection between the binding of Isaac and the blood of the Passover lamb, which marks the doorposts of Israelites in Egypt and protects them from the plague of death (Exod. 11:1–12:33). The blood of the lamb is the means and sign of liberation from bondage and God's covenant with Israel at Sinai. Likewise, the offering of the Son (pre-

26. Young, *Sacrifice*, p. 80.

27. Young, *Sacrifice*, pp. 27-28.

28. Young, *Sacrifice*, p. 72. Young argues that the translation of "propitiation" in Heb. 2:17 and Rom. 3:25 is correct; however, she also holds that these references do not indicate a propitiatory sacrifice as a placation of God's anger. In the wider context of Rom. 3 and Heb. 2, it is clear that — in conformity with the Old Testament — "it is God alone who can remove or expiate sin" (p. 72). Propitiation is a means for humans to deflect the effects of their own sins.

29. Young, *Sacrifice*, p. 28.

30. Young, *Sacrifice*, p. 70.

figured in the binding of Isaac) is the gift of a new Passover Lamb and new covenant.[31]

In the Easter Vigil the exodus is connected to new life in Christ. Fleeing from the Egyptians, Israelites enter the sea (Exod. 14), and the parting of the waters shows the power and goodness of the Lord. Within the Christian tradition the opening of the sea is an analogy to our baptism. The Egyptian armies are "the rulers" of the world and "the spiritual forces of evil" (Eph. 6:12). Like Egyptians on the heels of the Israelites, these evils "attempt to follow, but you descend into the water and come out unimpaired. . . . You ascend 'a new man' [Eph. 2:15] prepared to 'sing a new song' [Isa. 42:10]. But the Egyptians who follow you are drowned in the abyss."[32] These themes of entering and emerging from the water emanate from the reading of Romans 6:3-11 during the Easter Vigil. In Romans Paul unites the waters of baptism with paschal themes of death and the resurrection. "We have been buried with him by baptism into death, so that, just as Christ was raised from the dead by the glory of the Father, so we too might walk in newness of life" (Rom. 6:4).

Likewise, the sacrifice of Isaac, ironically, is understood as rebirth. According to a traditional reading, Abraham's willingness to obey God's command to sacrifice his son is considered a mirror image of his willingness to receive the promise that, even though he and his wife Sarah were barren, a son would be born.[33] For his part, Isaac shows astounding obedience and trust. In the tradition of the church, Isaac's obedience to his father is an adumbration — a preliminary sketch in time — of the self-offering of the Son. As Abraham does not withhold his own son from God, God does not withhold the Son from us. Abraham sets out to sacrifice Isaac, but Isaac becomes the one through whom Abraham's descendants are multiplied.[34] Likewise, Jesus, the one actually sacrificed, is the giver of new life. We are heirs of this new way, and we, like Abraham and Isaac, are called to pattern our lives in the grace and mercy of Christ.

---

31. Notker Füglister, "The Biblical Roots of the Easter Celebration," in *Celebrating the Easter Vigil,* ed. Rupert Berger and Hans Hollerweger, trans. Matthew J. O'Connell (New York: Pueblo, 1983), pp. 18-24.

32. Origen, "Homily V: On the Departure of the Children of Israel," in *Origen: Homilies on Genesis and Exodus,* Fathers of the Church: A New Translation, vol. 71, trans. Ronald E. Heine (Washington, D.C.: Catholic University of America Press, 1982), pp. 283-84.

33. John Chrysostom, "Homily 47: 'Despite These Words God Put Abraham to the Test,'" in *Saint John Chrysostom: Homilies on Genesis 46–67,* Fathers of the Church: A New Translation, vol. 87, trans. Robert C. Hill (Washington, D.C.: Catholic University of America Press, 1992), p. 18.

34. Chrysostom, "Homily 47," p. 24.

This new life in Christ is the power of the resurrection. The Easter Vigil's liturgy of the word culminates in the reading of Matthew 28:1-10, where Jesus appears to "Mary Magdalene and the other Mary" and tells them, "Do not be afraid; go and tell my brothers to go to Galilee; there they will see me" (Matt. 28:10). Monika Hellwig notes a twofold commission in this command: to go into the world as disciples, brothers and sisters of Christ, and "to be where Christ is."[35] The resurrection is liberation to live in a new way, a new exodus, and it is also "a freeing of the imagination with explosive force to embrace possibilities for human life in peace and non-violence and in communities of creative reconciliation. Nothing that pertains to the Reign of God in human society is unthinkable anymore."[36] In this way the resurrection and the liturgy of Easter give us words to express and a way to see the world as redeemed and loved by God.

The Proclamation of the Kingdom

The Easter Vigil is the culmination of Holy Week, a week that begins with Jesus' triumphal entry into Jerusalem. When Jesus enters Jerusalem, it is shortly before the Passover holiday, which is the remembrance of Israel's liberation from Egypt. He is hailed as the would-be redeemer, the Son of David (Matt. 21:1-11). Welcomed into the capital city in David's name, he is considered a promising heir to the great monarch who unified the people and put Israel on the world map among the nations. Jesus is hailed as the anointed one of the new exodus.[37] As the Son of David, he will liberate Israel from the reigning powers of the world — from its own unfaithfulness and its current bondage to Rome. But on the eve of the Passover, Jesus is condemned to death. If great kings and kingdoms of the world are represented by military power and great wealth, then by suffering under the power of Rome he brings an entirely different kind of kingdom. It is a kingdom that draws on the hopes and expectations of God's work in Israel — to be faithful to the Lord and a light to the nations. After Christ's resurrection

---

35. Hellwig, *Gladness Their Escort*, p. 50.

36. Monika Hellwig, *Jesus: The Compassion of God* (Wilmington, Del.: Michael Glazier, 1983), p. 104.

37. N. T. Wright, *The New Testament and the People of God*, Christian Origins and the Question of God, vol. 1 (Minneapolis: Fortress, 1992), pp. 268-69. Wright argues that most Jews of the Second Temple period "believed that in all the senses which mattered, Israel's exile was still in progress."

his disciples see that God's reign is present in him. His life, death, and resurrection carry forward the coming kingdom of God.

In *Jesus in Latin America*, Jon Sobrino proposes that the kingdom of God — that is, new life in Christ — is the antithesis of what deprives people of life. He holds that to gain a "working idea of the content of the kingdom of God, we must adopt the viewpoint of those who lack life, power, and dignity. . . . The poor, the sinners, and the despised are the necessary, though not absolutely sufficient, starting point for an understanding of what is meant by the good news of the kingdom."[38] Sobrino cites a few passages from the Gospels of Matthew and Luke. Consider Luke 4:18-19:

> The Spirit of the Lord is upon me,
> because he has anointed me to bring good news to the poor.
> He has sent me to proclaim release to the captives
> and recovery of sight to the blind,
> to let the oppressed go free,
> to proclaim the year of the Lord's favor.

The good news is that God's kingdom comes through healing and restoration, through the gathering of people on the wrong side of fortune and power — the wayward and ill-fated people who were left out but now will make Israel, God's people, whole again.

Sobrino also cites the first of the beatitudes in the Gospel of Matthew: "Blessed are the poor in spirit, for theirs is the kingdom of heaven" (5:3). Poverty of spirit is not the same as material poverty, but in the Christian tradition (particularly the lives of the saints) the two are connected. The ancients would not make the modern dualistic claim that money does not change a person. They were wary of being controlled by things in the world. For example, Gregory of Nyssa (ca. 335-395) tells us that money and material riches are often gained and lost at the expense of others, while spiritual wealth is like the sun "which communicates itself to all who seek it."[39] It is clear to Gregory that giving to the poor is the way to follow God's justice. In doing so, we use things of the earth to draw us near to others. In contrast, hoarding wealth isolates a person (as in the gated communities and exclusive neighborhoods of today). Worse, we lose touch with divine justice and the brothers and sisters of God (Matt. 25:31-46).

Saint Gregory sees that our goal should be spiritual riches, and thus

38. Jon Sobrino, *Jesus in Latin America* (Maryknoll, N.Y.: Orbis, 1987), p. 143.

39. *St. Gregory of Nyssa: The Lord's Prayer and the Beatitudes,* trans. Hilda C. Graef (Westminster, Md.: Newman Press, 1954), p. 87.

thinks of "the poor in spirit" in terms of greater spiritual wealth, which creates communion with others and adds to the spiritual riches of all. Poverty of spirit is the opposite of standing on one's own spiritual achievements; it is our solidarity with others and openness to God — for Jesus Christ took on spiritual poverty, being one with God but emptying himself to be a servant (Phil. 2:5-7).[40] In modern terms, "the more one is aware of the need for God, the more one is going to be receptive to the reign of God. . . . The proud, who bask in their reputations, learning, and titles (Matt. 23:5-8), will shut themselves from the kingdom of heaven (Matt. 23:13)."[41]

It should be noted, at this point, that in Matthew the "kingdom of heaven" refers not to a place that we reach after death, but to "the rule of heaven, that is, of God, being brought to bear in the present world."[42] Compare the Lord's Prayer,

> Your kingdom come.
> Your will be done,
>   on earth as it is in heaven.
>
> (Matt. 6:10)

The "kingdom of heaven" names the conviction "that the creator God intend[s] to bring justice and peace to his world here and now."[43] When the remaining beatitudes and sayings in Matthew 5 are considered, it is clear that poverty of spirit — receptivity to God — is required to see the ways of God's reign. Consider, for instance, "Blessed are those who hunger and thirst for righteousness, for they will be filled" (Matt. 5:6). I must admit that I have learned to be numb to newspaper and television news because I lack hope about war, hunger, and other injustices in the world. If I were not to anesthetize my compassion, a yearning for a better world would ruin my nice, satisfying life. The news would leave me starving for righteousness. When Jesus proclaims, "Blessed are those who hunger and thirst for righteousness," he turns my world upside down.

The very nature of sovereignty (at least in the usual terms) includes a government or a people's ability to secure its territory and impose its will upon an insecure and competitive world. But when Jesus sends disciples

---

40. *St. Gregory of Nyssa*, p. 91.

41. David E. Garland, *Reading Matthew: A Literary and Theological Commentary of the First Gospel* (New York: Crossroad, 1995), p. 55.

42. N. T. Wright, *The Challenge of Jesus* (Downers Grove, Ill.: InterVarsity, 1999), pp. 36-37.

43. Wright, *The Challenge of Jesus*, p. 37.

into cities and towns, he tells them to take no walking stick or purse and to depend entirely upon the welcome of their hosts (Matt. 10:5-15). Likewise, Jesus' parables of the kingdom show God's reign not in terms of conquest, but as a bountiful offer. The parable of the sower (Matt. 13:1-23) indicates that the word of the kingdom cannot be imposed on inhospitable soil; yet the seed, when it finds fertile ground, will yield an abundance of fruit. When telling the parable, Jesus points out that the very purpose of parables is to offer a peaceable word.[44] He will not coerce a closed heart. "Seeing they do not perceive, and hearing they do not listen, nor do they understand" (Matt. 13:13).

At first glance Matthew 13:13 might seem to suggest that Jesus is intending to be obscure. On the contrary, parables tell stories about ordinary life (like planting seeds) where surprising events transpire. This transformation of the ordinary is precisely the nature of the kingdom of God, so that parables are the clearest way to present the ways of God. Anyone who has sown seeds (even grass seeds) knows that it is foolish to toss them on hard paths and untilled soil. We wouldn't sow this way. But God does. If we are captivated by protecting our interests and controlling our life plan, we will cringe at the waste of valuable resources. We are likely to see this extravagant sowing, not as bounty and grace, but as a hopeless or inefficient undertaking. Unwittingly, we have let our picture of things obscure the kingdom. In doing so, we will see but we will not understand.

In a world of violence, greed, and fear, it is not easy to trust in Christ's way of hospitality, reconciliation, and peace. Most of us are unwilling to take the way of peace and hospitality unless we have a way to ensure our safety and financial security first. Ironically, the more we focus on our own safety and security, the more we are controlled by a world of violence and indifference. Fear and vulnerability control our lives. No wonder the most frequent command in the Bible is "Do not be afraid."[45] The self-seeking that invulnerability requires blinds us to seeing and responding to God's presence in the world. All at once we desire God's peaceable kingdom, and yet we are likely to be unable to trust it, to take its risks, to see the kingdom (not merely our own private salvation) in the way of Jesus Christ.[46]

The expectations for God's reign were high in Jesus' time. He and his fellow Jews lived under foreign domination and internal corruption and op-

---

44. Wright, *The Challenge of Jesus,* pp. 40-41.

45. N. T. Wright, *Following Jesus: Biblical Reflections on Discipleship* (Grand Rapids: Eerdmans, 1994), p. 66.

46. Stanley Hauerwas, *The Peaceable Kingdom* (Notre Dame, Ind.: University of Notre Dame Press, 1983), pp. 86-87.

pression.[47] In Jesus' time the Roman Empire controlled the lands of Jews through client kings like Herod the Great and his son, Herod Antipas, whom John the Baptist denounces. According to N. T. Wright, "zealous Jews had long regarded their own local rulers as compromisers, and the Jewish leaders of Jesus' day fell exactly into that category. The powerful Chief Priests were wealthy pseudo-aristocrats who worked the system and got what they could get out of it. Herod Antipas . . . was a puppet tyrant bent on wealth and self-aggrandizement."[48] Many hoped Rome and its local leadership would be overthrown, and Israel would be vindicated. Instead, Jesus turned his attention to Israel's unfaithfulness, its need for repentance, and its call to be the light of the world (Matt. 5:13-16).[49]

For example, the Sermon on the Mount (particularly Matt. 5:13-48) moves directly from Jesus' call to be the light of the world to his teaching about Mosaic Law. Jews thought of law not in the way many today think of it, as a set of external rules and regulations, but as the very structure of life and the way of following God day to day. Jesus declares, "Do not think that I have come to abolish the law or the prophets; I have come not to abolish but to fulfill" (Matt. 5:17). After this there is a litany of Jesus' commentary on the law: "You have heard that it was said. . . . But I say to you . . ." (5:21-22). With these antitheses Jesus "does not add more laws or raise the standards of what is right. Instead, he recovers what God has always required."[50]

His teaching against "an eye for an eye" (5:38-42), which prohibits retaliation, is not a reversal of the law. "'Eye for eye, tooth for tooth,' in the ancient Israelite setting, actually meant a limitation placed on vengeance."[51] We, ironically, are likely to use "eye for eye" to defend retaliation — for instance, as an argument for capital punishment. Jesus' reversal of an "eye for an eye" is not a change in God, but a call to us to turn ourselves around and follow the ways of God as they are fulfilled in Jesus. The same reversal of our attitudes and behavior is required of Jesus' rejection of oaths in Matthew 5:33-37. The reason for oaths is truthfulness ("I promise to God"), but we have made them a sign that we are not to be held to our word in ordinary things. Again the call for truthfulness has not changed; Jesus brings the ways of God to their fulfillment.[52] "Let your 'Yes' mean 'Yes,' and your 'No' mean 'No'" (Matt. 5:37 NAB).

47. Wright, *The Challenge of Jesus,* p. 36.
48. Wright, *The Challenge of Jesus,* p. 36.
49. Wright, *The Challenge of Jesus,* p. 49.
50. Garland, *Reading Matthew,* p. 63.
51. John H. Yoder, *The Original Revolution* (Scottdale, Pa.: Herald, 1971), p. 44.
52. Yoder, *The Original Revolution,* p. 44.

In *The Original Revolution* John Howard Yoder notes that Matthew 5 is properly understood in terms of Jesus' call for repentance and his announcement of the coming kingdom: "Repent, for the kingdom of heaven has come near" (Matt. 4:17). Yoder explains that biblical repentance is not merely sorrow for one's sins, but "a transformation of understanding *(metanoia),* a redirected will ready to live in a new kind of world."[53] Jesus' teachings in the Gospel of Matthew point us to the visible witness of the kingdom in Jesus' person and work. The Sermon on the Mount is an ethic of discipleship, according to Yoder, that is guided not by prevailing political and economic standards of success but "by the Lord it seeks to reflect."[54] Jesus calls us to reconciliation with one another (5:21-26). Then Jesus instructs us, "If anyone wants to sue you and take your coat, give your cloak as well" (5:40). He calls us to "love your enemies and pray for those who persecute you" (5:44). We are called to the love and faithfulness of the Son of God, who gathers the lost and gives himself up for us on the cross.

Crucified and Risen

Jesus proclaims God's reign in a world of Roman oppression and strife in Israel. When he announces the kingdom, he puts it into action through teaching, healing the leper and sending him to the priest as proof of his restoration (Matt. 8:1-4), eating with sinners, gathering and sending out disciples, calling for repentance, and calling for the fulfillment of God's purposes for Israel (Matt. 5). Further, Jesus forces the issue and brings kingdom expectations to a climax by challenging and claiming prerogative over the temple. Upon entering the temple he overturns its tables and, during his brief time there, is the center of its activity (Matt. 21:12-17). According to N. T. Wright, "Jesus' Temple-action led straightforwardly to the question about Messiahship; his unequivocal claim to Messiahship would translate without difficulty into the charge with which Pilate would confront him: 'Are you the king of the Jews?'"[55]

There are three basic options available to Jesus among the Jews of his day, and he claims a "kingdom-model" from Israel's scriptures that differs from these three.[56] The first option is quietism and withdrawal into desert

53. Yoder, *The Original Revolution,* p. 38.
54. Yoder, *The Original Revolution,* p. 39.
55. N. T. Wright, *Jesus and the Victory of God,* Christian Origins and the Question of God, vol. 2 (Minneapolis: Fortress, 1996), p. 547.
56. Wright, *The Challenge of Jesus,* p. 37.

communities (in the Jordan Valley) like the one at Qumran, which produced the Dead Sea Scrolls. The second is the way of compromise "taken by Herod: build yourself fortresses and places, get along with your political bosses as well as you can, do as well out of it as you can and hope that God will validate it somehow." The third is violent resistance (the zealot option): "God will give you a military victory that will also be the theological victory of good over evil."[57] Jesus' way is remarkably different. He takes up a battle with oppression and sin "through turning the other cheek, going the second mile, loving [our] enemies and praying for [our] persecutors . . . a revolutionary way of being revolutionary."[58] He confronts the powers in Jerusalem, and "defeat[s] evil by letting it do its worst to him."[59]

Why does Jesus die? The backdrop for the answer is Israel's commission to be a light to the nations, to bear God's holiness, and to be a redeemed and reconciled people. To do so, this people would have to be gathered, called to repentance, and forgiven. Jesus shows the way of love, compassion, and reconciliation, so that the question remains as to why such a man would be put to death. First of all, Jesus is "executed as a rebel against Rome," and crucifixion is the kind of public and humiliating death that the Roman Empire used to display its power.[60] However, Jesus is hardly the kind of rebel that Romans were accustomed to executing; we can rightly say that Jesus is executed by Pilate as a would-be king because there is nothing else that Pilate, as a self-interested and cynical instrument of Caesar, could do with him after he is accused.[61] Jesus is accused by the leaders of his own people as a false prophet, leading people astray, making pronouncements against the temple, and conjuring up revolutionary activity that "might well bring the wrath of Rome upon Temple and nation alike."[62] Instead, Roman wrath comes down only upon Jesus, but as a representative of the people — as king of the Jews.

These historical reasons for Jesus' death coincide with theological ones. Jesus is innocent. He is neither false prophet nor guerilla warrior; however, he does give the procurator of Roman affairs, the temple leadership, and the Jewish aristocracy reason to want him dead. He seeks to gather and restore Israel, and as noted above, he brings expectations for God's reign to a climax. He brings the battle to his opponents. He does not

57. Wright, *The Challenge of Jesus*, p. 37.
58. Wright, *Jesus and the Victory*, p. 564.
59. Wright, *The Challenge of Jesus*, p. 85.
60. Wright, *Jesus and the Victory*, pp. 541-42.
61. Wright, *Jesus and the Victory*, pp. 546-47.
62. Wright, *Jesus and the Victory*, p. 551.

withdraw into the desert, or compromise, or take up arms, but faces the powers of the world with God's reconciling love — with a means to start anew. Jesus Christ is the incarnate Son of God who is sent into the world, to Jerusalem to die, but it is humans (not God) who make his death necessary. Throughout his ministry Jesus can foresee his death, and it is rightly called a sacrifice, but not a sacrifice to satisfy God's need for payment in blood. The sacrifice is a gift to us and to God. Jesus' death is inevitable because a world of hatred and violence will deem it necessary to kill the Son of God (Matt. 21:33-46). In Christ, God will not take the human way of enmity and bloodshed. Our victory is that God does not withdraw from us or compromise with our sins, but joins with us in Jesus Christ. He is God's offer of reconciling love to us, a new beginning and a new way, and he is (as fully human) our representative and (as divine) our cleansing sacrifice. He is our representative who unreservedly offers God's self-giving love back to God.

The resurrection is the new beginning, our reconciliation and new life. It is the crowning of Jesus as the Lord, not only as Savior and Messiah, but also as "the one in whom the living God, Israel's God, has become personally present in the world."[63] The resurrection is the triumph of God's justice, which is not credible, intelligible, or consistent without the cross. The cross is the consummation of "God's nearness to human beings, initiated in the incarnation, proclaimed and rendered present by Jesus during his earthly life. . . . The cross says, in human language, that nothing in history has set limits to God's nearness to human beings."[64] Jesus' resurrection is our foretaste of the kingdom that he proclaims.

Scripture and Ethics

The proclamation of the risen Christ is at the center of Christian scripture; therefore, the relationship between the Bible and Christian ethics is one of call and response. Hearing God's call to us in the Bible is a common experience among Christians. The saints have been inspired by passages such as Matthew 19:21 and Matthew 25:40: "If you wish to be perfect, go, sell your possessions, and give the money to the poor, and you will have treasure in heaven" and "Whatever you did for one of these least brothers of mine, you did for me" (NAB). Many of us have passages that speak to us at a specific

---

63. N. T. Wright, *The Resurrection of the Son of God*, Christian Origins and the Question of God, vol. 3 (Minneapolis: Fortress, 2003), p. 733.

64. Sobrino, *Jesus in Latin America*, p. 153.

time in our lives. I have been moved by Romans 12:2, "Do not be conformed to this world, but be transformed by the renewing of your minds, so that you may discern what is the will of God — what is good and acceptable and perfect." Listening for God's message to us is a time-honored view of the relationship between the biblical text and our lives.

However, this view also seems to encourage two mistaken ideas. One mistake is to consider the Bible a plain and simple book. It may be that someone who knows very little about matters of faith or Christianity can read the Bible and be inspired immediately (rather than bored, confused, or dismayed). Such inspiration is possible, but the image of a "plain and simple" book is false as a standard framework for how an understanding of Scripture becomes intimate and vital. According to ancient Christian belief, the message of salvation is indeed simple; however, understanding the Bible well requires the wisdom, compassion, and humility that come through a long life of study, prayer, and living faithfully with others.[65] Hearing the call in Scripture is not an individualistic endeavor.[66] We are called to be part of a community where we learn the skills and perspective necessary to read and hear God's call truthfully. We are called (in the words of Sandra Schneiders) to be "fit interpreters" in relationship to the Spirit of God.[67]

The idea that the Bible is simple and requires no study or prayer leads to a second misunderstanding, that the message of Scripture will always offer comfort. It is certainly true that texts like Romans 8:28-39 and Psalm 23 offer great reassurance and consolation, but most of the Bible, as a call to us, is likely to put more questions to our lives than to provide answers. Opening the Bible and ourselves to the Spirit is risky business and might bring discomfort rather than satisfaction with the way we are living our lives. Jesus' proclamation at the beginning of his ministry is to repent and prepare for the kingdom of God. It may be true that the Bible embodies a simple message, but its simple call will take all of who we are and our whole lives to answer. It is a call of transformation and new life. Sometimes our transformation is immediate, but usually it takes an entire life.

In other words, the "fit" interpreter of Scripture is "one who 'acts out'

65. Douglas Burton-Christie, "Oral Culture, Biblical Interpretation, and Spirituality in Early Christian Monasticism," in *The Bible in Greek Christian Antiquity*, ed. Paul Blowers (Notre Dame, Ind.: University of Notre Dame Press, 1997), pp. 415-35.

66. The modern study of the Bible, for its part, has emphasized that biblical texts have a complex history and are composed and first read in cultural contexts that may be strange and obscure to the untrained reader.

67. Sandra M. Schneiders, I.H.M., "The Paschal Imagination: Objectivity and Subjectivity in New Testament Interpretation," *Theological Studies* 43, no. 1 (March 1982): 66.

the material before him so as to give it intelligible life."[68] This approach to understanding the Bible is part of the incarnational approach developed earlier in the chapter. The incarnation is God with us in the humanity of Jesus Christ and in our continuing life in Christ's Spirit. It is an embodied (an "in the flesh" or "in the people") approach. From a modern point of view, this incarnational or "in the people" approach appears to be too vulnerable to human prejudices and weaknesses. Recall that the same problem was discussed at the beginning of the chapter in terms of the authority and inspiration of Scripture. How do frail human words convey the Word of God? Particularly in terms of applying the Bible to ethics, aren't we susceptible to fashioning Jesus in our own image?

This ancient model of the incarnate and embodied word provides an illuminating contrast to typically modern methods of studying the Bible. Here I am speaking of "modern" in a philosophical or ideological sense; the ancient model is time-honored and still used widely today. In the academic sense of "modern," the real meaning of the Bible is thought to exist apart from us in the historical past. The Bible's meaning "is conceived of (at least implicitly) as a sort of property," which is in the text like iron in iron ore.[69] According to this view, we find meaning by mining the text and separating out impurities. The "iron" or "real meaning" might be hidden behind the portrait of Jesus in the Gospels, or it might be considered the real intentions of the writer of Matthew in the composition of his portrait of Jesus. Whatever is considered the "property" or the good article of the text, the meaning is found by disinterested techniques: from historical study, literary criticism, sociology, and anthropology.[70] According to this "disengaged" view, faith and doctrine are too prejudiced, so that we must detach ourselves from the immediate impact of Scripture in our lives to get the real Jesus and the real meaning of the text.[71]

Stephen Fowl, in his *Engaging Scripture,* outlines this typical modern (disengaged) approach and also the postmodern (relativist) response to the

---

68. George Steiner, *Real Presences* (Chicago, 1989), cited in Burton-Christie, "Oral Culture," p. 431.

69. Stephen Fowl, *Engaging Scripture: A Model of Theological Interpretation* (Oxford: Blackwell, 1998), p. 33.

70. Fowl, *Engaging Scripture,* pp. 33-40.

71. In "The Bible and Christian Ethics," in *Christian Ethics: An Introduction,* ed. Bernard Hoose (Collegeville, Minn.: Liturgical Press, 1998), Tom Deidun argues that "the interpreter's involvement" should not be part of a constructive methodology and that the exegete should do "one's utmost to prevent one's 'exegesis of existence' colouring one's interpretation of biblical texts" (p. 4).

problems of biblical interpretation. On the modern side, he explains that separating the Bible from us as a "freestanding" text seems far more dependable than relying on people, who continually develop, change, and often fail to live out the love and faith they claim to have. Scripture can seem far more trustworthy if we locate the meaning "in" the text or in a historical reconstruction of the text. On the postmodern side, we might argue that the meaning "in" the text is inaccessible to us, so that no interpretation can claim to be better than another. All readings of Scripture are relative, and one relative reading is as good as the next. On the modern or disengaged side, the meaning exists apart from us; on the postmodern or relativist side, the "meaning" is so much a part of our point of view that there is no real meaning.[72]

We can deal with the weaknesses of people without retreating to either this disengaged or this relativist point of view. The vulnerability of the incarnational approach or what Fowl calls the "engaged" understanding of Scripture ought to be taken very seriously. People are liable to self-centered, sinful interpretations of Scripture. But Fowl argues that the way to overcome our inclination to self-centered readings of the Bible is to experience Scripture as part of a worshiping community. We cannot follow Jesus or understand his words faithfully alone. Following Jesus requires the confession of our sins. Jesus gathers disciples, the poor, lame, and blind, the tax collector, fisherman, rebel, and Pharisee into community. Insofar as we learn the virtues and practices of Christian community, we are learning how to approach Scripture well. An incarnational approach to the function of Scripture and the significance of Jesus for today will invite us into practices of steadfast love, the confession of our sins, forgiveness, reconciliation, and a discernment of the Spirit in our lives.[73] By answering the Spirit's call, we will begin to understand Scripture truthfully.

This incarnational approach is not opposed to historical, literary, and other modern methods of analysis. Many biblical scholars and moral theologians want to hold both kinds of inquiry together. The contrast between a technical/detached approach and an incarnational approach is a matter of which set of questions will provide the basic and most inclusive framework. The incarnational approach understands that morality and Scripture are first of all embodied, that they are sustained and intelligible insofar as they are carried out and lived out within communities of faith and a tradition over time.

72. Fowl, *Engaging Scripture,* pp. 32-61.
73. Fowl, *Engaging Scripture,* pp. 91-95, 97-127, 145-50.

William Spohn, in his *Go and Do Likewise,* proposes that the Christian profession of faith, that Jesus Christ is God revealed to us, indicates that he "plays a normative role in Christians' moral reflection. His story enables us to recognize *which* features of experience are significant, guides *how* we act, and forms *who* we are in the community of faith."[74] Spohn's reference to "which" features of experience helps clarify the incarnational model. Spohn proposes that a primary function of Scripture in the moral life is to allow us to begin to see the world from God's point of view (however challenging that might be) and to experience our lives in light of this vision of the world. We are called not only to experience the call of God in Scripture, but also to become experienced listeners and readers of Scripture. We become experienced not merely by opening a book, but through prayer, common worship (especially the celebration of Eucharist), and following Jesus' way of love.

Spohn's title, *Go and Do Likewise,* is evocative. It dispels the notion that we have to get the theory right or have expert knowledge before we put our understanding into practice (i.e., that we must know precisely what a biblical text means before we can put it into practice). This notion does not hold for any practical ways of knowing, whether one is a medical doctor, basketball player, teacher, or biologist. One is initiated into a community of practitioners, given guides and teachers, and must go and do in order to understand. Likewise, we must enter a community of shared faith and begin to follow Jesus before we know the significance of Jesus for the moral life. Spohn's *Go and Do Likewise* also suggests that the "meaning" of Scripture is an ongoing encounter, that our lives are brought into the way of God in Jesus Christ, and that Christ's way becomes part of our lives. We do not simply or mechanically repeat Jesus' actions. Rather, we go and do "likewise" in our time. Through our biblically formed vision and imagination, we are open to be instruments of God's loving presence in the world.

This new vision of life is identified, by Sandra Schneiders, as the paschal (or eucharistic) imagination. It is a "whole cognitive-affective capacity of the person" that is attained through the influence of Christ's Spirit and an experience of new life in Christ. It comes on the heels of a "transformation according to the new self-understanding and possibilities" that becomes available in Jesus.[75] Schneiders argues that this paschal imagination is the connecting link between Jesus of Nazareth, early Christians, their part

74. William C. Spohn, *Go and Do Likewise: Jesus and Ethics* (New York: Continuum, 2000), p. 2.
75. Schneiders, "The Paschal Imagination," p. 65.

in the composition and canonization of Scripture, and us. This paschal imagination is not a private experience but a shared conviction that the world has been changed by the life, death, and resurrection of Christ.

Conclusion

This chapter leaves many questions unanswered. The astute reader is likely to be wondering why I have not provided a more exact method for interpreting biblical texts and applying them to issues of our day. One might ask, "What does the Bible say about sex, divorce, marriage, and homosexuality?" These questions are important, but the answers do not hinge on a method of application, and using issues like these as a basis for a chapter on Scripture and ethics would misconstrue the foundational place of Scripture in our lives. Scripture is, first of all, not an encyclopedia where we look for sentences or a paragraph to answer essential questions, but a proclamation of salvation and a call to follow Jesus — to *go and do likewise.*

This chapter on Scripture fits with the methodological approach of the book as a whole, especially the second part that deals with issues of our calling, human fulfillment, and virtue; that is, the issue of moral formation precedes issues of how we approach moral issues. In the chapter, quite a few methods of textual analysis have been used. For example, from the ancient world I have used Origen's typological interpretation of the sacrifice of Isaac and Gregory of Nyssa's explanation of the Beatitudes as an ascending stairway of holiness. From modern sources I have used N. T. Wright's historical analysis of Jesus' ministry and crucifixion, David Garland's literary study of the book of Matthew, and Monika Hellwig's theological exposition of the liturgy. None of these methods provides the framework for interpretation, but each has been indispensable. To use them well we are called to pray, worship, share God's love for the world, and become part of a people, a tradition of study and action. We are called, to cite Sandra Schneiders once again, to be "fit interpreters" in relationship to the Spirit of God. For this reason the Easter Vigil and Jesus' proclamation of the kingdom are central to the chapter. We are called to be initiated to life in Christ, to be those who proclaim and extend the Bible's salvation history, to repent and seek to live anew.

Concurrent Readings

Biblical texts: Matthew 5-7; 18; Luke 4; 13-19; Romans 12-15; Philippians 2.
These texts are just a few that could be considered; these are recommended because the chapter provides a liturgical and ecclesiological context for them to be read fruitfully.

Hays, Richard B. *The Moral Vision of the New Testament: A Contemporary Introduction to New Testament Ethics.* New York: HarperCollins, 1996. Hays provides a comprehensive study of New Testament ethics by providing interpretive guides and studies of particular issues.

Lohfink, Gerhard. *Jesus and Community: The Social Dimension of Christian Faith.* Translated by John P. Galvin. Philadelphia: Fortress; New York: Paulist, 1984. Lohfink's work sets an account of discipleship in the context of biblical, salvation history.

Spohn, William C. *Go and Do Likewise: Jesus and Ethics.* New York: Continuum, 2000. This is one of the best works available for understanding the relationship between the Bible and contemporary ethics. Its basic approach has been outlined in the chapter.

Wright, N. T. *Following Jesus: Biblical Reflections on Discipleship.* Grand Rapids: Eerdmans, 1994. This book is the best companion to this chapter during a course in moral theology. It gives brief but incisive analysis of various books of the New Testament.

Chapter 3

The Trinity

FREDERICK CHRISTIAN BAUERSCHMIDT

Mystery and Irrelevance

There's a joke about an old, slightly deaf bishop who comes to confirm a group of teenagers. The bishop decides that, prior to conferring the sacrament, he will quiz the young people. So he asks, "What is the Trinity?" After a long silence, and a lot of downcast eyes and shuffling feet, one of the teenagers finally mumbles in a low voice, "The Father, the Son, and the Holy Spirit." The bishop, cupping his hand to his ear, says, "I'm sorry; I didn't understand that." Looking irritated, the kid replies, "You're not supposed to understand it. It's a mystery."

I will admit, this isn't a very funny joke, but it does make a point about how many of us think about the doctrine of the Trinity. Imagine yourself confronted with this fragment of the so-called Athanasian Creed:

> Almighty is the Father, almighty is the Son, almighty the Holy Spirit; yet, they are not three gods but one God. Thus, the Father is Lord, the Son Lord, the Holy Spirit Lord; yet, they are not three lords but one Lord. For, as the Christian truth compels us to acknowledge each person distinctly as God and Lord, so too the Catholic religion forbids us to speak of three gods or lords. The Father has neither been made by anyone, nor is he created or begotten; the Son is from the Father alone, not made nor created but begotten; the Holy Spirit is from the Father and of the Son, not made nor created nor begotten, but proceeding. So there is one Father, not three Fathers; one Son, not three Sons; one Holy Spirit, not three Holy Spirits.[1]

1. Complete text in J. Neuner and J. Dupuis, eds., *The Christian Faith in the Doctrinal Documents of the Catholic Church*, 7th ed. (New York: Alba House, 2001), §16-17.

Presented with such a document, one might be forgiven for suspecting that it espouses some sort of peculiar math that we're not really supposed to understand, in which 3 × 1 = 1, or that it functions as a kind of loyalty test for Catholics, showing that we are willing to believe any sort of nonsense that the church proposes for our belief. Despite the intense interest shown by professional theologians in the Trinity in the past few decades, its relevance is not readily apparent to many, even to many devout believers.

The theology of the Trinity might seem particularly unrelated to moral theology. The philosopher Immanuel Kant (1724-1804) opined that "the doctrine of the Trinity, taken literally, has no practical relevance at all, even if we think we understand it; and it is even more clearly irrelevant if we realize that it transcends all our concepts. Whether we are to worship three or ten persons in the Deity makes no difference."[2] Kant, for whom religion was a matter of practical reason (i.e., ethics), believed the Trinity to be bereft of both religious and moral significance because he could not see what possible impact it might have on human behavior. Even if it made sense, which it doesn't, one could still not derive moral maxims from it.

In this chapter I propose to do three things. First, I will briefly describe what the doctrine of the Trinity is by describing its genesis in the Christian tradition. Second, I will sketch two different strategies that have been employed in recent years in the attempt to overcome the irrelevance of the Trinity to moral theology, and will offer some remarks as to why I think they are wrongheaded. Finally, I will offer my own suggestions for thinking about how belief in God as Father, Son, and Spirit might shape the being-in-the-world of Christians.

One *What?* Three *Whats?*

Christian doctrines are usually generated by specific problems confronted by the Christian community at certain points in history. For the doctrine of the Trinity, the problem is how the Christian claim to worship the God of Israel, about whom the fundamental profession of faith is "Hear, O Israel: The LORD our God is one LORD" (Deut. 6:4 RSV), can be compatible with Christian claims regarding the divinity of Christ. Put differently, the problem is how one reconciles the uncompromising monotheism of Judaism with the claim that Jesus of Nazareth is God.

---

2. Immanuel Kant, *The Conflict of Faculties* (1798), trans. Mary J. McGregor (Lincoln: University of Nebraska Press, 1979), p. 67.

First, regarding the monotheism of Israel, we must realize that the Jewish people's awareness of the uniqueness of the God of Abraham, Isaac, and Jacob was hard won. The writings of the prophets testify to Israel's constant temptation to conform to the polytheistic practices of her neighbors, seduced by the attractions of deities whose power was limited in scope, deities who could provide aid in some carefully circumscribed area of life but who did not require the kind of unlimited allegiance demanded by the God of Israel. The claim that Israel's God was the only true God, and therefore the God of *all* people, was a radical claim that implied a new understanding of the cosmos and the place of human beings within it. The one God was the unique source of all that is, Lord of every time and place. As the psalmist prayed:

> Where can I go from your spirit?
>   Or where can I flee from your presence?
> If I ascend to heaven, you are there;
>   if I make my bed in Sheol, you are there.
> If I take the wings of the morning
>   and settle at the farthest limits of the sea,
> even there your hand shall lead me,
>   and your right hand shall hold me fast.

(Ps. 139:7-10)

To introduce a second god would be to compromise the universal scope of God's power and love.

Second, regarding Christian belief in the divinity of Jesus, it has been the common wisdom for the past century and a half that this is a late development, appearing only in the later books of the New Testament, and representing a "Hellenization" (i.e., a recasting into Greek language and thought) of the Christian gospel. However, more recently some biblical scholars have argued that belief in the divinity of Jesus can be found in the earliest writings of the New Testament.[3] Of course, we do not find the bald statement "Christ is God" or "Jesus is divine," which would be unthinkable in the context of Jewish monotheism. Rather, the divinity of Christ is on the whole indicated indirectly, by treating him as an object of worship and ascribing to him things that could only be true of God. To take one example, in Paul's letter to the Philippians he writes that Christ,

---

3. See, for example, the extensive evidence collected in Larry Hurtado, *Lord Jesus Christ: Devotion to Jesus in Earliest Christianity* (Grand Rapids: Eerdmans, 2003).

though he was in the form of God,
>   did not regard equality with God
>   as something to be exploited,
but emptied himself,
>   taking the form of a slave,
>   being born in human likeness.
And being found in human form,
>   he humbled himself
>   and became obedient to the point of death —
>   even death on a cross.
Therefore God also highly exalted him
>   and gave him the name
>   that is above every name,
so that at the name of Jesus
>   every knee should bend,
>   in heaven and on earth and under the earth,
and every tongue should confess
>   that Jesus Christ is Lord [*Kyrios*],
>   to the glory of God the Father.

(Phil. 2:6-11)

Here Paul presents Jesus as having been "in the form of God" prior to his "being born in human likeness." His resurrection from the dead is understood as God exalting him and giving him "the name that is above every name," which is *Kyrios,* or "Lord," the same word used in the ancient Greek translation of the Old Testament to indicate the unspeakable name of God (in Hebrew, *YHWH*). Furthermore, because he bears this name, Jesus receives the worship of all creation. Thus in this very early Christian writing we find Jesus presented as one who receives those things that are the sole prerogative of God. Faith in the divinity of Jesus lies at the very origin of Christianity.

This passage also provides us with a clue as to what could have led Christians to make such a radical claim about Jesus: his resurrection from the dead. Paul identifies this as the moment when God bestows upon him the divine name, so that, even though he had been "in the form of God" prior to his birth, he now is acknowledged and worshiped as God by creatures. It was in light of their experience of the risen Christ that the disciples came to understand Jesus' own attitude during his earthly ministry. Jesus had consistently acted as if one's adherence to him took precedence over any of Israel's religious institutions, whether this be the law or the temple. Being a follower of Jesus was what determined one's place in God's kingdom; all else was secondary.[4] This implicit placing of himself in the position of God is seen in a new light after the resurrection of Jesus.

With the Gospel of John, which was most likely written near the end of the first century, we reach the end of a trajectory that begins with Paul. In the prologue of his Gospel, John speaks of Jesus as the *Logos,* or "Word," who is "in the beginning" *with* God, and who *is* God (John 1:1). This Word comes forth from God his Father in such a way that he shares everything that is the Father's. And it is only with John's Gospel that we arrive at the explicit confession that Thomas makes before the risen Christ, "My Lord and my God" (20:28).

John's Gospel also speaks of the Holy Spirit as "another Advocate" (14:16), who continues Jesus' saving activity within his followers, and thus shares, though perhaps not so clearly, in the divinity that the Father and Word have in common. This same understanding of the Spirit is found in earlier texts as well, particularly in Paul, for whom the "Spirit of God" dwells in Christians and leads them so that they are sons and daughters of God, and cry out "Abba" — that is, "Father" — to God (Rom. 8:9-17). Certainly the baptismal formula at the end of Matthew's Gospel seems to present the Father, the Son, and the Holy Spirit as constituting together the "name" into which the nations are to be baptized (Matt. 28:19).

At first, Christians seemed content to simply let the claim of Jesus' (and the Spirit's) divinity exist side by side with monotheism. Certainly the New Testament contains no real attempt to address the problem. But by the second century Christians had begun to ponder how best to speak of the relationship of Jesus, as Son and Word of God, to the God he called Father. Two options initially presented themselves. The first, which is commonly called subordinationism, sought to distinguish the Son from the Father by thinking of the Son as a being that mediates between the created world and the Father, who is absolutely transcendent and the one true God. The Spirit, who receives relatively less attention, is treated in a similar way. According to the subordinationist view, the Son and Spirit are not God in the same sense that the Father is, but they are also not simply creatures; they seem to exist in an ill-defined middle ground between God and creation. The second option, commonly called modalism, interpreted "Father" and "Son" and "Holy Spirit" as different ways or "modes" in which God has acted in history. Thus when speaking of God's activity of creation, we speak of God as "Father"; when speaking of God's activity of redeeming us through Jesus, we speak of

---

4. See E. P. Sanders, *The Historical Figure of Jesus* (London: Penguin Books, 1993), pp. 238-48.

God as "Son" or "Word"; and when speaking of God's activity of indwelling Christians and leading them to holiness, we speak of God as "Spirit." According to the modalists, there is only one God, about whom we speak in three different ways based on three different divine activities.

Modalism clearly preserved monotheism, and seemed an easily graspable way of relating Father, Son, and Spirit, but it raised a host of difficulties. The chief of these is that throughout the Gospels the Father, Son, and Spirit are presented as "characters" who are distinct, though intimately related. Put most simply, when Jesus prays to the Father, is he talking to himself? When the Spirit descends upon Jesus at his baptism, is he descending upon himself? As the second-century writer Tertullian said pointedly regarding Jesus' crying out to God on the cross, "If it was the Father who was suffering, to what God was it that he addressed his cry?"[5] Subordinationism, on the other hand, preserved the distinctness of the Father, Son, and Spirit, and thus preserved the sense of their relatedness to each other, as well as a sense that it is through the Son and the Spirit that we are related to the Father. The difficulty arose when people, to preserve monotheism, began asking whether the Son and the Spirit are beings created by God, like all other creatures. If they are mere creatures, how could Christians claim to find salvation in Jesus through the Spirit without losing the sense of salvation as the sole prerogative of God; how could Christians worship the Son and Spirit without falling into idolatry? But if they are not creatures, then in what sense are Christians still monotheists?

Perhaps because it rendered the Gospel accounts nonsensical, modalism was fairly quickly rejected by the mainstream of Christianity. But subordinationism seemed to remain an attractive option. The most sophisticated and consistent subordinationist scheme was worked out by a priest from Alexandria, Egypt, named Arius, who lived at the beginning of the fourth century. Whereas earlier subordinationism had fudged the question of whether the Son and Spirit had been created by God the Father, Arius was clear that they were creatures, and therefore the Father alone was truly God. The Father, who was utterly transcendent, interacted with the world through the Son and Spirit as created intermediaries. But Arius's bishop, Alexander, rejected the views of Arius and his followers as being "invented by them, and spoken contrary to the mind of Scripture."[6] This controversy

---

5. Tertullian, *Against Praxeas* 30, in *Ante-Nicene Fathers,* vol. 3 (Peabody, Mass.: Hendrickson, 1994).

6. Alexander, Encyclical Letter of 319, §2, in *Ante-Nicene Fathers,* vol. 6 (Peabody, Mass.: Hendrickson, 1994), p. 297.

quickly became the source of bitter division in the church. The emperor Constantine, who had recently legalized Christianity, in part because he hoped it could be a unifying force in the Roman Empire, called a meeting of bishops in 325 at the town of Nicea in what is today Turkey.

The three hundred bishops who gathered for the Council of Nicea adopted a creed that explicitly rejected the views of Arius and his followers, proclaiming that the Son is "begotten, not made" — that is, the Son comes forth from the Father (i.e., is "begotten"), but yet is not a creature (i.e., "not made"). The creed goes on to say that the Son is "one in being" *(homoousious)* with the Father, making clear that the Son is fully divine. This term would prove to be controversial in the following decades, since it sounded to many as if it were saying that the Son was identical to the Father, as in modalism. It would fall to Athanasius of Alexandria (ca. 296-373), who attended the council as a young deacon, to become the champion of the theology of Nicea in general and the language of *homoousious* in particular.

Athanasius's argument centered around his understanding of salvation. Because of sin, which was a turning away from the God who is the source of our life and existence, human beings had become subject to suffering and death. In taking on human flesh the Son had united human mortality to divine immortality, thus renewing human nature and conquering death. But this can only be the case if the Son shares fully in the divine nature of the Father, for anything less than union with the divine nature is insufficient for the defeat of sin and death. And the best way to express the Son's full share of the Father's divinity is with the term *homoousious*. At the heart of Athanasius's argument is the same instinct that we find in the New Testament: in encountering Jesus we encounter the saving power of God, not through any intermediary, but directly. After decades of controversy, Athanasius turned the tide of opinion in favor of Nicea and *homoousious*. The final vindication of Nicene trinitarian theology occurred at the Council of Constantinople in 381, at which an expanded version of the Nicene Creed was adopted as the definitive version of the Catholic faith. The chief difference between the two creeds is the attention the expanded one pays to the Holy Spirit, affirming that the Spirit is "the Lord and giver of life" and that the Spirit is also a proper object of human worship and glorification. This is the creed that is said to this day in the Catholic Mass.

Of course, while the triumph of Nicene theology set the parameters of acceptable belief, this was not the end of theological reflection on the Trinity. In particular, there was an ongoing clarification of terminology, particularly with regard to the question, "If God is one in three, then one *what* and three *whats?*" This was worked out somewhat differently in the Greek-speaking East and the Latin-speaking West. In the East, God was one *ousia* (as in *homo-ousia*), or "essence," and three *hypostases,* or "concrete instances of existing." In the West, God was one *substantia,* or "substance," and three *personae,* or "persons." This difference in terminology has been the occasion for mutual suspicion and misunderstanding between East and West, though it is today generally accepted that both traditions express the same faith. There was also ongoing reflection on the interrelatedness of the persons, and particularly on their mutual indwelling of each other (or *perichoresis*), a reflection growing out of Jesus' words "I am in the Father and the Father is in me" (John 14:10). There was also a search for analogies that could cast some light on how God could be three persons and yet only one God. Some suggested that we think of the way in which three human beings share the same humanity; others suggested we think of the way in which a single human mind is made up of memory, reason, and will. On every side, however, it was agreed that all such analogies fail, either by obscuring the absolute unity of God or by slighting the absolute distinctiveness of the persons. The Trinity remains an abiding mystery that incites our minds to ponder and our hearts to adore.

Making the Trinity Relevant

I believe that the admittedly sketchy account I have given of the historical development of trinitarian doctrine will give some sense of how and why certain choices were made, certain paths followed. But it does not necessarily tell us why we should care about trinitarian theology today. Particularly, it does not indicate directly the implications of the Trinity for how Christians ought to live. What does trinitarian theology have to do with moral theology?

One possible answer to this question is "not all that much." As a friend once said to me, "The doctrine of the Trinity is important because it is true, not because it is practical." Thus, even among theologians who accept the truth of the Trinity, some strongly resist the idea that the Trinity can be "saved" for modern Christians by showing how norms for human action can be derived from it.[7] But other authors have maintained that unless this doctrine can shape and inform the moral lives of Christians, it will remain at best a historical artifact, set up on some dusty shelf. Thus, various

7. For a subtle and sophisticated form of that critique, see Matthew Levering, "Beyond the Jamesian Impasse in Trinitarian Theology," *Thomist* 66 (2002): 395-420.

paths have been pursued to relate the Trinity and ethics. In this section I will trace two such paths, and offer critical suggestions as to why I think, in the end, they will not take us where we wish to go.

The Trinity as Theological Traffic Cop

The first approach works from the presumption that the doctrine of the Trinity, like any statement about God, tells us nothing about God in himself, but only about how we perceive God. We see this view in the work of the twentieth-century American Protestant theologian H. Richard Niebuhr, who writes, "Trinitarianism is by no means as speculative a position and as unimportant for conduct as is often maintained." Rather, it is a way of addressing the different ways in which we derive our ideas of right conduct; specifically, it helps us keep straight "the relation of Jesus Christ to the Creator of nature and Governor of history as well as the Spirit immanent in creation and in the Christian community."[8] Niebuhr sees the Trinity as a way of resisting the three different "unitarianisms" that constantly tempt Christians in their reasoning about how they should live their lives: the unitarianism of the Father, which focuses on creation, reason, and natural law; the unitarianism of the Son, which focuses on redemption, revelation, and the Sermon on the Mount; and the unitarianism of the Spirit, which focuses on present experience, spiritual awareness, and conscience.[9]

For Niebuhr the doctrine of the Trinity is a way of saying that none of these unitarianisms is adequate to the demands of Christian moral reasoning. Christians must find a way of holding together reason, revelation, and experience while keeping them from coming into conflict. In terms of ethics, Christians must look to both natural law *and* the teachings of Christ, as well as individual conscience. If one focuses exclusively on the Father/Creator, one tends toward a rationalist morality based on the created order, which ignores both the teachings of Jesus and the lived spiritual experience of Christians. If one looks only to Jesus the redeemer, while ignoring the Father and the Spirit, one runs the risk of a legalistic fundamentalism that is both irrational and joyless, and that confines one to a sectarian ghetto. And if one sees God only in terms of the Spirit, then one has an ethics based en-

8. H. Richard Niebuhr, *Christ and Culture* (New York: Harper and Row, 1951), pp. 80-81.

9. This is spelled out with greatest clarity in "The Doctrine of the Trinity and the Unity of the Church," *Theology Today* 3, no. 3 (October 1946): 371-84; reprinted in H. Richard Niebuhr, *Theology, History, and Culture: Major Unpublished Writings*, ed. William Stacy Johnson (New Haven: Yale University Press, 1996), pp. 50-62.

tirely on intuition, without any stable principles. The doctrine of the Trinity helps us to avoid all these distortions in our moral reasoning, acting like a traffic cop keeping reason, revelation, and experience all running along in their proper lanes, making sure none is abandoned, but also avoiding collisions among them.

There is clearly some value in what Niebuhr says. We certainly want a moral reasoning that draws upon the full range of sources available to the Christian. Yet does the doctrine of the Trinity really help us do this? Jews and Muslims, without belief in the Trinity, look to reason, historical revelation, and personal inspiration for moral guidance. What does the Trinity add? Further, is Niebuhr's account of the Trinity itself adequate?[10] There are clear affinities between his account and the modalist view that "Father," "Son," and "Spirit" are nothing more than ways of speaking about the activity of God as eternal creator, historical redeemer, and personal inspirer. We might say that Niebuhr, somewhat like modalism, treats the Trinity as a kind of organizational chart of divine activity, though for Niebuhr this is only about how we perceive divine activity, and not a doctrine that says something true about God or God's activity in itself. So, in the end it seems that Niebuhr's approach turns the Trinity into simply a way of speaking about our ethical resources, and keeping them sorted out and in balance, rather than a way of speaking about God.

The Trinity as Social Blueprint

The second approach is much more prevalent among theologians today than Niebuhr's. This "social trinitarianism" sees a model for human community in the perfect communion of Father, Son, and Spirit. The doctrine of the Trinity calls human beings to live lives that reflect the relationship of love shared by the trinitarian persons. The equality and reciprocity of the persons of the Trinity show us that human beings ought to live lives of justice and mutuality, and in this the Trinity is shown to be a thoroughly prac-

---

10. The following critical remarks on Niebuhr's trinitarian theology are indebted to John Howard Yoder's "How H. Richard Niebuhr Reasoned: A Critique of *Christ and Culture*," in Glen H. Stassen, D. M. Yeager, and John Howard Yoder, *Authentic Transformation: A New Vision of Christ and Culture* (Nashville: Abingdon, 1996), pp. 31-90. To be fair, Niebuhr says at the end of "The Doctrine of the Trinity and the Unity of the Church" that what he has said is "only one approach, and that not the most significant or promising" (p. 62). In other words, he implies that much more could, and perhaps should, be said about the Trinity. However, it is the only way in which Niebuhr himself ever spoke of the doctrine.

tical doctrine. Thus, for example, the theologians Michael Himes and Kenneth Himes argue that "a trinitarian vision sees the individual and community as co-existent," and therefore "the most fundamental human right is the right to exercise the power of self-giving, the opportunity for entrance into relationship, for deeper participation in the life of the human community."[11]

The theologians who take a "social trinitarian" approach differ among themselves on a whole host of issues, but they also share certain things in common, in addition to their claim that the Trinity provides a model for human society. The chief theological point they share is an emphasis on the distinctness of the trinitarian persons and a critical attitude toward the emphasis on the unity of the divine nature that they see growing out of the theology of Saint Augustine, and as characteristic of Western theology in general. For social trinitarians the unity of the divine persons is a unity of *perichoresis,* a unity-in-relationship, allowing us to see the trinitarian unity as something that human beings in relationship with each other can aspire to. This approach to trinitarian doctrine is "social" not only because it takes the Trinity as a model for human societies, but also because it sees the Trinity itself as a kind of divine society into which the divine persons enter.

This approach has certain commendable features. Unlike Niebuhr's approach, social trinitarianism is not simply about how we know God, but rather makes a genuine claim about the divine nature: God is a community of persons. Also, the emphasis on the relational nature of the trinitarian unity clearly avoids the pitfall of modalism. In addition, this approach can find support in authoritative church documents: the Second Vatican Council's *Pastoral Constitution on the Church in the Modern World* says there is "a certain similarity between the union of the divine persons and the union of God's children in truth and love."[12] At the same time, this approach has certain weaknesses.

As with Niebuhr's approach, we might ask about the adequacy of this approach simply from a doctrinal viewpoint. A desire to maintain a clear distinction between the persons has, at times, motivated a subordination of the Son and Spirit to the Father, even to the point of Arius's denial that the Son and Spirit share the same divine nature as the Father. This is counter-

11. Michael J. Himes and Kenneth R. Himes, O.F.M., *Fullness of Faith: The Public Significance of Theology* (Mahwah, N.J.: Paulist, 1993), p. 61.

12. Second Vatican Council, *The Pastoral Constitution on the Church in the Modern World (Gaudium et Spes),* §24, in *Decrees of the Ecumenical Councils,* vol. 2, ed. Norman Tanner (Washington, D.C.: Georgetown University Press, 1990), p. 1083.

balanced in social trinitarianism, however, by a strong emphasis on the mutual equality of the persons. So while an approach that emphasizes the distinction of the persons needs to be careful to avoid subordinationism, this does not seem to be the real issue. A more serious difficulty is posed by the tendency of social doctrines of the Trinity to project onto God, in an unwarranted way, aspects of human interpersonal relatedness. The danger here is that we imagine the persons of the Trinity to be something like independent centers of consciousness and willing, who, as it were, "join" the Trinity of their own free will. This fails to take into account that the persons are constituted by their relatedness — they do not enter *into* relation, the way human persons do, but they rather *are* that relation. Social trinitarians at times seem to imply otherwise.[13]

There are further aspects of this tendency toward projection. The theologian Karen Kilby argues that what we find in social trinitarianism is a three-step process in which theologians, first, identify *perichoresis* (mutual indwelling) as the name of whatever it is that makes the Father, Son, and Spirit one; then fill out the meaning of *perichoresis* by projecting onto God what we value most in interhuman relations (e.g., warmth, love, empathy, equality, etc.); and finally, present the divine *perichoresis* as the model for human interrelation. While acknowledging that all human language about God involves some degree of projection, by which we speak of God according to human qualities and values, what Kilby finds problematic about the projection involved in social trinitarianism is the way in which "what is projected onto God is immediately reflected back onto the world, and this reverse projection is said to be what is in fact *important* about the doctrine."[14] In other words, the Trinity is reduced to a way of commending certain things that we value in human relations.

Another contemporary theologian, Kathryn Tanner, notes that the values derived from appeals to *perichoresis* tend to be somewhat vague. "[U]nless one purports to know much more about relations among the trinitarian persons than is probably warranted, one is still left with very vague recommendations — about the social goods of equality, a diverse community, and mutual relationships of giving and receiving. All the hard,

---

13. This is, of course, a matter of degrees. Leonardo Boff, for example, says "the trinitarian interplay of perfect perichoresis displays co-existence between personal and social, between the happiness of each and the well-being of all" (*Trinity and Society*, trans. Paul Burns [Maryknoll, N.Y.: Orbis, 1988], p. 119). Others are a bit more sober with regard to identifying divine and human personhood.

14. Karen Kilby, "Perichoresis and Projection: Problems with Social Doctrines of the Trinity," *New Blackfriars* 81 (May 2000): 956, 442.

controversial work of figuring out exactly what any of that might mean . . . seems left up to the ingenuity of the theologian to argue on other grounds."[15] These "other grounds" tend to be the ideological positions that the theologians already hold. Thus Michael Novak, a strong supporter of the market economy, sees in the trinitarian "pluralism-in-unity" a "dark illumination" of "a political economy differentiated and yet one" — that is, democratic capitalism,[16] while the liberation theologian Leonardo Boff claims that within trinitarian communion "mutual acceptance of differences is the vehicle for the plural unity of the three divine Persons," and that "by their practice and theory, capitalist regimes contradict the challenges and invitations of trinitarian communion."[17]

As the examples of Novak and Boff illustrate, social trinitarianism, even apart from its temptation toward a misunderstanding of the persons of the Trinity as separate centers of consciousness and will, runs a serious risk of simply projecting onto the Trinity our preheld ideals of human community — whether these be capitalist or socialist, egalitarian or hierarchical, conservative or liberal. In other words, it runs the risk of turning the Trinity into a means of giving a divine underwriting to whatever social ideology we happen to hold, without ever significantly challenging that ideology.

The Holy Trinity as the Grammar of Christian Belief

Does this mean that the Trinity has no relevance to Christian ethics or moral theology? Should this chapter simply have been omitted from this book? Is the Trinity simply a "mystery" in the sense of something that is beyond intelligibility, something we simply believe but that casts no light whatsoever upon our moral lives and our behavior? This could hardly be the case, since the Christian life is a single whole that cannot be neatly divided into "believing" and "behaving." To believe that God is a Trinity is not simply to twitch a particular mental muscle, but rather entails a holistic pattern of human knowing, speaking, acting, and suffering that reproduces the divine pattern of action in the world, a pattern that is the expression of

15. Kathryn Tanner, "Trinity," in *The Blackwell Companion to Political Theology*, ed. Peter Scott and William T. Cavanaugh (Oxford: Blackwell, 1994), p. 325.

16. Michael Novak, *The Spirit of Democratic Capitalism* (New York: Simon and Schuster, 1982), pp. 338-39.

17. Boff, *Trinity and Society*, p. 150. For Novak and Boff as examples, I am indebted to Miroslav Volf, "'The Trinity Is Our Social Program': The Doctrine of the Trinity and the Shape of Social Engagement," *Modern Theology* 14, no. 3 (July 1998): 419 n. 14.

God's own being and is summed up by the naming of God as Father, Son, and Spirit. When Christians are baptized "in the name of the Father and of the Son and of the Holy Spirit," they are inserted into the center of that pattern of divine action.

One way of thinking about the role of the doctrine of the Trinity in Christian believing is to say that the claim that God is Father, Son, and Holy Spirit — three distinct persons who are yet one God — is something like a remark one might make about the grammatical structure of a language. Like grammar in relation to a sentence, the doctrine of the Trinity has a regulative function for the proper reading of Scripture, and if we ignore this "trinitarian grammar," we will misread Scripture, as Athanasius claimed the Arians did.[18] Further, the trinitarian grammar of the Christian faith can help us identify "well-formed" theological statements, as well as figure out what it is about ill-formed statements of faith that makes them ill-formed. Thus, if we are confronted with Jesus' statement in John's Gospel, "The Father is greater than I" (John 14:28), we might, like the Arians, understand this to mean that the Father is God but the Son is not. Athanasius, however, proposes the trinitarian rule that "the same things are said of the Son, which are said of the Father, except his being said to be Father";[19] in other words, unless Scripture is speaking of that which makes the Father and Son different — that is, the fact that the Son comes forth from the Father and not vice versa — we ought to read all that Scripture affirms of the Father as affirmed of the Son as well, including divinity. Read in this way, according to this grammatical rule, Jesus' statement is clearly not a denial of divinity, but a statement about the coming forth of the Son from the Father by which the Son and Father are distinguished.

My suggestion is that the doctrine of the Trinity can be understood as playing an analogous role in the Christian moral life. That is, while we cannot read even general ethical recommendations directly off of the doctrine of the Trinity, this doctrine guides the shaping of the Christian moral life in a determinative way. To put it somewhat cryptically, the Trinity offers our moral reflection a grammar of imitation and improvisation. Let me explain

---

18. See, e.g., Athanasius, *Second Oration against the Arians* 1, in *A Select Library of Nicene and Post-Nicene Fathers,* 2nd ser., vol. 4 (Peabody, Mass.: Hendrickson, 1994).

19. Athanasius, *Third Oration against the Arians* 4, in *A Select Library of Nicene and Post-Nicene Fathers,* 2nd ser., vol. 4. We read a similar statement in Thomas Aquinas: "It is also a rule of Holy Scripture that whatever is said of the Father, applies to the Son, although there be added an exclusive term; except only as regards what belongs to the opposite relations, whereby the Father and the Son are distinguished from each other" (*Summa Theologiae* I.36.2ad.1).

what I mean by returning to some of the points made in my account of the origins of trinitarian doctrine.

The Grammar of the Christian Life:
Imitation and Improvisation

First, the doctrine of the Trinity affirms the unity of God. Like their Jewish forebears, Christians affirm that there is but one God. And as in Judaism, this affirmation of the unity of God by Christians gives a distinctive cast to the moral life. If there is but a single divine source of all that is, then we must presume a fundamental unity of the human race, indeed of all creatures. There is a similar unity to the life of each individual. The Shema, the Jewish profession of faith quoted in the second section of this chapter, which begins, "Hear, O Israel: The LORD our God is one LORD," continues by spelling out the ethical import of this belief in the unity of God: "You shall love the LORD your God with all your heart, and with all your soul, and with all your might" (Deut. 6:5). This means that human loyalties cannot be parceled out among the various gods charged with care for the different sectors of human life: one deity for successful business dealings, a second for human fertility, and perhaps a third for rain. The claim that there is but a single God who is concerned for the entirety of each and every human life challenges us to integrate the various sectors of our life into a whole. Indeed, the idea that a human life ought to be characterized by "integrity" seems somehow tied to the notion that there is an overarching good, transcending every particular good, which is the goal of every person, and which people call God. Our lives ought to be lives of integrity because each life, in all of its aspects, finds its source in the one God. This God who is one calls us to live our lives wholeheartedly devoted to the cause of God. Indeed, belief in the unity — the integrity — of God calls us to an integrated goodness that mirrors the goodness of God.

Thus this belief in the unity of God ought not to be thought of as something held "between the ears" that, once we have it, has somehow to be put into practice. Rather, to believe that God is one quite simply *is* to love God with all our heart, soul, and might, in the ordinary and extraordinary actions and passions that make up our lives. And for one who loves God in such a wholehearted way, the sorts of divisions and compartmentalizations that we are so tempted to make in our lives — between the personal and the political, the professional and the familial, the sacred and the secular, us and them — come to be seen as the barriers to integrity that they are. They show themselves to be the hedges in which we hide to avoid the consequences of living belief.

Second, the doctrine of the Trinity affirms the full divinity of Jesus of Nazareth. In other words, to believe in the Trinity is to look always to Jesus as that comprehensive, transcendent goodness that calls us to lives of integrity, a goodness now made flesh and dwelling among us. At least since Aristotle, those concerned with the moral life have recognized that we cannot grow in goodness unless we possess models of moral excellence, exemplars that we can look to and imitate as examples of a life well lived. The difficulty is that, as humans, we must obviously take our models of what it means to flourish as the particular kinds of beings that we are from among human beings, because what we are seeking is *human* moral excellence and not the moral excellence of angels or of nonrational animals. Yet to believe, as Christians do, that human beings are called to unite themselves to an integrated goodness that exceeds any and every finite, limited goodness — to unite themselves to God — seems to imply that we need a model that is at the same time a particular instance of human moral excellence *and* the unsurpassable revelation and embodiment of the transcendent, comprehensive goodness that is God.

The doctrine of the Trinity, along with the christological affirmation of Jesus as fully divine and fully human, gives us a way of cleaving to Jesus as just such an exemplar. Paul, in his letter to the Philippians, speaks of Jesus in precisely this way. He first exhorts the Christians of Philippi to "do nothing from selfish ambition or conceit, but in humility regard others as better than yourselves. Let each of you look not to your own interests, but to the interests of others" (Phil. 2:3-4). To the moral philosophy of the pagan ancient world, this would hardly seem a recipe for virtue. Such self-forgetfulness would indeed seem a recipe for moral disaster. How can we cultivate excellence in any area of life if we do not attend to our own development, if we do not look to our own interest? Even if we are generous toward another, it is only to increase our own status. As Stephen Fowl has noted, "In the competitive economy of honor which framed Greco-Roman friendships, money was something one spent or gave in order to solidify or increase one's status."[20] If we restrict our moral reflection to the horizon of the limited, finite goodness to which humans naturally aspire, such a view makes perfect sense and Paul's exhortation seems to propose a dubious course of action.

But Paul breaks through the horizon of limited, finite goodness by di-

---

20. Stephen E. Fowl, *Philippians* (Grand Rapids: Eerdmans, 2005), p. 24.

recting us to Jesus as exemplar: "Let the same mind be in you that was in Christ Jesus" (Phil. 2:5) — or, as Fowl translates this, "Let this be your pattern of thinking, acting and feeling, which was also displayed in Christ Jesus."[21] Paul goes on to spell out precisely what is the pattern displayed in Jesus in six verses that I have already quoted, but that are worth quoting again in this context:

> who, though he was in the form of God,
>> did not regard equality with God
>> as something to be exploited,
> but emptied himself,
>> taking the form of a slave,
>> being born in human likeness.
> And being found in human form,
>> he humbled himself
>> and became obedient to the point of death —
>> even death on a cross.
> Therefore God also highly exalted him
>> and gave him the name
>> that is above every name,
> so that at the name of Jesus
>> every knee should bend,
>> in heaven and on earth and under the earth,
> and every tongue should confess
>> that Jesus Christ is Lord,
>> to the glory of God the Father.
>
> (Phil. 2:6-11)

As we have seen, this text is one of the foundational scriptural texts for the development of the Christian doctrine of the Trinity, presenting Christ as "in the form of God" prior to his birth, and ascribing to him the divine name of *Kyrios* upon his exaltation. But this text also serves as a foundational text for the Christian moral life, holding out the humility of Jesus and his self-giving unto death as the appearing in history of the exemplar of infinite, unrestricted goodness. Paul is telling the Philippians, and us, that if we wish to break out of the restricted horizon of particular finite goodness, we must possess the "mind" of Christ Jesus, the pattern of thinking, acting, and feeling that we see in his pouring himself out for our sake, even to the point of death on a cross. Such unrestricted self-giving seems absurd

---

21. Fowl, *Philippians,* p. 88.

by human standards; Paul elsewhere speaks of "the message about the cross" as "foolishness" when judged by human standards (1 Cor. 1:18). But here a different standard is being appealed to, a standard that can never be attained by human reason, but is still a genuine human possibility, because it has become actual in the human life of Jesus. In imitating the pattern of Jesus' unique, particular human life, in taking this as our exemplar of goodness, we are participating in the pattern of divine generosity.

Third, the doctrine of the Trinity affirms that the Spirit poured out on the church is God in the same sense that the Father and the Son are. This is significant in Christian moral reflection because participation in the pattern of thinking, acting, and feeling, which was also in Christ Jesus, is never simply a matter of slavish imitation but is rather a matter of constant improvisation upon the fundamental theme sounded in Jesus' incarnation, ministry, death, and resurrection. While the question "What would Jesus do?" might be useful for getting adolescents to reflect for a brief moment before embarking upon some incredibly stupid course of action, it is often insufficient for the nitty-gritty complexities of many moral questions. This is not because the human life of Jesus is in some sense inadequate; rather, it is because it is only through the Spirit that the risen Jesus, who has not ceased to be human, remains present to us as our exemplar. We must always repeat the pattern found in Jesus, a pattern discerned by careful attention to his life as recounted in Scripture, but we inevitably repeat that pattern differently. Identical gestures in different contexts end up being different actions (think about the difference between swinging a bat during a baseball game and during a bar fight), so to faithfully follow Jesus as exemplar we must exercise discernment, we must "read the signs of the times," as the Second Vatican Council's *Pastoral Constitution on the Church in the Modern World* puts it.[22]

Reading the signs of the times does not involve simply applying the example of Jesus in present circumstances, but also includes tracing the movement of the Spirit in the church's tradition, particularly as the life of the Spirit has been embodied in the saints. If in Jesus we are offered the human exemplar of unrestricted goodness, in the saints we can perceive the Spirit's improvisation upon that exemplar; we might say that the saints are our exemplars of the kind of Spirit-filled improvisation that is required if we are to be faithful imitators of Jesus. Because the Spirit who fills the saints is the Spirit of Jesus, breathed forth from the Father and the Son as from a single source, the example of the saints must always point us back to

---

22. *The Pastoral Constitution on the Church in the Modern World (Gaudium et Spes)*, §4.

Jesus, while at the same time guiding us in how to repeat it differently. The divinity of the Spirit points us to the fact that this improvisation is never accomplished simply by human effort. Our repetition of the pattern of Christ Jesus in ever-novel ways is faithful repetition only if the Spirit takes possession of us. All our human cleverness will finally fail in moral discernment if we are not Spirit-filled people.

These remarks have been somewhat abstract, and have not delved into the moral quandaries that face Christians today. Does the doctrine of the Trinity really have a role to play in our thinking about the morality of embryonic stem cell research or preemptive military action or the death penalty? Can it guide us toward justice for the poor and disenfranchised or greater equity among different races or between men and women? My suggestion here is that, strictly speaking, we ought to answer no to these questions. The doctrine of the Trinity is neither about our sources of moral knowledge nor about the ideal of human community, and as such it cannot be pressed into direct service for deciding moral questions. The doctrine of the Trinity is rather the grammar of Christian belief about the Father, the Son, and the Holy Spirit.

Yet if this doctrine is not of direct ethical relevance to Christians, I hope my remarks have made clear that the triune God very much is relevant to Christian moral discernment, for it is through our Spirit-filled, improvisational imitation of the incarnate Son that we are led back to the unrestricted goodness of the one God. In this sense, by guiding our beliefs about God, the trinitarian grammar of the Christian faith does articulate, albeit at something of a distance, the rhythm of imitation and improvisation that characterizes the Christian life. And in this rhythm we glimpse something of the true mystery of the Trinity, which is nothing less than the mystery of God's own life poured out into the world for our salvation, a mystery of salvation into which we are invited to enter through lives of holiness.

Concurrent Readings

Athanasius. *On the Incarnation*. New York: St. Vladimir's Seminary Press, 1993.
     A classic early Christian treatment of what difference it makes to Christians to believe that Jesus is the second person of the Trinity.
Basil the Great. *On the Holy Spirit*. New York: St. Vladimir's Seminary Press, 1980. Another early Christian classic, which explains the doctrine of the Trinity as growing out of the grammar of Christian prayer.
Hill, William J., O.P. *The Three-Personed God: The Trinity as a Mystery of Salvation*.

Washington, D.C.: Catholic University of America Press, 1982. A reliable, if at times dense, survey of classical and modern approaches to the doctrine of the Trinity.

McCabe, Herbert, O.P. "Aquinas on the Trinity" and "The Trinity and Prayer." In *God Still Matters*. New York: Continuum, 2002. These two essays are amazingly lucid introductions to some of the more technical aspects of trinitarian theology, as well as a reflection on the difference that Christian trinitarian beliefs make.

Richardson, Alan. *Creeds in the Making: A Short Introduction to the History of Christian Doctrine*. London: SCM, 1935. Though somewhat dated in its scholarship, this book provides a brief and well-written introduction to the theological developments of the first five centuries of the Christian era.

Chapter 4

Pilgrim People

WILLIAM T. CAVANAUGH

It is popular these days to say "I'm into spirituality, but I'm not into organized religion." The church scandals that have made the news in recent years have certainly contributed to this sentiment. But let's face it: the church has always been sinful. Listen to Paul scold the Christian community in Corinth for its jealousy and quarreling (1 Cor. 3:3), arrogance (4:18), sexual immorality (5:1), lawsuits against one another (6:1), humiliation of the poor (11:22), and so on. Scandal in the church is nothing new, nor is turning away from the church because of these scandals. There is something new, however, in the preference for "spirituality" over "organized religion." Here we encounter the idea that the spiritual life is essentially an individual thing that is hindered by the trappings of organization: prescribed rites, communal judgments, hierarchical leadership, and rules. These tend to be what many people think of when they think of the church. At best these trappings seem like a means to a greater end. At worst they seem like an unnecessary evil, a way for humans to interfere with the free movement of the individual to God.

Does one need the church to be a Christian? What is the church, and what is it for? Those who defend the need for the church often see it in instrumental terms, as a means to a higher purpose. They might describe this means negatively: the church — like a child safety seat in a car — is there to keep us from error. They might describe the church more neutrally: the church — like a hotel banquet room — is there to provide us a place and a means to gather. Neither of these responses, however, gives us a positive reason to think that the church is actually an essential part of the Christian life, and not merely a means to the Christian life. And both responses treat the church as something external to us, as the hierarchy alone or as the church building. Neither response treats the church as a community of people. Neither contemplates the possibility that when we say "church" we mean a community of people — we mean us. What are *we* for? Is our gathering just for the purpose of those individuals who need it, or do *we together* have a role to play in the cosmic drama of salvation?

In this chapter we will explore the role of the church in the Christian life. We will not confine ourselves to asking, "Does the church serve the spiritual needs of the individual Christian?" We'll start with a different question: "Does the church — that is, the gathering of God's people together — have a role to play in God's plan for the world?" To answer this question we will have to ask what it means to say that God "saves" the world, and what that plan of salvation entails.

The Story of Salvation

In Fyodor Dostoevsky's great novel *The Brothers Karamazov*, the character Grushenka tells the following story:

> Once upon a time there was a peasant woman and a very wicked woman she was. And she died and did not leave a single good deed behind. The devils caught her and plunged her into the lake of fire. So her guardian angel stood and wondered what good deed of hers he could remember to tell to God; "She once pulled up an onion in her garden," said he, "and gave it to a beggar woman." And God answered: "You take that onion then, hold it out to her in the lake, and let her take hold and be pulled out. And if you can pull her out of the lake, let her come to Paradise, but if the onion breaks, then the woman must stay where she is." The angel ran to the woman and held out the onion to her. "Come," said he, "catch hold and I'll pull you out." He began cautiously pulling her out. He had just pulled her right out, when the other sinners in the lake, seeing how she was being drawn out, began catching hold of her so as to be pulled out with her. But she was a very wicked woman and she began kicking them. "I'm to be pulled out, not you. It's my onion, not yours." As soon as she said that, the onion broke. And the woman fell into the lake and she is burning there to this day. So the angel wept and went away.[1]

---

1. Fyodor Dostoevsky, *The Brothers Karamazov,* book 7.3, at http://www.freebooks.biz/Classics/Dostoevsky/Karamazov/Karamazov_VII03_4.htm.

When we think about the question of salvation, many of us think in terms of whether or not an individual person is going to get into heaven. As Grushenka's story illustrates, however, salvation in the Christian tradition has not always been thought of as an individual achievement. In the story, the precise moment that the onion breaks is when the woman tries to claim salvation as her own. In the biblical story too, salvation is not primarily depicted as the rescue of the individual, but rather as the regathering of a creation that has been torn apart by violence and sin.

The first eleven chapters of Genesis are an attempt by the ancient Israelites to explain the human predicament, and point to a way out of it, a way to salvation, in other words. When the ancient Babylonians looked around at the violence of the world, they decided that was just the way things have always been; the Babylonian creation account, the *Enuma Elish,* has the earth created in violence, in a war among the gods.[2] The ancient Israelites, on the other hand, wrote that the world was created in peace and harmony, and only later fell away from it through sin. Harmony, in other words, is the way things really are. Humans are all made in the "image of God" (Gen. 1:27), so we all participate in one another through our participation in God. The story of Adam and Eve's "fall," therefore, is not a cause for pessimism, but for optimism; there is something originally good to fall away from. Sin and violence are a departure from the norm, not the way things are meant to be. We thus have hope that we can be saved from our predicament, and recover the harmony that was meant to be.

Nevertheless, sin and violence are here. How did they come from a creation that is all good? Genesis describes sin as coming out of something good: human freedom. Once this good gift is used to claim autonomy, to put humans in rivalry against God — "when you eat of it your eyes will be opened, and you will be like God" (Gen. 3:5) — then the original harmony among humans, and between humans and God, breaks up. Immediately, the man blames the woman (3:12), and there is enmity between the humans and creation (3:15-19). Chapter 4 of Genesis records the first murder, and by chapter 6 "the earth was filled with violence" (6:11). This introductory section of Genesis ends in chapter 11, with the story of the tower of Babel. In this story the consequence of human self-assertion is the scattering of humanity (11:9).

When the early church reflected on the doctrine of original sin, they did not think of it so much as a stain on the individual soul, but more as the very condition of humanity being broken up into self-asserting individ-

---

2. For an English translation of the *Enuma Elish,* see Alexander Heidel, *The Babylonian Genesis: The Story of the Creation* (Chicago: University of Chicago Press, 1951).

uals. Origen, a theologian of the third century, put it succinctly: "Where there is sin, there is multiplicity." This judgment was shared by many theologians of the early church.

> True to Origen's criterion, Maximus the Confessor, for example, considers original sin as a separation, a breaking up, an individualization it might be called, in the depreciatory sense of the word. Whereas God is working continually in the world to the effect that all should come together into unity, by this sin which is the work of man, "the one nature was shattered into a thousand pieces" and humanity which ought to constitute a harmonious whole, in which "mine" and "thine" would be no contradiction, is turned into a multitude of individuals, as numerous as the sands of the seashore, all of whom show violently discordant inclinations.[3]

We in the twenty-first century often trivialize the word "sin." "Sin" means thinking dirty thoughts or indulging in a piece of "decadent" chocolate cake. In the Christian tradition, however, "sin" names the condition of a world in which people view each other and God as threats to their freedom and use violence against each other to get what they want. Pick up any newspaper today, and this is largely what you see. Though written more than twenty-five hundred years ago, Genesis's analysis of the human predicament sounds remarkably fresh.

What is God's plan for saving us from this predicament? It begins to unfold in the twelfth chapter of Genesis. Salvation begins by gathering a people. Abraham is called to become a great people, and told that all the peoples of the earth will be blessed through this people (12:2-3). If sin is scattering, then salvation from sin will be gathering. According to biblical scholar Gerhard Lohfink, "gathering" is a prominent theme throughout the Old Testament, and is even used as a technical term for the event of salvation.[4] For example, Psalm 106:47 implores,

> Save us, O LORD our God,
>   and gather us from among the nations.

Salvation in the Old Testament is not about individuals trying to gain admittance to a place called heaven after death; it is about gathering people in

---

3. Henri de Lubac, *Catholicism: Christ and the Common Destiny of Man*, trans. Lancelot C. Sheppard and Sister Elizabeth Englund (San Francisco: Ignatius, 1988), pp. 33-34.

4. Gerhard Lohfink, *Does God Need the Church? Toward a Theology of the People of God*, trans. Linda M. Maloney (Collegeville, Minn.: Liturgical Press, 1999), pp. 51-52.

communion, thereby restoring the good creation that sin and violence have torn apart.

The theme of gathering does not change in the New Testament; the only change is that the promises of the Old Testament are said to be fulfilled in Jesus Christ. Jesus himself describes his mission in these terms: "Whoever is not with me is against me, and whoever does not gather with me scatters" (Matt. 12:30). Jesus dies for the nation Israel, "and not for the nation only, but to gather into one the dispersed children of God" (John 11:52). People are gathered now not merely into Israel, but into Christ himself. Jesus declares that his body is the temple (John 2:21). Salvation is being gathered into the body of Christ, which Paul identifies with the church, meaning *us*: "Now you are the body of Christ" (1 Cor. 12:27), with Christ himself as the head of the body. As Paul stresses, there is diversity in the body of Christ; there are hands and feet and eyes, and each is indispensable. And precisely because of this diversity and uniqueness, we need each other, even the weakest members (1 Cor. 12:14-26). For the Christians at Ephesus, the body of Christ is the reconciliation of the two mutually hostile groups of humanity, the Jews and the Gentiles.

> For he is our peace; in his flesh he has made both groups into one and has broken down the dividing wall, that is, the hostility between us. He has abolished the law with its commandments and ordinances, that he might create in himself one new humanity in place of the two, thus making peace, and might reconcile both groups to God in one body through the cross, thus putting to death that hostility through it. So he came and proclaimed peace to you who were far off and peace to those who were near; for through him both of us have access in one Spirit to the Father. So then you are no longer strangers and aliens, but you are citizens with the saints and also members of the household of God, built upon the foundation of the apostles and prophets, with Christ Jesus himself as the cornerstone. In him the whole structure is joined together and grows into a holy temple in the Lord; in whom you also are built together spiritually into a dwelling place for God. (Eph. 2:14-22)

In the biblical view, the church is not just a Moose Lodge or a stamp collectors club, where individuals with similar interests come together to share those interests. The church has a role to play in the drama of the salvation of the world. Our very gathering as church is the beginning of a new kind of humanity, a humanity where we cease to see ourselves as mutually competitive individuals, but rather experience ourselves as we really are, as members of the same body, all humans made in the image of the one God and re-united in Christ. Heaven is the completion of this process.

A Chosen People

If we grant that God works this way, gathering a scattered humanity, why is God so sneaky about it? Why does the creator God, the one God of the whole universe, choose to work salvation through one obscure Middle Eastern people? If you are going to start a universal movement to salvation, choosing a goatherd from Ur is probably not the quickest way to get the message out. What's more, God's choice of Abraham and his descendants seems positively contrary to God's own purpose. Having one chosen people among all the peoples of the earth seems divisive, not unitive. It seems guaranteed to encourage ethnocentrism and parochialism, a claim of privilege over others. Is this what the biblical view implies?

To take the second objection first, the Scriptures make clear that, although salvation is *through* the Jews, it is not only *for* the Jews. God tells Abraham that all the peoples of the world will be blessed through him. But, to address the first objection, surely there is a quicker way to transform the world. According to Lohfink, that is always what revolutionaries think. God, like every revolutionary, wants a radical transformation of the way the world operates. The difference is that revolutionaries, unlike God, are short on time and impatient of human freedom. Lifetimes are short, and the masses are weighed down by inertia. Revolutionaries seek a sudden overthrow of power structures by open and direct violence. God works differently, however, for God wishes to respect the dimension of human life that most closely expresses the image of God in humans: freedom. God cannot vanquish violence through violence, but only by refraining from coercing the human will. If humans are to come to salvation, to find harmony with God and with one another, they will have to do so without being coerced. Lohfink writes:

> [H]ow can anyone change the world and society at its roots without taking away freedom? It can only be that God begins in a small way, at one single place in the world. There must be a place, visible, tangible, where the salvation of the world can begin: that is, where the world becomes what it is supposed to be according to God's plan. Beginning at that place, the new thing can spread abroad, but not through persuasion, not through indoctrination, not through violence. Everyone must have

the opportunity to come and see. All must have the chance to behold and test this new thing. Then, if they want to, they can allow themselves to be drawn into the history of salvation that God is creating. Only in that way can their freedom be preserved. What drives them to the new thing cannot be force, not even moral pressure, but only the fascination of a world that is changed.[5]

The emphasis on human freedom here is not an emphasis on the human autonomy and self-assertion at the root of sin and violence. It is not freedom from God, but freedom for God. "Clearly this change in the world must begin in human beings, but not at all by their seeking through heroic effort to make themselves the locus of the new, altered world; rather it begins when they listen to God, open themselves to God, and allow God to act."[6]

The salvation of the world occurs not through coercion but through attraction. Salvation history is a cosmic love story, the story of the erotic attraction between God and humanity. Here "erotic" indicates not something literally physical but rather the intense desire to be united to the other, to overcome separation and become one whole. The sensual love poetry of the Song of Solomon — "I found him whom my soul loves. / I held him, and would not let him go / until I brought him into my mother's house, / and into the chamber of her that conceived me" (3:4) — has been included in the Bible and interpreted as an allegory for the love between God and God's people.

This kind of attraction does not occur in a general and universal way, any more than one falls in love with men or women in general. Attraction to the Christian life occurs when one can see a concrete community of people living out salvation, living reconciled and hopeful lives in the midst of a violent world. Rarely are people converted by well-argued theories. People are usually converted to a new way of living by getting to know people who live that way and thus being able to see themselves living that way too. This is the way God's revolution works. The church is meant to be that community of people who make salvation visible for the rest of the world. Salvation is not a property of isolated individuals, but is made visible only in mutual love.

The cosmic love story between God and God's people is not always, or even usually, a carefree tale of romance, however. Juxtaposed with the Song

---

5. Lohfink, *Does God?* p. 27.
6. Lohfink, *Does God?* p. 27.

of Solomon is the book of Hosea, in which God instructs the prophet to marry a prostitute, just as God has married a "wife of whoredom" (Hos. 1:2) by entering into covenant with Israel. Hosea marries the prostitute Gomer, who bears three children, all of different fathers, then leaves Hosea. But he pursues her and brings her back. "The LORD said to me again, 'Go, love a woman who has a lover and is an adulteress, just as the LORD loves the people of Israel, though they turn to other gods and love raisin cakes'" (3:1). Raisin cakes were used in pagan festivals, which the Israelites were fond of frequenting. There was hardly a variety of idolatry and sin of which the Israelites were not capable. We would be hard pressed to find a book more full of treachery, misdeeds, lust, and violence than the Bible. Indeed, the biblical authors seem to go out of their way to emphasize the sinfulness of the chosen people. Abraham himself, not even a whole chapter removed from being named great patriarch of the chosen people, is seen having his wife lie to protect him (Gen. 12:13). A few chapters later, he gives up on God's promise of an heir with his wife, and impregnates his slave girl (Gen. 16:1-2).

Clearly the claim of Israel, and later the church, to have a special role in God's salvation of the world is not a claim of the moral superiority of God's people. The biblical writers emphasize the sinfulness of God's people to highlight the goodness and faithfulness of God. God loves the people unconditionally, contrary to anything the people deserve. The claim of a unique role for the people of God is a claim based not on human effort but on the forgiving love of God. The reason the biblical authors are able to name the people's sin so bluntly and so truthfully is that the truth has been revealed to them in the Law of the one true God. The only reason God's people can witness to the rest of the world — even by their own sinfulness! — is that they have been enabled to name sin truthfully through the revelation of the living God. If it were not for their relationship with the God of Abraham, Isaac, and Jacob, they would not be able fully to recognize their sin as sin.

Despite their sinfulness, the Israelites understood themselves as different because they had been given the Law. In the Law, God spells out exactly how the people of God are not to be like other peoples. At the heart of this command is the remembrance that they were once slaves in Egypt (Deut. 15:15; 24:22). As Walter Brueggemann points out, the Israelite witness to the world was to be built upon the basic contrast between Israel's God and the Egyptian pharaoh. Pharaoh is an absolutist who, propelled by anxiety about not having enough, rules through exploitation and domination of those more vulnerable. The true God, by contrast, projects a vision of abundance based on the communal sharing of goods and responsibilities, an enactment of the original noncompetitive harmony at the basis of creation. The vulnerable — widows, orphans, aliens, the poor (Deut. 24:17-22) — are to be treated with special regard, based on Israel's own remembrance of oppression. "You shall also love the stranger, for you were strangers in the land of Egypt" (Deut. 10:19). The most dramatic provision for the vulnerable stipulated that debts be remitted every seventh year, in the "Year of Release" (Deut. 15:1-18).[7]

It is easy for us today to understand the attractiveness of these particular provisions of the Law, but the Law in general tends to leave us cold. The rabbis tell us there are 613 separate statutes of the Mosaic Law, and they cover everything from forbidding boiling a kid goat in its mother's milk (Exod. 23:19), to how many loops to put on the outermost edges of the curtains of the tabernacle (Exod. 26:4-5), to what to do when food is touched by water from a vessel into which a dead weasel has fallen (Lev. 11:29-35). We scratch our heads at Psalm 119, a rapturous and very lengthy love song to the Law: "With open mouth I pant, / because I long for your commandments" (Ps. 119:131), and so on and on. We today have a tendency to associate faith and spiritual matters with immaterial things and interior dispositions. For the Israelites, however, faith was not a feeling; it was something visible in the concrete everyday way they dealt with the material world. The Law was a way of training in the practices of the community. Jews were made, not born. Furthermore, if God's plan of salvation depends on an aesthetic and erotic attraction to a people living a particular way of life — a "contrast society," as Lohfink says — then it is crucial that that community and that way of life be *visible*, that is, manifest in concrete practices. The Law is the primary way the Israelites had of maintaining their distinctive visible identity as God's people. Through centuries of exile, dispersal, and rule by others, the Israelites maintained their identity and their visibility through the concrete, material practices of the Law.[8]

The Body of Christ

When we come to the New Testament, the basic theme of a people that witnesses to salvation does not change. The only difference between Israel and the church is that Christians believe that all the promises made to Israel are

7. Walter Brueggemann, "Old Testament," in *The Blackwell Companion to Political Theology*, ed. Peter Scott and William T. Cavanaugh (Oxford: Blackwell, 2004), pp. 7-20.

8. Lohfink, *Does God?* pp. 74-88.

fulfilled in Jesus Christ. In the Sermon on the Mount, Jesus says, "Do not think that I have come to abolish the law or the prophets; I have come not to abolish but to fulfill" (Matt. 5:17). It is true that Christians do not continue to follow all 613 precepts of the Mosaic Law. While Christians hold the Ten Commandments in high regard, they no longer require males to be circumcised, nor do they keep most of the cultic and purity statutes of the Torah. Christians may eat raisin cakes and have considerable freedom of action regarding dead weasels. Nevertheless, the core of the Law abides: "I am the LORD your God, who brought you out of the land of Egypt, out of the house of slavery; you shall have no other gods before me" (Exod. 20:2-3). This means that all aspects of human life must be brought into relationship with the one true God. There is no autonomous "secular" realm of things to which God does not apply or over which God has no say. The Old Testament community tried to accomplish this by bringing even the most minute details of daily life into the Law. Jesus radicalizes this sovereignty of God in the Sermon on the Mount. "You have heard that it was said to those of ancient times, 'You shall not murder.' . . . But I say to you that if you are angry with a brother or sister, you will be liable to judgment" (Matt. 5:21-2). "You have heard that it was said, 'An eye for an eye and a tooth for a tooth.' But I say to you, Do not resist an evildoer. But if anyone strikes you on the right cheek, turn the other also" (Matt. 5:38-39). Here Jesus is not abolishing the Law or making it just a matter of internal dispositions and feelings. In Jesus the final gathering of salvation has come. It is now possible to live a new way, to live fully in the restoration of the whole creation to its original harmony, even to the point of loving one's enemies and not returning their violence (5:44).

The theme of gathering God's people also does not diminish, but rather comes to a climax in the New Testament. Jesus chooses twelve disciples in a deliberate symbolic act to show that the final gathering of the twelve tribes of Israel has begun. When Jesus announces at the beginning of Mark's Gospel that the kingdom of God is at hand (Mark 1:15), he signals that the final reign of God over all of history has come to fruition. As the word "kingdom" indicates, this is not a reign over hearts and minds only, but a visible, tangible community that continues as God's chosen people. Only now, both Jews and Gentiles together in peace will come to signal what the new humanity will look like, saved from violence and divisions. Jesus the Christ is the focal point of this new humanity, this new community. As the passage from Ephesians quoted above makes clear, the gathering of humanity will begin in the very body of Christ, the church. In the incarnation, whereby God assumed human flesh (John 1:14), God has actually taken humanity into the very being of God. The cosmic love story between God and humanity comes to its definitive point in the birth, life, death, and resurrection of Jesus Christ. In Christ, God unites with humanity, is rejected by humanity, but once again, as in Hosea, pursues humanity and lovingly invites us to become a member of Christ's very body, God's people, the church. The body of Christ is the visible witness to God's final gathering of humanity.

All of this sounds very grand for a carpenter from an obscure outpost of the Roman Empire. It sounds even preposterous when one considers Jesus' fate. He was executed as a common criminal, publicly tortured to death on a cross. And now some people claim that God raised him from the dead, and that this was the focal point of all of history, the very moment in which all of history changed course for good, and creation was restored. It is not hard for us to imagine why many Jews and pagans scoffed at these claims. "What has changed? I look around and I see a world still full of sin and violence. What evidence can you give me that the world has changed because of this Jesus?" The only response Christians could give to this challenge was to point to communities of people living as if everything had changed. The only evidence of salvation they could give was to point to people living peacefully and communally, living visibly different lives in which violence, greed, and lust had been vanquished. Look: "All who believed were together and had all things in common; they would sell their possessions and goods and distribute the proceeds to all, as any had need. Day by day, as they spent much time together in the temple, they broke bread at home and ate their food with glad and generous hearts, praising God and having the goodwill of all the people. And day by day the Lord added to their number those who were being saved" (Acts 2:44-47). The witness of people living visibly different lives remains the best, and perhaps the only, proof we have to offer.

There is a famous dictum associated with the third-century Christian writer Tertullian: "The blood of the martyrs is the seed of the church."[9] Tertullian noted the historical fact that the more the Romans put Christians to death, the more the church grew. People were attracted by the sheer radiance of the truth that shone from the martyrs' deaths. On the one hand, their deaths were evidence that nothing had changed because of Jesus; innocent people continued to be victimized. On the other hand, their deaths were proof that everything had changed because of Jesus. Here was

9. The actual quote appears in Tertullian's *Apology,* chapter 50, as "The oftener we are mown down by you, the more in number we grow; the blood of Christians is seed"; *The Ante-Nicene Fathers,* vol. 3, ed. Alexander Roberts and James Donaldson (New York: Scribner, 1926), p. 55.

this group of people, the church, living as if death no longer mattered. Here were these people living as though it was possible to absorb violence with love, and not return the violence. Here were these people living as though God had changed history and made it possible to live a totally new way. People were attracted to this way of salvation, and freely joined the church even though it could get them killed. This dynamic continues today. There were many more Christian martyrs in the twentieth century than in three centuries of Roman rule.

The church, then, is regarded as itself a sacrament, a visible sign of God's salvation of the world. As the Second Vatican Council declared: "All those who in faith look towards Jesus, the author of salvation and the principle of unity and peace, God has gathered together and established as the Church, that it may be for each and everyone the visible sacrament of this saving unity."[10] Vatican II even calls the church "necessary for salvation."[11] Does that mean that all those who call themselves members of the church are saved? Not necessarily. The people of God remains as full of sin as it was in Hosea's time. Does that mean that non-Christians cannot be saved? No. Vatican II upholds the possibility of salvation for those of other faiths and even for those who do not yet explicitly acknowledge God.[12] The Spirit blows where it wills, and as Vatican II says, "many elements of sanctification and of truth are found outside [the church's] visible confines."[13] The boundaries of the church are permeable, and people's relationships to the people of God are many and varied. It is perhaps best to say, as Dorothy Day was fond of saying, that all people are "members or potential members of the body of Christ." To say this, however, is to acknowledge the indispensability of the body of Christ for witnessing to the salvation of the world.

Christian Life and the Church

For a Christian, not believing in organized religion is like not believing in organized hospitals; the church must be organized to do what it does, though it is perhaps better thought of as an organism than an organization. Another way of putting it is that having faith in Christ is more like joining a movement than having a personal philosophy. The individual

---

10. Second Vatican Council, *Dogmatic Constitution on the Church (Lumen Gentium)*, §9.
11. *Dogmatic Constitution on the Church (Lumen Gentium)*, §14.
12. *Dogmatic Constitution on the Church (Lumen Gentium)*, §16.
13. *Dogmatic Constitution on the Church (Lumen Gentium)*, §8.

Christian life is swept up into a larger movement of cosmic proportions, the healing of the cosmos. This does not mean that one's own personal faith life is unimportant. It just means that one's faith life unfolds within a story much larger than the self.

Sometimes today we think of faith as a purely interior decision of the heart, a warm feeling of assurance and trust. Traditionally, however, faith was much more than this. Saint Thomas Aquinas classified faith as one of the virtues, which were a kind of good habit. Aquinas thought habits were necessary for the moral life because of our freedom. Imagine how messed up your life would be if every time you walked into a store, you had to decide whether or not to steal something, or if every time you opened your mouth, you were not sure if the truth or a lie would come out. You would have no stable identity or character, and you would be isolated, because people would not be able to trust you. According to Aquinas, habits are necessary, therefore, so that you do not have to make decisions at every moment. The virtuous person does not have to decide not to steal when she walks into a store; it simply does not occur to her to steal. Good actions simply are second nature to a person with the virtues. It becomes easy for such a person to do the right thing, with the right intention, at the right time, with the right emotions.[14]

How does one obtain these habits and become a virtuous person? In much the same way that one becomes a master carpenter. First, one must be apprenticed to someone who is already a master. The apprentice follows the master around and watches what the master does. Then the apprentice begins to do some simple tasks, under the watchful eyes of the master. At first the tasks seem difficult, and the apprentice has cut and bruised fingers to show for it. Eventually, though, by repetition and guidance, the tasks become easier. It becomes second nature to drive a nail in perfectly straight with a few swift strokes. In time the tasks become more complex, and the apprentice is on his way — subject to the approval and certification of the carpenter's union — to becoming a journeyman and perhaps a master someday. Once he becomes a master, he does not simply repeat what has always been done, but applies his own creativity to new tasks that present themselves.

The Christian life is like this. Faith is not usually a sudden inspiration that comes out of nowhere. Faith is a habit that is built up over time by doing faithful actions. Faith, as it was for the ancient Israelites, is not just a feeling or interior assurance, but is constituted in the real, material world by

14. Thomas Aquinas, *Summa Theologiae* I-II.49-56.

concrete practices. Faith is skillfully and wisely dealing with strangers, loved ones, money, genitals, and pots and pans. Faith is not usually something that comes in a flash of blinding light, but is built up over time by small actions like saying a prayer for a friend, cutting vegetables at a soup kitchen, putting one's rear end in a pew every Sunday morning. If faith takes hold, these sorts of actions and a thousand others become second nature.

But faith is not a property of individuals in isolation from others. As we have seen, God attracts us to the life of salvation by the witness of others. We see what faith looks like by seeing people living reconciled lives together. As apprentices in the faith, we become faithful by learning from the masters of the faith, the saints and other exemplars of what faith actually entails in the here and now. Faith is a complex skill that requires many such exemplars. For some of us the masters include the great saints of the tradition: Saint Perpetua, who was martyred rather than renounce Christ; Saint Francis of Assisi, who gave up all his worldly possessions to embrace the freedom of poverty; Saint Catherine of Siena, who called popes and princes to holiness in dark times. But often the exemplars are closer to home: parents, friends, priests, teachers, all the people who show up with us at church on Sunday, set out doughnuts afterward, and call when we are sick to see if we need anything. The habit of faith — as well as the other good habits or virtues, such as love, hope, courage, prudence, justice, and temperance — is built up in community. And we do not just need the witness of others when we are children in the faith. Not only is practicing the virtues a lifelong process, but also the very practice of faith is the gathering of people together. The church, in other words, is not simply a "school of virtue" that teaches individuals so that they can go out and use those virtues on their own. The whole point of virtue is to build community, to gather a broken humanity together. The virtuous life is a life lived as members of one another, where faith, hope, and charity circulate and give life to the whole body. The Christian life is not about building up heroic individuals through the sedimentation of virtue in the individual self; it is rather about the participation of the individual self in a larger whole. Virtue is not so much a property of individuals as it is the condition of the larger body of Christ in which individuals find their own unique place.

Even when we think of virtues as something acquired through repetition and hard work, therefore, it is more honest to regard them as gifts that we receive from others by the grace of God. None of us is an autonomous individual, standing back from reality and choosing our actions and our character as if we were shoppers in a grocery store. The truth is that we are immersed in reality, swimming in an ocean of grace. Who we are is an intricate web of our freedom made possible by others — our family, friends, and community, by the grace of God. Who we really are in Christ is a product of that web of relationships we call "church," which is made possible only by the life of the Holy Spirit breathed into it. When Aquinas distinguishes between moral virtues that are *acquired* by upbringing and practice, and moral virtues that are *infused* by God's grace, he is talking about the same virtues looked at from two different points of view.[15] Aquinas does not mean to imply that there are some virtues that we can acquire purely on our own merits by our own efforts without God. The fact is that all of our natural life is suffused and elevated by God's supernatural grace. When we come to taste and see the beginnings of salvation in communion with others, we recognize that we did not get here on our own, but were drawn to it by the erotic attraction of God, the pull of God's grace into participation in divine life.

Sacrament

It is in the sacraments that God's grace comes to us especially in a visible form. The *Catechism of the Catholic Church* says, "The sacraments are perceptible signs (words and actions) accessible to our human nature. By the action of Christ and the power of the Holy Spirit they make present efficaciously the grace that they signify."[16] The sacraments are the visible practices that constitute the communal life of the people of God. They are the social order of the church. And they do not simply symbolize another reality; they actually do what they signify.

This type of social order is especially apparent in the Eucharist. "The Eucharist makes the church," in Henri de Lubac's phrase. The Eucharist is not just a symbol that "means" certain things, nor is it just a special supernatural nourishment for the individual soul. The Eucharist is an action that arranges people into a certain order that makes them collectively into the body of Christ. "Body of Christ" refers both to the consecrated bread and — as we have already seen — to the assembly of people. "The cup of blessing that we bless, is it not a sharing in the blood of Christ? The bread that we break, is it not a sharing in the body of Christ? Because there is one bread, we who are many are one body, for we all partake of the one bread" (1 Cor. 10:16-17). In a strange way, then, we are what we eat. We become the body of Christ by eating the body of Christ (and drinking the blood). A

---

15. Aquinas, *Summa Theologiae* I-II.63.3-4.
16. *Catechism of the Catholic Church* (Mahwah, N.J.: Paulist, 1994), §1084 (p. 282).

sermon attributed to Saint Augustine says: "You are on the table and you are in the chalice, you along with us are this. We are this together. We are drinking this together because we are living this together. . . . Since what is realized is one reality, you too must be one by loving one another, by keeping one faith, one hope, one indivisible love."[17] Elsewhere Augustine reports the voice of God saying to him, "I am the food of the fully grown; grow and you will feed on me. And you will not change me into you like the food your flesh eats, but you will be changed into me."[18] In the Eucharist the cosmic love story comes to its consummation, as humanity is united with God in Christ through the Holy Spirit. We come to an actual participation in Christ in the Eucharist, such that we become members of the body of which Christ is the head. The original harmony of the creation is restored, as we lose our preoccupations with our small selves and become part of others, members of a larger self that is taken up into divinity. We are not divinized by the Eucharist as individuals; we are gathered together as a larger body. Thus in the *Didache,* an early Christian document, we find this eucharistic prayer: "As this broken bread, once dispersed over the hills, was brought together and became one loaf, so may thy Church be brought together from the ends of the earth into thy kingdom."[19]

This gathering is accomplished not just for the sake of the church, but also for the sake of the world. The people of God is not an elitist enclave meant to stay separate from the world. The people of God is a pilgrim people, on a journey through this world to its heavenly home. On the way the church is a sacrament of salvation for the world. The Eucharist is especially important in this regard. To become one bread is to be made food for the world. As theologian Louis-Marie Chauvet points out, the essence of bread is realized only when it is consumed; bread that is not food has not accomplished its purpose. Only bread as food, bread as meal, bread broken for sharing reveals the true being of bread. This is especially apparent in the Eucharist. The Eucharist is bread to be broken and shared. When Jesus appears after his resurrection on the road to Emmaus (Luke 24:13-35), his disciples do not recognize him until he breaks bread and gives it to them. The

---

17. Sermon Denis 6, quoted in Jean-Marie-Roger Tillard, *Flesh of the Church, Flesh of Christ,* trans. Madeleine Beaumont (Collegeville, Minn.: Liturgical Press, 2001), p. 43. Tillard notes that some question whether this sermon was in fact from Augustine, but it is certainly Augustinian in flavor.

18. Augustine, *Confessions* (7.16), trans. Henry Chadwick (Oxford: Oxford University Press, 1991), p. 124.

19. *Didache* 9, in *Early Christian Writings,* trans. Maxwell Staniforth (Harmondsworth: Penguin Books, 1968), p. 231.

eucharistic significance is unmistakable; from now on they will know Christ in the breaking and sharing of the bread. The real presence of Christ is not a static presence, but an active giving. Christ's presence becomes real in being given away for others.

The same is true of those who follow Christ. We become who we are by giving ourselves away. As we have seen, the root of sin is the desire to be autonomous, to stand in competition with others, build walls around the self, and stuff it full. Salvation is being saved from the confinement of the self. It is an opening to the other, a pouring out of the small self into a wider communion with God and with others. Service is therefore intrinsic to the Christian life, an important part of becoming who we really are. Service, however, is radicalized in the Christian tradition beyond its usual meaning of me giving to you. In the Christian vision, the very boundaries between me and you, between mine and thine, as de Lubac says, are blurred. We are not simply asked to do good things for poor people; the very distinction between us and them is called into question.

Consider the account of the final judgment in Matthew 25:31-46. The Son of Man will gather all the nations of the world before him and separate those destined for eternal life from those destined for eternal punishment. To the former group he says, "Come, you that are blessed by my Father, inherit the kingdom prepared for you from the foundation of the world; for I was hungry and you gave me food, I was thirsty and you gave me something to drink, I was a stranger and you welcomed me, I was naked and you gave me clothing, I was sick and you took care of me, I was in prison and you visited me" (Matt. 25:34-36). They do not remember seeing him hungry and thirsty, a stranger and naked, sick and imprisoned. Christ tells them that whenever they did this for the least of his brothers and sisters, they did it to him. The reverse is the case for those condemned to punishment. Insofar as they did not perform these acts of mercy, they did not do them for Christ. What is most radical about this passage is not simply that service to others is rewarded, and its lack is punished. What is most remarkable is that in this passage Christ is identified not with those who serve, but with those who are served. The downtrodden are in fact Christ. The body of Christ effects a strange economy in which the difference between us and them, those who serve and those who are served, is radically confused. We are all members of one another, so that what is mine and what is yours become what is ours. In the body of Christ, all belongs to God, and none can claim absolute ownership of God's abundance. We find this same idea in Paul's image of the body of Christ. There is weakness in the body of Christ (1 Cor. 12:22), but the weakest parts are treated with the greatest honor. The strong do not simply try to alleviate the suffering of the weak, but actually share in that suffering. "If one member suffers, all suffer together with it; if one member is honored, all rejoice together with it" (1 Cor. 12:26).

If the church is the body of Christ, then this dynamic of sharing the fate of others must be true of the church as a whole. The church does not stand apart from the world, but tries to make Christ visible and tangible for the world, and tries to absorb the suffering of the world. As Vatican II put it, "The joys and the hopes, the griefs and the anxieties of the [people] of this age, especially those who are poor or in any way afflicted, these are the joys and hopes, the griefs and anxieties of the followers of Christ."[20] The church exists to create spaces where the salvation accomplished by Christ is made real. It is a public space where competition gives way to a deep sharing of life, including the material things of this world. It is a public space that questions the boundaries erected by human beings, not least the borders around countries that carve up creation into mutually hostile nationalities. The church, in short, is vital to the Christian life, because it makes us — with all our sinfulness and imperfections — *live together,* and thereby give hope to the world that God is restoring creation to the way it was meant to be.

Concurrent Readings

Day, Dorothy. *The Long Loneliness.* San Francisco: HarperSanFrancisco, 1952.

De Lubac, Henri. *Catholicism.* San Francisco: Ignatius, 1988.

Lohfink, Gerhard. *Does God Need the Church? Toward a Theology of the People of God.* Translated by Linda M. Maloney. Collegeville, Minn.: Liturgical Press, 1999.

Nichols, Terence L. *That All May Be One.* Collegeville, Minn.: Liturgical Press, 1997.

---

20. Second Vatican Council, *Pastoral Constitution on the Church in the Modern World (Gaudium et Spes),* §1.

Conclusion to Part 1

Theology matters for moral theology. Theology matters for how we see the world, make decisions, and live our lives. As Bauerschmidt states in chapter 3: "The Christian life is a single whole that cannot be neatly divided into 'believing' and 'behaving.'" What we live is what we truly believe. What we really believe will be embodied in our lives, whether we realize it or not.

Part 1 has outlined four important loci for sustaining a *theological* approach to moral theology. These four components of the Christian life are rooted in fundamental claims about God's relation to the world, claims that shape the context for how we are to see and understand our relationships, roles, and duties in daily life. We have looked at liturgy, Scripture, Jesus' ministry, and the doctrines of the Trinity and the church. What conclusions can we draw about moral reasoning to carry into parts 2 and 3? At this juncture, let us briefly name four topics for further discussion: identity, church, practice, and apprenticeship.

Identity — Whose We Are

What we ought to do, how we ought to act, and the ways in which we ought to live are intrinsically related to who we are and who we see ourselves becoming in the days and years ahead. Part 1 presents a number of proposals about what it means to be claimed by the identity "Christian." The authors hope to be faithful to this identity as a *gift:* we are who we are by virtue of God's love for us. God acts first to call us, to claim us, to love us. We will delve more deeply into that conviction and God's ever-present creativity in part 2. What difference ought our faith to make, and what can we give to the world? What difference does it make to be open to the possibility that the God of love, the God of all things, has chosen and called us and waits for us to follow?

As Bauerschmidt and Cavanaugh note, living out this call could mean something as simple and as simply profound as living the Shema. What would our lives look like if we were to embody the conviction that the Lord our God, the Lord is One? How would we live if we were to bring all aspects of life in relation to God, if we were to have no other gods before him? What does it mean, in other words, to return God's love for us, to love God above all others, and all others in relation to God? Do these questions sound extreme? Would such passion for God cloud our moral reason? (Chapter 8, in part 2, will ask these same questions.)

The sources of the Christian life as described in part 1 (and as developed further in part 2) do not create a barrier and cordon Christians off from the world. They open Christians to the world. Moral reasoning, in general, is always set within a history and culture. For religious and nonreligious folk alike, practical judgments and moral reflection depend upon underlying questions about identity, community, and formation in day-to-day practices. Who am I, and who do I hope to become? With whom and how do we share everyday matters of life? What holds us together? How does what we do shape how we see the world and act in it? Our hope is that the four loci that we have investigated (liturgy, Scripture, Trinity, and church) give a context for understanding our identity as Christians, in such a way that will help others (other Christians and non-Christians) ask about the sources of life. Hopefully we will live in such a way that encourages us and others to see God as our source.

Church — Who We (Plural) Are

The conception of faith and the church in part 1 challenges the individualism that plagues most modern accounts of moral reasoning. According to each chapter in part 1, one's "personal faith" is embedded in a story much larger than the individual self. The whole of Scripture suggests that God calls the people Israel and then the church into being. To be "Christ-ian" means to be "of Christ," and the way that Christ has made himself present in the world is in his body, which is extended in the world through the Spirit — through a peculiar group of people we call the "church." How amazing is it to think that "we together," as Cavanaugh notes, have a role to play in the cosmic drama of salvation? It is a strange thought that actually fits perfectly with the "foolishness" of the incarnation (1 Cor. 1:23) and the "scandal" of the cross (1:18-21). In the incarnation, God empties himself to join in solidarity with humanity (Phil. 2:1-11). Jesus gathers disciples to live as a part of a new people that will be the beginning of a new kind of human community — that will make salvation visible for the rest of the world. According to the foolishness of the incarnation and the scandal of the cross, this people will be comprised of regular people (fishermen and tax collectors), saints and sinners, who learn to live by grace.

Participating in the common life of the church, through worship and service, is crucial for learning to see our lives truthfully, because through these activities we learn ever more deeply who we are called to be. Practical knowledge and wisdom are not attained by individuals set apart from others. We come to reason well about the moral life by seeing it embodied in others — in those around us as well as in those exemplars remembered in an ongoing tradition. The church has the *saints,* those holy ones (sometimes recognized officially by the whole church) through whom we see the power and love of God. What we learn from the generations that come before us is, not that being a Christian means rigid uniformity, but that we become increasingly more unique, more truly who we each are as we cleave closer to God, as we follow Christ more closely. The holy ones among us, surely, are uniquely different from one another. Examining how the saints have reasoned in their own particular contexts can inform our own struggles as we seek to discern how to live in our own day. There are no fixed formulae or calculations for embodying Christian identity in our day-to-day lives.[1] To do this — to reason prudently from identity to action — requires a community of discernment, colleagues and friends with whom we can think together, who will listen to our reasoning and challenge it when our thinking veers off track, when our vision is distorted by lesser "loves," or when we slide, almost without notice, into narrow and self-serving love.

Christians have been discerning together in this way for the better part of two thousand years. One benefit of being part of the church is that one does not have to reinvent the wheel every time one seeks to act. The accumulated wisdom of the tradition finds a home in part in the teaching office of the church, also known as the magisterium. The magisterium finds analogies elsewhere. Think of the U.S. Supreme Court, an authoritative body whose job is to evaluate particular reasoned judgments (laws) in light of a foundational text (the Constitution). The Supreme Court determines

---

1. Recall the discussion entitled "Modern Moral Theories and Practical Reasoning" in the introduction.

that particular ways of acting (laws) are in keeping, or not, with what it means to be an American, a citizen of the United States. Analogously, the magisterium evaluates particular practices (e.g., human embryonic stem cell research) in light of Scripture and the broad tradition of Christian history, determining that certain courses of action are consistent with Christian identity while others are not.

To recognize the authority of a body like the church's magisterium is indeed countercultural. The modern world has attempted to privatize both morality and religion. But clearly, the authors in part 1 (and in the remaining chapters of the book) do not see it this way. For Catholics, sound moral reasoning takes seriously the institutional church, including the teaching office. It recognizes that this authority is not arbitrary; it does not create or hold its authority as an exertion of a powerful and coercive will that is imposed upon other wills. Authority is not to be followed blindly or mechanically but must be engaged in faith that the Holy Spirit guides the church. The authority of church teaching is primarily an intellectual one, an engagement that is a matter of the assent of faith and reason. Arguments must be made, and they should have the power to convince on the grounds of faith. Reasoned assent recognizes that the magisterium cannot set its own path but must listen to the tradition of the church; we should call the magisterium to be unlike our own limited, local, and partial perspectives and to take into account the living tradition of the church as a whole.

Practice

Once again we note that practical reason depends upon a practical context. Medical students learn to become physicians by watching what experienced practitioners do. Golfers learn what to do by hitting putt after putt on green after green. For Christians, well-reasoned action arises out of an identity that is inescapably ecclesial. Such an identity is something that we grow into over time, something that becomes more deeply rooted in us as we become more deeply immersed in it. In other words, living into "being a Christian" takes practice. Thus, the practices of the Christian life — the Eucharist, sacraments, prayer, worship, and the works of mercy — are necessary for members of the church to develop sound and farsighted moral reasoning.

The dispositions and skills required to reason well and wisely are not attained easily, especially when we are called "into" the broad span of salvation history. It takes faith and practice. We have to learn to see the world in terms of this overarching narrative. Learning to see in this way comes from being immersed ever more deeply in the story and stories of Scripture, in both corporate worship and private prayer. As Christians, our moral vision comes through participation: as we participate in God's love for the world in worship, we learn more and more to see the world under this aspect. We learn that God is the Lord of all; we learn that God invites us to friendship; we learn that the shape of God's love is "charity." Finally, if we are to live differently than the ways dictated by the dominant cultures and markets in the world (see chapter 11), we need times and places where we can "practice," to learn how to act in these simple but powerful new ways.

Practice is also necessary for knowledge. In the Christian tradition, *lex orandi lex credendi* has long been recognized as the process through which we come to know and to do. This Latin phrase can be translated in various ways, but it essentially suggests that it is by praying *(orandi)* that we come to know, to understand, and to believe *(credendi)*. Through the Eucharist and the sign of peace, for instance, we come to begin to act out what it means to call Christ the Prince of Peace and to be called to "go forth" to live Christ's peace in the world. Through baptism and prayer "in the name of the Father, the Son, and the Holy Spirit," we move to a deeper understanding of God as Trinity. Thus, Christian knowledge, reasoning, and wisdom are necessarily shaped by immersion in the new reality that God has introduced into the world through the life, death, and resurrection of Jesus Christ.

Embodied Apprenticeship

Another name for the Christian life is discipleship; the "Christian life" is nothing other than following Jesus the Christ. To be a Christian might be described as "apprenticing" oneself to Jesus. Thus, for the church, representations and explanations of who we believe Jesus to be, where Jesus is lived in the world, and how Jesus is present in the church are indispensable for judgments about how we ought to live. Like the disciples on the way to Emmaus, we are most likely to encounter Jesus when bread is blessed and broken (Luke 24:30), when we come to the eucharistic table.

The chapters in part 1 have returned again and again to common theological convictions. For example, the important *kenosis* hymn from Philippians 2:1-11 is mentioned in each chapter of part 1. McCarthy advocates an "incarnational" approach to biblical interpretation. This approach hears the biblical call to be an embodiment of God's Spirit — the Spirit of God who is incarnate in the Son, who empties himself in solidarity with humanity. Through hearing this call we become "fit interpreters" of God's word. Bauerschmidt, likewise, notes that the trinitarian conviction that Jesus is fully human and fully divine renders his whole life exemplary for us. By carefully attending to his life as recounted in Scripture, we can discern a pattern for imitation, which we can then live out in our time.

We are called to be open to God's presence in the world, and to "go and do likewise" (chapter 2). This pattern of knowing and doing is not a lockstep formula, but rather a framework for the necessary work of improvisation, for the creative work of living the gospel over time, the kind of work embodied in the living witness of the saints. Our love for God is necessarily linked with our love for neighbor (Mark 12:29-31). Moral theology begins with claims about God's relation with the world, not as philosophical ends-in-themselves, but because such claims point us toward the pattern of our relationships with each other and with the world, where we are called to follow Jesus: to incarnate God's love, to serve and to be engaged in issues of justice and human well-being.

The four chapters of part 1 provide an outline of the theological and social context from which Christians begin to think about moral reasoning. With this context in view, we can now begin to explore topics that are traditionally set within the field of moral theology (e.g., human acts, conscience, and so on). Beginning with baptism, part 2 introduces the important considerations of the goal of human life ("happiness"), natural law, human freedom, and virtue. These topics are not abstract philosophical categories. For Saint Thomas Aquinas, thinking through the moral life (*Summa Theologiae* II) is bounded on one side by the conviction that all creation proceeds from and returns to God (*Summa Theologiae* I), and on the other side by redemption in Christ and Christian worship (*Summa Theologiae* III). We move, in other words, *from* theology *to* theological anthropology and back again.

As we move into part 2, let us not forget the social and practical environment of moral reasoning. For Christians the virtues we seek to embody are not only for our own sake, but also to build up the community, to gather a broken humanity together, and to have something to give to the world. Let us also remember that the Christian life is not about a minimum, not about merely getting "the right answers." It's as much — or more — about holiness, a character of life that is developed over a lifetime, through ongoing study and formation, and maintained by the practices of prayer and mercy. This way of the Christian life begins with baptism.

Part 2

Pilgrim's Progress:
Virtues and the Goal of the Journey

When a person is unable to put words on a page, she is likely to say she has "writer's block." When a person is attempting to fix a computer problem and his efforts are not progressing, he is liable to say he has hit "a dead end." When we begin to see the effects of our housecleaning, we will say we are "getting somewhere." On a couple's twentieth wedding anniversary, the two will have a sense that they have "come a long way" together. The metaphors of roadblocks, dead ends, and getting somewhere put our practical activities in the framework of traveling from point A to point B. The idea and language of a journey are how we conceptualize matters of practical life and how we give meaning to our lives as a whole.[1] So it is in Catholic moral theology; each of us is a pilgrim along the way. Part 1 has attempted to give a context, or "home," for moral reasoning — a formative place from which practical reasoning proceeds. Part 2 shifts from the metaphor of place to one of a journey. It offers a framework for understanding and analyzing the moral life as a pathway.

A journey implies a direction and a destination. In moral inquiry our direction is found in the purposes of our actions, and the destination is our fulfillment as persons in community with others and with God. The first two chapters of part 2 attend to our purposes and fulfillment. James Donohue, in chapter 5, attends to our "callings" as members of the church, that is, as baptized members of the body of Christ. He describes the common mission and ministry of us all, as well as the diversity of roles among those who are called to follow Christ. In chapter 6 David

---

1. Steven L. Winter, *A Clearing in the Forest: Law, Life, and Mind* (Chicago: University of Chicago Press, 2001), pp. 22-42.

Cloutier moves to the level of philosophical argument. He raises the time-honored question of human happiness and shows the logic of the Aristotelian idea that our conception of "happiness" is bound within and makes sense of our actions.

When the contributors to part 2 were discussing the plan for the book, the question of the order of chapters 5 and 6 was raised. Cloutier, in fact, argued that it might make more sense to place the philosophical arguments first, and then move subsequently to the more particular callings, purposes, and conceptions of fulfillment that are now in chapter 5. After some discussion we settled on the existing order: the particular callings of baptism come before the philosophical arguments. Why? First of all, chapter 5 deals with our call as members of the church and provides a bridge between part 2 and part 1, which concludes with the chapter on the church. The second reason is pedagogical. We think it best to begin with the substantive and particular rather than a more abstract conception of actions, purposes, and ends. Finally, chapters 5 and 9 (the final chapter of part 2) give symmetry to this section of the book. Chapter 5 begins with the call from God in Scripture, and chapter 9 concludes with the tasks of discipleship — directing our "this-worldly" activities to God. The two chapters represent the beginning and end of the Christian's sojourn in the world.

Directly following the chapter on human fulfillment is chapter 7, on natural law and freedom. In this chapter Dana Dillon and David McCarthy give a broad overview of the natural law tradition, and focus especially on the *nature* of how humans *naturally* reason, or, we could say, how human beings reason according to the *law* of our *nature*. These references to *nature* and *law* might seem awkward. The words "nature" and "law," as understood in natural law tradition, are often misunderstood. In the modern world the terms tend to mean something less than human. The "natural" is identified with the instinctual, and law is considered mechanical and wooden. Both nature and law are usually considered structures that limit our freedom as human beings. The chapter on natural law attempts to restore the distinctively human meanings of nature and law, especially in relationship to human freedom.

Two additional comments need to be made about the chapter on natural law. First: As editors we decided that the best place to deal with conscience would be within this chapter's discussion of law and freedom. The importance of conscience in the modern Catholic tradition ought not to be overlooked. The contemporary idea of conscience, among Catholics, arose within what are called the manuals of moral theology, where conscience and law were the principal means of determining moral obligations.[2] The trained reader will see that our treatment of conscience relocates it from a setting more suited to moral conflict to a more fundamental context of the development of virtue.

Second: Another important issue set within this chapter is moral authority. The reference in the chapter is brief, but we will highlight it here. An essential feature of law is that it is promulgated/declared and transmitted. Law is an externalized structure of common life. Because human life is necessarily social, law and institutional authority are natural and essential, albeit external, aspects of sharing a common good. Certainly the institutional promulgation of law is not sufficient; it is well ordered when it shares a source with our inner inclinations toward the good. Without personal assent, law is hollow. For this reason, both deliberating about and interpreting pronouncements by authorities are necessary. Engagement and argument are how a people calls a way of life its own. One of chapter 7's main arguments is that moral law and freedom are not opposed. The same can be said for freedom and institutional authority; both are aspects of common life insofar as we are bound by a common good.

The preceding two paragraphs have emphasized issues of conscience and authority, but they do not stand out as separate subjects in the chapter on natural law. They are integrated within a consideration of human reason and freedom, and it is this discussion that forms the link between chapter 6 on human fulfillment, chapter 7 on natural law, and chapter 8 on freedom and grace. Chapter 8 begins with a presentation of the theological virtues: faith, hope, and love. These virtues are given to us by God's self-giving grace. If this is the case, then the question arises as to whether faith, hope, and love limit or enliven our freedom and personal fulfillment. Do the theological virtues and God's grace in general intrude on our choices and free action? In the chapter, Michael Miller argues the contrary, that God's creative and self-giving grace both restores and elevates our freedom for happiness — for fulfillment in what is good for us.

In the final chapter in part 2, William Mattison offers an explanation of moral virtue, where our object of concern is "this-worldly" activities (e.g., eating, confronting disagreements, giving our loved ones and neighbors their due, making practical judgments, and so on). Chapter 9 is another spot where the contributors discussed the ordering of the chapters. To some it made more sense to place Mattison's chapter on the "chief" or

2. See Dominicus Prömmer, *Handbook of Moral Theology,* trans. Gerald W. Shelton, ed. John Gavin Nolan (New York: P. J. Kennedy, 1957).

"hinge" moral virtues before Miller's chapter on faith, hope, and love. Their view was that the book should present a theory of acquired virtue and this-worldly activities first, and then move to the theological virtues and our destiny with God. Although this proposal is sensible, the current order won the day for a few reasons.

First, the present arrangement makes clear that our lives are not divided into a moral part and a theological part. Chapter 8, on grace and freedom, explicitly argues that grace is not a "topping" placed upon an already completed nature. It argues that God is ever-active in creation as well as in the redemptive self-giving of Jesus Christ. Second, beginning with the relationship between grace and human freedom facilitates the discussion, in chapter 9, of the relationship between this-worldly human fulfillment and our ultimate happiness with God. Mattison offers an account of our journey in this life that is both animated by grace and attentive to life with our neighbors and with the basic matters of life in the world.

In sum, the contributors in this part of the book have attempted to present basic themes in the Catholic moral tradition. Looking at the second part of Thomas Aquinas's *Summa Theologiae*, one will see that we address its main topics of human happiness in relationship to human acts, the virtues (including theological and moral virtues), sin, law, grace, and stations or vocations in life.[3] In our attempt to be as concise as possible, we have neglected explicit mention of how emotions, like anger, sorrow, and joy, are actively formed by us, participate in virtue, and contribute to our journey in life. We ask the reader to keep the passions in mind, especially when considering our inclinations and movement toward the good we desire (chapters 6 and 9). After working through part 2, readers will see that a discussion of the passions is a logical outcome of our analysis: the moral life engages all of who we are and encompasses the entirety of our lives.

3. Thomas Aquinas, *Summa Theologiae*, trans. Fathers of the English Dominican Province (New York: Benziger Brothers, 1948).

Chapter 5

Baptism, Mission, and Ministry

Rev. James M. Donohue, C.R.

A Call from God

The Bible is filled with intriguing stories of people who are called by God. Abraham was called to leave his father's house in Haran and set out to the land of Canaan, where God made a covenant with him (Gen. 17). Moses, encountering God in the burning bush, was called to confront Pharaoh and lead God's people out of captivity in Egypt to the Promised Land (Exod. 3). King David, anointed as a youth by the prophet Samuel, was called by God to shepherd the people of Israel in the newly united kingdom (2 Sam. 5). The great prophets, such as Elijah (1 Kings 17), Isaiah (Isa. 6), Jeremiah (Jer. 1), and Ezekiel (Ezek. 3), were each called by God to speak God's words to Israel, which had lost its way. We read stories in the Synoptic Gospels of how Jesus called his first disciples, sending them out two by two, enabling them to participate in his ministry of proclaiming the good news of forgiveness and salvation (Mark 6). In the Gospel of John, when Jesus' first two disciples ask Jesus where he is staying, Jesus invites them to "Come and see" (John 1:39).

And we know that others have been called by God as well. We remember God's call to great saints such as Saint Francis of Assisi, Saint Vincent de Paul, Saint Thérèse of the Child Jesus, Saint Ignatius of Loyola, Saint Frances Xavier Cabrini, Saint Maximilian Kolbe, Saint Elizabeth Ann Seton, and so many others whom the church venerates as living witnesses to the imitation of Christ in their service to the church and the world. In addition, we recognize many modern-day people whose holiness seems rooted in God's call to make a difference in the lives of others: Dorothy Day of the *Catholic Worker,* Jean Vanier of L'Arche, Mother Teresa of Calcutta, Archbishop Oscar Romero of El Salvador, and Pope John Paul II.

We might find it surprising, however, to realize that many if not all of these people whom we hold in such high esteem were initially unable, or quite reluctant, to hear God's call. The prophet Samuel, for instance, was confused about hearing God's call, thinking it was the voice of another person. He needed the assistance of Eli, who told him what to do the next time he thought he heard God's voice: "If you are called, reply: 'Speak, Lord, for your servant is listening.'" In addition, many of these great people, having heard God's call, did not consider themselves the ideal candidates for the mission for which God had selected them.

The classic examples of "reluctant responders" in the Old Testament are Jonah and Moses, who both tried to avoid God's call altogether. Jonah, for instance, tried to run away from his divine commission. In the process, he was thrown overboard, swallowed by a big fish, and rescued in a spectacular manner, before he accepted his call to go to Nineveh to preach a message of repentance (Jon. 1-3). For his part, Moses, after encountering God in the burning bush, continued to plead his unworthiness five separate times (Exod. 3:11, 13; 4:1, 10, 13). After God reveals God's plan to Moses, Moses asks: "Who am I that I should go to Pharaoh and lead the Israelites out of Egypt?" And even after God reassures Moses each time Moses raises new questions doubting his own ability. Moses, in the end, declares, "If you please, Lord, send someone else!"

Similarly, the New Testament contains stories about how those called by God are unable to imagine how God could work through them. Saint Peter, at first skeptical about any results from putting out from shore to fish after a night of catching nothing, turns to Jesus after a bountiful catch and says, "Go away from me, Lord, for I am a sinful man!" (Luke 5:1-8). Indeed, Peter, sinful as he is, embodies the frailty of all disciples. On the same night that he boastfully declared before Jesus and the other disciples, "Even though I should have to die with you, I will not deny you" (Mark 14:31 NAB), he, in panic and fear, later declared, "I do not know this man you are talking about" (14:71). Yet, despite his failings, this same Peter accepts the forgiveness and reconciliation offered by the risen Lord and becomes, indeed, a great leader and fisher of people (see Luke 24:34; Acts 1:15; 2:14-41; 10:11-48; 15:7-12; John 21:15-19).

The other great apostle of the New Testament, Saint Paul, has a similar story. Initially a persecutor of early disciples who followed "the Way" (Acts 9:1-2), Paul encounters the risen Lord and becomes the "Apostle to the Gentiles." Despite this lofty call, Paul never forgets his former sinful self and the transformative power that has healed him and enabled him to respond generously to the task God set before him (see 1 Cor. 15:8-10 and

2 Cor. 12:6-10). He realizes that it is only "by the grace of God [that] I am what I am, and his grace toward me has not been in vain" (1 Cor. 15:10). Realizing his own human inadequacies in following Jesus, Paul comes to understand the transformation that has occurred within, revealing that "I have been crucified with Christ; and it is no longer I who live, but it is Christ who lives in me. And the life I now live in the flesh I live by faith in the Son of God, who loved me and gave himself for me" (Gal. 2:19-20).

We continue to observe evidence of God's callings in our world today. For instance, Archbishop Oscar Romero of El Salvador stands as one example of a contemporary person who, hearing God's call, made a difference in his world. Described as cautious and conservative, he initially wanted to believe in the basic goodness of those in power in El Salvador in the 1970s.[1] But faced with the escalation of the government's oppression against the poor, as well as the murder of Father Rutilio Grande, Romero began to "see" differently. In the words of the Salvadoran Jesuit theologian Jon Sobrino, when Romero gazed at the body of Father Grande, it was as if "the scales fell from his eyes."[2] From this point he committed himself through nonviolence to make the lives of the poor in El Salvador better. Ultimately, he gave his life to the poor, being brutally slain on March 24, 1980. He was shot while celebrating the Eucharist, but not before preaching his final words: "We know that every effort to better society, especially when injustice and sin are so ingrained, is an effort that God blesses, that God wants, that God demands of us."[3]

God Continues to Call Today

As we study more closely the lives of saintly people, it becomes clearer that each of them had shortcomings, limitations, and inadequacies. Some had difficulty in hearing God's call, and some resisted the call once they heard it. Yet, it still may seem as though these biblical characters and great people are very different from the rest of us. We might persist in thinking that God speaks to special people only in dramatic ways. There is, however, a wonderful story in 1 Kings 19 that might offer a different model for us as we ponder

1. Marie Dennis, Renny Golden, and Scott Wright, *Oscar Romero: Reflections on His Life and Writings* (Maryknoll, N.Y.: Orbis, 2000), p. 8.

2. Jon Sobrino, *Archbishop Oscar Romero: Memories and Reflections* (Maryknoll, N.Y.: Orbis, 1990), p. 5.

3. Oscar Romero, "Homily on March 24, 1980," in *Oscar Romero: The Violence of Love,* compiled and translated by James R. Brockman, S.J. (Maryknoll, N.Y.: Orbis, 1988), p. 206.

God's call in our own lives. In this story the prophet Elijah is being pursued by Queen Jezebel, whom he has angered because he put all her prophets of Baal to the sword. He is told that God will appear to him on the mountain of God, Horeb. Elijah expects to find God in some rather spectacular manifestations — after all, that seems to be how God works in the Old Testament! But Elijah does not encounter God in the strong and heavy wind that was "rending the mountains and crushing rocks." Nor does Elijah encounter God in the earthquake or the fire. Instead, God comes to Elijah in a "tiny whispering sound" (1 Kings 19:11-12 NAB).

This "tiny whispering sound" is the way that many people — even those we consider great saints and moral exemplars — begin to hear God's call in their own lives. Concentrating on and anticipating drastic and dramatic actions on God's part may prevent us from hearing the gentle and tranquil call that emerges from everyday encounters with God through family, friendship, prayer, church, school, work, service, and recreation. The very ordinary encounters and events in our lives will serve as the most important places to "hear" God's call. Perhaps to say it differently, religious experiences happen in and through the ordinary experiences of our lives: personal encounters with family, friends, neighbors, and colleagues; prayer and liturgy; musical, athletic, and artistic experiences; and social, economic, and political experiences.

Characterizing God's call as a "tiny whispering sound" also should tell us there are many other "sounds" in our world, and some are quite dominant in our culture: materialism, consumerism, and individualism, to name a few. In addition, our fast-paced world can seduce us into a kind of manic busyness where reflection time, peace and quiet, and wholesome recreation are sought after but rarely attained. In the face of these obstacles, hearing God's call requires the nurturing of personal time and space where we are able to cultivate an "open and listening heart."

While the obstacles to hearing God's voice may seem daunting today, the good news is that people do not have to search and listen in isolation from each other. The Christian community is the gathering of Jesus' disciples who journey together to hear God's call. Here Christians continue to tell the many fascinating stories of God's call, and of the generous responses of women and men in every age, and the many and varied obstacles and challenges they have faced. All these stories are part of the church's story, handed on to each new generation. The thread woven most deeply within this story remains the Word of God's steadfast love for God's people and God's enduring call for us to live a most truly fulfilled and human life. Jesus, the Word made flesh, the image of the invisible God (Col. 1:15), reveals most fully who we are called to be.

The Call to Follow Jesus

Immediately after the call of the first disciples, Jesus begins his ministry with acts of healing. He cures a demoniac (Mark 1:21-28), Simon's mother-in-law (1:29-31), a leper (1:40-45), a paralytic (2:1-12), and "many [others] who were sick with various diseases" (1:34). Each healing is a sign that Jesus, the incarnation of God, has entered the world, offering health, salvation, and peace. Each healing is an indication that Jesus has entered the "strong man's house" and has begun to "plunder" it (3:27), restoring God's original plan for humanity. Each healing is a manifestation of Jesus' proclamation that "the kingdom of God is at hand." Each healing is a microcosm, for particular persons and their communities, of God's coming reign realized here and now.

We can identify certain characteristics and attitudes that Jesus manifests throughout his saving ministry. He uses touch with Simon's mother-in-law, is empathetic and responsive to the request of the leper, and admires the faith of those who bring the paralyzed man to him. Although the numbers of those who need healing often seem overwhelming, Jesus is attentive to the needs and faith of each individual, such as the woman afflicted with hemorrhages for twelve years (5:31-34). And whenever someone is overwhelmed by whatever keeps that person from being a whole and healthy human being, Jesus not only maintains that "all things can be done for the one who believes," but also responds positively to the plea of the father of the boy possessed by a demon, who cries out in response: "I believe; help my unbelief!" (9:23-24).

Jesus is the way, the truth, and the life (John 14:6), who embodies all the qualities that are worthy of imitation by his followers. Jesus reveals "the way" as integrity and compassion, listening attentively and responsively to others in their suffering from sickness and disease, their alienation from others, their poverty, and their marginalization in the world. Jesus reveals "the truth" as he communicates through his words and deeds that no one is beyond God's concern, healing, and forgiveness. Jesus reveals "the life" through his own suffering, death, and resurrection, revealing that true fulfillment in life comes from service, self-sacrifice, and learning to lose oneself so that others may have life.

Compared to our usual desires for success, defined as wealth, fame, independence, self-aggrandizement, and power, Jesus models and invites his followers to live differently. Following Jesus entails living in imitation of him: taking up your cross and losing yourself for his sake and the sake of the gospel (Mark 8:34-35), learning to become "last of all and servant of all"

(9:35), and coming to understand that "whoever wishes to become great among you must be your servant, and whoever wishes to be first among you must be slave of all" (10:43-44). This, according to the gospel, is the path to fulfillment, one to which every follower of Jesus is invited to participate.

At the very beginning of his public ministry, Jesus called others to come after him so that he could make them fishers of men and women (1:17). He began to teach them, and sent them out two by two, giving them authority over unclean spirits. Mark's Gospel reports that they enjoyed great success, as the disciples "cast out many demons, and anointed with oil many who were sick and cured them" (6:13). But we might wonder at this point how the disciples were able to be so successful, while at the same time thinking, once again, that this type of call is only for "holy" or "special" people.

In his Gospel account, Mark intimates that the positive results of the disciples' ministry came from dependence upon Jesus, not themselves. Notice that the disciples are instructed to take a walking stick and sandals, but nothing else for the journey — no food, no sack, no money in their belts, and no second tunic (6:8-9). These instructions may seem rather obscure unless we have in mind a passage from the Old Testament, Exodus 12. There, like Jesus' disciples, the Israelites have sandals on their feet and a staff in their hands. They gather on the night that the angel of death will pass over them, for they are about to be freed from their bondage in Egypt and to begin their journey to the Promised Land. The Israelites begin their hurried journey, taking with them the dough before it was leavened and, as they leave Egypt, they "despoil" the Egyptians, taking with them "jewelry of silver and gold, and . . . clothing" (Exod. 12:35). Jesus' disciples, however, are instructed to take no sack, no money, and no second tunic, for Mark's Gospel suggests that — in contrast to the Israelites in Exodus 12 — the ministerial success of Jesus' disciples will depend — ultimately — upon their ability to rely, not upon themselves and their own gifts, but upon their relationship with Jesus, who is the way, the truth, and the life. This was a difficult lesson for the early disciples of Jesus to learn, as it is for those who strive to follow him today. We often think a response to God's call depends solely upon ourselves, and thus become hesitant and reluctant to respond generously.

But that the God who calls us will also be there to guide and support us is also something we often forget! Returning from their ministry journey, the disciples wanted to share with Jesus all they had done and taught. However, people were coming and going in great numbers, and there was no opportunity for them to share their stories. Jesus suggests that they go to a deserted place, but when they arrive by boat, Jesus and the disciples encounter a vast crowd. Jesus "had compassion for them, because they were like sheep without a shepherd; and he began to teach them many things" (Mark 6:34). Suddenly it becomes clear why Jesus' disciples need a walking stick or staff: Jesus calls them to shepherd people with care and compassion, following his example as the Good Shepherd, who is willing to lay down his life for his friends (John 10:11).

As the story continues, however, the disciples are frustrated and want to send the crowds away. After all, Jesus has told them not to bring any food or money, so how could they possibly provide for this huge crowd? The disciples seem to have forgotten the lesson they had learned earlier: if they have Jesus, they have all they need. Turning to Jesus, and depending upon him, the crowd of people "all ate and were filled" (Mark 6:42). In fact, there was an overabundance of food, for ministry rooted in Jesus is the fulfillment of his promise that he has come that we "may have life, and have it abundantly" (John 10:10).

Through the arrangement of these stories, Mark reminds his hearers that discipleship is a call and that God works through our generous responses, bringing forth abundant fruit in ways that we might not imagine or expect. God wants to use our gifts and talents to further God's reign. But these stories remind us that even in the face of our inadequacies, we do not have to be afraid, for the God who calls people to serve others is faithful and steadfast in love to those who respond generously. It is this insight that led Saint Paul, reflecting upon the love of Christ that had transformed him, to say: "Glory be to God whose power, working in us, can do infinitely more than we can ask or imagine" (Eph. 3:20 NJB).

Baptism: The Source of the Call for All Who Serve

The Second Vatican Council continually speaks of baptism as the source of all Christian service, clerical and lay. For instance, the *Dogmatic Constitution on the Church (Lumen Gentium)* identifies baptism as the source of all Christians' participation in the threefold mission of Christ as priest, prophet, and king (§10-13).[4] To reinforce the idea that this is not a call reserved only for priests and religious, the same document reiterates this teaching specifically in relation to the laity, stating that by baptism laity "are in their own way made sharers in the priestly, prophetic, and kingly functions of Christ,"

---

4. *Decrees of the Ecumenical Councils,* ed. Norman P. Tanner, trans. Edward Yarnold, vol. 2 (Washington, D.C.: Georgetown University Press, 1990), pp. 849-98.

carrying out "their own part in the mission of the whole Christian people with respect to the Church and the world" (§31).

While distinguishing between the common priesthood of the faithful and the ministerial or hierarchical priesthood (§10), the document clearly indicates that all the faithful, whatever their condition or state, are called by the Lord, each in his or her own way, to a life of perfect holiness (§11). In the words of the "General Introduction: Christian Initiation," the three sacraments of initiation — baptism, confirmation, and Eucharist — combine "to bring us, the faithful of Christ, to his full stature and to enable us to carry out the mission of the entire people of God in the Church and in the world" (§2).[5]

The baptized person is able to carry out this mission, for having become a member of the church, he or she belongs no longer to himself or herself, but to Christ, whose dying has destroyed our death and who, rising, has restored our life. As a member of Christ's body, the church, the baptized Christian is now called to a life of service, following the example of Christ, who at the Last Supper proclaimed, "I am among you as one who serves" (Luke 22:27). As a new creation in Christ, the baptized person has been purified from sin and given new birth in the Holy Spirit. An adopted son or daughter of God, a member and coheir with Christ, and a temple of the Holy Spirit, the Christian now partakes in the divine nature (see 2 Cor. 5:17; 2 Pet. 1:4; Gal. 4:5-7), enabling him or her to believe in God, to hope in God, and to love God, to live and act under the prompting of the Holy Spirit through the gifts of the Holy Spirit, and to grow in goodness through the moral virtues.[6]

The Call to Service for Priests and Religious

The *Dogmatic Constitution on the Church* notes that the common priesthood of the faithful and the ministerial or hierarchical priesthood are interrelated, but differ from one another in both degree and essence (§10).[7] Each priest-

---

5. *The Rites of the Catholic Church,* vol. 1, study edition, revised by decree of the Second Vatican Ecumenical Council and published by authority of Pope Paul VI, approved for use in the dioceses of the United States of America by the National Conference of Catholic Bishops and confirmed by the Holy See, prepared by the International Commission on English in the Liturgy: A Joint Commission of Catholic Bishops' Conferences (New York: Pueblo, 1990).

6. *The Catechism of the Catholic Church,* 2nd ed., revised in accordance with the official Latin text promulgated by Pope John Paul II (Vatican City: Libreria Editrice Vaticana, 1997; Washington, D.C.: United States Catholic Conference, 1997), 322.

7. *Decrees,* 2:849-98.

hood participates in the one priesthood of Christ, but in its own special way (§10). The part of the chapter devoted to the hierarchical structure of the church maintains that the ministerial priesthood is meant for the nurturing and constant growth of the people of God, working for the good of the whole body. The service that priests provide to their brothers and sisters through their sacred ministry enables all who are the people of God to work toward a common goal freely and in an orderly way, arriving at salvation (§18).

The rites of ordination for a bishop, a priest, or a deacon include an instruction that outlines the duties of each, underlining the particular call to the service of God's people. As representatives of the people of God, bishops, priests, and deacons are entrusted with certain roles and duties within the community. For instance, the priest who is to be ordained to the episcopacy hears:

> You, dear brother, have been chosen by the Lord. Remember that you are chosen from among men and appointed to act for men and women in relation to God. The title of bishop is one not of honor but of function, and therefore a bishop should strive to serve rather than to rule. Such is the counsel of the Master: the greater should behave as if he were the least, and the leader as if he were the one who serves. Proclaim the message whether it is welcome or unwelcome; correct error with unfailing patience and teaching. Pray and offer sacrifice for the people committed to your care and so draw every kind of grace for them from the overflowing holiness of Christ. . . . As a father and a brother, love all those whom God places in your care. Love the priests and deacons who share with you the ministry of Christ. Love the poor and infirm, strangers and the homeless. . . . Attend to the whole flock in which the Holy Spirit appoints you an overseer of the Church of God — in the name of the Father, whose image you personify in the Church — and in the name of his Son, Jesus Christ, whose role of Teacher, Priest, and Prophet you undertake — and in the name of the Holy Spirit, who gives life to the Church of Christ and supports our weakness with strength. (§18)[8]

The instruction spoken to the one about to be ordained to the priesthood outlines his sacramental duties and notes that the priest is chosen from among the people of God to serve the people of God, especially as a minister of the sacraments:

> My son, you are now to be advanced to the order of the presbyterate. You must apply your energies to the duty of teaching in the name of

8. *The Rites of the Catholic Church,* vol. 2.

Christ, the chief Teacher. Share with all mankind the word of God you have received with joy. Meditate on the law of God, believe what you read, teach what you believe, and put into practice what you teach. . . . When you baptize, you will bring men and women into the people of God. In the sacrament of penance, you will forgive sins in the name of Christ and the Church. With holy oil you will relieve and console the sick. You will celebrate the liturgy and offer thanks and praise to God throughout the day, providing not only for the people of God but for the whole world. Remember that you are chosen from among God's people and appointed to act for them in relation to God. Do your part in the work of Christ the Priest with genuine joy and love, and attend to the concerns of Christ before your own. . . . Always remember the example of the Good Shepherd who came not to be served but to serve, and to seek out and rescue those who were lost. (§14)

We see that service to God's people is also central to the instruction given to those who are to be ordained to the deaconate:

He will draw new strength from the gift of the Holy Spirit. He will help the bishop and his body of priests as a minister of the word, of the altar, and of charity. He will make himself a servant to all. As a minister of the altar he will proclaim the Gospel, prepare the sacrifice, and give the Lord's body and blood to the community of believers. It will also be his duty, at the bishops' discretion, to bring God's word to believer and nonbeliever alike, to preside over public prayer, to baptize, to assist at marriages and bless them, to give viaticum to the dying, and to lead the rites of burial. Once he is consecrated by the laying on of hands that comes to us from the apostles and is bound more closely to the altar, he will perform works of charity in the name of the bishop or the pastor. From the way he goes about these duties, may you recognize him as a disciple of Jesus, who came to serve, not to be served. (§14)

Acting on behalf of the people of God, bishops, priests, and deacons are called to exercise servant leadership, caring for and nurturing the people of God through teaching and the ministration of the sacraments. No longer acting only on their own authority, they become "public" people through their ordination, representing and acting on behalf of the church in service of the church.

While religious life is not included among the hierarchical structures of the church, many men and women continue to be drawn to commit themselves with others of similar vision to follow Christ, poor, chaste, and obedient in a community life guided by a particular charism and mission. The *Dogmatic Constitution on the Church* stresses that the call of professed religious is to be Christlike, providing through their prayer and service an effective image of "the real Christ" (§46).[9] Similar exhortations are given in the Second Vatican Council's document on religious life *(Perfectae Caritatis)*, which states that the committed religious "abandons all for Christ (see Mark 10:28), follows him (see Matt. 19:21) as the only good (see Luke 10:42), and accepts his teaching (see Luke 10:39) concerning what is dear to him [or her] (see 1 Cor. 7:32)" (§5).

Religious men and women provide a service to the church, even when they are cloistered, with limited contact with the world. Rooted in their baptism with a yearning to be dedicated totally to God, religious men and women are moved by the Holy Spirit to follow Christ more nearly, to give themselves to God who is loved above all, and, pursuing the perfection of charity in the service of the kingdom, to signify and proclaim in the church the glory of the world to come.[10] In a world that often glorifies wealth, personal freedom, and sex above all else, religious men and women who practice poverty, obedience, and chastity in celibacy for the sake of the kingdom provide a striking witness to other values and the way to a fulfilling life.

The Call to Service for Us

As mentioned above, the *Dogmatic Constitution on the Church* notes that the common priesthood of the faithful and the ministerial or hierarchical priesthood are interrelated, but differ from one another in both degree and essence. Each member of both priesthoods participates in the one priesthood of Christ, but in his or her own special way (§10).[11] Susan K. Wood, writing about the ecclesiological foundations of ministry, notes that the offices of priest, prophet, and king are not exercised in the same manner by the ordained and nonordained.[12] We note differences in *how* priests and laity are called to exercise the offices of priest, prophet, and king.

---

9. *Decrees,* 2:849-98.

10. *Catechism,* p. 241. See also *Code of Canon Law,* §573, in *New Commentary on the Code of Canon Law,* ed. John P. Beal, James A. Coriden, and Thomas J. Green, commissioned by the Canon Law Society of America (New York: Paulist, 2000).

11. *Decrees,* 2:849-98.

12. Susan K. Wood, S.C.L., *Sacramental Orders* (Collegeville, Minn.: Liturgical Press, 2000), p. 18. The differences in the exercise of the three offices that follows is taken from this source.

In the priestly office the ordained minister is identified with the person of Christ, the head of the body, while the baptized become a priestly community through baptism, which incorporates them into the ecclesial body of Christ and orients them to participation in Christ's eucharistic body (§10). Dedicated to Christ and anointed by the Spirit, the baptized in this particular way can offer all their work as a spiritual sacrifice: their prayers and apostolic works, their married and family life, their daily work, their mental and physical recreation, and even life's troubles if they are patiently borne (§34).

In the prophetic office the ordained minister — particularly the bishop — is identified with authoritative teaching. As successors of the apostles and members of the college of bishops, the bishops throughout the world, in union with the pope, share in the apostolic responsibility and mission of the whole church. (As an aside, the church documents used as sources in this chapter are an example of the fruit of this teaching function and the office of apostolic unity of the hierarchy.) For their part the baptized members of the common priesthood exercise their prophetic office with the testimony of their daily social and family life. This work is understood as evangelization, for the laity carry forth the message of Christ through their words and the witness of their lives in the ordinary worldly situations of life (§35).

In the kingly office the ordained minister provides pastoral leadership within the church, particularly in administering the sacraments to all the baptized. For their part the baptized members of the common priesthood are called to spread the kingdom of God, particularly in the secular world, "so that the world may be penetrated with the Spirit of Christ" (§36). This is the principal role of the laity: penetrating the world with the spirit of Christ so that the world will more effectively attain its purpose in justice, in love, and in peace. Specifically, this will entail such efforts as working for a more equitable distribution of the world's goods and improving secular structures and conditions that are sinful and unjust. Through the activities of those baptized into Christ, the whole of human society will be enlightened by the saving light of Christ (§36).

The role of the laity is specified in the section of the *Dogmatic Constitution on the Church* devoted to the laity. Here the council fathers note that the particular vocation or call of the ordained is to sacred ministry, while the particular vocation or call of the laity is to "seek the kingdom of God by engaging in temporal affairs and ordering them in accordance with the will of God" (§31). The document points out that laymen and laywomen live in the world, are engaged in all the secular professions and occupations of the world, and are occupied with all the ordinary circumstances of family and social life. Being closely involved in temporal affairs of every sort, laypeople are called to "work for the sanctification of the world as it were from the inside, like leaven, through carrying out their own task in the spirit of the gospel, and in this way revealing Christ to others principally through the witness of their lives, resplendent in faith, hope, and charity" (§31).

Another document from the Second Vatican Council, the *Decree on the Apostolate of the Laity (Apostolicam Actuositatem),* maintains that the laity are called to participate in the church's mission and that no member can be purely passive, for each shares in the life and functions of the body of Christ (§2).[13] Initiation into Christ's body, the church, is the source and foundation of ministry for laypeople: "They are brought into the mystical body of Christ by baptism, strengthened by the power of the Spirit in confirmation, and assigned to the apostleship by the Lord himself. They are consecrated as a royal priesthood and a holy people (see 1 Pt 2:4-10), so as to offer spiritual sacrifices in all their works and to bear witness to Christ throughout the world" (§3).

Pope John Paul II, in his Apostolic Exhortation on the Laity, *Lay Members of Christ's Faithful People (Christifideles Laici),* reiterates the teachings of Vatican II, emphasizing that "everyone, the whole people of God, shares in this three-fold mission [of priest, prophet-teacher, and king]" (§14).[14] He maintains that as baptized members of Christ, all members share a common dignity from their rebirth in Christ, all have the same filial grace, and all have the same vocation to perfection (§15). John Paul II, consistent with Vatican II, notes that among the lay faithful this one baptismal dignity takes on a manner of life that is proper and particular to them: *a secular character* (§15). Living "in the world," the lay faithful — if they are to respond to their call — must see "their daily activities as an occasion to join themselves to God, fulfill his will, serve other people, and lead them to communion with God in Christ" (§17).

John Paul II continues to speak of the involvement of laymen and laywomen as a "call," wherein each member of the church "is entrusted with a unique task that cannot be done by another and which is to be fulfilled for the good of all" (§28). Prepared by the sacraments of initiation and the gifts of the Holy Spirit, each follower of Jesus is called by name, and no disciple

13. *Decrees,* 2:981-1001.

14. John Paul II, *Lay Members of Christ's Faithful People,* in *Origins* 18 (February 1989): 567.

can withhold making a response. To emphasize this point John Paul II makes reference to Saint Paul, who, in this light, declared: "Woe to me if I do not proclaim the gospel!" (1 Cor. 9:16) (§33).

The gospel proclamation will be transformative in a world infused with secularism, atheism, and indifference to God, but also particularly relevant in so-called First World countries, in which economic well-being and consumerism — coexisting with poverty and misery — inspire and sustain a life lived "as if God did not exist" (§34). In this light John Paul II encourages laymen and laywomen to make the inviolable dignity of every human person the central and unifying task of their service in the church to the human family (§37). He cites charity toward one's neighbor, through contemporary forms of the traditional spiritual and corporal works of mercy (see Matt. 25), as the most immediate, ordinary, and habitual way that enables the faithful to animate and transform the temporal order (§41). In addition, he reminds us that "a charity that loves and serves the person is never able to be separated from justice" (§42). Hence, laymen and laywomen are called to participate in "public life," that is, in the many different economic, social, legislative, administrative, and cultural areas that are intended to promote the common good (§42).

In more recent times the church has experienced the emergence of a new group of laity who, responding to God's call, transcends a too-narrow distinction between sacred and secular ministry. The *Dogmatic Constitution on the Church* recognized some overlap but maintained that by reason of their vocation, those in sacred orders "are principally and professedly ordained for sacred ministry," while it is the special vocation of the laity "to seek the kingdom of God by engaging in temporal affairs" (§31).[15] Cardinal Avery Dulles points out that the *Constitution on the Sacred Liturgy (Sacrosanctum Concilium)*, the *Decree on Religious Education (Gravissimum Educationis)*, the *Decree on the Church's Missionary Activity (Ad Gentes)*, and the *Pastoral Constitution on the Church in the Modern World (Gaudium et Spes)* recognize that many laypeople are involved in "ministry": those involved in liturgical roles such as servers, readers, commentators, and choir members; religious educators; missionary workers; and workers on behalf of justice, the defense of human life, and peace.[16]

Since the Second Vatican Council, the United States Conference of Catholic Bishops has published three noteworthy documents on lay minis-

15. *Decrees*, 2:849-98.
16. Avery Dulles, "Can Laity Properly Be Called 'Ministers'?" *Origins* 35 (April 2006): 727-28.

try: *Called and Gifted,*[17] *Called and Gifted for the Third Millennium,*[18] and *Co-workers in the Vineyard of the Lord.*[19] They provide a snapshot of the development of "ecclesial lay ministry" — laypeople who do not simply "work" in and for the church, but are called by God to exercise ministry in and on behalf of the church. The American Catholic bishops characterize lay ecclesial ministers as having: (1) authorization of the hierarchy to serve publicly in the local church; (2) leadership in a particular area of ministry; (3) close mutual collaboration with the pastoral ministry of bishops, priests, and deacons; and (4) preparation and formation appropriate to the level of responsibilities assigned them.[20]

Some might prefer to reserve the words "ministry" and "minister" for the ordained and never allow them to be applied to laypeople, while others contend that the overemphasis on the word "ecclesial" obscures the particular secular mission of the laity. A middle ground is staked out by American bishops who recognize that this particular call of the laity is both "ecclesial," because it has a place within the community of the church while being submitted to the discernment, authorization, and supervision of the hierarchy, and "ministry," because it is participation in the threefold mission of Christ.[21]

Conclusion: Four "Calls" in the Life of Every Christian

On the thirtieth anniversary of the *Decree on the Apostolate of the Laity* and the fifteenth anniversary of *Called and Gifted,* the U.S. Catholic bishops offered some reflections on the ways laymen and laywomen were answering God's call and using their gifts to take an active and responsible part in the mission of the church to the world. In their document *Called and Gifted for the Third Millennium,* the bishops note four "calls" — to holiness, to community,

17. Secretariat for the Laity, National Conference of Catholic Bishops, *Called and Gifted: The American Catholic Laity,* Reflections of the American Bishops commemorating the fifteenth anniversary of the issuance of the *Decree on the Apostolate of the Laity* (Washington, D.C.: United States Catholic Conference, 1980).

18. Secretariat for the Laity, National Conference of Catholic Bishops, *Called and Gifted for the Third Millennium,* Reflections of the U.S. Catholic Bishops on the thirtieth anniversary of the *Decree on the Apostolate of the Laity* and the fifteenth anniversary of *Called and Gifted* (Washington, D.C.: United States Catholic Conference, 1995).

19. Committee on the Laity, United States Conference of Catholic Bishops, *Co-workers in the Vineyard of the Lord: A Resource for Guiding the Development of Lay Ecclesial Ministry* (Washington, D.C.: United States Catholic Conference, 2005).

20. *Co-workers in the Vineyard,* p. 7.

21. *Co-workers in the Vineyard,* p. 8.

to mission and ministry, and to adulthood/Christian maturity — and identify several challenges confronting each one.[22] These "calls" are the foundation upon which all service, in the church or in the world, must be based.
They can be used to reflect upon the vocations of all in the church — clerical, religious, and lay.

The bishops cite the *Catechism of the Catholic Church,* which talks about
holiness as the call to "ever more intimate union with Christ" (§2014).[23] As we
hear the call to holiness, we have to discern our role within the body of Christ.
The call is always applied in practical terms within community:

- to hear the call of good work, to work for conditions where work is
  not only profitable but serves the worker and the common good;
- to hear the call of service to community, in civic organizations and
  public life, to resist a culture of greed, violence, and superficial fame
  and to persist in seeking to do good for our neighbors;
- to hear the call of marriage and family, to take the journey of discipleship, to resist the individualism of modern life, and to be a community of fidelity, hospitality, and generosity;
- to hear the call of service to the church as laypeople who work to pene-
  trate the world with the spirit of Christ; and
- to hear the call to the priesthood and religious life to provide servant
  leadership for the people of God and to signify and proclaim in the
  church the glory of the world to come.

The bishops recognize the great desire Christians have for experiences
of deeper community, especially in their families and parishes. As we hear
the call to community, we are challenged to live faithfully, to be life-giving
and caring to others, to reach out to the needy, and to grow in mutuality as
we recognize our equality as persons created in God's image.[24]

The bishops reiterate that through the sacraments of baptism, confirmation, and Eucharist every Christian is called to participate actively and
coresponsibly in the church's mission of salvation in the world. And they
acknowledge that the Holy Spirit pours out gifts that make it possible for
every Christian man and woman to assume different ministries and forms
of service that complement one another and are ordered for the good of all
people.[25] Bishops, as well as priests and deacons who collaborate with them,

22. *Called and Gifted for the Third Millennium,* p. 1.
23. *Called and Gifted for the Third Millennium,* p. 3.
24. *Called and Gifted for the Third Millennium,* p. 10.
25. *Called and Gifted for the Third Millennium,* p. 15.

are called to teach, sanctify, and guide the community. Vowed religious, through their particular charism and mission, are called to a life of service, especially among the poor and marginalized. It is also crucial today for the church to communicate the importance of the laity's witness and service within the family; within the professional, social, political, and cultural life of society; and within new and developing ecclesial lay ministries.[26]

The bishops note that the three previous "calls" to holiness, community, and mission and ministry will come to full expression only by development and growth toward Christian maturity. Among the various signs that would manifest a "mature Christianity" is the laity's exercise of responsible participation both individually and in groups, not only at the invitation of church leadership, but also by their own initiative.[27] In so doing, laity, along with ordained clergy and vowed religious, will have heard their particular call and, gathered on the journey of discipleship, will work together to transform the world more fully into the kingdom of God.

Concurrent Readings

Committee on the Laity, United States Conference of Catholic Bishops. *Co-workers in the Vineyard of the Lord: A Resource for Guiding the Development of Lay Ecclesial Ministry*. Washington, D.C.: United States Catholic Conference, 2005. This is a resource document approved by the U.S. Bishops to guide the development of lay ecclesial ministry. It discusses the theological foundations, the discernment of suitability, the formation, and the workplace policies and practices of such ministries.

Fox, Zeni. *New Ecclesial Ministry: Lay Professionals Serving the Church*. Rev. ed. Chicago: Sheed and Ward, 2002. Fox has served as an adviser to the Bishops' Subcommittee on Lay Ministry since its inception in 1994. This very readable work traces mission and ministry from the perspective of the tradition and provides an overview of the present reality of emerging "ecclesial lay ministries."

Wood, Susan K., ed. *Ordering the Baptismal Priesthood: Theologies of Lay and Ordained Ministry*. Collegeville, Minn.: Liturgical Press, 2003. This collection of essays explores baptism and its implications for mission and ministry within the contexts of the ordained, religious, and laity.

---

26. *Called and Gifted for the Third Millennium,* pp. 15-16.
27. *Called and Gifted for the Third Millennium,* pp. 20-23.

Chapter 6

Human Fulfillment

DAVID CLOUTIER

What Causes Human Action?

The simplest way to understand what ethics is about is to say that it is the study of human actions. Just as chemistry is the study of atoms and molecules, so ethics studies what humans do. Its raw material is the fact of human action, and it seeks to analyze and understand how and why humans act.

So we start by asking the questions: What causes human action? Why do anything at all? In our overly scientific world, we tend to look for causes somewhere "before" the thing we are analyzing. If we ask why it is raining outside, we look at atmospheric conditions and reactions that resulted in the rain. That is to say, we look at the object under study as an effect of some prior cause. We can and do look at human action in the same way. If we ask what caused a marriage to break up, for example, we may look at the arguments a couple had, or dispositions they brought into the marriage, or family problems from their childhood. If we are particularly scientific, we may look for explanations in the chemistry of the brain, suggesting (as some have) that the excited "feelings" we have when we enter a romantic relationship are caused by certain chemical reactions in the brain, but as with any drug, the reactions adjust after constant use, and so the same drug no longer produces the effect. Our brain seeks stimulation elsewhere.

These explanations may suffice if we are trying to explain a car engine, or even certain phenomena of nature (though there is some argument about this), but we sense that they are inadequate for why humans act. And we would be right. For human action is not simply human movement. It's not just a human version of physics. Human action is driven not primarily by past causes, but by causes situated in the future.

If I ask a student why he has decided to go to college, he might reply that his parents forced him to do it. But the very word "forced" should indicate to us that this action is a bad candidate for human action. We naturally assume that genuine human action, the action of mature adult persons, is voluntary or free.[1] It does not involve being forced by another, but involves intentional choice. We recognize this in our legal system. When we look for who is primarily responsible for a crime, we may not only look for the henchman who, because perhaps of fear of stronger gang members, actually committed the crime. We also look to those who planned the crime. Those persons acted freely.

And why did they act? Put simply, they wanted something, and it is this interior inclination and knowledge of it that mark human action as voluntary.[2] My student, if she has gone to college freely, has gone because she desires something in the future, whether it be a liberal education or a credential for a job. That is to say, her action has a *purpose*. It aims, as if trying to hit some target in the future, and it is her desire for that purpose that "causes" her to act. Were she to learn that she could have the job she wants right now, without completing her college courses, she would drop out and stop doing the action (if her sole purpose was to get a job). If a man is paying special attention to a woman in the hopes of dating her, but then learns that she is unavailable, he will stop taking those actions. (Or perhaps he will continue, but only because he has it in his head that, at some future time, she may be available.) In both of these examples, we can see that what causes the action is its purpose, its directedness toward a desired end.[3]

Is There an Ultimate Purpose/End?

The moral theology of Thomas Aquinas, following on the non-Christian Greek philosopher Aristotle, argues that just as individual actions happen

---

1. Thomas Aquinas, *Summa Theologiae* I-II.6, introduction and 1. All references to this work are to *Summa Theologiae,* trans. Fathers of the English Dominican Province (New York: Benziger Brothers, 1948).

2. Aquinas, *Summa Theologiae* I-II.6.1: "for the word *voluntary* implies that their movement and acts are from their own inclination."

3. Aquinas, *Summa Theologiae* I-II.1.1: "Now it is clear that whatever actions proceed from a power, are caused by that power in accordance with the nature of its object. But the object of the will is the end and the good. Therefore all human actions must be for an end." I-II.6.1: "But those things which have knowledge of an end [purpose] are said to move themselves because there is in them a principle by which they not only act but also act for an end."

because we have purposes or aims, the action of our entire life must happen because it too has a purpose. Thomas suggests that if all we do is perform individual actions for individual purposes, without some larger, further purpose, we would (again) cease to act.[4] All our action must be aimed at an ultimate end, or *telos,* as the Greeks called it.

But where do all our actions take us? Is there any destination? Some philosophers of the twentieth century argued (essentially) that the overall action of our life has but one possible end: death.[5] No matter what we do and what end we aim at, it cannot endure; eventually we will die, and it will be meaningless. Hence, when looking at the overall meaning of life, many people (both yesterday and today) invest themselves in "immortality projects," in ways of sustaining their lives after they die — they give handsome sums of money to build buildings on college campuses, for example, or they educate children, or they strive after fame and honor. Some, sensing the futility of these immortality projects, instead follow some ancient philosophical wisdom recently refurbished by Dave Matthews: eat, drink, and be merry, for tomorrow we die.[6] Rather than striving after something enduring, let's just sit back, relax, and enjoy ourselves.

All these perspectives are perspectives on human fulfillment, on the ancient question: What will ultimately satisfy us? What do we ultimately want out of life? Ancient philosophy suggested that what everyone wanted was happiness — not meaning some sort of temporary contentment or momentary feeling of elation, but rather a state of complete and utter satisfaction of our true desires, called *eudaimonia.*[7] But you don't need to be a philosopher to recognize that this answer begs the further question: What is happiness? What truly satisfies our desires? If we are looking at the cause of human actions, we can't be satisfied just to look at the purposes of individual human actions, but rather we need to ask about the overall purpose for all our actions. This is the question of human fulfillment.

---

4. Aquinas, *Summa Theologiae* I-II.1.4: "Since if there were no last end, nothing would be desired, nor would any action have its term."

5. I have in mind primarily the work of Friedrich Nietzsche and Jean-Paul Sartre. However, this position that life ends in death is also found in ancient philosophers, such as Lucretius.

6. See the Dave Matthews Band song "Tripping Billies."

7. Aristotle, *Nichomachean Ethics,* trans. Martin Oswald (Indianapolis: Bobbs-Merrill, 1962), no. 1097b.

What Is Human Fulfillment?

So take a minute and ask yourself what you're really looking for in life. What do you really want, not just tomorrow, but for your life as a whole? What are your goals and dreams? What drives you? Most of us, I suspect, will conjure up a certain picture of adult life — a nice house, a nice family, a job we like that provides us with somewhat more money than we need, a set of friends with whom to go hunting or fishing or (insert your favorite hobby here), perhaps good health, perhaps the admiration of others for our work.[8] Some, motivated by different ideals, may have a different picture: motivated by Derek Jeter or Michael Jordan or President Bush or Martin Luther King or (God forbid!) Britney Spears, they may have a more single-minded dream, focused less on the ordinary picture above and more on sacrificing some of those goods in order to find superior achievement in some field or another.

But wait, this is another trick question, just like the one about what "causes" action. What unites the many answers that might be given above is that they are focused on achieving certain goals, accomplishing certain tasks. They are, to put it more technically, interested in achieving certain states of affairs, and they motivate actions that are like tools for achieving such states of affairs. The actions are the tools that build the building of life.

The problem here (and again, our scientific and technological age is particularly susceptible to this) is that humans are not machines. Or at least, we hope they are not. As John Paul II puts it, things are supposed to serve the development of persons, not the other way around.[9] Do we devote our lives to the perfect house or the perfect World Series ring? The key difference between acting persons and acting machines is that machines construct something outside themselves. Machines build a building. But for humans, the Christian tradition suggests, the building of your life is not your house or your car or your family. It's you. The purpose of human life,

---

8. Aquinas argues that the ultimate end must be single, though we may will other purposes as means to the final end. See *Summa Theologiae* I-II.1.5: "It is impossible for one man's will to be directed at the same time to diverse things, as last ends." On the failures that happen in our thought and action if we lack some conception of a last end or highest good, see Alasdair MacIntyre, "Plain Persons and Moral Philosophy: Rules, Virtues, and Goods," in *The MacIntyre Reader*, ed. Kelvin Knight (Notre Dame, Ind.: University of Notre Dame Press, 1998), pp. 136-52.

9. John Paul II, *Laborem Exercens* (Encyclical on Human Work, 1981), §12. This idea underpins all of John Paul II's social encyclicals.

what will fulfill you, is not simply achieving certain external goals, but rather it is the task of becoming yourself.[10]

This is very much a challenge to the way we are tempted to think about our lives and all aspects of them. We are tempted to look at actions (and things and, sadly, people) as *instruments* to achieve our desired purposes. We set up school systems, economic systems, and employment systems where the premium is put not on the development of the person but on the achievement of certain external goals (e.g., test scores, economic growth, profits for shareholders, etc.). The people working in such systems are supposed to subordinate themselves to the external goal of the system. This is just as true in our personal lives. We enter into friendship and romances and even marriages looking not for the good of the other person, but for what we get out of the relationship, whether it be with a girlfriend, a spouse, a church, or even God. In short, we *instrumentalize* others, and insofar as we do this to achieve wealth or fame or power, we enslave both ourselves and others in the service of things, inanimate dead things. We make these things (rather than persons) our ultimate end. We think if we achieve these external goals, then we will find happiness.

We have to be careful here: the external goals themselves are not necessarily a problem. As a friend of mine commented, Derek Jeter's World Series rings are a genuine sign of excellence, but if Jeter simply played *for the ring* and *not for the excellence of the game,* we would question his achievement. Again, we see here the importance of looking at the *purpose* of an action to determine its goodness or badness. We need to know whether Jeter just wants the ring and the money and the fame, or whether he really loves baseball. Are all our actions ultimately directed to the accumulation of possessions, of power, or of our own glory? Or are they directed to the development of people, both ourselves and others?

So perhaps we should restate the question as: What are your goals in life? A first crack might be: What sort of person do you want to become? Philosophers and theologians, for a long time, have suggested that there are many practical problems with investing your deepest desires in external things. They are often very much out of your control, for example, or subject to the whim of others.[11] You may get them and discover they are not all you thought they would be. But your character, your self, that is safe from

10. For a recent defense of human fulfillment in terms of becoming a certain sort of person, rather than in achieving external goods, see Jean Porter, *Nature as Reason: A Thomistic Theory of the Natural Law* (Grand Rapids: Eerdmans, 2005), pp. 141-203.

11. See Aristotle struggling with this problem in *Nichomachean Ethics* 1099a-1100b.

all these problems. If you are a person who knows yourself, you may not worry or care about these externals.

But how do we become a certain sort of person? How do we build our character? Simply by our acts. Human actions, unlike machine actions, are what philosophers called "reflexive" — they create effects not only in the external world, but also on the agent performing the action. Put simply, you become the person your actions determine. If you perform a lot of greedy actions, you will in fact find yourself a greedy person. Actions make persons. You are what you do.

So perhaps the question, What are you doing? which becomes the question, What are you striving for? can further become, Who do you want to be? Ethics is therefore a question first about identity (or character) and not about accomplishments. Our actions in the world do not simply make institutions or products or buildings. They make us. They are the way we shape our identity.[12]

Who Am I Called to Be? What Is My Identity?

So, who are you? Are you who you want to be? Here we're going to cross into some muddy waters. Perhaps, at least for some of you, the way you think about your identity is that there is some "true you" underneath all the trappings, like a little acorn or seed or magic grail at the center of your soul. No one can find it except you. And human fulfillment consists in finding it and always being true to it.[13] If you made a circle that represented you on the board, you might fill it in with a whole bunch of pieces: your activities, your friends, your religion, your political views. But "you" are not exactly any of these things. The "you" lies underneath. So in the center of your identity circle, you might simply put your name.

But what if you are (to invoke a favorite ethics example) a Nazi? Are you just being "true to yourself"? What if that deepest voice inside you tells you to go abuse children? If you think these examples are twisted, then you might want to rethink the whole idea that there is a "true you" buried deep

12. See Charles Taylor's description of someone struggling with whether to stay at a job that feels uninspiring or to run off for high adventure in Nepal, in "What Is Human Agency?" in his *Human Agency and Language: Philosophical Papers I* (Cambridge: Cambridge University Press, 1985), pp. 26-27.

13. This is the classic position of American transcendentalism, crystallized by Ralph Waldo Emerson in his essay "Self-Reliance." However, it is now as common as the air we breathe.

inside. Obviously, your identity is not simply or primarily constituted by static facts about yourself, such as appear on your driver's license. But it is not a matter of a static, permanent identity buried inside your soul, either. The ethicist Herbert McCabe writes that we should never speak about human beings. We are not human beings, as if being human was simply a matter of bodily existence, but rather we are human becomings.[14] This naturally follows from the earlier comments about action — you act with a purpose, and in this case the purpose is to become a certain sort of person. Presumably this implies you are not yet that person.

As with action and with ultimate purpose, so with identity. We have to dislodge one common picture to take a fresh look at the matter. But as we've dislodged these pictures, we haven't wanted to discard them entirely. Just because wanting to date someone is what causes your pursuit of that person, doesn't mean there aren't hormones involved, too. And just because our actions primarily shape our character and identity, doesn't mean they don't also lead to houses or World Series rings. So, too, just because our identity is not about finding some "essential me" underneath our everyday lives doesn't mean we give up soul-searching. But let's stick close to see how that might look different.

So we have this nagging sense that our everyday self is not the self we want it to be. We have a restlessness about ourselves. How do we go about gaining that identity? A popular form of changing your identity, well displayed on certain reality shows, is by creating a "new you," getting a makeover. Our culture is constantly suggesting to us that if we buy certain products or gain certain external goods, we will actually feel better about ourselves. That's why, for example, a recent ad campaign for Diet Coke featured flashy commercials where attractive people were whizzing around and engaged in various happy activities, holding cans of Diet Coke that magically gave off sparkles as they moved around. The tag of the commercial was simply: "Sparkle." Now if you were walking around campus and saw someone with sparks shooting out of her Diet Coke can, you'd probably think it was on fire. The commercial is not selling sparkling cans; it's selling a feeling and an identity, a feeling and an identity ("sparkling") you get when you're drinking Diet Coke. Now in some sense this must be true, or else it wouldn't work. We do feel better about ourselves with a new car or a new outfit . . . or even when drinking Diet Coke (though "sparkling" probably makes a safer tag than the more accurate "legal stimulant"). But are we

---

14. Herbert McCabe, O.P., "Teaching Morals," in *God Still Matters* (New York: Continuum, 2002), p. 189.

really different? Are we really about the products we buy and have? Do clothes really make the man?

Despite all these messages, we also have a sense that such identity change is only skin-deep. Who you are is deeper than that, but not in the sense that there's some innate and hidden spark in your soul. Rather, in the sense of possessing character or, as we might put it today, having a certain sort of personality makeup. The way Aristotle and Aquinas talked about personality or character was in terms of having virtues.[15] They didn't think having a certain amount of money should define your identity, or having a certain job, or wearing certain clothes, or even cultivating certain tastes. When they asked about who you wanted to become, they were interested in the virtues you had. Later on in the book, other authors will spend a great deal more time expanding on the notion of virtue. Here we can simply think of it by comparing self-descriptions: instead of answering the question "Who are you?" by saying "I am a banker" or "I am wealthy" or "I am a fan of country music," you would answer "I am courageous" or "I am cowardly" or "I am perceptive" or "I am lustful" or "I am friendly" or "I am deceitful." In other words, you would answer by identifying certain lasting dispositions toward action that you have. And, as anyone will tell you, if you are cowardly and want to be courageous, it's not going to happen by being hit by a lightning bolt. It's going to happen when you start doing courageous things instead of cowardly things. ·

Now, raising the importance of the virtues is going to leave a lot of questions unanswered. For example, is being deceitful good or bad? What are desirable qualities for human beings? And these are important questions. But for now we need to relate virtue back to our overall question of human fulfillment. Does human fulfillment simply consist of possessing certain inward qualities called virtues? Is being virtuous enough?

But the virtues present certain problems, particularly for Christians. Aristotle didn't think very many people could achieve virtue, for example.[16] And virtuous people were also supposed to be self-sufficient, according to him. To us that might often look like arrogance or self-righteousness.[17] The

15. Aristotle, *Nichomachean Ethics* 1098a: "The good of man is an activity of the soul in conformity with excellence or virtue, and if there are several virtues, in conformity with the best and most complete." Also Aquinas, *Summa Theologiae* I-II.56.3: "Virtue is a habit by which we work well."

16. Aristotle, *Nichomachean Ethics* 1095b.

17. Biblically, those enchanted with their own virtue are called self-righteous and severely chastised by Jesus. See, for example, the debate with the Pharisees in the story of the man born blind in John 9.

picture we have drawn of human action so far has left out one crucial component: human life and human action are *not solo performances, but group performances.* They are like baseball or basketball, rather than like running or
golf. So far, the picture of life we've drawn has been of the solitary actor. But
there are no solitary actors, and really, even if there were, who would want
to be them or offer them as ideals of human fulfillment? Virtuous . . . and
alone. Is that happy and fulfilled? I think not.

The virtues are skills or dispositions that are important because we
are called to life with others.[18] The good baseball player cannot simply develop "his own skills," but has to develop skills that allow him to coordinate
with others. Ask a baseball player who he is, and he might say "I am a shortstop" or "I am a Minnesota Twin." In either case, identity is defined by being part of certain relationships. "Shortstop" is an identity defined by its relationship to other fielders, for example.

Thus the question of identity is really a question of the relationships
in which we participate. When we say "I am a sister" or "I am a mother" or "I
am so-and-so's best friend" or "I am so-and-so's husband," we are perhaps
finally getting to the bottom of the question about human fulfillment. We
are seeking to become a certain sort of person, but our personhood comes
to us in our relations with others.

Who Loves Me and Whom Do I Love?

Hence, action depends on identity, and identity depends on participation in
relationships. It is in relationships of giving and receiving with others that
we find ourselves, that we become who we are called to be, and that we learn
how to act well. This is a complex way of stating the simple truth that the
meaning of human life is to love.[19] For Aquinas and many other writers in
the tradition, the purpose of life is to be in love with God, to share in the life
of communion that is God.[20] When we say that God is love, we mean that
God has chosen to invite us to participate in his own life of love by coming
to us in the flesh, in Jesus, so that we might have communion with him.

18. This underlies the emphasis on the role of practices in the understanding of virtue presented by Alasdair MacIntyre, *After Virtue,* 2nd ed. (Notre Dame, Ind.: University of
Notre Dame Press, 1984).

19. Aquinas, *Summa Theologiae* II-II.23.7-8. Note that Aquinas explicitly identifies this
love as friendship (II-II.23.1).

20. Aquinas, *Summa Theologiae* I-II.3.8. Compare the famous quotation from Augustine's *Confessions:* "Our hearts are restless until they rest in Thee."

But, as Jesus himself says in giving us the greatest commandment, the love of God and the love of others are inseparable parts of the same whole.[21] As we have seen in prior chapters describing Jesus' mission, the biblical narrative, and the church, we come to participate in God's life through Jesus in the Holy Spirit by being drawn into the community called the church. This is the concrete form of Jesus' command to love God and love neighbor. To be drawn into participating in the love of God is to be drawn into a life where we love and are loved by others, the life of the community called the church.

But what is love? In the English language, few words are as complicated to understand as "love." When we think of "being in love" with someone, we almost automatically think of romantic love, and while this is part of what it means to love, it is not the whole. We could easily use terms like "affection" and "friendship" to mean what we mean here by love. To be in a relationship of love is to offer oneself as a gift for the good of the other, to lay down one's life for a friend. Love is designed to be mutual, so that the gift offered is also a gift received. A community of love is a community characterized by sharing, by a sense that we are *interdependent*, that we need to help each other toward our common fulfillment, so that my fulfillment and your fulfillment are tied together. Love is a sharing of gifts, a sharing of lives, allowing the lives to intertwine with one another, and that can happen in many different ways.

It can also *not* happen in many different ways. Are all human relationships of this sort, nourishing us and allowing us to reach out of ourselves to another with generosity and help? Hardly. Quite to the contrary, Christianity teaches. The challenge of thinking about human action as a Christian is the recognition of the brokenness of the world, and specifically the brokenness of relationships among humans and of humans with God.

This is the challenge that sin presents to the foregoing description of human happiness. Rather than a world in which human relationships involve harmonious and mutual sharing between persons and with God, we live in a world where we have systematically distorted these relationships, so that they are ones of competition, domination, and self-seeking. In our own culture, a high premium is placed on independence, on making your own choices. Obviously, in terms of the model of human fulfillment being developed here, this is a poor way of finding fulfillment. Nevertheless, we are also aware that such an independence is a bulwark against forces that wish

---

21. *Gaudium et Spes* (Vatican II, *Pastoral Constitution on the Church in the Modern World*, 1965), §24: "The love of God cannot be separated from love of neighbor."

to use us for their own ends, against being manipulated and destroyed by others who want to hurt us. Hence, human relationships, wherein we find our fulfillment, can also become sources of our destruction.

The spiritual writer Henri Nouwen describes the point to which we can be driven when we allow the expectations and definitions of others to determine our actions and our very identity.[22] Nouwen describes the construction of a false self, a managed self that exists precisely to meet others' needs and expectations, which we manipulate to place us in the best possible light with others. Our actions are driven by the needs of others in bad ways. As we grow in this false self, we expect the same from others, we act toward them in manipulative ways, we even use our false self to gain goods from them. Nouwen suggests that the antidote to all this is found in the writings of the Desert Fathers and Mothers, a group of early Christians who fled cities for the desert in search of God and of themselves, away from society's distortion. We might find this extreme, but many other writers on the early church see the same impulse in the formation of early Christian communities, their departure from their families (a key source of distortion), and their commitment to mutual sharing and to celibacy.[23] Jesus himself, in the Gospels, is constantly beckoning people he meets away from themselves, from their families, their jobs, and their identities that are constructed not to help others, but to put them down and diminish them.

This pattern can be summed up in Jesus' pithy saying: "Those who want to save their life will lose it, and those who lose their life for my sake, and for the sake of the gospel, will save it" (Mark 8:35; Matt. 10:39; Luke 9:24; John 12:25). This saying, if we think about it, will throw all our thoughts about human fulfillment into confusion. Doesn't fulfillment consist in finding yourself? In finding happiness? Jesus doesn't deny that, but he suggests that we have to allow our selves to die, to be lost, if we are truly to go about the task of finding ourselves. He is not here talking about the fires of hell, but rather about the necessity of dying to self, of letting go and leaving behind all the distorted relationships we cling to, that give us false meaning, that form our false self. Unless we die to the distorted relationships, we can't find the true relationships of love. All this is to say that the path to human fulfillment is not a straight line, but rather a path that passes

22. The following digest of Henri Nouwen's thought is principally drawn from *The Way of the Heart* (New York: Seabury Press, 1981) and *Lifesigns* (New York: Image/Doubleday, 1986).

23. See especially Peter Brown, *The Body and Society* (Berkeley: University of California Press, 1984).

through conversion, through various ways of dying to our false self in order to rise into the true self given to us by following Jesus.

We see this in the story of the rich young man who comes to Jesus seeking an answer to the question of ultimate fulfillment. The rich young man has done all the right things, but (interestingly) we don't even learn his name. All we know about his identity is that he's rich. So what does Jesus go and do? He asks him to give away all his riches, the very thing that constitutes his identity. And do what? Simply follow Jesus. Thus, in place of all the false selves we construct, Jesus offers himself as the center of our identity, as the true relationship of love and fulfillment. The rich young man walks away sad, the story tells us, and perhaps we often do too (Matt. 19:16-30).[24]

Thus, one of the most unique and challenging dynamics of Christian teaching on what fulfills us as humans is *the necessity of conversion and renunciation*. We do not start as normal, healthy, neutral human persons, but rather we begin life saddled by distorted relationships, both personal and societal, that (before we know it) begin to distort our sense of self. For Christians the ultimate distortion of our relationships is our alienation from God, not because God is angry with us, but because we as humans have wanted to reject God's love in favor of our own autonomy. We have imaged God as a rival, as a competitor, as a threat to us — or even worse, as a god who takes the side of our identity in order to diminish and destroy others. Because this is the sorry situation in which we live life, all of us (to a greater or lesser extent) grow up with distorted images of what will fulfill us, and so instead of a straightforward path to happiness, we must walk the way of the cross, the way of renunciation, to find our true fulfillment.

How Do We Lose Ourselves to Find Ourselves?

The way of renunciation is both an inward journey and an outward journey. The inward journey begins when we start to recognize the confusion, fear, and insecurity about who we are. We often seek to cover over this confusion by projecting various images of self-assurance, or simply by immersing ourselves in the distractions of many activities and pursuits. These movements seek to deny the hollowness and insecurity we may find if we give ourselves

24. Pope John Paul II uses the story of the rich young man as the set piece for his encyclical on moral theology, *Veritatis Splendor*. For the idea of Jesus as God offering himself as the center of our lives, see Robert Barron, *The Strangest Way: Walking the Christian Path* (Maryknoll, N.Y.: Orbis, 2002).

the space and silence of solitude.[25] When we are with ourselves, we come to see all our weaknesses and vulnerabilities, our true frailty, our need for others and for God. When we encounter ourselves as vulnerable creatures, we can let go of all the masks and disguises we project, let go of all the things we have created in our lives that appear to make us strong and likeable. That letting go is certainly a dying of self, but through the death we are finally able to receive the love of God (and hopefully of others) for the self we really are.

The outward journey of renunciation is similar. Perhaps our favorite way of reassuring ourselves about our identity is by identifying ways in which we are superior to others. Often enough, these judgments are more or less valid, though sometimes they can also be deceptive. But in either case, we have set ourselves above our brothers and sisters. We have purchased our identity by constructing a relationship in which we live by somehow denying the full dignity and personhood of others. And again, these judgments may *seem* entirely justified. Nevertheless, the gospel calls us to give them up, to engage in the practice of forgiveness in the hopes of restoring a relationship of love with the other. Similarly, we also can recognize ourselves as in need of the forgiveness of others and of God. Forgiveness is the process by which relationships that are distorted can be reconciled.

As we noted before, Christianity teaches a gospel of love, teaches that love is the meaning of life. However, the journeys of renunciation do not take on the cheery, joyous tenor of love. Especially initially, as we embark on the Christian journey, they look to us like loss and misery, like how giving away all his possessions looked to the rich young man; in short, they look like the cross. But it is only through the way of the cross, the dying of self, that we are received into full life. And we can take some consolation: when we fall truly in love, the giving away of our possessions becomes almost easy, as it was for the man who, finding a treasure in a field, goes away and sells all he has to buy the field (Matt. 13:44-46).

As with most Christian ideas, these ideas are played out or enacted for us in the sacraments. The mystery of our need for a death of self and a rising to new life through forgiveness is enacted in the drowning that happens at baptism. In the Eucharist we show how the broken body of Jesus becomes the source of life to feed the whole community, but only if it is broken and poured out. In the sacrament of reconciliation, when rightly understood, we enact the inner journey of revealing our vulnerable and weak selves and

---

25. Besides Henri Nouwen, see Thomas Merton, *Contemplative Prayer* (New York: Herder and Herder, 1969).

being received not with condemnation, but with words of forgiveness and reconciliation. In the sacraments we show forth the new world of loving relationships in the midst of the present world.[26]

The sacraments, therefore, are all *communal* embodiments of the conversion of life into which we are drawn when we live in the church. Our conversion, our movement from one set of relationships to another, is a social movement. It is a move, you might say, from identifying with one family to identifying with a new family. That new family is the church.[27] Now, of course, playing on this team in this league requires developing in virtue and sustaining life through the making and sharing of external goods. In other words, it involves the very external goals and virtues that are aims of our action. But these aims are transformed by being put in the service of the community, or, as Saint Paul puts it, the upbuilding of the body of Christ. Like any good team, not everyone aims at the same thing (Paul also recognized this). And so the concrete content of fulfillment for each Christian might be said to be his or her vocation, an idea we will discuss elsewhere. But vocation is not simply about you and your fulfillment. It's for the team, and for the ongoing good of the game that the team is playing. Ultimately, it's for the life of the whole world.

Summary

This chapter is aimed at understanding human fulfillment. I have suggested that human fulfillment ultimately is a matter of participation in relationships; it is sharing in the lives of others and of God. The object of the game of life is not to win or lose, but to sustain the game of love, to keep it going . . . by becoming a skilled player, a virtuous person, in building and sustaining relationships of love and mutuality. We do so in a marvelous variety of ways, playing many interlocking games in which we learn how to friend and be "friended," love and be loved, how we make a home together, not simply with those we like or those to whom we are related, but espe-

---

26. This conception of sacraments is indebted to Herbert McCabe, O.P., *The People of God: The Fullness of Life in the Church* (New York: Sheed and Ward, 1964); and Alexander Schmemann, *For the Life of the World: Sacraments and Orthodoxy* (Crestwood, N.Y.: St. Vladimir's Seminary Press, 1973).

27. The concept of the church as "new family" is explained extensively by Gerhard Lohfink, *Jesus and Community: The Social Dimension of Christian Faith*, trans. John P. Galvin (Philadelphia: Fortress, 1984), pp. 39-44. It is also employed summarily in the first encyclical of Pope Benedict XVI, *Deus Caritas Est*, paragraph 25.

cially with the stranger, the outcast, the sinner — who is often enough us. The promise of the resurrection is that even death, which always threatens our ability to keep the game going, by breaking down a group or by instilling fear in us, cannot stop the game. When we are baptized into Christ, we are baptized into the new life of God's own love and God's people. That life is the life of the Holy Spirit, which eternally builds us into one body in Christ so that we share more and more in each other's lives and in the communion that Jesus has eternally with the Father. That life never ends.

Further Questions You Might Have
That Relate to Human Fulfillment

Isn't the goal of the Christian life heaven? Why don't you talk about that in the chapter?

Properly speaking, according to the Gospels, the goal of the Christian life is to live in the kingdom of God. But God's kingdom (as we pray always in the Our Father) is breaking in on earth, it is being established right now: "Thy kingdom come, thy will be done *on earth* as it is in heaven." The marriage of heaven and earth, which is fully consummated only at the end, has already begun. And let us note that "heaven" is nothing more and nothing less than the communion with God and with others that we have been describing here.

But don't you get to heaven by following God's laws?

Remember the story about the rich young man? He followed all the commandments. The story says so. But he didn't follow Jesus, and so he went away sad, not fulfilled. (Nor does a simple confession of personal faith in Jesus suffice — rather, active following is required.) A later section of the book will discuss God's laws. But we must understand that any sort of law exists only to direct us to some sort of fulfillment. God's laws exist not to restrict or test us, but to provide wisdom for us on how to sustain and build human relationships. Their "reward" is simply that they instruct us on how to play the game of love. For example, if as a four-year-old you went with your mother to the grocery store and started acting up, Mom might say, "If you behave, I'll buy you a candy bar when we get to the checkout." That's sometimes what you have to do with four-year-olds: bribe them. However, if you go to the store tomorrow and start acting up, Mom might say, "Knock it off." If you say, "If I behave, will I get a candy bar at the checkout?" I hope your mother would give you a dirty look and refuse, or at the very least laugh and call your offer ridiculous. Heaven is not the "bribe" God offers us for obeying his rules. The laws exist to guide us to better human relationships, and hence to our fulfillment.

Does all this mean that I have to give up my desires to have a family and buy an SUV, or any sort of external goods?

Well, I don't know. What you have to ask yourself is what you are aiming at when you want those things. Having a family can make you a very self-centered person, spending much time insulating your family from exactly the sorts of strangers and outcasts that Jesus insisted we need to share life with. On the other hand, for many people the great challenge of truly loving a spouse and truly loving children is exactly the sort of activity that forces them to die to their false self and really find communion with others. Thus, in terms of particular career goals or family goals or any concrete state of affairs, the question is usually not a matter of yes or no, but a matter of how and why. As for the SUV, well. . . . The point is to recognize that all these external goods should be directed toward the fulfillment of persons. If you're wondering whether you should be a doctor, for instance, ask why you want to be a doctor.

Can someone who doesn't know God find fulfillment, or is that person out of luck?

This is a very hard question. Classically, it involves the question about whether human fulfillment comes in two varieties — the natural variety (which anyone and everyone can achieve here on earth) and the supernatural variety (which involves sharing in God's life in some way). The problem comes in trying to figure out how these two ends are related to each other. My description above, which attempts to be faithful to the overall story of Scripture, suggests that in some sense there are not two ends, but one. Herbert McCabe, perhaps a bit more precisely, suggests that we have a human end, which is the sharing of genuine human friendships with one another, and a divine end, which is the sharing in God's own friendship, to which God lifts us.[28] The church is the body in which we find and share in the restored human relationships *by* receiving a share in the divine friendship (a share we call "the Holy Spirit"). In this context, it is not clear that the two ends are really separable. Writers in the tradition of Augustine have been doubly skeptical of confusing the ends, since they tend to view our human loves as inevitably in competition with our love of God. I side with more modern authors, such as Germain Grisez and C. S. Lewis, who suggest that

28. See McCabe, "Teaching Morals," p. 191.

this sort of dualism is not faithful to the gospel.[29] Although loving others can get in the way of our ability to love God, this is not "the way it is," but rather the result of distorted loves. Genuine loves, genuine human goods, are good and are not in competition with God. Recall here the love commandment of Jesus: it does not say love God *or* love others, it says love God *and* love others. Genuine human love does not compete with the loving God. Grisez uses the formula that proclaims Jesus as "fully God and fully man" to show that there is no inherent incompatibility between human and divine goods.

However, I have avoided the precise question of whether someone who does not know God can find fulfillment if, as we have described, communion with God is our final end. According to *Gaudium et Spes,* one of the major documents of Vatican II, the pattern of Christ's life, death, and resurrection, into which Christians are drawn, is present for all: "All this holds true not only for Christians, but for all men of good will in whose hearts grace works in an unseen way. For since Christ died for all men, and since the ultimate vocation of man is in fact one, and divine, we ought to believe that the Holy Spirit in a manner known only to God offers to every man the possibility of being associated with this paschal mystery."[30] There is no way of construing an ultimate purpose for human life that somehow excludes communion with God, and (except for those who explicitly and systematically reject God) the Council suggests that this communion with God and neighbor is available to those who are not Christian.

Don't all people define what they want and what will fulfill them in different ways? Who are we to say what fulfills someone else?
Well, in some sense, yes, people are fulfilled in different ways, and that is a good thing for all of us. Not everyone is attracted to the same sort of significant other, for instance. Some people devote their time to reading lots of books, some people devote their time to fixing lots of cars, and it is clear we need both sorts of people. Some people love baseball, while others love football. I do not fully understand the latter group, but I can accept that baseball is not going to be for everyone. This points us toward the idea of vocation, and the fact that we are pursuing fulfillment as a community, not alone.

---

29. Germain Grisez, *The Way of the Lord Jesus,* vol. 1, *Christian Moral Principles* (Quincy, Ill.: Franciscan Herald Press, 1983), pp. 16, 807-10; C. S. Lewis, *The Four Loves* (New York: Harcourt Brace, 1960), pp. 119-21.
30. *Gaudium et Spes,* §22.

However, the fact that no one is fulfilled alone means that certain ways of fulfilling yourself that rest on the destruction or diminishment of others may be ruled out. Everyone needs to be in relationship with others, even to do the things listed above. And because we need to be in relationship with others (and with God, who loves all that he has created), no one can truly be fulfilled by doing things that attack another person's ability to be fulfilled, to become human, as described above. Thus, as I insist to my classes, Hitler's definition of what fulfills him is not as good as Mother Teresa's. I may not be able to challenge your allegiance to football, but I will challenge your allegiance to killing other people.

Hence, while there are many paths to human fulfillment, they all tread along the same pattern developed above. Examples that *contradict* that pattern, however, cannot be included. So while it is correct to say that different people find fulfillment in different ways of life, the possibilities are bounded by ways of life that cannot fit the end of loving God and neighbor. These boundaries are articulated most clearly in the articulation of the Law, to which we turn in the next chapter.

Concurrent Readings

Barron, Robert. *The Strangest Way: Walking the Christian Path.* Maryknoll, N.Y.: Orbis, 2002. Barron extends and thickens the spiritual development outlined in writers like Henri Nouwen (see below), embedding it within a conception of practices and tradition (see Alasdair MacIntyre below). Numerous students have told me this is the book that brings it all together for them, for Barron's three "paths" of the Christian life address the questions of identity, of the paschal mystery, and of vocation with a unique combination of the intellectual, the personal, and the practical.

Guignon, Charles, ed. *The Good Life.* Indianapolis: Hackett, 1999. Guignon offers the best available anthology of different and competing accounts of human fulfillment. While some academics may quibble with the omission of some classic readings, the anthology is effective in giving students a sense of how these questions have been negotiated at different times. The mix is excellent — excerpts from Emerson, Russell, and Sartre capture the sense of today's plain person far better than any postmodern; the inclusion of a couple texts from Asian traditions is illuminating in exposing certain persistent biases (e.g., toward "achievement") in the "Western" traditions; the inclusion of four classic "religious" texts (including William James and Dostoevsky) is unusual in these sorts of anthologies; and the MacIntyre excerpt (from *After Virtue*) is extremely helpful.

MacIntyre, Alasdair. "Plain Persons and Moral Philosophy: Rules, Virtues, and Goods." In *The MacIntyre Reader*, edited by Kelvin Knight, pp. 136-52. Notre Dame, Ind.: University of Notre Dame Press, 1998. Although quite dense, this is a very accessible overview of MacIntyre's account of the aspects of moral development. In particular, MacIntyre argues for why "we are all proto-Aristotelians," indicating why the search for fulfillment will take on the shape assumed in this chapter (and by this text as a whole). He also explains fully why, in the absence of a highest good, our attempts at practical reason will fail.

Nouwen, Henri J. M. *Lifesigns: Intimacy, Fecundity, and Ecstasy in Christian Perspective*. New York: Image/Doubleday, 1986. Any number of Nouwen's books might work here, but this text works the inner journey from fear to love most effectively, particularly because it simultaneously pushes outward toward community and service.

Vanier, Jean. *Happiness: A Guide to a Good Life*. Translated by Kathryn Spink. New York: Arcade Publishing, 2001. The best introduction to the basic Aristotelian shape of the moral life, with the added bonus of Vanier's extraordinary background combining a doctorate in philosophy and the founding and sustaining of L'Arche, an ever-expanding group of homes that build shared Christian community between the mentally handicapped and able-bodied assistants. Vanier treats the dynamics of desire, friendship, virtue, and the gradual unfolding of the good life.

Chapter 7

Natural Law, Law, and Freedom

DANA DILLON AND DAVID MCCARTHY

Abigail McCarthy, in her eleven short years, has had a lengthy relationship to the piano. It began at age six with curiosity, went through a few years when practicing was punishment, and is now reaching a point where there are flashes of grace. She and the piano are becoming friends. The analogy of playing the piano will be used later in the chapter when we discuss the connection between freedom and law. Musical performance offers an interesting example of the interplay of an established order and freedom, natural capacities and discipline, and rote learning and creativity. One must develop basic skills of play before one can even know the extent of one's natural abilities. One needs to conform to an established form and discipline in order for one's individuality and creativity to emerge. It is the same in the moral life. As David Cloutier has pointed out in the previous chapter, the question of human fulfillment is a question of identity, "Who am I?" Cloutier explains that our fulfillment with God and in this life depends upon "becoming a certain sort of person" through the grace of God and our actions.

In this chapter we will discuss the questions of identity and fulfillment at a basic level: Who are we as human beings? What is human nature? What are human beings for? These questions about the order and purpose of human life — about the "law" of our nature — have a long history in the Catholic faith, and they have been one way that our theological perspective has joined in conversation with other peoples and faiths and with philosophers and scientists, ancient and modern. The chapter begins with an exploration of natural law as the human impulse to ask questions about the order and purpose of the world. We proceed with an extended discussion of the terms "nature" and "law" as they apply to human beings. Then we turn to the relationships between law and freedom, and freedom and our moral conscience. The next chapter, "Freedom and Grace," will take up these questions of human nature and human freedom in relationship to God's action, as sovereign, creator, and redeemer of the world.

Why Natural Law

The impulse to the sort of thinking that we call "natural law" is generally spawned by the confluence of three basic convictions about the world. First, the world has a certain kind of order to it. Each thing in the world has a nature, a role, a place, and a purpose. Second, human beings can recognize the ordering of the world. We have use of reason and can perceive and name the right relationships between the things of the world. Third, the order of the world is a good thing and should be maintained. Each thing in the world should more or less function in accord with its nature, role, place, and purpose. Notably, human beings are among these things. In other words, human nature matters when it comes to thinking through human conduct. In this broad sense, one can be a "natural law thinker" without being a Christian, or without being even a theist of any sort. Consider Plato's emphasis in the *Republic* on justice as the right ordering both of the human person and of the human community. For a more recent example, consider Charles Darwin. Long after he had given up the faith of his youth, he remained deeply convinced of a very precise order and process by which nature works. Natural law, at its most basic level, is the impulse to give an account of the world and our place within it, and the belief that such an account will indicate the sorts of actions that might or might not lead to our flourishing.

For Christians (and for the Jews whose scriptures we have inherited), the natural order of things is far from accidental. Rather, this order results from God's creation of the world, down to its most intricate detail. This picture of creation runs throughout the whole of the Old Testament. Genesis describes God's creative work: in the beginning God creates heaven and earth, the sea and sky, all the plants and animals, and finally human beings, and God pronounces all of his handiwork good. The psalmist celebrates the creative power of God:

> He spoke, and it came to be;
> he commanded, and it stood firm.
>
> (Ps. 33:9)

In the book of Job God reminds Job that he not only sets the foundation of the earth and the limits of the sea, but also commands everything from dawn to death and oversees such details as the birthing of mountain goats and the flight of the eagle (Job 38–39). The Hebrew scriptures thus describe the world as ordered and ordained by God. Nature is not simply nature, but creation. The order of things is the work of God, and it is good.

Christian scriptures reaffirm and deepen this sense of creation as God's design and plan. The beginning of John's Gospel affirms the same Word of God who becomes flesh in Christ Jesus: "All things came into being through him, and without him not one thing came into being" (John 1:3). The God who creates all that is, is the same God who becomes flesh in Jesus. The God that Jesus reveals in his life, death, and resurrection is the same God who made the universe. The God that Jesus reveals is the same God whose providence guides the universe. Christians see continuity between God's saving action in Christ, God's saving action in the history of Israel, and God's action in the world more generally. This observation has shaped the Christian conviction that creation itself can reveal something about God. Perhaps the earliest expression of this is found in Paul's letter to the Romans: "Ever since the creation of the world [God's] eternal power and divine nature, invisible though they are, have been understood and seen through the things he has made" (Rom. 1:20). Christians affirm in their creed a God who is "creator of heaven and earth, of all things seen and unseen." All that exists owes its existence to God. Because of this, Christians believe that the order of creation is in keeping with God's design, and can even reveal much about God, particularly when considered in the light of Christ.

So, as we consider creation, we see that all things are subject to the laws or principles with which God designed them. In the words of Augustine, "Nothing evades the laws of the most high Creator and Governor, for by Him the peace of the universe is administered."[1] God sets every creature on its course, giving each a nature and a purpose and certain inward principles that move it to its goal. The human person is no exception. Humans are naturally inclined to preserve their own lives, to procreate, to seek the truth about God, and to live in society.[2] As rational creatures, however, human beings actually participate in God's governance of the world in a second way as well. Using the faculty of reason, human beings are able to know

---

1. Augustine, *City of God* 19.12, quoted in Thomas Aquinas, *Summa Theologiae*, trans. Fathers of the English Dominican Province (Allen, Tex.: Christian Classics, 1981), I-II.93.6.

2. Aquinas, *Summa Theologiae* I-II.94.2.

and to recognize the order of creation as springing from God, and therefore participate in God's eternal law through this knowledge.

Thus, all of creation — each creature, each action, each movement — is subject to the eternal law. Nonrational creatures participate through their natural instincts. They are thoroughly ordered to their natural ends by God's design. This appeal to divine order does not require Christians to reject modern science. On the contrary, attention to science can help us avoid simplistic accounts of God's relationship to creation (views that picture God as a watchmaker or a huge person moving pieces around on a game board). However, Christians must question scientific proposals that attempt to reduce the meaning of creation and the role of human beings to merely natural mechanisms. "Natural," in Christian theological thought, always means "designed by God." Human beings, as rational creatures, participate in the eternal law not only through their natural inclinations but also through their knowledge and understanding of God's order and our God-given purpose. Though the movement of all things according to God's design is an imperative component of natural law, it is the participation of rational creatures in the knowledge of God's eternal law and governance that constitutes natural law proper.

Law, for Thomas Aquinas (d. 1274), is "an ordinance of reason for the common good, made by one who has care of the community, and promulgated."[3] If the natural law is "law" in this sense, then it is promulgated by God into the minds and hearts of all humankind. Herbert McCabe, in *Law, Love, and Language,* points out that attention to natural law, as law of human nature, demands attention to the ways in which humankind is a community. "To be subject to law is to be a member of a community; law is, if you like, the bearing of the community as such on its individual members."[4] We human beings are a biological unity in that we are linked genetically to one another, and we are a linguistic unity in that we are at least theoretically able to communicate with one another through "conventional signs."[5]

Insofar as law is the "bearing of the community" upon the individual members, this bond or bearing generally takes the form of the type of community that it is. Therefore, a species of wolves will have a different bearing on "wolf-ness" than humanity on being a human being. McCabe draws from the work of ethnologist Konrad Lorenz to show that in a biological community such as that of wolves, this "bearing" takes place biologically.

---

3. Aquinas, *Summa Theologiae* I-II.90.4.

4. Herbert McCabe, O.P., *Law, Love, and Language* (New York: Continuum, 2003), p. 36.

5. McCabe, *Law, Love, and Language,* p. 37.

For instance, when one wolf clashes with another wolf, it has an inescapable biological instinct to fight to the death, but to refrain from killing when its opponent ritually surrenders its unprotected neck.[6] McCabe observes that "when [an animal's] behaviour is influenced by its membership of the species, it is not suffering violence from outside. . . . When it acts in accordance with the inhibition, let us say, it is not submitting to some exterior force, but to a depth within itself."[7] Deep down, the wolf does not wish to kill, and its biology carries this "want" for him.

McCabe connects this observation about biology to human beings, not reducing human behavior to instinct, but pointing out that our human membership bears on us from within rather than without. "When a man obeys the law of his 'species,' the natural law, he is being true to a depth within himself, and . . . to act contrary to this law is to violate himself at his centre."[8] Natural law seeks to identify the depths of what it means to be human, in order to offer insight and guidance for human action in accord with who we are at our deepest. Inquiry into the natural law seeks to understand the basics of human fulfillment. We are not a merely biological species (like the gray wolf), but are a self-conscious, linguistic, historical, and self-directed community. Therefore, there is no aspect of human life that is merely biological. Our biology is always already linguistic, already rationally understood. Although our biological reality is always operative, it is always operative as understood within the language, practices, and consciousness of the communities in which we live. For this reason, though natural law cannot be understood without a sense of natural inclinations and instincts, these are not its central feature. The heart of natural law is virtue, our acquisition of habits that give form to our inclinations toward what is good and good for us.

McCabe explains that "the demands made upon a man by his membership of his 'natural community,' the human race, represent his own deepest desires." He proposes that we each have a "double set of desires, the shallow and the profound, the personal, superficial, temporary desires, and the inner, impersonal, great desires."[9] On this view the work of the moral life becomes sorting through one's desires to ascertain which are deep and great enough to merit following and which are merely shallow and superficial. But we cannot be told merely what these deeper desires are; we have to

6. McCabe, *Law, Love, and Language,* p. 40.
7. McCabe, *Law, Love, and Language,* pp. 44-45.
8. McCabe, *Law, Love, and Language,* p. 45.
9. McCabe, *Law, Love, and Language,* pp. 60-61.

learn to recognize them through thorough investigation.[10] Inquiry into natural law (i.e., into our human nature) is based upon the conviction that what each of us desires is neither self-evident nor the mere preference of individuals. Only through investigation of what it means to be human can each of us come to a genuine sense of our desires and of how our actions succeed or fail in moving us toward them. This investigation is necessarily a shared endeavor, a conversation shared over time with Christians and non-Christians, encompassing voices from many different times and cultures. The tradition of natural law is this investigation.

Natural Law and Human Fulfillment

The Catholic tradition of natural law presupposes that we human beings are inclined by nature to the good that fulfills us. This section offers a brief sketch of natural law that is derived from two sources, a chapter entitled "Natural Law and Freedom" by Servais Pinckaers, O.P.,[11] and Pope John XXIII's *Peace on Earth*.[12] Pinckaers develops his outline of natural inclinations from article I-II.94.2 of the *Summa Theologiae*, and his purpose is to present five inclinations that "flow from the essential components of our nature and are linked to the general notions that the philosophers call the 'transcendentals' or the 'universal attributes.'"[13] In *Peace on Earth* Pope John appeals to the natural law in a section on the order that exists between human beings. He outlines rights and obligations that are attributable to men and women by their nature. The content of these rights and obligations develops within the Catholic tradition's understanding of the physical, spiritual, and social goods that fulfill human beings. Pinckaers and John XXIII provide us with two modern yet classic texts that appeal to natural law to show the connection between human nature and human flourishing.

The first natural inclination outlined by Pinckaers is "the inclination for the good . . . the spontaneous attraction and taste for the good, as well as a repulsion from evil, or more precisely, an attraction and repulsion according to our perception of how things are, according to our reason and

10. McCabe, *Law, Love, and Language*, p. 66.

11. Servais Pinckaers, O.P., *Morality: The Catholic View*, trans. Michael Sherwin, O.P. (South Bend, Ind.: St. Augustine's Press, 2003), pp. 96-111.

12. John XXIII, *Pacem in Terris: Peace on Earth*, in *Catholic Social Thought: The Documentary Heritage*, ed. David J. O'Brien and Thomas A. Shannon (Maryknoll, N.Y.: Orbis, 1992), pp. 129-62.

13. Pinckaers, *Morality*, p. 98.

our conscience."[14] Because we are inclined to the good, our reasoned judgments about our common goods as human beings lead us to an ordering of our lives together that both reflects and expresses the natural law. It is within this framework that John XXIII presents an order of rights and duties in human community. The order of human life "is by nature moral" (§37) and has its ultimate source "in the one true God" (§38). Pope John specifies our inclination to the good in "the right to freedom in searching for truth" (§12); in the pursuit of truth in cultural advancements, art, science, and education (§13); in our relationship to God (§14); and in our responsibilities of justice to others (§30). In short, our inclination to the good gives form to the kind of social, institutional, cultural, and personal life that fulfills us as human beings.

The second natural inclination that Pinckaers attends to is "the inclination to preserve being." It includes not only the natural desire to live, but also "the love of health" and well-being. As is the case with each of these natural inclinations, precepts of the natural law flow from it. The desire to preserve our life, health, and well-being "establishes our right to legitimate self-defense," and also "pushes us toward what fosters our thriving" in physical and spiritual ways.[15] Likewise, John XXIII begins with basic physical goods and moves to social and spiritual fulfillment. Human beings have a "right to life, to bodily integrity, and the means which are suitable for the proper development of life; these are primarily food, clothing, shelter, rest, medical care, and finally the necessary social services" (§11). In the Catholic tradition these rights include the opportunity for good work, freedom from harsh conditions of labor, and the goods of family and private property. Fitting with our desire for what is good, our inclination to preserve life is "dynamic."[16] It includes our desire for fulfillment in education, culture, and participation in social institutions.

Pinckaers's third topic is "the inclination to marry." By placing the procreative drive within the social institution of marriage, Pinckaers highlights a point made by McCabe in the previous section. As human beings, our sexual inclinations and desire to procreate are not merely biological instincts, but are also social instincts, and interpersonally meaningful by their nature. Through our intelligence and freedom, our sexuality is directed to interpersonal and social fulfillment. Sexuality "engages the entire personality," and marriage is the form of life where the goods of sexuality can be ex-

14. Pinckaers, *Morality,* p. 99.
15. Pinckaers, *Morality,* p. 102.
16. Pinckaers, *Morality,* p. 102.

pressed without contradiction.[17] "First there is generation — the gift of life and the education of children, who ensure the growth and continuance of the human species and its cultural heritage. Second, there is the love and mutual support of the couple."[18] In short, our sexual inclination is fulfilled in family. When dealing with social questions, John XXIII, in *Peace on Earth,* adds that "most careful provision must be made for the family both in economic and social matters as well as in those which are of a cultural and moral nature, all of which look to the strengthening of family and helping it carry out its function" (§16).

Fourth in Pinckaers's outline is the inclination to know the truth, which is proper to our natural unity of body and spirit. As noted above, our fulfillment in pursuit of the truth is implied in our inclination to the good. "There is *science,* understood as the capacity to study and direct one's actions, and also *wisdom,* which draws together knowledge and experience into a unified view of life and action. More specifically there is *prudence,* which discerns the good of an individual act."[19] The pursuit of truth, particularly in moral judgments, is not a mechanical or disinterested application of norms, but the development, within us, of our relationship to God and creation. For this reason John XXIII indicates that our duties of justice, basic human rights, and our freedoms for intellectual development and religious expression are conditioned by the goods that we human beings share. "Inasmuch as God is the first truth and the highest good, he alone is that deepest source from which human society can draw its vitality" (§38).

The final inclination in Pinckaers's sketch summarizes what has been implied in the first four inclinations: "society is natural to the human person."[20] According to a common individualist perspective, personal rights have a natural antagonism with our responsibilities to others. In the individualist frame, freedom is opposed to the constraints of social life, and the goals of personal fulfillment are opposed to moral duty. For example, it is often said that one has a responsibility to release oneself from burdensome promises, because one has the responsibility to take care of oneself first. In the natural law frame, however, this antagonism between the individual and social obligations is understood to be a mistake. We are fulfilled in relationship to others, in friendship, justice, and love; therefore, our desires for ful-

---

17. Sexual activity is not a natural mandate, but if one does seek the fulfillment of sexual desire in sexual activity, marriage is the way of fulfillment. In other words, the celibate life accords with our natures as well.

18. Pinckaers, *Morality,* pp. 103-4.

19. Pinckaers, *Morality,* p. 105.

20. Pinckaers, *Morality,* p. 108.

fillment as individuals are well ordered when we seek to attain the "excellences" required of family, friendship, citizenship, and religion. With this reference to "excellences," we are foreshadowing a discussion later in the chapter on law and freedom. We human beings are created to know and to seek freely what is our common good. Natural law is distinctively human, and its application cannot bypass our capacities to see the world rightly and act toward our good end.

The Law of Reason

The inclinations outlined above do not come out of nowhere; they provide a good encapsulation of the kinds of issues to which natural law thinking applies. Examining human life through the lens of natural law has a long history, through which theologians, at various times, have engaged diverse sources and streams of thought of their own day (from Aristotle to evolutionary science). From the outside the history of natural law reasoning — as a history and tradition of thought — might look haphazard and "all too human" in contrast to mathematics or the natural sciences. Indeed, from a modern, rationalist point of view, a theological conception of human nature is not adequately reasonable. In this section we challenge this rationalist view and deal with the very issue of what makes something "reasonable," as well as with common notions of "nature" and "law." Our task is to give account of natural law as a rational, coherent picture of human reasoning within a theological conception of human life. First we outline a theological framework of natural law, and then we connect this framework of reasoning with the law that is both in us by nature and directed to our fulfillment as human beings.

Nature as God's Creation

For several centuries the reference point for discussions of natural law has been the thirteenth century. More specifically, anyone setting out to deal with natural law needs to attend to Thomas Aquinas's analysis and explanation of law in his *Summa Theologiae*. Aquinas's treatise on law is a small section of his *Summa*, but it is considered the focal point of a golden — Scholastic — age of natural law theory. Scholasticism refers not only to a period in history but also to a method of study that was dominant from the beginning of the eleventh century to the close of the fifteenth. This method raises disputed questions, notes the standpoints of various authorities on the topic, argues for and against the opposing views of these authorities, and arrives at a synthesis of the views. In short, natural law is developed through the study of a set of common texts and authoritative authors — common among the Scholastics yet diverse in origin — from Aristotle to Cicero and Roman law, to Augustine and the Bible.[21]

While modern scholars tend to see a great divide between philosophical reasoning and Scripture (revelation), the Scholastics do not. For example, Saint Paul's assertion in Romans 2:14-15 is important: the Gentiles, who do not have the laws of Moses revealed to them, can "do instinctively what the law requires" and, in doing so, "show that what the law requires is written on their hearts." Paul's statement, however, does not offer a foundation upon which to construct the norms of natural law — given that Paul's purpose is to indicate that the Gentiles are responsible for their failure to follow and to recognize this law (rather than a positive declaration that this internal law is in good working order). Nevertheless, Paul's pronouncement does highlight the idea developed later by Augustine and others that creation and Scripture have the same source and end. "All authentic orders of existence, together with the order of the universe taken as a whole, are grounded in the eternal law of God, which can be seen from one perspective as the creative and providential wisdom of God, and from another perspective as God's will for the existence and preservation of the created order."[22]

Natural law is not a written legal code; it is not a distinct body of laws that can be bound and carried from place to place and read out for all to hear. Rather, it is considered a standard and basis of just laws; the natural law is the root of human law. It is not known apart from customs and codes of particular peoples; we do not have direct access to it as "law," but only through the commands of God in the Bible and the laws of human communities (called "positive" law). Natural law is instantiated in human life (and law) in such a way that different peoples will express the same natural capacities and tendencies in somewhat different ways.[23] In this sense the natural law is a shared capacity, a general structure of human embodiment, and a common end to which various peoples are moving from and toward,

21. Michael Bertram Crowe, *The Changing Profile of the Natural Law* (The Hague: Martinus Nijhoff, 1977), p. 111.

22. Jean Porter, *Natural and Divine Law: Reclaiming the Traditions for Ethics* (Grand Rapids: Eerdmans, 1999), pp. 125-26.

23. In this sense Porter calls the natural law "underdetermined" in *Nature as Reason: A Thomistic Theory of Natural Law* (Grand Rapids: Eerdmans, 2005), p. 19.

and which we all, more or less and in different ways, instantiate in our laws and customs. Natural law is the higher law of human life.[24]

As a higher law, natural law will be genuinely biblical inasmuch as the Bible is the source of a higher law, the divine law (the law that God reveals). However, an authentically biblical approach to natural law is far more nuanced than today's "literalist" and "fundamentalist" approaches to Scripture. By considering the Bible more carefully than modern literalists, theologians (past and present) recognize that the Bible includes a variety of kinds of law and commands and a diversity of what we in modern times call religious and cultural practices. This diversity is not unified easily. To understand the unity, medieval theologians categorized the variety of principles and commands of Scripture according to their different purposes. For our concerns here, the main distinction is between moral and ceremonial laws, where, for instance, the commands in Leviticus pertaining to sacrificial offerings would not impinge upon the moral law. For the Scholastics the content of the moral law draws upon specific texts of the Bible, such as the Ten Commandments (Exod. 20:1-17) and the Golden Rule (Matt. 22:39-40).[25]

Natural law is a way of thinking that unifies diverse sources, such as Greek philosophers and modern scientists, through a conception of the God-given purposes of human life.[26] According to Gratian's *Decretum* (ca. 1140), both creation and revelation accord with God's ordering of human life, so that "whatever is contrary to the divine will or canonical Scriptures is also contrary to natural law."[27] This claim is possible because Scripture is not merely a set of commands but also the very framework of deliberation. Scripture is a living document rather than an inert depository of commands. As God's Word, spoken and revealed to God's people, Scripture is not simply read but lived, not simply words on a page but God's self-communication that forms the way Christians speak and think and live. Likewise, a theological understanding of natural law requires, not a static or lifeless conception of nature, but an account of creation alive with the presence of the trinitarian God who creates and sustains it. In other words, a natural law consideration of the creation accounts in Genesis 1–2 is not concerned with dating the beginning of human life or determining the geo-

---

24. Russell Hittinger, *The First Grace: Rediscovering the Natural Law in a Post-Christian World* (Wilmington, Del.: ISI Books, 2003), pp. 36-37.

25. Porter, *Natural and Divine Law*, pp. 134-35.

26. Stephen Post, *The Evolution of Altruism and the Ordering of Love* (Washington, D.C.: Georgetown University Press, 1994).

27. Gratian, *The Treatise on Laws* (Decretum DD.1-20), trans. Augustine Thompson (Washington, D.C.: Catholic University of America Press, 1993), D. IX. C. 11.

graphical location of Eden. Rather, it is concerned with the truth of creation: that creation is good, that human beings are created for community with others and union with God, and that our relationship to God as God's image gives us a distinct calling and relationship to the earth.

Human Reasoning

Natural law accords with reason, but this claim can be readily misunderstood because the terms "natural," "law," and "reason" have common meanings that undermine a sufficiently human account of our nature and reason. Consider, first, the various meanings of the terms "natural" and "nature." We might take a romantic view, which would use "natural" as the opposite of calculated and logical. In this sense the law of our nature would rule when we acted spontaneously and avoided premeditation and reasoned intentions. In this view intellectual deliberation is likely to inhibit what is natural.

In a different but not contradictory approach, we might think about nature in a modern scientific sense, so that immutable laws of nature (analogous to the laws of gravity and motion) determine our purposes and actions. For instance, behaviorist psychology undermines the freedom of reasoned choices when it attributes human action to laws of environmental conditioning. Evolutionary biologists and psychologists account for human behavior by appealing to survival as the fundamental purpose of our genes.[28] Within this framework we cannot propose what we *ought* to do or what is best to do in moral terms. We can only point out how basic genetic motivations are working through us to reinforce what we do. When using evolutionary explanations, any given cultural conventions are justified as adaptive behavior.[29] According to this kind of evolutionary view (not shared by all evolutionary biologists), the law of survival determines what is good for us (genetically speaking), and in a factual sense we are bound to serve this law of nature.

In the Catholic tradition of natural law, our rational nature is of a piece with our freedom. Human freedom will be discussed in more detail in the following section, but let it suffice here to say that our powers of reasoning and our freedom are fundamental to our nature — to human fulfill-

28. Richard Dawkins, *The Selfish Gene* (Oxford: Oxford University Press, 1976).
29. Jack A. Palmer and Linda K. Palmer, *Evolutionary Psychology: The Ultimate Origins of Human Behavior* (Boston: Allyn and Bacon, 2002).

ment and to responding to God as the divine image. It is the law of human nature that we are not bound by nature in the same way as dogs and tigers. Dogs, for instance, are locked into following their instincts. They may be trained into adept use of those instincts by a master, but they cannot go against their instincts. Human nature is different. By our very nature, human beings participate in who we are and who we are becoming. Though we too have our instincts and inclinations, as rational creatures we are not bound simply to follow our instincts for our basic good. Rather, we constantly rank and order the goods available for us to pursue. Thus, mere survival is not our highest good, but instead we may aspire to heights of goodness, truth, and beauty that are worth dying for. As we choose the goods we will pursue, we help shape the person we are becoming. On one hand, the natural law tradition rejects the view that we are bound by natural and technological mechanisms. On the other hand, it presumes that freedom is not opposed to law. The natural law tradition proposes that we cooperate with God in our "self-creation" through the use of our reason and the promulgation of law.

Natural law is not invariant in the same sense as something like the law of gravity (a different sort of "law of nature"), but it is also inaccurate to assume that it is "law" in the same manner as a state or nation's legal codes (positive law). In any case, positive law is diverse enough in kind, from parking restrictions, speed limits, and tax codes to penalties for murder, that simple analogies are difficult to make. In the first section of the chapter, "Why Natural Law," we noted that natural law is conceived as participation in eternal law, which is God's providential ordering of the diversity of creation to its common good and end.[30] Natural law is a share in God's nature as we are images of God, and in these terms a share in God's ordering of life. It is similar to an inherent tendency and similar to inherent knowledge of what is good, but more properly, the natural law is an ordering of reason: to do good and to avoid evil and to avoid contradictions in our reasoning about our good-seeking. If the law of animal nature works on instinct, the law in us by nature works on our capacity to order the good. However, part of this ordering by God is that the very ordering is "underdetermined."[31] We are designed to respond freely to what is good and to order our common life — in our place and time — to what is purposeful and good.

It is in our nature to develop customs and to form laws (civil and ecclesiastical) that are established, promulgated, and enforced by the inter-

---

30. Aquinas, *Summa Theologiae* I-II.93.6.
31. Porter, *Nature as Reason*, p. 49.

change of authority and consent. The dissemination of law by an authority is natural to natural law. What we typically think of as enacted law is an outcome and process of the law in us by nature. If directed to the common good, the content of the law (which includes its purpose) is our participation in God's ordering of human life. Examples include not only a law against murder, but also laws that establish safe driving speeds above which we endanger ourselves and others and undermine a common good. Natural law is the means through which we reason toward the good. It can be seen through how we write our statutes and are able to judge these civil laws as good or bad.[32] This is one reason why the bishops have a teaching office and theologians have a teaching role where they are called (among other things) to make judgments about civil laws and customs, and to make pronouncements on matters such as war, labor law, and sexual practices in our culture. We might question what bishops, theologians, philosophers, or civil leaders have to say, but we should not question (but encourage) their evaluation of civil law in terms of the ordering of human life toward the good. This process of promulgation, evaluation, and argument is a primary instantiation of natural law.

This connection between natural law and a conversation about our common good moves us to an understanding of "reason" in the claim that "natural law is reasonable." Natural law is a law of participation with God's design for human life in our particular time and place. It points to the way that we as human beings (bound by time, history, culture, and tradition) order human life to our common good, that is, to the good that is our Creator and to the goods of creation that we share in common. Human reason is purposeful, good-directed, and participatory (in relation to God) in our very human — historical and embodied — way.

Much of the modern history of natural law thinking has run aground on this point. When modern scientific and philosophical reason emerges in opposition to ancient and medieval authorities, reason is conceived as free-standing and disengaged from our fulfillment as human beings. Early modern thinkers claimed that reason is too often adulterated by local customs, faith in authorities like the Bible, and claims about the purposefulness and ordering of life. Modern natural law theories, by and large, have tried to compete on this terrain of so-called "pure" reason. What emerges is an understanding of reason that looks a lot like the kind of reasoning done in mathematics. No matter who we are and where we grow up, one plus one equals two. Likewise, we ought to be able to place things and ideas in differ-

32. Hittinger, *The First Grace*, pp. 63-91.

ent sets, according to their attributes and apart from their purpose or place in common life, and manipulate them with the logical equivalent of one plus one equals two.[33] In reference to the moral law, this way of thinking often appears to work. In fact, this seems to be precisely the kind of approach required of a natural law theory, the kind of theory that applies to nature apart from historical or cultural conditions. Typical modern formulas, described in the introduction of this book, such as the Kantian categorical imperative, are still in use today. As noted in the introduction, this kind of formula offers no shared conclusions (it fails as a formula) when tacit cultural assumptions (the input into the formula) cannot be taken for granted. Ironically, the attempt to be universal — even when applied to modern natural law theories — arrives at moral conceptions that are either too general to be helpful or too specific to secure wide agreement.[34]

The natural law perspective that we are proposing assumes that the very human (all-too-human) elements of reasoning are not barriers to moral reasoning but are required for such reasoning to be possible, practical, and effective. The same could be argued for scientific reasoning, that the budding scientist is initiated into a tradition of thinking and practices of study without which she would not be able to adequately reason in the community of scientists. But we will limit our remarks to practical reason and to speculation on the goods of human life. For instance, the very terms that we (English speakers) use for thinking about life are metaphors drawn from our embodiment: we think about life as a journey and purposes as destinations.[35] When we are frustrated with a task or our state of life, we are likely to say that we are "going nowhere." We even think about thinking with metaphors of bodily motion: we think things through, or get a mental block, or get sidetracked. Our bodily-social-historical nature is an essential part of how we think.

We think about day-to-day matters in terms of functions and purposes that are embedded in our ways of life. For example, the moral life might be considered something like an art or craft. We have potential, and we learn and work on our skills and excellences for living well. In a more recent framework, economic and market metaphors are beginning to shape how we think about life and relationships. Many of us persist in talking about our bodies as property, even though we cannot talk this way without

---

33. Steven L. Winter, *A Clearing in the Forest: Law, Life, and Mind* (Chicago: University of Chicago Press, 2001), pp. 69-103.

34. Porter, *Nature as Reason,* p. 334.

35. Winter, *Clearing in the Forest,* pp. 22-42.

strange implications. Can we "possess" a body? Are we both the owner and the thing owned? Likewise, we often think about loyalty in terms of cost and benefit, and when we have been betrayed we might say that we have been sold out. Fortunately, we have alternative practices for Christians, those shaped by the life of Christ in worship and discipleship. Through these social practices we begin to see ourselves and our world in a certain way. When we look at the poor, for instance, we see not the indignity of outcasts, but the dignity of Christ embodied (Matt. 25). This way of seeing bears directly on how we understand human nature.

We think through our lives by the only means available to us, the structures of thought that are "embodied" and "embedded" in the structures of everyday life. Natural law reasoning is not a set of rules or formulas for determining moral norms, but a way of rationally engaging and evaluating a variety of sources (both sacred and secular) for understanding the common good of human life, and for arriving at moral norms. The natural law tradition does not say that one can simply "read" the natural law as though it were written upon the design of the world, although some have seen it this way. Natural law names a capacity for reflecting upon and reasoning about the world. It has its basis in our free and rational nature and is a process by which we make judgments about human customs, laws, and conventions. It is an ongoing conversation about human history and culture with a view to how these historical "embodiments" either enhance or undermine our understanding of the human being as created for community with God. Natural law is participation in eternal law in the manner by which we are able to reason about our humanity. We do so, not from beyond or from God's point of view, but in our place and time with a view to understanding our deepest desires, that is, by understanding the demands (the law) of our membership in the human race.

Law, Sin, and Freedom

Saint Thomas's *Summa* includes nineteen questions on law (I-II.90-108), only one of which (94) specifically addresses natural law. The treatise on law comes between Thomas's treatment of sin and vice (71-89) and his treatment of grace (109-114). At the beginning of this section of the *Summa,* the *Prima secunda,* Thomas sets forth to consider human beings insofar as they are the principle of their own actions (I-II, prologue). And so he attends to the goal of human life, and then considers how we human beings are able to move toward this fulfillment through our own actions, passions, and habits. Then he attends to sin and vice as that which undermines our progress toward our goal. All these things are intrinsic principles of human acts. As Thomas begins the treatise on law, which will be followed immediately by the treatise on grace, he moves away from the intrinsic causes of human action and into consideration of the extrinsic causes of human actions. As Fergus Kerr puts it, "his consideration of law is part of his consideration of the 'exterior principle' moving us to good, namely God, who 'instructs us through law and helps us through grace.'"[36]

Thomas Aquinas adopts Augustine's definition of sin: "an utterance, a deed, or a desire contrary to the eternal law."[37] Sin is, simply speaking, a bad human act. But what makes a human act bad is its failure to conform to its proper measure. For Thomas, human action has two such proper measures: human reason and God's eternal law. Human reason is the more proximate measure, because it is intrinsic to us. Eternal law, though less immediate, is the first measure of human action. Thus, sin is counter to what is good, good in us and for us, which is also to say that it is counter to God (against God) and to God's law. If we separate the very idea of "sin" from our fulfillment in God, "sin against God" appears to be an arbitrary constraint against "what I want" or "what really doesn't hurt anyone." When set within a frame of human fulfillment, sin against God can be seen also to violate our own good. Sin moves us away from God and neighbor insofar as our acts change us. With each act contrary to reason and to our true end in God, we become more disposed to similar acts, and form ourselves into persons of vice rather than of virtue. Vice undermines our capacity for fulfillment, which is to say it undermines our receptivity and responsiveness to God. The more we sin, the more difficult it becomes for us to see what is truly good for us and to work toward that good. The more we sin, the less free we become, because we become less able *not* to sin.

What we do, whether good or bad, affects others and who we are becoming. In a practical sense (in everyday life), freedom is not neutral or detached from who we are. At the beginning of the nineteenth century, Immanuel Kant expressed a typically modern conception of detached freedom. Kant attempted to ground morality in the autonomy of human reason, with reason providing for our self-legislation. According to Kant, we are reasonable (and therefore legislate good and evil for ourselves) when our

---

36. Fergus Kerr, *After Aquinas: Versions of Thomism* (Oxford: Blackwell, 2002), p. 105.

37. Aquinas, *Summa Theologiae* I-II.71.6. This definition continues to shape the Catholic understanding of sin today. It is quoted in *The Catechism of the Catholic Church* (1997), #1849.

reason sets us free from the constraints of our natural inclinations. Kant believed that natural human inclinations lead us to be ruled by self-centered interests. For Kant, moral reason lifts us out of ourselves, allowing us to transcend our specific histories, our embodiment, our commitments, and all the things that shape us in our particularity. Through reason we attain a universal perspective.

By the middle of the twentieth century, this detached freedom began to be criticized widely because its conception of objectivity and universality requires that we view human life as if from no particular point of view — a view from nowhere. This critique of Kant holds that we, as human beings, all see life from somewhere and that the view from nowhere is an illusion at best and a source of intolerance and oppression at worst. This backlash against the "view from nowhere" leads to moral relativism: all have a view from somewhere, and no perspective is better than another. Although set against Kantian universality, relativists accept that objectivity requires a view from nowhere. They sustain the view *in theory,* in order to hold that empirical evidence is against it. Though we all agree on certain goods, including truth, freedom, compassion, and justice, we find it difficult to agree on what these ideals look like in particular. What they look like seems to be a matter of perspective.

As a result, in our age of moral relativism morality is seen to be a matter of particular perspective. People try to free themselves from their membership in the human community by proclaiming that they have their own personal ethics. We are likely to think of ourselves as free to choose our own morality, free to determine what is good and evil *for us.* I can choose what's good for me, and you can choose something else to be good for you. This anti-Kantian relativism is oddly Kantian in its neutral sense of freedom. Although I might be a history-bound creature immersed in various customs and habits of my culture, moral freedom — by means of the detachment of reason — lifts me to a view from nowhere. Freedom is indifference, and anything that might compromise that indifference — from God's law to one's own virtue or vice — is a violation of freedom.

Such a concept of freedom, however, is not in keeping with the Christian tradition of thought on human freedom or human nature. Human life is not a neutral proposition; being created in God's image carries a purpose. God has designed us such that union with God is our happiness, and our freedom is designed to move us toward that end. Our own freedom and God's law and grace all work for that purpose. In this way, as mentioned above, our freedom is an intrinsic principle through which we move to the good, while God moves us to the good extrinsically through law and through grace. Law and grace serve as training and support for our freedom, not as constraints on it. Freedom is not a freedom of indifference but a freedom for excellence in our common good and in a multitude of good things and ways of life. Dominican theologian Servais Pinckaers offers two wonderful images of what freedom for excellence might look like: learning a musical instrument and studying a foreign language. Either effort involves discipline, commitment, practice. Each requires the mastery of certain tools or skills, be they rhythm and dexterity or grammar and vocabulary. Once one has developed a certain proficiency, one's freedom to express oneself has grown. Are we all equally free to sit down at a piano and play? If by "play" we mean striking a few keys, whatever their pitch, then our freedom is no doubt equal. If everyone in the room is truly indifferent to whatever noise might be produced at our hands, then, again, we are equally free. But if there is some value in, for instance, playing in a single key, with chords that match a melody, or perhaps in even playing a particular piece, then clearly those with training and practice behind them have developed a greater freedom to play for us.[38] Pinckaers offers a definition of such "musical freedom": "the gradually acquired ability to execute works of [one's] choice with perfection."[39] Likewise, our true freedom involves the gradually acquired ability to live our lives with increasing perfection. As the virtuoso musician becomes such through disciplined practicing of her instrument, so too the person of moral virtue becomes such by disciplined practice of the virtues.

On this view, human freedom is never merely freedom in a vacuum, but is always both situated in a particular context and directed to some purpose. A typically modern conception of freedom sets our freedom over against our historical, cultural, and bodily constraints. Rightly understood, freedom is always constituted in terms of who we are, including our particular gifts and skills and training. The desire to be outside of these is a desire to be superhuman. This modern notion actually takes us back to our very first temptation, Adam and Eve's desire to become like gods (Gen. 3:5). The contingencies of our own particularity do not make us less free; they are simply the character of human freedom. In Catholic moral thought, we all have basic freedoms due to us as creatures made in the image of God, such as a right to be free from physical, political, and economic oppression.[40]

---

38. Servais Pinckaers, O.P., *The Sources of Christian Ethics*, trans. Mary Thomas Noble, O.P. (Washington, D.C.: Catholic University of America Press, 1995), p. 355.

39. Pinckaers, *Sources of Christian Ethics*, p. 355.

40. John XXIII, *Pacem in Terris*, §8-38.

These freedoms are a matter of how God has made us who we are. But key to this freedom is how we also participate in our own becoming. Freedom is constituted by who we are; therefore, our own actions, efforts, and experience are an essential part of our freedom. The more we pursue mastery of a language, or of a musical instrument, the freer we become to express ourselves in that medium. In other words, we use our freedom to make ourselves more and less free.

God is the source of our freedom, so that God working in us does not make us less free, but in every free act we reflect the image of God in us. Because good acts are in keeping with the eternal law, we participate in the good that moves us toward God when we act in accord with reason and our human nature. Freedom is not an end in itself, but is directed to our fulfillment as human beings, ultimately in communion with God. God's law and God's grace work in us to direct us to our fulfillment. Ironically, even though we tend to think of God as competing with our freedom, the principle limitation to the fulfillment of our freedom is our own misdirected acts or sin. For instance, the more we act according to greed, the less we become able to spend our goods for the sake of those in need. We isolate ourselves, and the more we sin, the less able we are to act for our own true good and that of our neighbors. The more we sin, the less free we are to act in ways that draw us closer to God. Grace and law are two different means God uses to liberate us from our own efforts to thwart our freedom.

Law and Conscience

One of the places where questions about law and freedom meet is in conscience. One certainly hears much about "respecting the freedom of the conscience." The Second Vatican Council upheld conscience as the "most secret core and sanctuary" of the human person.[41] In its *Declaration on Religious Freedom* it insisted as well that the freedom of the conscience be protected from coercion. However, it is important to note that the church's protection of this freedom is always an insistence upon the conscience's freedom from coercion from external influences, such as oppressive human laws, unjust social customs, and other constraints. However, for the church the conscience must be free from such external constraints precisely because it is the internal place in which "men and women discover a law which

41. *Gaudium et Spes: Pastoral Constitution on the Church in the Modern World*, §16, in O'Brien and Shannon, *Catholic Social Thought*, pp. 174-75.

they have not laid upon themselves and which they must obey."[42] Conscience names the place within the human person where we carry the law inscribed there by God, where God's voice echoes within the depths of the person (Rom. 2:15-16). Freedom of conscience, therefore, from a Christian point of view, is not freedom from God's law; rather, it is freedom from human interference in order to choose and move toward the good — an inclination that is carried within us. The dignity of the human person requires human beings "to act out of conscious and free choice, as moved and drawn in a personal way from within, and not by their own blind impulses or by external constraint."[43]

In the Catholic tradition conscience refers to a capacity to know the truth, a process of discernment, and a particular judgment about what is to be believed or done.[44] The way Thomas Aquinas attempts to sort through these different ideas is helpful. Thomas tries to sort through whether conscience is a power of the soul (a capacity), a habit (which would be like structure of a process), or an act (an act of judgment). For Thomas, these concepts are interrelated but distinct.

The powers of the soul are not related to particular acts by their nature but by habit (virtues and vices). In the *Summa Theologiae* I.79.13, Thomas says conscience, properly speaking, is not a power but an act. In fact, he traces conscience to *cum alio scientia,* literally a "thinking with" something, or knowledge applied to a particular situation. The primary habit that shapes the intellect's application to practical situations is *synderesis. Synderesis* is not a power itself but rather a "special natural habit" whereby the principles of practical reason are bestowed upon us. *Synderesis* is thus not a power of the human soul, but rather the set of most basic practical principles by which our intellect works.[45] For Thomas, conscience, properly speaking, is an act of the intellect that may be formed through a variety of habits, but primarily through the habit of *synderesis.* When we refer to conscience as though it were a power or faculty of the soul, we are referring to the power of the intellect acting in an act of conscience, informed by the principles contained in the natural habit of *synderesis.* Thus, we sometimes name as "conscience" the power (intellect) or the habit *(synderesis)* that is brought to bear in an act of conscience.

When we think of conscience in this way — as the power of the intel-

---

42. *Gaudium et Spes,* §16.

43. *Gaudium et Spes,* §17.

44. Richard M. Gula, S.S., *Reason Informed by Faith* (New York: Paulist, 1989), pp. 136-51.

45. Aquinas, *Summa Theologiae* I.79.12.

lect, informed by the natural habit of *synderesis* and acting in a particular situation — it becomes evident that conscience is a place of connection between law, especially natural law, and freedom. Natural law is, as we have said, the participation of the rational creature in God's eternal law. Therefore, conscience may be seen as the act through which our reason brings God's law "written on our hearts" to bear upon us in our particular acts. Christians, however, are not only left to the powers of their intellect in sorting this through, but also have the gift of the theological virtue of faith, which heals, perfects, and surpasses the powers of the intellect alone. Likewise, divine law, as well as the New Law that is the outpouring of the Holy Spirit within our hearts, completes and perfects these natural capacities within us. The more deeply our consciences are formed in accord with divine law and the guidance offered by church teaching, the better equipped we are to be "in good conscience."

Freedom of conscience, like every freedom rightly understood, is a freedom to know and to do the particular good that will move us toward our greatest good and our greatest happiness, union with God. Conscience is bound to the truth. For this reason the conviction of conscience must be followed even when it puts a person at odds with his or her community, culture, and government. Although conscience is inviolable and at the heart of the person, it is not usually part of our day-to-day moral language. In a difficult situation at work, a person is likely to say to herself or a coworker, "I need to have the courage to deal with this situation." She is not likely to say, "As a matter of conscience, I need to be honest," unless a superior or coworker is pushing her to lie. Conscience tends to be used in a moral appeal made over against cultural conventions, law, and authority. It becomes an active part of our moral language in times of crisis, and for this reason our day-to-day moral formation and decision making depend more on words like "honesty," "loyalty," "courage," "justice," and "love." We are likely to worry about the "formation" of conscience when these primary moral terms seem to be in conflict and when our pathway of action is uncharted or unclear.

Because conscience is usually introduced in situations of conflict, it might be wrongly understood in opposition to law. However, since law is always also for the purpose of moving us to the good, law and conscience can never truly be in conflict. A freedom that is not directed toward attainment of the good is not true freedom. In the same way, a law that does not direct those it binds to the good is not truly law. ("An unjust law is no law at all.") Voluntarism and antinomianism are two sides of the same coin. Voluntarism gives the will the power to legislate good and evil; antinomianism reacts against an assumption that law could do so. Both imagine a morally neutral situation into which either the will or the law then enters. But all of creation is good, not neutral, by God's design. The human person is designed to know and to seek freely that good. Intrinsically, reason, through the act of conscience, works to direct us to that good. Extrinsically, God's law serves as an instruction and a guide to that same good. The two are designed to complement one another in drawing us to the good.

Law and Virtue

We began this chapter with the image of eleven-year-old Abigail, who, after five years of practice, is beginning to show some real expertise at the piano. Just as the structure of pitch and key gives a structure and order to music, so we say, in view of natural law, that there is a structure and order to creation. In the goodness of God's design we human beings are ordered to our fulfillment and our good through our freedom and free thinking. Natural law is the ordering of human life through which we identify moral norms through participating in God's ordering of creation. We determine what we are to do in our distinctively human way, through our common life and our shared history. Just as her practice on the piano allows young Abigail both to recognize and to perform good music better and better, so too our capacity for knowing and doing the good is rooted in how we learn to see ourselves and our world truthfully.

There are certain truisms that most of us who have practiced anything have heard a thousand times from a teacher or a coach. "The way you practice is the way you play." Or "*Practice* doesn't make perfect; *perfect practice* makes perfect." We can practice and play well or badly. We can learn and reinforce the skills that we need for excellence in music, or we can simply practice bad, sloppy habits that detract from our achievement, our learning, and our freedom. In the same way, we find that in the moral life we are shaped by our common life, our shared histories, and our particular actions over time. We may attend carefully to our lives and our choices and develop the skills (virtues) to live well and the freedom to move well toward our fulfillment, or we may reinforce the bad habits (vices) of sinful living and fail to develop the freedom to move well toward our fulfillment. The two chapters that follow attend to our freedom of movement toward our end in terms of God's activity in the world (chapter 8) and our "this-worldly" activities in relationship to the good that is our God (chapter 9). They assume an order and design to creation that, with God's help, we can learn, practice, and be shaped by, to become virtuosos of the moral life.

Concurrent Readings

Hittinger, Russell. *The First Grace: Rediscovering the Natural Law in a Post-Christian World.* Wilmington, Del.: ISI Books, 2003. Hittinger gives an excellent overview of natural law within the Catholic tradition, and he deals with key questions and cases in the American legal tradition. One of his most important criticisms of modern accounts of natural law is their neglect of authority as essential to natural law.

John XXIII. *Pacem in Terris: Peace on Earth,* nos. 8-38. In *Catholic Social Thought: The Documentary Heritage,* edited by David J. O'Brien and Thomas A. Shannon, pp. 132-37. Maryknoll, N.Y.: Orbis, 1992. In *Peace on Earth,* John XXIII summarizes the Catholic tradition of social thought and gives what is now a classic outline of human rights and duties based on the natural fulfillment of human beings.

McCabe, Herbert, O.P. *Law, Love, and Language.* New York: Continuum, 2003. The book was originally published in 1969 under the title *What Is Ethics All About?* It is at once simple and profound. It provides the best introduction to Christian ethics and natural law.

Pinckaers, Servais, O.P. *Morality: The Catholic View.* Translated by Michael Sherwin, O.P. South Bend, Ind.: St. Augustine's Press, 2003. Pinckaers develops the conceptions of law and freedom that are presented in our chapter. He also gives an outline of natural law in relationship to human fulfillment and the Ten Commandments.

Porter, Jean. *Nature as Reason: A Thomistic Theory of Natural Law.* Grand Rapids: Eerdmans, 2005. Porter provides a comprehensive account of the natural law tradition, Scholastic and modern. Her work is especially helpful for its understanding of nature, reason, law, and the relationship between natural law and virtue.

Chapter 8

Freedom and Grace

MICHAEL R. MILLER

The brilliant thirteenth-century Dominican saint and theologian Thomas Aquinas wrote much about virtue, which he defined as habits "by which we work well."[1] Much of the discussion in this chapter is influenced by his writing, especially his *Treatise on the Virtues* in his masterpiece *Summa Theologiae*. Aquinas, adopting the advice of the great ancient Greek philosopher Aristotle, generally encouraged his readers to live a life of holy moderation. That is, Aquinas recognized that there can be too much of a good thing, so he cautioned against living most of the habits "by which we work well" to the extreme. For example, although the habit of jogging can help keep us fit, running 150 miles or more a week would very likely wear our body down. Aquinas, however, did write that everyone should live the virtues of faith, hope, and love — commonly called the theological virtues — to the extreme. He argued that since we can never "love God as much as He ought to be loved, nor believe and hope in Him as much as we should," we become better people the more faith, hope, and love we have.[2]

Many in our day are very worried about Aquinas's recommendation of extremism. They hold that doing anything in the extreme, especially a theological virtue like faith, is to be avoided because extremism harms others and limits one's own freedom. Concerning harm to others, critics are quick to point out that the extreme Christian faith of the Crusaders directly led to remarkable suffering of countless Muslims and Christians. Likewise, they note that the extreme interpretation of the Qur'anic call to jihad led a

1. Thomas Aquinas, *Summa Theologiae* (hereafter *ST*), trans. Fathers of the English Dominican Province (New York: Benziger Brothers, 1948), I-II.56.3.
2. Aquinas, *ST* I-II.64.4.

small number of radical Muslims to kill over 3,000 innocent people on September 11, 2001. Extreme religious convictions also limit human freedom, so say these critics, because such faith commitments severely restrict our options to think and act as we want. That is to say, these critics believe that deeply religious people are forced by their faith commitments to live a certain kind of life, and hence cannot find true personal satisfaction because their extreme faith severely restricts both the scope and the possible attainment of their desires. Taken together, these criticisms suggest that if God plays too great a role in our lives, we will act in such a way that harms both our good and the good of others.

Aquinas makes the exact opposite point when he argues that we should live the theological virtues to the extreme. That is, Aquinas argues that possessing extreme faith, hope, and love of God (traditionally known as charity) does an unlimited amount of good for us and others. Such a claim reveals the importance of the theological virtues, given by God through grace. Aquinas valued them so because he understood that they transform the lives of those who possess them, shaping our character and directing us toward union with God. Aquinas also well understood that this transformation does not destroy our human freedom, but fulfills it. Explaining this extraordinary interplay between God's grace and human action, as exhibited in the gifting of the theological virtues, is the primary concern of this chapter. In it I will argue that God's action and God's grace are not opposed to human freedom; on the contrary, God makes us truly free.

Theological Virtues

All people are disposed to act in particular ways when presented with a choice. Over time these dispositions help shape our capacity to act in one way or another, which in turn accounts for the kind of person we will be. For example, if you are disposed to be impatient, it is likely you are an underachiever. Why? Because if you are prone to settle for the first good thing to come your way, it is likely that you do not actively desire the highest good. Therefore you probably are not especially interested in the higher good of developing your talents, since many talents require great patience to master them. The more often you decline to perfect your talents, the harder it becomes to orient yourself toward the good; your bad dispositions are reinforced and your impatience becomes a vice, a tendency to reject what brings human fulfillment. However, if you are disposed to be patient, you do not find it difficult to work for long-term goals like your personal development; hence, you probably have started and successfully completed many projects to develop your talents. The good that comes from the gradual perfection of your talents reinforces your efforts to improve. Thus, your good disposition to patience is called a virtue, for it directs you to the good and helps you do good actions; it is, as Aquinas said above, the habit "by which we work well." It must be noted, however, that although virtues give us a steady aim at the good, the possession of any virtue does not guarantee that good actions come easily. For example, we may have a disposition toward the love of our enemies, but we may struggle to seek their good. Virtues shape our capacity for good, but they do not necessarily free us from hard work or the possibility of failure.

Every person, if so inclined, can do things that will help him or her acquire many virtues, such as courage, temperance, or honesty. For example, if people want to become brave, their efforts to overcome relatively mild fears (standing on a step stool) help them face larger fears in the future (such as standing on a ladder). Although all good things, including all virtues, come from God, these virtues are commonly thought of as "acquired virtues" since our efforts help us obtain them. In contrast, the theological virtues of faith, hope, and love are dispositions that we cannot develop or bring to perfection by our efforts, for they are completely given to us by God through the grace that joins us with God in Jesus Christ. That is, the theological virtues have their origin in God's movement in us and with us; nothing we can do outside of God's operation in us necessarily gives us these virtues. For this reason they are traditionally called "infused" virtues, in a logical contrast to the "acquired" virtues we can help bring about by our efforts. The use of the term "infused" should not imply that they are suddenly poured into us by God against our human nature, as some mistakenly suggest. Rather, God complements and perfects our very nature with these infused virtues, for these dispositions bring us both to our fulfillment as human beings and to life with God. Thus, the great gifts of faith, hope, and love dispose us to a special relationship with God, established in us by the self-giving friendship of God, which is holiness. In this way the theological virtues give us the remarkable gift of unity with God, which ultimately is found in our embrace of the beatific vision.

The New Testament makes it clear that it is these virtues (and not other virtues like courage, temperance, determination, or even wisdom) that give us a share in God's nature. For example, Jesus praises the Roman centurion for his faith, not his courage (Luke 7:1-10). The thief on a cross is praised for his hope in Jesus' forgiveness (and was given the gift), despite living a very unjust life (Luke 23:39-43). The woman who washed Jesus' feet was not a virtuous person in the eyes of the world; yet Jesus praised her great love (Luke 7:47). Jesus' parables also praise faith, hope, and love over and above all other good traits, talents, and advantages. In the parable of the separation of the sheep and the goats, the blessed are praised for loving others, not for being patient (Matt. 25:31-46). The rich man, whom we can assume has the talent of making money and is likely very smart, is condemned because he did not properly love Lazarus (Luke 16:19-31). The persistent woman, pounding at the judge's door, received satisfaction because of her persistent hope that justice would be done (Luke 18:1-8). Saint Paul too praises the virtues of faith, hope, and love (1 Thess. 1:3). He notes that they open the way for our other virtues and talents to ring true. Love, for instance, is not patience, but it gives facility to patience and unifies it with what is good (1 Cor. 13:1-13).

Having faith, in a general sense, is believing what is true without definitive proof. In the theological sense, faith is belief in God who is revealed in Jesus Christ. Faith in this God is necessary because no argument can provide all the evidence necessary to accept every doctrine of the faith, such as God's existence, the Trinity, or the incarnation. The virtue of faith shapes our ability to affirm the truth of such claims in spite of doubts and open questions. Faith, however, is not illogical or irrational. Faith believes without seeing, but it is not mere optimism; in a world of hatred and sin it allows us to see signs of God's love and to begin to accept the evidence for what we believe. Like all the theological virtues, faith takes us out of ourselves and focuses our entire being on another, on Jesus. In this way faith is less about believing doctrines and more about receiving a person into our lives, he who is the way, the truth, and the life (John 14:6). In an age that doubts the existence of objective truth, the church's emphasis on faith may seem quaint or hopelessly old-fashioned. However, the Christian tradition recognizes that faith is extraordinarily important, especially in our age of skepticism, because faith proclaims the existence of truth. Like the light of the lighthouse that reveals both the dangerous rocks of the coast and the safety of the harbor, faith leads us to the love that distinguishes what is false and what is true. The virtue of faith is necessary for salvation, for without faith we cannot know God and enter the kingdom of heaven.[3]

Hope, as the second theological virtue, helps us live with trust in our eventual fulfillment in union with God. Hope is not simply anticipation for some future event or reality. In its theological sense, hope is confidence in

3. See Mark 16:16; John 3:36; 6:40; Matt. 10:22; 24:13; Heb. 11:6.

the promises of God, such as the forgiveness of our sins, our resurrection, Christ's return at the end of time, and his mercy. The virtue of hope also has a more general sense, for the person with hope is certain that there is a reason to live and a good end for which we strive. But it is not mere optimism, for hope gives us the ability to face the possibility that important matters of life might turn out badly. With hope we can strive onward without despair, even in the face of grave difficulties. Confident in the promises that God transforms us, hope profoundly changes our relationship with other people and to things. In a manner that those without hope may deem foolish or reckless, those with hope understand that the victory has already been won and they are free to live a life without anxiety or fear. Thus, in the face of violence and hatred, we need not turn to violence and hatred. That is, hope in Jesus and his reign makes it possible for us to live without fear, without seeking dominance over others, and without isolating ourselves from the needs and suffering of others. With a Christ-centered hope, we are able to live the life we are called to live and to live it to the fullest. In this way hope prepares us for heaven, our eternal home, as we pray that God's kingdom may come on earth as it is in heaven (Matt. 6:10).

Saint Paul tells us that the love of God is eternal and the greatest of all virtues (1 Cor. 13:13). He explains that in heaven there is no need for faith, since all there will clearly see God and know the truth. Likewise, hope in heaven is unnecessary, since everything promised by God will already be fulfilled. The love of God, in contrast, will always be present in heaven for it is an inexhaustible source of pure self-giving and other-receiving action. Through God's love we are called to live the ways of heaven here on earth, for to be in love with God is to be in love with the entirety of God's creation. God's love teaches us to not only love others, but to love ourselves with the unmerited love of God. This profound love gives us the capacity to follow Jesus, and sets us on the way to be more fully human.

In today's world love has lost much of its sacredness because the term itself is both overused and misunderstood. Many false forms of love exist in society, and many fail to recognize true love's life-giving and transformative power. Worldly loves are not bad in themselves; rather, they are limited, for they cannot be self-sustained and self-sufficient. They become "false" forms of love only when they seek to be complete in themselves. For example, a sexual expression of love is good in itself, but it devolves into lust when a person ignores the fullness of a loving relationship and puts physical desire at the center. Romantic love seems much closer to Christian love, for romantic love focuses the attention of the individual in love upon the beloved. This attentive care for the other and not oneself follows the pattern given to us by Jesus. However, romantic love tends to be inwardly directed; we seek romantic moments alone with our beloved. The love of God is not this kind of isolated and limited resource. God's bountiful love naturally expands to include others (especially the outcast, the poor, and the sick). In this way Christian love is more akin to the enduring faithfulness of marriage (Eph. 5:21-32). Even marriage, however, devolves into a mistaken view of love if it attempts to represent love in its fullest. Many of the biblical passages often read during wedding ceremonies, such as 1 Corinthians 13, are actually descriptions of love in a community of faith, where the individual gifts and talents of each are given to serve the good of all. In short, God's love is better represented, not by the wedding, but by the wedding banquet, where the poor and outcast are invited in, where we are invited into an ever widening bounty of God's hospitality (Luke 14:15-24).

Divine Action, Human Freedom, and Fulfillment

The theological virtues raise difficult philosophical questions. For example, does God — who gives us the disposition of faith, hope, and love — make us act in accord with those gifts? That is, do the theological virtues undermine our human freedom by discounting the need for human choice and action? And if we struggle with the virtues of faith, hope, and love, do our doubts, moments of despondency, or lack of love mean that God's grace is not working in us?

I am going to tackle these questions by explaining how God operates in his creation, notably in human life, through grace. Attempting to do so is probably foolish, for trying to explain one thing about God's nature usually ushers in several more issues, each requiring extremely nuanced answers. Like fighting the mythical hydra, who grows two heads for every one the hero hacks off, any effort to "explain" God often leads to more questions than answers. Whatever the difficulties, I believe the effort is necessary. We need to understand how grace — so attractive, effective, and powerful — influences us to live a better life without destroying an essential part of what makes us human, our free will. I fully recognize that in attempting to do so I may be charged with making one process — the action of God's grace — overly complex, but I urge you to pay attention to the beautiful and complex details of this process, since understanding how God is at work in your life right now may actually help you find happiness both in this life and in the next.

The relationship between God's grace and human freedom is at the heart of the Christian moral life. When considering this complex and dynamic relationship between God and human beings, we naturally want to examine the relationship between God's power and our own, which is best seen in our ability to freely choose something. Given the possible combinations of divine power and human freedom, only four options exist — each made up of two propositions. Given the rules of logic, one of these four options must be true.

OPTION 1   Humans are *not* free and God is *not* absolutely powerful.
Implication: moral action and responsibility are not possible and life is not entirely ordered by God's providence.

OPTION 2   Humans are free and God is *not* absolutely powerful.
Implication: moral action and responsibility are possible but life is not entirely ordered by God's providence.

OPTION 3   Humans are *not* free and God is absolutely powerful.
Implication: moral action and responsibility are not possible because life is entirely ordered by God's providence.

OPTION 4   Humans are free and God is absolutely powerful.
Implication: moral action and responsibility are possible because human life is entirely ordered by God's providence.

To make sense of these four options, the terms used must be defined. First, the term "freedom" is often used indiscriminately, but we will use it here in a technical, philosophical sense. A person is "free" only if he or she is able to both choose and initiate what is chosen without external influence or coercion. This does not mean a person must have the power to complete the task in order to be free. Nor does it mean that we are solitary and have not been formed within a community; we all become persons within a social structure and our actions both influence and are influenced by others. Nor does it mean that a free person must be able to do things he or she is not physically or intellectually able to do (such as levitating or speaking Swahili if never before studying the language), or things that are logically impossible to do (such as becoming a cat). Such actions have no bearing on the liberty of human freedom. So, a person is rightly considered to be acting in a "free" manner when no external power coerced his or her choice; this choice is unbiased and undetermined, and chosen simply because he or she *wanted* to make it. Second, a being is properly defined as "absolutely powerful" only if the being has the ability to do anything it wants to do — bearing a logical impossibility.[4] This means that the actions of an absolutely powerful being could not be constrained by the material or metaphysical barriers that hinder those without absolute power. For example, the absolutely powerful being could change water into wine, restore life to those who are dead, and even create the universe out of nothing. The absolutely powerful being would not have to do these things, or others like them, but must be able to do them if desired. The absolutely powerful being would also have a preeminent place in the hierarchy of powers, for it would be the cause of all causes without being caused by (that is, dependent upon) anything else.

Rather than examining each of the options individually, it will be more efficient to examine the particular propositions that make up the four options. Why? Well, given the laws of logic, if it can be shown that one of the propositions is false, then the entire option that contains the false proposition must also be false. So, let's determine which propositions we should accept or reject.

First, should we accept the proposition "God is *not* absolutely powerful"? Scripture argues that the proposition is false, for the Bible is full of verses that clearly express that God governs all things: God creates the universe out of nothing, frees the chosen people, and raises the dead.[5] Each of these acts, and many more like them, demonstrates that God possesses absolute power and is the source of all things. Likewise, Christian theologians, such as Thomas Aquinas, consistently argue that the will of God is always fulfilled since everything (natural acts and human choices alike) happens exactly as God wills it to happen.[6] Aquinas notes that some theologians mistakenly thought that God causes humans to will but not "in such a way that He makes us will this or that."[7] Aquinas strongly rejects this solution. He holds that God is the real cause of every human choice because God

---

4. God does not have to be able to make a circle a square or 1 + 1 = 3 to be absolutely powerful. Such a claim is irrational since the rules of logic are not external to God, who is internally logical.

5. For example, see Gen. 1 and 2; Exodus; and John 11:1-44.

6. For more on this see Aquinas, *ST* 1.19.6.

7. Thomas Aquinas, *Summa contra Gentiles* (hereafter *SCG*), 3.89.1. Aquinas has Origen in mind. See Origen, *Peri Archon* 3.1 (Patrologia Graeca 11, col. 293); on this theory see Gilson, *History of Christian Philosophy* (New York: Random House, 1955), pp. 41-43.

gives people the power to choose.[8] Thus, given the scriptural claims and the authority of the arguments advanced by Aquinas, we should not easily accept the proposition "God is *not* absolutely powerful" as true.

Second, should we accept the proposition "Humans are *not* free"? At least two reasons argue against our accepting it. We know we are free, in part, because everyone feels that his or her choices are free. A much more sophisticated argument would need to be made to prove this claim, but this feeling is so universal and the intuition is so strong (even the most ardent determinist recognizes that it appears as if we are making choices without any coercion) that we should not easily accept the proposition "Humans are *not* free" as true. The Bible also makes it clear that we are responsible for our choices, for our condemnation or reward depends upon the freedom of the will.

If we follow the arguments presented and accept both that humans are free and God is absolutely powerful, options 1, 2, and 3 must all be rejected. Thus, the only option that remains (and hence must be true) is option 4: "Humans are free and God is absolutely powerful." Yet, how can this claim be true? Even though scriptural evidence and strong philosophical authorities support both human freedom and God's absolute power, doesn't the existence of absolute power destroy all freedom in the universe, including human freedom? Conversely, doesn't the existence of human freedom (if it is to be real freedom) deny God's ability to wield absolute power? Something must be wrong here. The universe just isn't big enough for both human freedom and God's absolute power.

Fully aware of this apparent problem, Aquinas offers a philosophical explanation that allows us to simultaneously affirm human freedom and God's absolute power. That is, Aquinas recognized that a great number of things are true causes (including things that follow from free human choice) even if the causes were ultimately caused by God.[9] For example, imagine that a tree is destroyed by lightning in a storm. Aquinas would think it reasonable to consider the lightning bolt the cause of the tree's destruction — even though the bolt itself was caused by a large number of topographical and meteorological factors, all of which ultimately can be traced back to laws of nature that were ordered by God. In a somewhat similar fashion, Aquinas argues that a human choice is a real cause even if it is not completely independent from the influence of another cause.

8. Aquinas, *SCG* 3.89.5. Aquinas uses this false teaching to drive home the point that "acts of choice and movement of will are controlled by God" because "every movement of the will must be caused by the first will, which is the will of God." Also see *SCG* 3.91.2 and 3.89.6.

9. Aquinas, *ST* I.19.5.ad3.

To explain his answer, Aquinas highlights the difference between instrumental and secondary causes. Instrumental causes are those that act only because an agent makes them act. For example, a hammer is an instrumental cause of the nail entering a board because a carpenter made the hammer drive the nail — the hammer could not do otherwise given the carpenter's will. Thus, to be an instrumental cause means not to be a free cause. Secondary causes, however, are different because they act as real causes, even if the initiation of the action depends upon an earlier cause, known as the primary cause. Consider the following example. A general orders a sergeant to fire his cannon at the enemy, and the sergeant does as ordered. Even though he is ordered to fire, the sergeant still had to choose to obey the general's direct order. Thus, the sergeant is not an instrumental cause of the cannon firing but a secondary cause, even though he fired the cannon, because he was ordered to do so by the general.

Aquinas contrasts instrumental and secondary causes to emphasize certain points. Both causes depend upon some prior agent to complete the effect: the instrumental cause completely and the secondary cause partially. The secondary cause is not dependent upon the primary cause in the same way that the instrumental cause is, but a certain level of dependence remains nonetheless. The difference between the two, however, should remain clear. Instrumental causes depend upon the power of the primary cause in order to be a cause at all, for the instrumental cause cannot act unless immediately directed to do so by the primary cause. Secondary causes also do what the primary cause wants them to do, but they already have within them the power to act. Thus, a primary cause may initiate and in some cases even direct the action in the secondary cause, but the secondary cause is acting as a real, albeit immediate, cause. Human beings are secondary causes since we act as real causes, even though we receive our power to cause from God.

In short, Aquinas's conversation about the nature of human freedom and God's power highlights the remarkable difference between the manner in which God operates and how God's creatures operate. Three observations follow. First, we must understand freedom and power from God's point of view and not our own. Most of us think that having freedom means having the power to do whatever we want to do without limits. Aquinas rejects this libertarian notion of freedom, for he believes true freedom means having the power to do what fulfills us as human beings. For example, who could freely choose to become a drug addict? Such a choice does not prove a person's freedom, but only his or her enslavement to the hope for physical pleasure. In contrast, true human freedom means that we are able to attain the fulfillment that God has planned for us; acting freely thus makes us more human, more virtuous, and more godlike.

If God directs us to fulfill our purpose in life, to become better and more fully human, God's influence, albeit powerful and directive, does not destroy our freedom to choose what God wills for us to choose. God creates us as beings that are fulfilled through our freedom. Philosopher James Ross puts it this way:

> God produces, for each individual being, the one that does such and such (whatever it does) throughout its whole time in being. Still, God is not the *agent* of the sun's motions. Nor, strictly speaking, does God cause the sun to move. Those motions of which you are *agent* (e.g., your gestures) are *your* motions; whereas those motions you produce but are not the agent of are still your effects. God does not move the sun; he makes the *moving sun to be*. So the movements of the sun are God's effects, even though he does not move it.

In a similar manner, Ross argues that God does not make any person act; rather, God makes *the acting person be*. That is, "God causes Adam, acting exactly as Adam actually does, to *be*, not like a wind-up toy that ricochets off objects in a path undetermined by the player, but to *be* wholly, including being able to do otherwise than as he actually does."[10]

Second, following upon this point, the fact that God is the creator of the universe forces us to think about causation differently. Given our typical experience with other things in this world, we typically believe that as long as a person is not forced to do something by an external force, then that person is free. That is, if nothing outside of our own internal desires "pushed us" to do something, we did so freely. Aquinas is quite clear in his agreement with this position in the sense that if any person is forced by an external cause to do something he or she does not wish to do, then that person is not responsible for that action.[11] However, Aquinas is equally clear that something can be voluntary and still be caused by an outside agent, because it is not essential to the notion of freedom that every internal impulse be the first cause of every choice.[12]

---

10. James Ross, "Creation II," in *The Existence and Nature of God*, ed. Alfred J. Freddoso (Notre Dame, Ind.: University of Notre Dame Press, 1983), p. 130.

11. See Aquinas, *ST* I-II.6, where Aquinas carefully qualifies a person's responsibility for voluntary and involuntary acts, a very important principle in the legal system of the West. Also see Aristotle's *Nichomachean Ethics* 3.1 (1110a5-20), the source of Aquinas's discussion.

12. For example, my choice to break my diet is voluntary yet caused by the ice-cream sundae placed before me.

If something is moved in accord with its natural tendencies, then such a movement is not violent, but natural or voluntary. For example, someone can throw a rock upward, or simply set it in motion by dislodging the stones and dirt that keep it in place. The first movement is violent, since the rock does not "want" to go upward. The second movement is not violent but natural, for by its very nature the rock seeks the lowest place. In both situations the rock is moving because of some external force, yet one is violent while the other is natural. And yet, Aquinas notes that the natural movement of the rock falling is only an accidental cause, because the person who causes the rock to slide down the hill does so "by removing an impediment, and thus uses a natural motion, or action, rather than causes it."[13] In fact, only the one who made the rock heavy (that is, made it so that it always falls to the ground when possible) truly causes the rock to move externally without violence. This being exists outside of the rock, causes the rock to move, and yet does not violently force the rock to move in a way it does not "want" to move. Now the only one who can cause such a movement is God, who is the cause of the rock's being and who sustains it in its being according to its nature. Therefore, God alone can truly cause the natural movement of any object from outside that object without violence.

Thanks to the fact that humans are naturally drawn to the good, the beautiful, and the true, Aquinas concludes that God alone influences the human will to act but does not take away human freedom.[14] Aquinas argues that no body, human will, or angel can move the will from within,[15] for: "The only agent that can cause a movement of the will, without violence, is that which causes an intrinsic principle of this movement, and such a principle is the very power of the will. Now, this agent is God, who alone creates a soul. . . . Therefore, God alone can move the will, in the fashion of an agent, without violence."[16] Only God can move the human will to act without destroying human freedom, for God's movement is internal and not coercive.

The result of these two points is the third, and in many ways the most interesting: God's power ensures that we are free because God wills us to be free. God, as the creator of freedom and our very nature, determines not

13. Aquinas, *SCG* 3.88.6.

14. Aquinas, *SCG* 3.88.4. A person, unlike a rock, does not have to capitulate to the pressure being levied upon him or her by another creature, even if the pressure is great. That is, a person may choose to lose a good job, lose a friendship, or even die rather than partake in an evil deed.

15. Respectively, see Aquinas, *ST* I.115.6; *SCG* 3.88; *Compendium of Theology*, trans. C. Vollert (St. Louis: St. Louis University Press, 1947), pp. 127-28; and *SCG* 3.92.4.

16. Aquinas, *SCG* 3.88.6.

only what God wants to happen, but also that those things happen in the manner he wills them to happen — necessarily or freely. This means that God's power is so great that God determines that natural causes, such as rocks falling to the ground, always happen, and that particularly human actions, such as eating pancakes for breakfast or wearing white socks, are chosen freely. That is, God's actions are not a threat to human freedom, for God's creative act does not impede liberty but guarantees it. "In this way," according to philosopher Brian Shanley, "human beings reflect the divine image and reveal something of the nature of the free divine creativity that originates free human creativity."[17] God's creative and transcendent act is the key, which ensures human freedom rather than limits it. God operates in all things without controlling any, for he is the cause of all being.

Clearly, God's mode of operation lies beyond anything the human mind can comprehend. This "otherness" of God does not mean, however, that we have no knowledge of how God operates in the universe. Instead, Aquinas suggests that one of the best ways to determine in a positive manner how God operates through his will is by examining our own free will, for in acting freely humans reflect the divine image.[18] This is remarkable, I believe, because it means that human creativity reveals something of the divine creativity that shaped the world and governs all. It is precisely such a reflection that leads Herbert McCabe to conclude that God directly and powerfully causes humans to be free: "God brings about my free action, however, not by causing other things to cause it, he brings it about *directly*. The creative act of God is there immediately in my freedom. My freedom is, so to say, a window of God's creating. . . . In human freedom we have the nearest thing to a direct look at the creative act of God (apart, says the Christian, from Christ himself, who *is* the act of God)."[19] Paradoxically, it appears that human activity is more directly caused by God than any other

---

17. Brian Shanley, "Divine Causality and Human Freedom in Aquinas," *American Catholic Philosophical Quarterly* 72 (1998): 122. Shanley writes: "God is not a rival to human freedom like some Homeric deity or the modern idol that Nietzsche rightfully saw as a threat to human freedom. Instead, the radical transcendence and distinction of the Creator God from the created world means that God empowers rather than overshadows creaturely freedom. God generously allows created beings to share in divine providence as bearing the dignity of causes in their own right. This is especially true of the human person, who falls under divine providence as a secondary cause of a particular kind because it belongs to him to reflect the Creator's own mode of causation through his free, rational, provident and self-determining actions. In this way human beings reflect the divine image and reveal something of the nature of the free divine creativity that originates free human creativity."

18. Aquinas, *ST,* prologue, 1-2.

19. Herbert McCabe, *God Matters* (London: Geoffrey Chapman, 1987), p. 14.

earthly thing and yet remains the most free of all earthly activities, for when we act we share in God's own creative freedom. God's direct and immediate action in each of our free choices not only ensures our freedom but also places upon humans a dignity no other earthly creature has. Therefore, thanks to God's generosity, when we choose to act we are not only being fully human in doing so, but we are also acting as God acts. Humans possess this remarkable gift of freedom, simply because God wishes us to be free.

Aquinas stresses that real freedom is not independence from the transcendent Creator, for he creates humans to be free. Since God is the guarantor of human freedom, it is wrong to think that a person must be a first cause to be the real cause of his or her own movement. Aquinas argues:

> Free-will is the cause of its own movement, because by his free-will man moves himself to act. But it does not of necessity belong to liberty that what is free should be the first cause of itself, as neither for one thing to be cause of another need it be the first cause. God, therefore, is the first cause, Who moves causes both natural and voluntary. And just as by moving natural causes He does not prevent their acts being natural, *so by moving voluntary causes He does not deprive their actions of being voluntary: but rather is He the cause of this very thing in them;* for He operates in each thing according to its own nature.[20]

God, therefore, guarantees human freedom by being actively and immediately involved in all causes as the creator of all things, the first cause that makes secondary causes be free, and the transcendent being who insures that humans have the power to choose freely. Remarkably, we are free, not in spite of God's great power, but because of God's great power. Therefore, God ordains our freedom, determines that we choose, and guarantees our liberty because we are made free creatures with the inherent power to choose. Thus, we must accept the apparent contradictory statements as true: God is in complete control of his creation, for nothing happens that he does not will to be, and we humans are free to choose what we want.

God's Gift of Grace

If the arguments above have been convincing (that God is in complete control of the entire universe *and* that we human beings are totally free), an-

20. Aquinas, *ST* 1.83.1.ad3, emphasis added.

other question quickly arises concerning God's role as creator. Does God the creator also act in creation? That is, did God just create all and step back so as to let the universe run its course, or does God "get involved" in our lives? If God is involved, does that mean God "steps in" and fixes things or circumstances in our lives? For example, does God give us strength when we are tired, courage when we are afraid, or knowledge when we are confused? Even more importantly for us, does God give us the particular virtues that we may need to share life with God, or does he just let us muddle around by our own devices, hoping to live the life worthy of eternal reward?

The immediate response to these questions is to affirm God's active involvement, for as Christians we intuitively know that God is intimately concerned with our lives. God demonstrates his profound commitment to our well-being by his incarnation and death. His willingness to answer our prayers, sometimes with miracles, provides further evidence that he actively intervenes in our lives. This divine activity, where God "steps in" and makes us or the situation better, is best defined as grace. Simply put, grace is the love and life of God, freely shared with us for our well-being. Grace is the reason why we are alive, for our life itself is a grace. Grace is also divine help, which transforms our lives and motivates us to act in godlike ways, loving, encouraging, and forgiving others.

There is an old story, which has become a popular modern fairy tale, which many think illustrates well the role God and his grace have in our lives. It is the story of "the Natural," a young man who has remarkable athletic skills, and as the story is usually told, plays baseball.[21] The Natural wows all who see him play with his phenomenal strength, speed, and quickness; none, not even historians of the game, can remember a more talented athlete. However, for all his athletic ability the Natural is a dreadful player: since he wants only to hit home runs, he often fails to advance his teammates with a higher-percentage base hit; the Natural doesn't study opposing pitchers, so a smart pitcher can overcome his superior strength; he is a foolish base runner, often running into an out or failing to tag up for an extra base; and he does not play defense, for he expects others to cover the field. Worst of all, the Natural is not a team player, caring more for personal statistics than for helping the team win.

As a result, few managers want the Natural on their team, in spite of his great physical talents; the Natural becomes known throughout the league as an underachiever. However, one wise Coach (who typically is a lit-

---

21. A well-known version of this story is found in the movie *The Natural* (1984), directed by Barry Levinson and starring Robert Redford.

tle cantankerous but with a big heart) takes an interest in the Natural. The Coach sees beyond the Natural's limitations and recognizes the diamond in the rough. He shapes the Natural up. That is, the Coach teaches the Natural to be disciplined, to work hard, and to study the game. Almost overnight, with the Coach's help, the Natural achieves what he could not achieve on his own, and he becomes an all-star. The team goes on to win multiple championships, and years later the Natural enters the Hall of Fame. At his introduction to the Hall, the Natural thanks the Coach for making him into a superstar, for giving him the know-how and discipline to best use his natural gifts.

Many believe that this story illustrates how God operates in our lives. We, like the Natural, have certain natural abilities. We are successful because we make good use of what we can naturally do, but we recognize that we can only go so far on our own; we need a little help so we can go further than our natural abilities can carry us. Grace is that help. God sees the potential that is in us and gives us a little push so we can now do remarkable things — even supernatural things. For example, I may be naturally brave and fear no one, but with God's grace added onto my natural virtue I become willing to die for my faith. My courage is put into overdrive, and becomes a kind of turbo-bravery. Likewise, I may have disciplined myself over the years to "say no to drugs" and other harmful addictions, but now God helps me complete a difficult religious fast. In the same manner, I may be a "good guy" who always helps others when I can, but now God's grace gives me the "extra push" I need to love others in the manner of a saint. God, the wisest of coaches, blesses me with grace and I do supernatural things; God gives me his help and my natural talents are perfected and I become more than I was without him.

This image of grace at work, although very common, is flawed for several reasons. First, graces are not earned, as this story suggests. Just as the rightly condemned criminal cannot demand or expect leniency, we humans cannot demand that God restore to us what we undo and lose through our sin. We do not work ourselves out of disorder through fear of punishment and a bit of divinely inspired discipline. This means that we do not earn God's help to love in a supernatural way because we have mastered the art of loving in a natural way. Nor are we graced with the ability to complete a sacrificial action because we successfully completed a somewhat demanding action. Saint Paul, in explaining one of the most profound mysteries of the faith, tells us that God's grace is completely unearned and totally free. He explains that if God's grace was earned it would not be grace, but payment for a deed done (see Eph. 2:8-10 and Gal. 2:16). God's grace cannot be bought because God is in need of nothing — not our worship, praise, service, or love. Acting in love and as love, God generously gives of himself to us for our benefit. Thus, try as we might, there is no human explanation for why God gives as much as God does.

Second, the popular image of God at work in our lives is also wrong because it suggests (a) that we can work independently of God's action in our lives, and (b) that God's action, namely, grace, is something added on top of what we do. In other words, this notion suggests that we are able to do things completely on our own. These actions are thought to be our natural powers, free from God's control. As the first part of this chapter explained, nothing that happens in the universe is independent from God's activity, even though some things (our choices, for example) are free. As the creator, therefore, none of God's actions in our lives are coercive because God causes us to act from within. Even more problematic, the popular image suggests that God's operation in our lives is limited to certain actions that transform (or raise up) our natural powers to supernatural powers. As a result, God is not properly credited with being the origin and movement of these "natural talents" as well.

It is certainly right to praise God for giving us the "supernatural graces" that bring us to heaven, our final fulfillment and friendship with God. But this is not the only way God is active in the world. We must also recognize and praise what God has done in giving us certain talents that help us in our ordinary life. These natural abilities too are from God, since he is responsible for our very nature, which includes our capacities for intelligence, strength, temperance, determination, and so on. God is fully at work here, in the "natural" realm. His "supernatural graces," which the popular image would see as the only way that God works, are just part of God's operation in our lives. Likewise, it is equally wrong to deny the operation of grace in our earthly and ordinary lives, to give exclusive attention to God's operation in the actions we do that direct us to heaven. Grace is grace, whether it helps us live our life on earth well or helps direct us to our supernatural end.

The old story about the Natural and the Coach must be rewritten if it is meant to mirror how God operates in our life, because it overemphasizes the independence of the Natural's ability. What is natural to us is not static but develops in relationship to others and to our efforts. We are always in the process of coming to be. That is, the Natural does not receive his physical talents in a genetic vacuum; nor does he develop them without the actions of others. His parents, playmates, and Little League coaches all contributed to who he is. The Natural may have always been able to run fast and throw hard, but many others taught him the rules of the game and helped him develop into a talented athlete. They also contributed to his becoming a selfish player. So-called raw talent is not entirely set apart from our habits, desires, and relationships. We are always in the process of working on our natures. One problem for the Natural is that he continues to work on his nature in such a way that his abilities are becoming more and more "raw" (uncultivated) and at odds with the good of the game.

The story also needs to be rewritten because it misconstrues God's activity as the mere "influence" of a coach. Here the human analogy fails to articulate the way we should understand God's action and our freedom. Recall the problem discussed in the first half of the chapter, that we often make the mistake of thinking of God's action and power as external to us. Our rewritten story will have to emphasize the internal workings of the Coach in order to stress the operation of God's grace within our lives. In the popular version of the story the Coach gives the Natural what the Natural apparently lacks, an *influence* that instills drive, wisdom, and a sense of personal sacrifice for the well-being of the team. In fact, the Coach could not have presented these qualities to the Natural, as if they were articles of clothing that he simply could slip on over his athletic ability. These qualities could be developed only *within* the Natural, and not from any external force. Only God could have done so, since only God could give the Natural a second nature, which shares in the divine nature. This second nature provides the possibility of unity with God through a reconciliation. God's grace has given the Natural the capacity not only to love what he can do while he is playing the game, but also to truly love the game. God, as the creator of the Natural's talents, also offers the grace of redemption that is God's own self-offering. The Natural receives God's self-giving love, which gives him the capacity to live outside of himself for the love of life, for God is the source of life itself. Ironically, the Natural's talents reach a greater "this-worldly" fulfillment when his play is no longer directed to his own glory and merely to "this-worldly" achievement.

Another way of stating the Natural's problem is that he does not love doing what he is created to do. His love is too narrow and self-serving. The Natural is selfish and idle and does not look beyond his immediate circumstances and investigate what effect he is (or is not) having on the team. The Coach (God) does not simply challenge the Natural to actually love the game, but he offers a new capacity to do so. He gives the Natural the freedom to love what is beyond himself and his own glory. The disorder of the Natural's God-given ability is restored to its proper order, and therefore he freely can direct himself and his efforts to his proper natural end. In theological terms, the grace that elevates our nature to a life shared with God (ultimately experienced in heaven) also restores our natural capacity for doing good in the world. This restoration is a transformation, because the abilities necessary to be a great player are disordered and lacking in the Natural, even though he has extraordinary gifts. Certainly, the Natural could run fast and hit the ball hard, but he lacked the ability to put his game in order, to bring his talents to fulfillment. In grace, God gives himself to us so that we share in God's nature. In unity with God, we are given the capacity to join in loving as God loves. The same grace restores our natural abilities to their proper natural ends.

Once the Natural comes to love the game, he understands that the fundamentals of the game — sliding, fielding, laying down a bunt, and so on — are beautiful acts in themselves. Not surprisingly, his base running improves, as does his fielding and throwing. With his newfound love — his new nature — the Natural suddenly enjoys tasks he once avoided: practicing in the batting cage, talking to his coaches about strategies to use when batting against opposing pitchers, and lifting weights. The Natural now understands that trying for a base hit, a walk, or even a sacrifice fly could be better for his team than swinging for the fences. He now hustles to first every time, striving to beat the throw, rather than shuffling down the line expecting the worst. In theological terms, he is living with hope.

In this corrected version of the story, I have tried to move the Coach, as an external influence, toward an understanding of God as an internal movement that accords with our freedom, indeed, that offers through grace a capacity for greater freedom and fulfillment. Now I will have to progress beyond the analogy of the Coach. We are all given talents and abilities in our lives. These are gifts, for we do not earn them before our birth. Many of the gifts vary from person to person; some people have more athletic ability, intelligence, health, and so on, and some people have less. But each of us has the capacity to contribute to our human community and share the good of human life. Like the Natural, we limit our own freedom and fulfillment because of selfishness and sin. We are liable to narrow what we are able to see as freedom and the human good. Such sin and narrow vision lead us to harm and do evil to others in the name of our good.

Christians believe that God's self-giving gives new life. We are given a share in God's nature. This is where the Coach analogy breaks down, for he is an external influence. Because God's power accords with our freedom (as seen earlier in this chapter), the grace-given nature of God's self-giving does not violate but restores our created nature. In fact, because of sin, we (like the Natural) are often working against our freedom and fulfillment as human beings. Through the gift of faith, however, we are given the freedom to believe in God and to know something about God's relationship to humanity. In hope, we are given an ability to strive for unity with God in this life and the next. Through the grace of God's love, we are given the capacity to love freely as God loves. These three gifts — faith, hope, and love — serve as the foundation for all other graces in our life, direct us to our ultimate unity with God in heaven, and serve as a renewed foundation in this life.

God does not give us the dispositions of faith, hope, and love as an extra on top of our already-completed natural abilities. The theological virtues elevate us to share life with God by being an integral part of our natures. As dispositions, they give shape to how we are able to live now. In a world of sin, the grace that elevates us to life with God also gives us the ability to put our natural gifts in order. This is the point where the analogy of the Coach and the Natural is useful. We might think our natural talents and abilities (being able to throw a ball, being brave or temperate) are our own, but in fact all our talents are from God (a point too often forgotten). We (like the Natural) have a tendency (in sin) to undermine our abilities for justice and love through our very efforts to make them our own possessions and to serve our self-centered purposes. The grace that frees us for life with God, frees us to fulfill our nature as well.

Conclusion

I want to end this chapter by repeating Saint Aquinas's proposal that we should live the theological virtues to the extreme, and all other virtues in moderation.[22] There is a special wisdom here, for Aquinas understood the special role faith, hope, and love play in our lives. The myriad of gifts given to us by God are certainly worthy of praise, but the theological virtues alone give us what we need for peace, harmony, and well-being in both this life and life eternal. My main concern in this chapter has been to explain the relationship between faith and freedom, between God's grace and our moral action. Faith, hope, and love are infused in us by God, and as this chapter has explained, the movement of grace in us does not undermine our action or freedom. On the contrary, the infusion of grace restores our freedom for natural goods and elevates us to shared life with God.

In the introduction I raised the question of violence and extremism along with the issue of God's will and human freedom. I have shown that

22. See Aquinas, *ST* I-II.64.4.

God's power is the source of our freedom to act toward and be fulfilled in what is good for us. Insofar as faith is used to oppress others and undermine human dignity, it is a disordered faith — not ordered by the grace that makes us fulfilled and free. The next chapter will deal in more detail with our capacity to act on and attain "this-worldly" goods. It explains the relationship between God's grace and moral virtues, for instance, between faith and the moderation of temperance and between the abundant love of God and justice.

Concurrent Readings

Aquinas, St. Thomas. *Summa Theologiae.* New York: Benziger Brothers, 1948. Essential reading is Thomas's conceptions of freedom and grace, I.19 (God's Will), I.22 (Providence), I.25 (God's Power), I.102-105 (The Government of Creatures), and I-II.109-114 (grace). On the virtues, see the questions on faith, hope and love, II-II.1-46.

McCabe, Herbert. *God Matters.* London: Geoffrey Chapman, 1987. McCabe offers concise and profound analysis on the relationship of God to creation, freedom, and the problem of evil.

Ross, James. "Creation," *Journal of Philosophy* 77 (1980): 614-29; and "Creation II," in *The Existence and Nature of God,* edited by Alfred J. Freddoso. Notre Dame, Ind.: University of Notre Dame Press, 1983. My philosophical arguments on the relationship between human freedom and God are truncated. Ross offers a fuller account of the view that God creates us as beings that are fulfilled through our freedom.

Shanley, Brian, O.P. "Divine Causation and Human Freedom in Aquinas." *American Catholic Philosophical Quarterly* 72 (1998): 99-122. Like James Ross, Shanley offers a fuller philosophical account of the arguments about God and human freedom. He argues that the utter difference of the Creator from creation, God's radical transcendence from creation, allows the very possibility for God to work from within (not as an external force). Because of God's transcendence, God's power does not overshadow human freedom, but actually empowers it.

Chapter 9

Moral Virtue, the Grace of God, and Discipleship

WILLIAM C. MATTISON III

Moral theology has traditionally explored how people act in the world ("moral") in the context of their faith in God ("theology"). This volume purposely examines morality in the context of Christian belief. What difference does faith make in how a person lives his or her life? Surely a person of faith engages in certain distinctive activities, such as going to church, praying, and reading the Bible. But what about the myriad of activities that all people partake in every day, such as eating, facing difficulties, exchanging goods, and making decisions? Does the person of faith engage in these activities with the same "morality" as everyone else? As is already clear, a life of discipleship is not simply about performing certain types of actions. It is a vocation, a transformation of one's very self. Such a transformation of course impacts how we act. The primary question for this chapter is, how does discipleship, a life of following Jesus, transform not only who we are but also how we act in this world?

The ancient notion of virtue will help us answer this question. A virtue is an abiding part of a person that disposes the person to act well. Obtaining a virtue changes who one is. It also explains how such a change in a person disposes one to act differently. Thus the first section of this chapter explains the concept of "virtue" in order to illustrate how changes in who we are lead us to act differently. The second section examines more closely one type of virtue: moral virtue. It identifies and defines the four main moral virtues, traditionally called "cardinal virtues," which dispose us to good action in the types of activities noted above as shared by all persons, of whatever faith commitment. The third section explores how the four cardinal virtues have consistently been identified throughout the Western tradition (and even beyond) as the "hinges" to living a good life in this world. Even with this commonality, the cardinal virtues are also supple enough to invite interpretation by different worldviews. Thus, these virtues can lead people to different sorts of actions based upon people's varying belief commitments. This points us toward the fourth section, which defines a certain sort of cardinal virtue that Christians have traditionally labeled "infused." A fifth and final section explains why the infused cardinal virtues are essential to understanding how a life of discipleship transforms a believer's life in this world.

Defining Habits and Distinguishing Virtues

As human persons we have all sorts of capacities: to eat, to make decisions, to allot goods, to have sex, and so on. We can exercise these capacities in numerous ways. A virtue is a habitual inclination to use a certain capacity well, or simply a "good habit." Therefore, to understand a virtue it is necessary to understand the difference between simply performing actions and actually having a habit.[1] A habit is an abiding disposition that inclines one to exercise a specific capacity in a certain manner. It is a change of who one is, with a resulting change in what one does. Aristotle was making this point when he claimed that a person with a habit is still marked by that habit even when not exercising the habit's activities.[2] For instance, a mathematician is still a mathematician even in her sleep. As a habit, a virtue is a quality that abides in us, even when it is not being acted upon. This is not the case for sporadic actions.

Several things follow from the enduring nature of a habit. First, a person with a habit can be relied upon to consistently act in conformity with the habit. Someone could give occasional money to charity, but the generous person consistently gives money to the poor. Second, the person with a habit generally acts spontaneously out of that habit, seemingly without thinking. When someone has a habit, it often feels like "second nature" (or "natural") to act in conformity with that habit. We might say today that acting well for the virtuous person is a "no-brainer." Finally, a habit concerns not only exterior actions but also internal dispositions, particularly inten-

---

1. For a helpful introduction to this topic, see C. S. Lewis's *Mere Christianity* (San Francisco: HarperSanFrancisco, 2001), pp. 76-81, where Lewis describes the cardinal virtues and uses the example of a tennis player to distinguish having a habit from performing occasional actions.

2. See Aristotle's *Nichomachean Ethics*, pp. 927-1112, in *The Basic Works of Aristotle*, ed. Richard McKeon (New York: Random House, 1941), for a classic treatment of virtue. The discussion of habits (or "states of character") is found in book 2, pp. 954-62.

tions.[3] In other words, a habit not only inclines a person to do certains sorts of acts, but also to do them in a certain way and for particular reasons.

All these observations are true of habits in general. Habits incline us to act consistently, spontaneously, and with corresponding intentions. Virtues are good habits, and vices are bad habits. For example, people may give money to the poor to relieve their guilt, or to look good in front of others (as Christ himself describes in Matt. 6). And people do develop habits of doing good acts either to look good in front of others or to make themselves feel better. These habits are not virtues, but rather vices. The person with the virtue of generosity, however, gives money to the poor with the proper intention of seeking to alleviate distress out of genuine concern for people in need. A virtuous person not only consistently and automatically performs good actions, but also does so for the right reasons.

There are a myriad of different virtues and vices. Perhaps you have heard of the seven deadly sins, either from Dante's *Divine Comedy* or from the Brad Pitt movie. These are all vices. You have surely heard the expression "patience is a virtue." Perhaps now that has more meaning than just "patience is a good thing." There are many ways to group virtues (and vices, for that matter). One of the most important is by the type of activity being done well (or poorly, in the case of a vice). There is a virtue for using one's sexuality well (chastity — which does not mean simply "don't do it"), for enduring suffering well (patience), for believing true things about God and God's relationship to humanity (faith), for seeking pleasures well (temperance), for seeking union with God in this life and fully in the next (hope), and for distributing goods well (justice).

Each virtue is named for the sort of activity being done well. A technical name for the "sort of activity" is the "object." The numerous virtues can be placed into two broad groups based on whether their "type of activity," or "object," falls into one category or the other. The first category is called theological virtue, and includes the virtues faith, hope, and love.[4] What distinguishes these virtues is that their activities, or objects, all concern God directly.[5] We believe in God (faith). We love God above all else, and all things in God (charity, or love). We yearn for union with God, experienced fully only in the next life but tasted in this one (hope). When one engages in such activities well, one is said to have these "theological virtues." They were ex-

---

3. Recall David Cloutier's chapter 6 earlier in this collection. There he describes how we humans act with purposes, for the sake of fulfillment. Intentions are those purposes.

4. The classic place these are found in Scripture is 1 Cor. 13:13. But see also 1 Thess. 1:3.

5. See Thomas Aquinas's *Summa Theologiae* (New York: Benziger Brothers, 1948), I-II.56, for a detailed discussion of the theological virtues.

amined more closely in the previous chapter. Since they concern God directly, and direct us toward ultimate union with God, they are not accessible to us without God's help, or "grace." Therefore we say they are "infused" virtues because they are given to us through the grace of God. We cannot acquire them on our own. In sum, the theological virtues concern God directly (object). They are obtained by grace, or infused, and concern our ultimate destiny with God.

The second category of virtue consists not of virtues that concern God directly, but of those that concern inner-worldly activities. Such activities include eating, drinking, engaging in sexual relations, distributing goods, making practical decisions, and facing difficulties. Anyone who lives in our world must address how to engage in these activities.[6] Hence the objects of these virtues are called inner-worldly.[7] The group of virtues concerning such activities has often been labeled "moral virtues." Given that the term "moral" is used so frequently and broadly, "moral virtues" will be called "cardinal virtues" here. Though the number of inner-worldly, or moral, virtues is rather large, the four "cardinal" virtues (prudence, justice, fortitude, and temperance) have long been posited in the Western tradition as encapsulating the virtuous life in this world.[8] Saint Thomas claimed that every single one of the myriad of virtues concerning inner-worldly activities could be grouped under one of these four virtues.[9] So generosity is a subvirtue of justice; chastity a subvirtue of temperance; patience a subvirtue of fortitude; and foresight a subvirtue of prudence. Therefore, what distinguishes cardinal virtues from theological virtues is that the objects of cardinal virtues are inner-worldly activities. The rest of this chapter explores the four cardinal virtues in more depth.

Naming and Defining the Four Cardinal Virtues

The four cardinal virtues are justice, prudence, temperance, and fortitude. Each of these is easily misunderstood, so it is worth pausing to state exactly

---

6. This is true even of those who apparently decide not to do certain activities, such as the celibate person or the pacifist.

7. John Paul II used the term "innerworldly" in the encyclical *Veritatis Splendor*, §65.

8. This is seen in the work of Saint Thomas Aquinas, who actually uses the term "moral virtue" to refer to virtues concerning inner-worldly activities, but on certain occasions employs "cardinal virtue" to avoid confusion. See *Summa Theologiae* I-II.61. Thomas examines all moral virtues under the auspices of one of the four cardinal virtues. See II-II.47-170.

9. Again here he is following the likes of Gregory the Great and Cicero, both of whom he cites at *Summa Theologiae* I-II.61.2 and 61.3, respectively.

what type of inner-worldly activity is done well by those possessing it.[10] First, consider justice. Aristotle famously claimed that we humans are social animals. Our lives are interdependent, such that living a good life must entail good relationships with other people. Justice is the virtue that inclines us to good action in our interactions and relationships with others. We may immediately think of the courts and the law when we hear "justice," and such matters do indeed fall under justice. But any activity where we give another his or her "due" is a matter of justice. Honesty, generosity, keeping promises, respect, etc., are all matters of justice.

Another central component of human life in this world is bodily desire. We desire and act to obtain things that are pleasant to touch, taste, or experience. Such objects of our desire include food, drink, sex, and recreation. Any good life in this world will be marked by such desires, but these desires must also be well ordered. Temperance is the virtue of well-ordered desires for pleasures. When we hear the word "temperance," we may think solely of alcohol, or even more specifically of the temperance movement in the early part of the twentieth century in the United States. A moderate desire for alcohol is indeed important for temperance, but temperance also includes desires for food, sex, and recreation. The person who drinks too much is acting "intemperately." But so too is the person who is obsessed with video games, or who neglects important duties to spend leisure time with friends.[11]

Life in this world entails facing difficulties. Fortitude is the cardinal virtue that enables us to face difficulty well. "Courage" and "bravery" are synonyms of "fortitude." When we think of bravery, we may immediately think of soldiers on the battlefield risking their life for their friends and nation. This is indeed an example of bravery. In fact, since the greatest danger we can face in this life is our own death, a willingness to literally lay down one's life has always been seen as the paradigmatic act of fortitude. Yet this virtue may also be demonstrated in any difficulty in life, such as a sick person facing the sickness well, a student "stepping up" during stressful exam periods to perform well, or a person enduring pain after a hard breakup. These are all examples of fortitude.

---

10. C. S. Lewis's brief chapter on the cardinal virtues in *Mere Christianity*, cited above, was very formative for this section.

11. We commonly assume that vices are always examples of excess, in the case of temperance, excessive desire for pleasure. This is understandable since this problem is by far the most common. But Aristotle and Thomas are clear that one can be "intemperate" by having *too little* desire for, and too few activities seeking, pleasure. This is clearly the case with eating, but can even be true of people who prudishly condemn anything pleasurable as sinful.

The final cardinal virtue is perhaps the most difficult to understand. In all areas of life we have to make practical decisions that guide our actions. Even if we "mean well" and have good desires, we must choose well to effect those good desires. Prudence is the virtue of doing practical decision-making well. When we hear the word "prudence," we commonly think of being cautious and wary. At times the virtue prudence may indeed call for cautious hesitation. But it may also call for decisive action. In all cases, one acts prudently when one accurately sizes up the situation at hand and makes good practical decisions. This virtue is particularly important, because it is required for the exercise of the other cardinal virtues.[12] One may desire to drink moderately, but without an accurate grasp of what constitutes moderate drinking, one cannot effect that desire. One may desire to help those in need by giving money to a charity. But if one contributes to a fraudulent charity, then the poor are never served. Surely we can make poor decisions out of unavoidable ignorance.[13] But the prudent person uses the good sense she is capable of to choose well concerning all activities in this world.

Cardinal Virtues as the Path to the Good Life in This World

The cardinal virtues may rightly be called the path to the good life in this world. These four virtues, and all the "subvirtues" under each of the four, "cover" all aspects of a good life as it concerns activities in this world. In fact, the very term "cardinal" comes from the Latin word for "hinge," since a good life is said to "hinge upon" these virtues. There is actually remarkable consistency throughout the Western tradition in affirming the centrality of these virtues for the good life.[14] They may be found in Scripture, where the book of Wisdom, describing God's Spirit of Wisdom, claims

12. For this reason prudence has traditionally, in both Christian and non-Christian sources, been called the "charioteer of the virtues" or "preeminent among the virtues." See, for instance, *Catechism of the Catholic Church*, 2nd ed. (Vatican City: Libreria Editrice Vaticana, 1997), §1806.

13. We see here the close relationship between prudence and conscience. Conscience is defined by the *Catechism* as the concrete judgment by reason of the moral quality of an act, as good or bad (see §1778). Though a treatment of conscience is beyond the scope of this chapter, in such a treatment one would explore whether an erroneous conscience, or acting wrongly out of ignorance, is blameworthy (vincible ignorance) or not blameworthy (invincible ignorance).

14. There are even important commonalities between Western thought on the cardinal virtues and non-Western thought. See, for example, Lee H. Yearley's *Mencius and Aquinas: Theories of Virtue and Conceptions of Courage* (Albany: State University of New York Press, 1990).

> she teaches moderation and prudence,
>> justice and fortitude,
>> and nothing in life is more useful for men than these.
>>>> (Wis. 8:7 NAB)

Plato uses these four virtues to describe both the well-ordered society and the well-ordered individual.[15] Cicero also reduces all virtues to these four.[16] Saints Augustine, Gregory the Great, and Thomas Aquinas are just a few of the Christian thinkers who appeal to the four cardinal virtues when describing the moral life.[17] Thus there is a remarkably consistent emphasis in the Western tradition on the importance of the cardinal virtues in the moral life, and this witness extends beyond the Christian tradition.

What can account for this consistency? Since the cardinal virtues concern "inner-worldly activities," any person or society, regardless of beliefs or religious commitments, must have some vision (explicitly stated, or just implicitly seen in how people act) of how to engage in these activities well. All persons everywhere face difficulties, desire sensual goods, relate to others, and make practical decisions. Living in this world necessarily entails these activities. Therefore we say that the cardinal virtues are "accessible to reason" because all rational persons engage in these activities and can at least in principle discern how to do them well.

Nevertheless, it would not be accurate to say that therefore all these voices in the Western tradition share a solitary vision of what is morally right and wrong. This points us to another observation about the cardinal virtues. The cardinal virtues incline their holder to act well in different areas of life: making practical decisions, desiring pleasures, relating to others, and facing difficulties. Yet what exactly constitutes "acting well" in each of these areas? The traditional answer to this question has been that virtue resides in the "mean," or middle course. In other words, the brave person (i.e., fortitude) is neither too cowardly nor too foolhardy. The chaste person is neither too promiscuous nor too prudish. Virtue lies in the mean.

---

15. See book 4 of Plato's *Republic,* trans. G. M. A. Grube (Indianapolis: Hackett, 1974), pp. 85-109. This is one of the reasons why early Christians such as Justin Martyr thought Plato was exposed to the Old Testament (which is not true)!

16. Thomas makes this claim at *Summa Theologiae* I-II.61.3, where he cites Cicero's *De inventione rhetorica.*

17. See Augustine's *The Way of Life of the Catholic Church* (Washington, D.C.: Catholic University of America Press, 1966), book 1, pp. 15, 19-28. See Gregory the Great's *Morals on the Book of Job,* cited at Thomas's *Summa Theologiae* I-II.61.2. Thomas's own treatment of the cardinal virtues is cited above.

Perhaps we can all agree on this claim that virtue lies in the mean. But this really just pushes back one step further the question of what constitutes good or bad action. What constitutes promiscuity, or being too prudish? A virtue approach to morality has the advantage of being supple. It can accommodate individual, as well as cultural, differences as to what constitutes, say, temperance concerning alcohol. Nonetheless, a virtue approach is not so abstract or "formal" as to render anything potentially virtuous. What guards against such a contentless morality is the reliance of the virtue approach on paradigmatic actions to exemplify each virtue.[18] For instance, bravery is paradigmatically described as a willingness to lay down one's life for an important cause. We can certainly debate which of our country's wars are just and thus warrant laying down one's life, or whether the circumstances in a particular battle justify a retreat. But on no one's terms is it brave to abandon one's country-mates in the heat of battle. That is cowardice.

Nonetheless, though a virtue approach to morality is not completely contentless, it is flexible enough to require further specification. In other words, saying "be temperate in your use of alcohol" is a good start, but more is needed. And thus identifying the relevant virtue is only the start of this process of discerning how to act well in a particular situation. For instance, virtue discussions of alcohol use assume there is a mean of temperance, and ways to deviate in excess or defect. But where the lines are drawn is something that needs to be specified through further examination of the particular activity at hand. For what purposes is alcohol being used? How does alcohol impact the body? What social forces are at work inclining one toward or preventing one from alcohol use? What influence does an individual's history or physique have on the decision to use alcohol? Further prudential reflection, at both the individual and communal levels, serves to further specify the mean of temperate alcohol use.[19]

Yet if the cardinal virtues concern inner-worldly activities that are in principle accessible to reason, why are there so many different understandings of what constitutes a just, or brave, or prudent, or temperate act? How can some societies regard hara-kari as honorable and others condemn it as suicide, and wrong? How can societies hold such radically different views of gender or race relations, or of what constitutes virtuous sexuality or alcohol use? Some individual and communal differences as to what constitutes vir-

18. For more on this point, see Jean Porter's *Nature as Reason: A Thomistic Theory of the Natural Law* (Grand Rapids: Eerdmans, 2005), p. 190.

19. For the importance of the community in such reflection, see Pamela Hall's *Narrative and Natural Law: An Interpretation of Thomistic Ethics* (Notre Dame, Ind.: University of Notre Dame Press, 1994).

tuous action reflect the simple truism that the good life has many expressions. But some differences seem incompatible with each other, and not so easily explained. Even though the activity is inner-worldly and in principle accessible to unaided human reason, "the way things really are" concerning that activity may be contested. For instance, what is the true purpose of sexuality? Different people may disagree on this, or even that there is a "real purpose" of sex. Are men and women truly equal, and if so how should that equality be instituted in a society? Clearly people continue to disagree on this. This does not necessarily mean there is no such thing as temperance or justice. It simply means that people disagree on the meanings of inner-worldly activities, or "the way things really are" in this world. There are many possible explanations for these differences (such as malice, ignorance, etc.), but another important cause is that one's understanding of "the way things really are" concerning inner-worldly activities is importantly shaped by one's beliefs about "the way things really are" concerning God and God's relationship to humanity. In other words, what one believes about God does indeed shape how one regards inner-worldly activities, and judges whether or not they are being done well. Of course, all differences about cardinal virtues such as temperance and justice do not boil down to differences of faith. However, neglecting the impact of faith on how one lives in this world leads to an impoverished view of the cardinal virtues. Understanding the "infused cardinal virtues" prevents just such a mistake.

Explaining the Infused Cardinal Virtues

We have yet to attend to the question of how the cardinal virtues are obtained, or more dryly, the "efficient cause" of these virtues. Since virtues are good habits, the most obvious way they are obtained is through repetitive, intentional action. If you want to become a generous person, you must repeatedly, and for the right reasons, help those in need with what resources are available to you. By continually performing such actions, a habit develops such that you will be disposed to do more such actions (automatically, with proper intentions) in the future. Oftentimes developing a good habit, or virtue, means overcoming a bad habit, or vice.[20] If I am stingy or greedy, developing the virtue of generosity will mean first refraining from acting on

---

20. For a helpful discussion of the stages of development of virtue, see Paul Wadell's *The Primacy of Love: An Introduction to the Ethics of Thomas Aquinas* (New York: Paulist, 1992), pp. 106-24. Wadell bases his stages on Thomas's *Summa Theologiae* II-II.24.9.

my stinginess (by, say, not giving alms to the poor or not lending out my possessions to those in need) out of a desire to be generous (by, say, giving up some of my own goods to help those in need). An initial vice is an obstacle to overcome on the path to virtue, though it does not prevent one from developing a virtue. Thankfully, people do change. Of course, one can also change by losing a virtue, and so even those who possess a virtue must continue to act upon it lest they lose it in favor of a contrary habit, or vice.

When one acquires a cardinal virtue, one performs inner-worldly acts well with an eye toward how they contribute to human flourishing. In other words, I drink moderately (i.e., temperately) because I want to maintain bodily health and consistently enjoy this sensual good. I am generous because I want to contribute not only to my own well-being but also to that of others in my community, since I understand the two as intertwined. People are able to understand, through the use of their reason, natural human flourishing, as it includes things like bodily health and the common good. Since it is our created nature that flourishes here, and we can understand this type of flourishing with our reason, such flourishing is called our "natural end," or goal. It is "natural" to us not in the sense that everyone achieves it, or even that everyone fully understands what constitutes natural flourishing, but rather in the sense that it completes or perfects our created nature and is accessible to our human reasoning.

Yet, as already hinted at earlier in part 2, Christians believe that humans are invited by God to share in a greater destiny. This destiny is called, literally, a "supernatural" destiny, and is constituted by union with the triune God of Jesus Christ who became man for us to reconcile us with God and make us (astonishingly!) sharers in the divine nature (2 Pet. 1). This is a destiny that far transcends our unaided created nature and unaided powers of reasoning. We could not "get there" on our own. In fact, we cannot even begin to comprehend this invitation, let alone live it out, without the assistance of God's grace.

So how can it be understood or achieved? God gives us the grace to truthfully understand who God is, and his plan for humanity (faith). He bestows on us a love of God and others in God, such that we seek to be unified with God in communion with others (charity). He fills us with a longing for that union — tasted in this life and completed in the next — even when it is not fully available to us now (hope). Therefore Christians can be virtuous in their relationship with God thanks to God's help, or grace.

What does this have to do with the cardinal virtues? Christians, like all human persons, live in this created world and continue to engage in "inner-worldly activities." To do these well they, like all others, need the cardinal virtues of prudence, justice, temperance, and fortitude. At this point it would seem that the only thing distinguishing Christians and non-Christians is the presence of faith, hope, and love. Christians have the infused theological virtues to guide them to union with God, a supernatural destiny. But all persons — Christian or not — have the cardinal virtues that are acquired by the process of habituation and direct us to do inner-worldly activities well for the sake of natural human flourishing. On this read, in fact, there really is no difference between how Christians act well in the world and how virtuous non-Christians act well. There is simply a "human" ethic for inner-worldly activities, and so the cardinal virtues incline all people toward the same sorts of actions.

There are kernels of truth in saying that Christians and non-Christians both have these acquired cardinal virtues. First of all, for many inner-worldly activities, it simply does not matter whether or not one is Christian. If you want a good exercise trainer, it is probably not necessary to ask if he or she is Christian! Physical training is an inner-worldly activity accessible to unaided human reason that looks the same for Christians and non-Christians alike. The same is true of many questions of justice. A non-Christian judge can be just as knowledgeable in American law and render just judgments as a Christian judge. Second, it is true that Christians can work hard to obtain cardinal virtues concerning inner-worldly activities. So Christians can work hard to diet so as to be physically fit, or try to be more patient with people that may annoy us.

However, sometimes inner-worldly activities look different for Christians because of their Christian faith. Thomas Aquinas uses the example of fasting.[21] During Lent Christians may fast and eat less than three square meals a day on, say, Good Friday. To make a sacrifice joining us to the ultimate sacrifice of Christ, and to subordinate our more basic desires for the sake of our deeper desire for the Lord, we eat less than we normally do. This action concerns an inner-worldly activity, i.e., eating, and thus is a matter of the virtue temperance. So fasting Christians are said to be temperate. But on that same day virtuous nonbelievers may eat their standard three square meals. They, too, are eating temperately. How to explain this difference?

Some different virtuous actions are explainable by different circumstances. One person's temperance may entail more food than another's, simply due to a larger body size. But that is not the case here. Both actions are temperate, but they differ not due to circumstances but in their very *meaning*. Nonbelievers are temperate for the sake of natural human flour-

21. See Thomas's *Summa Theologiae* I-II.63.4.

ishing. Christians are temperate for the sake of union with God. The goal of the former's temperance is the natural end of humanity. The goal of the latter's temperance is the supernatural end of humanity's union with God. So the actions differ in meaning, or ultimate goal. They also differ in source. Though Christians may work hard to fast, ultimately these temperate acts require the assistance of God's grace. Since we are incapable of acting on our own for the sake of union with God, this temperance is rightly called "infused" because eating in this way would not be possible without God's grace. Hence in this example we have two different types of virtues: the infused cardinal virtue of temperance (fasting during Lent), and the acquired cardinal virtue of temperance (three squares a day for the nonbeliever).

Eating is certainly not the only inner-worldly activity that is transformed by a Christian's call to union with God, and assisted by God's infused grace. Many worldly activities of Christians are transformed by our relationship with God, and so are done differently. Consider the cardinal virtue fortitude. Firefighters and other first responders can develop this acquired virtue, risking their lives to help citizens in danger. Christians can do this as well, but they see the ultimate act of fortitude to be laying down one's life for one's faith in God, which is called martyrdom. The early church martyrs are fine examples of infused fortitude, as are contemporary figures such as Saint Maximilian Kolbe and Martin Luther King, Jr. Kolbe was willing to lay down his life in place of a fellow prisoner in a Nazi concentration camp, not simply for the natural end of saving a person with a family, but also in imitation of Christ's willingness to die for us and in hope of future union with God beyond this life.

As for the cardinal virtue justice, surely a virtuous non-Christian can be willing to lay down his life for social justice (e.g., racial or economic equality). But a Christian might do this differently. Anyone who has read Martin Luther King's work knows that he was committed to racial equality not only for the sake of humanity's natural end (social justice), but also for the sake of his and humanity's ultimate union with God. He pursued justice in a manner shaped by Christ's injunction to love the enemy, and turn the other cheek. Archbishop Oscar Romero spoke out for economic justice on behalf of the poor not simply because the conditions of his society impeded natural human flourishing, but also because they violated the dignity of people created in God's image, and particularly the poor, for whom God has a special love.

These examples reveal that cardinal virtues, while always concerning inner-worldly activities, actually come in two different stripes. And therefore there are ultimately three types of virtues. First, there are infused theological virtues. These concern God directly, and thus are obtained only with God's grace. Second, there are acquired cardinal virtues. They concern inner-worldly activities. They are accessible to unaided human reason and acquired by our own efforts. They direct us toward human flourishing considered simply at the level of our created human nature. Finally, there are also infused cardinal virtues. These concern inner-worldly activities as well. Yet they incline us to do inner-worldly activities well in the larger perspective of our supernatural destiny. They give a different *meaning* to those activities, commonly leading to different particular actions.

The Significance of the Infused Cardinal Virtues

Why is any of this important? Is it simply an abstract theological claim that there are not only infused theological and acquired cardinal virtues, but also infused cardinal virtues? Categorizations often help us understand more about what is being categorized. This is certainly the case with the infused cardinal virtues. People who neglect the existence of this type of virtue fail to see accurately a crucial facet of the Christian life. They may rightly note that people can acquire on their own certain cardinal virtues concerning inner-worldly activities. And they might even recognize that God helps people to be in right relationship with him by infusing the theological virtues of faith, hope, and love. But if these two categories of virtue were all that existed, something important would be missing. We suggest three reasons for why the infused cardinal virtues are so important in the Christian life, and thus why something is "missing" when they are not attended to.

First, Christian faith transforms not just a person's relationship with God, but also a person's inner-worldly activities. The problem with a twofold categorization of virtue, which attends only to infused theological virtue and acquired cardinal virtue, is its failure to account for how our worldly activities are transformed by our faith. Simply put, Christian faith matters for how we live, including those activities that nonbelievers can do virtuously. We have already seen the case of fasting, which provides an obvious example of Christian faith transforming how one goes about an inner-worldly activity. There are many other such examples. Consider the political example of Saint Thomas More, who refused to acquiesce to King Henry VIII's demand that he recognize an illegitimate marriage. More's infused justice precluded him from doing so, and his infused fortitude gave him the grace to endure martyrdom because of it. Or consider the contemporary example of the United States Bishops, whose stances on political issues differ from our prevailing Republican and Democratic views on justice in their attention to life at all stages, and to the preferential option for the poor. This "infused justice" is not simply the same as secular forms of justice, but rather is transformed by Christian beliefs. The very content of their positions is shaped by the infused cardinal virtue of justice.

As noted above, sometimes the action performed by someone with an acquired cardinal virtue does look the same as one performed by someone with an infused cardinal virtue. If you want a good trainer, his or her faith commitment is probably not very important. And surely people with either infused cardinal virtues or acquired cardinal virtues can pursue racial equality in the manner espoused by King. That said, even in these cases where the external act may be the same, the meaning of the action is still slightly different. The Christian trainer may understand her work as a way of honoring the bodies God gave us, as really a form of worship. The nonbeliever would not consciously share this perspective. Similarly with King, anyone who has read him knows that he understood his work for social justice to be directly related to his own faith and the larger Christian project of helping to instantiate the kingdom of God. A socially just atheist could surely join King, but the overall meaning of the act would be different.

Thus the first reason why we must attend to the infused cardinal virtues is to see how Christian faith transforms a person's inner-worldly activities. At times this leads the believer to different sorts of actions. Different ultimate ends can lead to different understandings of what constitutes truly just, temperate, brave, and prudent action.[22] Yet even when the one with infused cardinal virtue performs acts that appear the same to the external observer as the ones performed by someone with acquired cardinal virtues, those acts nonetheless possess a different overall meaning due to their relation to the supernatural destiny of the person.

The second reason why we must attend to the infused cardinal virtues is the Christian belief that people can *receive God's grace to help them become virtuous,* not just directly in their relationship with God (faith, hope, and love) but also in their inner-worldly activities. This is readily seen in our liturgical and prayer lives. We commonly pray for God's help in being more just, temperate, brave, and prudent people. We trust that God's grace "works" in these areas as well. Consider the example of Saint Paul from

---

22. Recall the third section's discussion about how competing views of "the way things really are" contribute to different understandings of virtuous inner-worldly activity.

Acts 9. He ceased his unjust persecution of Christians due to God's direct intervention. Or consider Saint Augustine, who begged for God's assistance in being rid of his lustful desires, and was granted that help in the famous story of his conversion in the garden.[23]

These are obvious — and dramatic — examples of God's grace helping people with inner-worldly activities. Unfortunately, due to the term "infused" and to the existence of such extraordinary stories of God's grace, people too often assume that infused cardinal virtue is present only when someone has been obviously "zapped" by God's grace in the manner of Saint Paul or Saint Augustine. But God's grace can be just as present and efficacious for people who have less dramatic stories of God's transformative impact on their lives. That grace can be present in the upbringing provided by holy parents, the challenging advice of a close friend, or the helpful example provided by a mentor. We say grace is present when someone is pointed toward his or her supernatural destiny of union with God. Such meaning and context for our virtuous action could not be present without God's help, even when that help comes in less dramatic forms.

Differing from Saints Paul and Augustine are Saints Peter and Thomas Aquinas, who clearly exhibited infused cardinal virtues without extraordinary stories of being "zapped" by God's grace. That does not mean God's grace did not transform their lives; it most certainly did. What makes their cardinal virtues infused was that they came from God, and led to actions whose ultimate purpose was to unite them to God and to neighbors in and through God, which is of course their supernatural end, a destiny unknowable, let alone achievable, without God's help. Acquired cardinal virtues may entail actions with the same "object," but the ultimate source and ultimate goal of those activities would nonetheless be different.

The third and final reason why we must attend to the infused cardinal virtues is encapsulated in the famous Scholastic dictum "Grace perfects — rather than takes away or leaves untouched — nature." We have talked a great deal in this chapter about humanity's natural and supernatural ends. But there are two mistakes that are easy to make when discussing these two distinct ends. First, some assume that they persist as parallel tracks, with no relationship between the two. This chapter has been very explicit in asserting that this is not the case. Even seemingly "nonreligious" activities like physical training, eating, and fighting for racial equality are indeed transformed in the context of one's supernatural destiny. We do not live hermeti-

---

23. Augustine, *Confessions,* trans. Maria Boulding, O.S.B. (New York: Vintage Books, 1997), book 8.

cally sealed "natural" (or inner-worldly) and "supernatural" lives. Grace perfects nature, rather than leaving it untouched.

There is a second error in attending to humanity's two distinct ends. Some people recognize that attention to our supernatural destiny impacts our inner-worldly activities, but go further and claim that believers should no longer seek and experience "natural" flourishing. The natural end is taken away and replaced by the supernatural end. Yet this opposite extreme also defies the Scholastic dictum that grace perfects — but *does not take away* or leave untouched — nature.

Some examples might help make this clear. Thomas again uses the example of fasting. Here is a case where infused temperance makes what one eats (e.g., during Lent) different for the believer. However, the "natural end" of eating is not taken away; rather, it is fulfilled and transcended in the broader context of one's supernatural destiny. How does fasting respect the natural end while transcending it? Doesn't it actually defy our natural end, since three square meals a day is the path to natural human flourishing as it concerns eating? Generally this is so. But just as we might fast a day before surgery, or "carbo-load" the day before a marathon, three square meals a day is not the only way of achieving our natural end. Furthermore, Thomas insists that if we were to fast so stringently that it actually harmed our natural bodily health, then we are fasting inappropriately.[24] Thus, grace fulfills and transcends, but does not destroy or leave unfulfilled, our nature.

In fact, Christians have consistently maintained that though natural human flourishing is in principle accessible to unaided human understanding and action, in reality people are *not* able to live naturally flourishing lives due to the reality and pervasiveness of sin. Saint Thomas claims it is possible to act well toward our natural end, but only occasionally and with much error, primarily due to the finite and broken human condition. Therefore, since God's grace perfects human nature even while transcending it, ironically complete "natural flourishing" is possible only for those who are assisted by God's grace.

A good example of this is the relationship between love and justice. It is in principle possible to be a just person and have a just society without the theological virtue of charity, or love. However, as both the Vatican II document *Gaudium et Spes* and the recent Pope Benedict XVI encyclical *Deus Caritas Est* make clear, charity enables one to more perfectly see the beauty and dignity of other persons. This perfects (rather than leaves untouched,

---

24. See Thomas's *Summa Theologiae* II-II.147.1ad.2. Jean Porter discusses this text in her *Nature as Reason*, p. 390.

or destroys) our ability to be just, giving other persons their due. Thus the person with charity has a different sort of justice. It is still justice since it concerns inner-worldly relations with others. Yet it is transformed by God's grace, and thus rightly called infused justice rather than acquired justice.

One more example may help illuminate this. Consider two believers who are married. As part of their shared life they go to church and understand their marriage to be a sacramental bond sustained by God's grace. But that same grace also sustains them in "natural" aspects of their marriage, aspects of marriage shared by believers and nonbelievers alike. So one spouse may be granted infused virtue to be patient in times of strife and generous with time and attention. The other spouse may be granted infused virtue to be just in handling of finances and chaste in interactions with other people. All these virtues are in principle accessible to unaided reason, and indeed may be acquired by repeated actions and without further reference to any supernatural end by effort. But these Christian spouses are granted not only the infused theological virtues of faith, hope, and love, but also infused cardinal virtues to assist them in the "natural" facets of their marriage, and indeed to transform how those aspects are done in light of their supernatural end. In this case grace has clearly perfected — rather than taken away or left untouched — nature in a manner that may well be more complete than without God's grace.

Conclusion

We have come a long way since the opening of this chapter and the seemingly simple question: What difference does faith make in how a person lives his or her life, especially with regard to those activities engaged in by all people, regardless of faith commitment? The concept of virtue provides a vehicle for explaining how persons can be transformed, and their actions subsequently impacted. The cardinal virtues in particular concern actions in this world, and apply to believers and nonbelievers alike. Nonetheless, how they are practiced is shaped by one's faith commitments. Thus the infused cardinal virtues are essential for understanding how God's grace can transform human action in this world. In dramatic or subtle ways, these virtues equip the believer to live an integrated life of discipleship, such that one's relationship with God truly shapes all one does.

Concurrent Readings

Lewis, C. S. *Mere Christianity*. San Francisco: HarperSanFrancisco, 2001. Lewis offers a helpful and very concise introduction to cardinal virtues in the context of a larger account of Christianity (pp. 76-81).

Porter, Jean. *Nature as Reason: A Thomistic Theory of the Natural Law*. Grand Rapids: Eerdmans, 2005. Porter offers an advanced treatment of Thomistic ethics, and especially the relationship between virtue and other topics such as happiness and natural law.

Thomas Aquinas. *Summa Theologiae*. New York: Benziger Brothers, 1948. The most formative text for this chapter is without a doubt Saint Thomas Aquinas's *Summa Theologiae*, particularly the *Secunda Pars* on the moral life. See especially Thomas's general discussion of habits and virtues (I-II.49-70), and his detailed examination of each theological (II-II.1-46) and cardinal (II-II.47-170) virtue. Thomas himself was very influenced by Aristotle's *Nichomachean Ethics* (books 2-6 are particularly important for the discussion of virtue).

Wadell, Paul. *The Primacy of Love: An Introduction to the Ethics of Thomas Aquinas*. New York: Paulist, 1992. Wadell offers a helpful introduction to Thomistic ethics and virtue in particular (pp. 106-24).

Conclusion to Part 2

Part 2 has examined the moral life from the perspective of Catholic moral thought. It begins, in chapter 5, with the callings embodied in baptism, and chapter 6 explains the formal connections between acts and purposes (such as callings), and between moral judgments and human fulfillment. Our action and activities set a pathway to becoming a certain kind of person who intends to do and does certain kinds of actions among and with others. The chapter on human fulfillment makes the point that our happiness comes through our desire, striving, and openness to be formed by the good. For this reason, happiness is found, not in self-centered grasping, but in self-giving love and includes not only attaining what is good, but also giving up our limited (or limiting) desires. It includes giving things and ourselves away. Likewise, the chapter on natural law attends to the nature of practical reason in terms of human inclinations toward the way of life that will fulfill us. In that chapter human freedom is understood in relationship to the "excellences" of human life — that is, in relationship to the virtues. Chapters 8 and 9 present a framework of the virtues: faith, hope, and love; prudence, justice, fortitude, and temperance. The theological and cardinal virtues are dispositions that not only incline us to act well, but also change who we are. The moral life is movement; life is a journey of transformation.

Part 2 attends to a broad range of topics in moral theory, but it certainly cannot stand on its own. Part 1 is the context or landscape for understanding the journey of part 2. The substance and texture of part 1 give flesh to the concepts in part 2: the categories of happiness, fulfillment, mission, and ministry; of practical reason, freedom, and natural inclinations; and of acquired virtue and infused grace. The conclusion of part 1 notes four themes that carry over from the first four chapters to the pilgrimage of part

2. In an attempt to make connections in this conclusion, we will revisit the four themes (in two groups of two).

Identity (Whose We Are) and Church (Who We Are)

Who we understand ourselves to be is intrinsically related to our choices, actions, and the kinds of everyday practices that we cultivate. Who we are makes sense of what we want to do, and conversely, what we desire to do is indicative of who we are. This point bears directly on the first two chapters of part 2. In chapter 5 James Donohue shows that the identity of baptized Christians puts us in a situation where we are face-to-face with God's call. Certainly, God's love goes to all people, but through baptism Christians are like the first disciples who receive the charge to "Follow me and I will make you fish for people" (Mark 1:17). The identity of the baptized implies a diverse set of callings, with a common call to ministry. In chapter 6 David Cloutier shifts the question from "Who am I?" to "Who am I becoming?" Although the phrase "human fulfillment" suggests that we might reach a point where we finish the job, in this life we are always in the middle of the journey, attracted by various things, conscious of different and sometimes conflicting "identities," and pulled this way and that by diverse communities and ways of life.

What are we to think of the diversity (or fragmentation) and the push and pull of a complicated life? Part 1 proposes a unity that is carried over into all the chapters of part 2. Chapter 1 on liturgy spells out how worship provides an environment and opportunity to respond to and live into God's love for the world. Chapter 2 discusses the liturgy of Easter in order to place the meaning of Jesus' life, death, and resurrection and us (as the readers of the New Testament) into salvation history. The chapter on the Trinity points us to the living out of this history, in all times and places, in the lives of the saints, and the chapter on the pilgrim people defines the church as a people who have been gathered to embody the drama of salvation — the story of sin, forgiveness, and God's invitation to share God's self-giving love for the world.

This drama of God's relationship with the world is the backdrop for the chapters in part 2 on natural law, grace, and freedom, and the infused cardinal virtues. The chapter on natural law proceeds from the presumption that human beings share a common good and inclinations that direct us to the goods that fulfill us. The tradition of natural law fits with the biblical narrative insofar as it focuses on the unity of humanity as created by

God. The tradition has engaged a variety of sources from Aristotle to modern evolutionary psychology, and in this way natural law constitutes a perspective and history of engagement rather than a single theory. Human knowledge and freedom, as human, are always defined within the place, time, and circumstances of our lives. To this degree natural law theories can point to basic human goods and principles of practical reason, but as theories they are always unfinished. Particular judgments include a context-dependent understanding of "what is going on," as well as the virtues of prudence and justice.

According to the chapter on natural law, human knowledge and the freedom to choose and to act on what is good are not neutral; that is, our choices to harm others or to contradict our own good make us less free. The same conception of freedom sets up the problem presented in chapter 8 — the apparent conflict between our moral freedom and God. Michael Miller's account of God's activity in relationship to creation assumes the distinctions between God and creation that are outlined in Bauerschmidt's chapter on the Trinity. Who is God, as God, and in relationship to us? It is this question of God's identity, as creator, that is the groundwork for Miller's point that God's ever-present activity in creation is the very possibility of our freedom. The high point of the drama of salvation is that God gives himself to us in order to set us free. We are quick to blame God for the ways that we (through sin) have made ourselves less free. But God's grace restores creation and elevates us to share life with God.

The chapter on grace, freedom, and the theological virtues (as well as the chapters on human fulfillment and natural law) assumes a distinction between natural and supernatural ends. In modern Catholic theology there is a tendency to separate the two possibilities for fulfillment (the two ends) into two stages or two parallel forms of life. A less widespread, but still problematic, approach is to unify these two kinds of human completion — to equate the "end" available to humans as created by God and the "end" available as redeemed and reconciled by God. On one hand, our nature is assumed to exist outside the realm of grace. Miller discusses this problem using the analogy of "the Natural." On the other hand, our created nature is elided by grace.[1] When distinguishing these two different kinds of potential-for-fulfillment, chapter 8 uses Thomas Aquinas's distinction for how grace operates in us. It restores our nature that has been disordered by

---

1. This problem of "ends" is outlined in the introduction of the book, where we shifted the primary metaphor from the "end" of the journey to our "capacity" for fulfillment.

sin, and it elevates us to a higher fulfillment of shared life with God. Put another way, the self-giving of God does not merely fulfill a capacity that we already have according to our created nature. Through Jesus Christ, we are given a new capacity for an ultimate fulfillment, which also effects our natural capacities and tendencies to attain "this-worldly" goods.

William Mattison's chapter on the cardinal (or moral) and infused cardinal virtues develops these distinctions. He extends Miller's definition of a virtue to the idea that good habits offer a "second nature" that is attained, in the cardinal virtues, through our sustained efforts. (Recall that Miller makes the point that a theological virtue is an abiding "second nature" given through God's grace.) Mattison, then, specifies the acquired virtues that are considered the "hinge" moral dispositions in the Western tradition: prudence, justice, fortitude, and temperance. Finally, he indicates how God's grace elevates the cardinal virtues and transforms how people of faith live in the world. With the infused cardinals, we have capacities for action that have worldly matters as their object (eating, giving our neighbors what they deserve, facing adversity, and so on), but have grace as their source and God as their end.

Practice and Apprenticeship (Discipleship)

These brief comments on the theological and cardinal virtues lead us directly to the themes of practice and apprenticeship. Because part 1 focuses on a theological context of moral reasoning, it attends to specific practices of the Christian life, like the Eucharist, prayer, hearing the word of Scripture, the confession of sin, and works of reconciliation and mercy. These practices reveal a complex interchange of receptivity and action. In relationship to God (in prayer, the Eucharist, and the like), we first of all receive and respond. We are called to follow. In theological terms (specifically in chapter 4: "Pilgrim People"), our action — our apprenticeship — is conceived as a willing openness to be filled by grace — to be an embodiment of God's love for the world.

The chapters in part 2 attend to how doing certain activities and acting certain ways consistently shape us so that we are disposed toward certain goods of life. Our day-to-day practices affect how we see the world and transform our character (i.e., we acquire a second nature), and if the practices are internally good, they dispose us to act on what is good for us and the world. Even the account of natural law, in chapter 7, uses this line of reasoning. Our "natures" are social, and the goods suitable to our natures do not stand apart from ways of life. Within this framework the contributors to parts 1 and 2 have attempted to offer an account of the moral life that attends to how the particular way of discipleship to Jesus Christ enhances our understanding of what it means to be human.

Part 3

The Imitation of Christ:
Issues along the Way

As we move to part 3, let us begin by noting how the structure of the book suggests a methodological claim. The overall shape of the book moves in three parts. We began with our gathering in worship and fundamental theological convictions (Trinity, Christology, ecclesiology). From there we moved to reflection on the human person and important ways of thinking about human action. Within the Catholic tradition such reflection on human persons and action is not separated from our convictions about who God is and how God acts, and the content in part 2 can also be referred to as "theological anthropology." The structure of the book thus far suggests that theological anthropology derives from theology. But for moral theology, this is not the end of the discipline. From the perspective of Christian claims about God's relation to the world, *Gathered for the Journey* intends to make clear, especially in part 3, that Christians are called to serve and to be engaged in issues of justice and human well-being.

We now turn directly to questions and problems of our time. Insofar as the second part of the book extended the sociotheological perspective of part I, we hope it has established a sufficient backdrop for dealing with contemporary issues. Part 3 takes up six issues, demonstrating how one might think about them from a Catholic (and, we hope, "catholic") theological perspective. Unlike the essays in the first two parts of the book, the essays in part 3 do not build on each other. The organization of the chapters is ad hoc. But we believe the chapters are unified by a consistent perspective, a perspective that holds that worship and discipleship shape (and *should* shape) how we see moral questions and act on them.

We hope these essays will complicate "the received wisdom" on their respective topics, pushing readers to think about these issues in new ways.

The essays weave together in compelling ways insights from a wide array of sources: the liturgy, virtue theory, feminist analysis, rhetorical analysis, magisterial documents, the saints, economic theory, cultural commentary, the preferential option for the poor, a commitment to peacemaking, and environmental science. Crossing over typical divisions of "liberal" and "conservative," the essays attempt to display the "grammar of imitation and reflection" or what it means to "incarnate" the faith of the Gospels in the world.

In chapter 10, "Catholic Social Teaching," Kelly Johnson develops connections between questions of justice and our everyday lives, especially in ordinary matters of life in the church. In moral theology, what is typically called "social ethics" is considered a distinct area, as opposed to moral theology in general or other specific areas like bioethics. Likewise, people tend to divide issues of "social justice" from ordinary matters of pursuing a career or raising children, as well as worship and life in Christian community. Johnson helps us understand the problems of this fragmentation, and she offers practical suggestions for integrating Catholic social teaching and everyday life. To do so, she turns to the issue of migration and the U.S. Bishops' pastoral letter *Strangers No Longer*.

William Cavanaugh begins chapter 11 ("Consumer Culture") by explaining that consumerism is "a spiritual disposition, a way of looking at the world around us that is deeply formative." In the body of the chapter he indicates how the modern market and habits of consumption shape a worldview, and he points to Christian worship, specifically the Eucharist, as a formative practice — an alternative pattern of life and consumption. Cavanaugh's key insight on consumerism is that it functions to frustrate and "undo" us; it disengages us from common life and even from the very things we seek to possess. On one level this disengagement produces a constant restlessness; on another level it helps us to be ignorant of the suffering and abuse that are all too commonly part of how our shirts and toys are produced. As an alternative, Cavanaugh spells out a traditional Catholic view of property and our practices of worship, where our consumption of the Eucharist binds us in life-giving community with God and neighbor.

Chapter 12, by Julie Hanlon Rubio, uses homeschooling as a case study to present essential themes in the Christian theology of marriage and family. Homeschooling presents an interesting case because it brings questions of moral formation and basic practices of home life into clear relief. For instance, homeschoolers intend to challenge the modern pattern of flight from home. The household has become like an airport or train terminal: a place to wait to go to the next place. In this way family life and home are increasingly becoming a reflection of the market culture as described by William Cavanaugh's chapter on consumerism. Homeschoolers work to make their homes alternative places of human "cultivation" — communities of production and moral formation. Within this contrast of cultures and cultivations, Rubio sets her discussion of Christian theology on children and parenting. In the background is the traditional idea of family as "domestic church." Rubio argues that Christian parents are called to take the time to develop their homes as schools of virtue.

In chapter 13 Tobias Winright — theologian and former police officer — turns to questions of just war and pacifism. Taking up the directive of the Second Vatican Council, as well as the increasingly imperative counsel coming from the U.S. Bishops and the Vatican, Winright explores what it might mean to "undertake an evaluation of war with an entirely new attitude." Winright, who would not classify himself as a pacifist, takes issue with the regnant attitude toward war in the United States, even among Catholic commentators, that takes the justice of our own nation's wars as a default position. He challenges those who would interpret the just war tradition as not being rooted in a presumption against war. Through careful analysis of the scriptural record (both Testaments) as well as a rich analysis of Catholic liturgy, Winright demonstrates the overriding nature of the Christian commitment to peace and peacemaking.

Chapter 14 displays what a commitment to peacemaking might look like within the field of bioethics. Here M. Therese Lysaught takes on the debacle of the Terri Schiavo case. The media war that surrounded the Schiavo case highlighted a conflict over whether or not medically assisted nutrition and hydration could be withdrawn from a woman in a persistent vegetative state. Lysaught identifies the layers of hostility, enmity, and violence that characterized the actions of parties to both sides of the case — even Christians! She demonstrates how behind this enmity lay particular theological convictions — ones deeply at odds with orthodox Christian beliefs. Yet, the final vigil for Terri Schiavo unfolded during Holy Week. Drawing on the Holy Week narrative, in which Christians participate year after year, Lysaught begins to build an alternative framework for responding to the end of life rooted in reconciliation. Such a framework she finds embodied in the life of Joseph Cardinal Bernardin, whose story shows what it looks like to "incarnate" Holy Week into the world.

Part 3 closes with Jeanne Heffernan Schindler's chapter on environmental ethics. Again, complicating categories, Schindler redescribes environmental ethics as social ethics. Making clear the extent of the world's growing environmental crisis, she calls for Catholics and Christians to both form their consciences around the issue of the environment and work toward developing a comprehensive ethic. She notes how such a call marks an important — and often overlooked — convergence of the Catholic/Christian and scientific communities. Such an ethic, she argues, would be rooted in the Christian commitment to the sacramentality of creation (a theological conviction), the tradition of Catholic social thought (theological anthropology), and the resources of the spiritual life (worship).

The editors and contributors have not intentionally integrated the chapters, as is the case in parts 1 and 2. However, we hope you will read these essays not only in relationship to the methodological chapters (chapters 1–9), but also as a real-time conversation among friends and colleagues about the shape of Christian service and love in the world. Schindler's chapter can be read fruitfully in conversation with Johnson's and Cavanaugh's chapters. Likewise, connections are readily apparent between Winright's and Lysaught's, as well as between Cavanaugh's and Rubio's. Part 3 reveals an unplanned yet common approach to contemporary issues.

Chapter 10

Catholic Social Teaching

KELLY S. JOHNSON

After the death of John Paul II, one of the more unexpected voices to join in honoring him was Bono, lead singer of U2 and social justice activist. The two met in 1999 regarding efforts to gain debt relief for the world's poorest nations. Bono praised the pope as a "wily campaigner on behalf of the world's poor" and claimed he had been moved to tears at the cost to John Paul to stand and speak on the issue. The pope's passion was unmistakable. But Bono also recalled that during the meeting the pope kept looking at his trademark sunglasses. Thinking perhaps they were offensive in that setting, Bono took them off. But at the end of the meeting, he realized that the pope still had his eye on them. When he received blessed rosary beads from the pope, Bono offered him the sunglasses, and John Paul not only accepted them but also immediately put them on with what Bono called "the wickedest smile."[1]

It's a peculiar moment: in the face of a serious, even grim, situation for millions of the world's poorest people, the pope makes a rock star laugh. Gathered to discuss a complex economic and political reality, a topic for grief, outrage, and attention to the tedious detail of finance and law, they crack each other up. It is disturbing in the same way as the scene in Mark 14, when a woman prophetically anoints Jesus, showing him to be "the Anointed One," which is to say the Messiah, the Christ. Onlookers protested, the Gospel says, that the oil should have been sold and its price, a year's wages for a laborer, given to the poor. Can concern for justice partner with the delightful wastefulness of comedy, worship, art, human affection?

---

1. Edna Gundersen, "Bono Recalls Pontiff's Affection for the Poor — and Cool Sunglasses," *USA Today,* April 4, 2005, p. 2D.

This is, in fact, a deep problem in the way Catholics think about the church and social justice. People loved John Paul II for his enthusiasm for youth, for his soccer playing and theatrical background, for forgiving his own attacker and asking forgiveness from the world's Jews, for his personal charisma. His positions on the importance of indirect employers in the global economy or the rights of migrants or, Bono's efforts notwithstanding, Third World debt are much less well-known and seem to many rather dour in comparison. Often in parish life and campus ministry, we find some tension between those most committed to social justice and those working on details of caring for the local church community and enriching its liturgy, between those who expect the church to focus on justice and those who expect the parish to be a place of contemplative beauty or a friendly community of families. Nevertheless, the answer in Catholic teaching is not merely that justice, prayer, and friendship can coexist, but that they must. To unpack this claim, we'll look first at the state of attempts to make Catholic teaching on social justice a more central element in Catholic life; then at reasons why that attempt has not been altogether successful; and finally at an example of what a better kind of integration looks like.

Principles of Catholic Social Teaching

In their 1998 pastoral letter on the church's social teaching, the U.S. Catholic bishops noted that a study done by a task force of the bishops conference showed that "far too many Catholics are not familiar with the basic content of Catholic social teaching. More fundamentally, many Catholics do not adequately understand that the social teaching of the Church is an essential part of Catholic faith. This poses a serious challenge for all Catholics, since it weakens our capacity to be a Church that is true to the demands of the Gospel."[2] The bishops commend to readers the documents that have become the canon of Catholic social teaching, a series of encyclicals, pastorals, and conciliar documents starting with *Rerum Novarum* in 1891. But they also devised a brief list of themes, the description of which takes up barely more than two pages, so that those not so eager to plow through the hundreds of rather dense pages of the major documents could gain quick access to the

---

2. United States Conference of Catholic Bishops (USCCB), *Sharing Catholic Social Teaching: Challenges and Directions* (Washington, D.C.: USCCB, 1988). The document can be found on the USCCB Web site, http://www.usccb.org/sdwp/projects/socialteaching/socialteaching.htm. The quotation is the epigraph and on page 4.

essential characteristics of the teaching. The bishops provided an introduction to Catholic social teaching through seven of its central themes: the life and dignity of the human person; the call to family, community, and participation; rights and responsibilities; the option for the poor and vulnerable; the dignity of work and the rights of workers; solidarity; and care for God's creation.[3]

Anyone who has faced a volume full of encyclical letters can understand that such simplification is helpful, and given the appalling state of ignorance among Catholics, we might even say it is necessary. Certainly the bishops' intention is admirable, but the resulting themes are a little lacking in punch. It is not that they are not important; they simply seem obvious and relatively uninteresting. Who, for example, isn't in favor of "human dignity"? As an abstraction, it simply does not have the kind of clear content that would call for passionate commitment. Christian slave owners once argued that they were supervising barely human creatures who had become more dignified in the process of being enslaved; many who witness the final stages of painful and debilitating diseases now wonder if human dignity does not require euthanasia; the dominant economic practices of the West honor the designers and marketers of weaponry far more than they do teachers and farmers. The value of human dignity as such is not contested. What is contested is who counts as a person, what "dignity" requires, and how it is to be upheld when it costs something to others.

In fact, the teaching to which these brief themes refer is far from vague or empty in answering those questions. In Catholic thought "human dignity" is connected to an anthropology that is really Christology. John Paul II spoke of the human person as the way of the church, because Jesus is the Way and he has united himself with the human family and with each person.[4] The church, he was claiming, is not about demanding that people fit into a system or ideology: it is about love of the actual persons who are God's family, even when those persons don't fit into political programs or even when they complicate received theological notions. The church works this way because God works this way. Each human is personally called to union with God, to be another Christ by adoption. The dignity of the person is not something we achieve ourselves or give to one another — it is intrinsic in a person's creation by the Father of Jesus, in his or her redemption, and in his or her destiny as a member of God's family. Human dignity is assured by God and is most fully seen in the holiness of the saints.

3. USCCB, *Sharing Catholic Social Teaching*, pp. 4-6.
4. John Paul II, *Redemptor Hominis* (Vatican City: Libreria Editrice Vaticana, 1979), §14.

John Paul II particularly developed this sense of human dignity in his encyclical letter *Evangelium Vitae,* where he contrasted a Christian sense of the human person with a "Promethean" anthropology, which holds that dignified humans make themselves, control their own lives, and therefore are strong and self-sufficient.[5] This heroic image of human dignity has led some societies to treat those who do not live up to the standard as better off dead. The weak, the sick, the dependent, the young, the old, the Jew, the foreigner, the manual laborer, the female: in each case a desire to "honor human dignity" can bear a strange resemblance to "the weak should be destroyed." Criminals are executed, the sick are encouraged to consider suicide, workers are left in sweatshops at starvation wages, bombs are dropped on residential neighborhoods, all in the name of building up a free and healthy society, one in which human dignity flourishes. The rhetoric of human dignity, when it refers to the glorification of independent strength, can end up meaning death for those who don't fit in.

John Paul II argued in *Dives in Misericordia* that as we meditate on the dignity of the person before the crucifix, we have to consider justice, dignity, and fragile, suffering humanity in a different way. The highest imaginable human life in the world as we know it is not one of strength and independence. It is, rather, Jesus' torn, immobile body, the weeping and helpless mother, the repentant thief, the cowardly followers. These are not failures of human dignity, but they are love enduring the horrors of a sinful world. In Catholic teaching, preserving human dignity means not escaping need and weakness, but loving each other in the midst of it.[6]

This embrace of weakness and self-sacrificial love does not however mean that self-destruction is somehow virtuous. Catholic teaching is about human *dignity,* rightly understood. The bishops' themes of Catholic social teaching regarding family, community, and participation illustrate that in Catholic thought, human dignity is always a social category, because humans are social and human fulfillment cannot be achieved alone. As the achievement of love, human dignity requires our connection to each other, mutual care, friendship. A full human life is one of participation in communities great and small by contributing to the shared good of the common life, which means by carrying out one's responsibilities and honoring the rights of others as they carry out theirs. In this cycle of mutual care and respect, we discover how interdependent we are, how our fates are connected — and as we embrace that connection, we carry out the call to soli-

5. John Paul II, *Evangelium Vitae* (Vatican City: Libreria Editrice Vaticana, 1995), §15.
6. John Paul II, *Dives in Misericordia* (Vatican City: Libreria Editrice Vaticana, 1980).

darity. John Paul II first took up the resonant term "solidarity" in the years when the labor union of that name was suppressed in his homeland, Poland. But as Catholic teaching attended more to globalization, the term came to name particularly the bonds of human unity that exist and must be fostered internationally. Financially, politically, in environment and culture, and even spiritually, humans are interconnected and can live well only when they attend to those bonds.

Conversely, human sin exists within a social context and can even be hardened into "structures of sin." The problem of debt in the world's most impoverished nations, for example, belongs not only to the category of individual sin. Certainly at the inception of the crisis, lenders looking for ways to invest capital behaved reprehensibly, providing loans that could not reasonably be expected to be repaid in full but that would, at least, bring in significant interest payments for years to come. Leaders of countries that snapped up such deals also in many cases sinned in their misuse of funds that should have been invested for the common good of their people. Now that the amount of the original debt has long ago been repaid but payments on the accumulated interest require cuts to health care, education, and infrastructure in already-fragile societies, those who could release the debtors but refuse to do so may be guilty of rapacious greed. For that matter, citizens who have access to information and potentially have influence over the way debt is administered but fail to act are themselves caught in sins, often of despair or sloth. But the problem of indebted nations cannot be defined correctly only in these terms. It is not a matter only of individual sin, but of structures of financial bureaucracy, economic habits, and international political systems within and among the world's nations. Debt has implications for trade balance, exchange rates, and international relations, and addressing it requires attention to the way those structures themselves have become sinfully disordered. Building up our ability to address such wrongs requires attention to social habits of consumption, investment, and leisure, because the sinfulness of individuals comes about within social structures and builds up such structures, which themselves complicate and perpetuate sin.

Because modern societies tend to abuse them, the bishops then name three areas for particular attention: the option for the poor, the rights of workers, and care for creation. Although Catholicism has always been concerned for those living in poverty, the "option for the poor" came out of recognition in the late 1960s and early 1970s that the church had to take sides in the political and economic issues of the day. Refusal to take a side on an issue like land reform in a society where the great majority of the population remained trapped in economic patterns established under colonial rule implicitly meant favoring the status quo, the power of those who already held money and influence and who had demonstrated a vicious addiction to them. Catholics are to choose in these cases to stand with the poor and to judge every decision by how it will impact those who are most vulnerable. More than that, solidarity with the poor means sharing in the risks they take as they defend their humanity.

John Paul II, with his own experience of World War II, held up as the model of solidarity Maximilian Kolbe, who offered to die in the place of another prisoner in a Nazi camp.[7] In this respect, the practice of Latin American Catholic leaders who defended the poor and therefore shared in their deaths — people like Ignacio Ellacuria, Oscar Romero, Rutilio Grande — has powerfully impacted the thinking of the church. More recently, the Brazilian landless movement, Movimiento Sem Terra, has used constitutional provisions in Brazil to argue for the redistribution of land, and as peasants occupy land to force the issue, Catholic leaders have supported them and shared in their struggle. Dorothy Stang, a Catholic sister from Ohio, sealed her solidarity with that movement with her death at the hands of assassins in 2004. As I write, the fate of four Western Christians who lived in Baghdad in solidarity with the suffering of civilians and fighters there, recently kidnapped by opponents of U.S. forces in Iraq, is still unknown.

Attention to the environment is a relatively recent addition to the social teaching of the church, but it has gained momentum, especially as leaders realize that human well-being is inseparable from care for creation and that environmental damages disproportionately affect the poor. Seen in that light, the recent environmental awareness continues the long-standing concern in Catholic teaching for farmers and rural communities, whose work is essential for the well-being of all and whose culture of interdependence, family, and hard work is so conducive to understanding of the common good. While the language of environmentalism is relatively new to Catholic social teaching, concern for the land and those who work it has been pivotal from the beginning. It is not surprising, given the sacramentalism and the long history of Catholic thinking, that agriculture remains in Catholic thought the heart of the economy. The production of food in all its phases, the more immediate work of each year's planting and harvesting as well as the long-range care of the land's fertility, is the sine qua non of all human productive activity, and those who

7. John Paul II, *Sollicitudo Rei Socialis* (Vatican City: Libreria Editrice Vaticana, 1987), §40.

specialize in producing healthful food are particularly honored among workers.

But it is not only farmers and farm laborers whose work concerns the church. In fact, the document usually referred to as the beginning of Catholic social teaching argues at length on behalf of factory workers' rights. Church teaching always rejected the materialism and presumption of class conflict in Marxism, but Leo XIII did teach that workers could not be treated as commodities, as mere "labor power." Rather, they are persons contributing to the common good of all, and as such, they have rights related to their duties: a right to rest, a right to a wage sufficient to keep a family in "comfort," a right to time off for worship, a right to safety in the workplace, a right to earn and keep property, and even a right to organize into associations that could keep the greed of owners in check.[8] Lest these rights be understood merely as limitations on the damage that can be caused to workers, Catholic teaching emphasizes the goodness and joy of creative labor. Humans are creative, and human dignity includes the power to do good work. Therefore a successful business not only makes a profit, not only contributes to the common good, but also honors and fosters the creativity of its workers, allowing them to participate as persons rather than as mere "labor." The aim of effectively producing goods (the objective aspect of work) should not override the aim of honoring and cultivating human activity (the subjective aspect of work). It is not a question of reducing effective production, but of recognizing that any organization of work that reduces humans to mindless cogs or mere units of production is harming, rather than contributing to, the common good.[9]

Catholic social teaching must by nature be general enough to apply internationally across a wide range of specific cases. It is not, however, lacking in challenging and coherent content that amounts to an impassioned argument for forms of life that build up the joy and beauty humans so long to know.

Why Don't More Catholics Know and Care about This?

The bishops, confronted with evidence that Catholics have little knowledge of or commitment to this rich tradition of social teaching, developed these

---

8. Leo XIII, *Rerum Novarum* (Vatican City: Libreria Editrice Vaticana, 1891), §40-50.

9. John Paul II, *Laborem Exercens* (Vatican City: Libreria Editrice Vaticana, 1981), §6, 9, 14-17, and passim.

themes to make the teaching more accessible. Ironically, though, the themes may themselves be part of the problem. Most devoted Catholics go to Mass, pray at night and before meals; they marry and have children; they struggle to act kindly and to speak truthfully, and they confess their failure to do as much (or at least they know they should). The Catholic social teaching of church documents — whether in weighty volumes or concentrated into a list of PowerPoint themes — is not part of the devotional, emotional, personal faith of most Catholics. It is quite possible to be a practicing Catholic and neither know nor be committed to social teaching, precisely because it is partitioned off as "social teaching." As such, it is distinct from Catholic life and faith, more broadly conceived.

The problem, then, is not just that people need to know about the teaching, but that the teaching needs to be more clearly integrated into the ordinary life of faith. Happily, such integration is not at all difficult. When we pay attention, we can see that it already exists and needs only to be named and encouraged. "Social issues" are the common stuff of Catholic lay life, when we talk about them in a more full-blooded way.

For example, most Catholics are more conversant with the church's teaching on sex and medicine than they are with social teaching. Perhaps that is because these teachings deal with our bodies and families, our most important emotional ties, and these, more than starvation or human rights, have priority of place in the hearts of U.S. Catholics these days. But it is also true that the sacraments accompany us through our sickness and our marriages and births and deaths. There are designated liturgical markers — baptisms, marriages, anointing, funerals — where moral teaching, our deepest emotional concerns, and our devotional lives meet. One cannot live an ordinary Catholic life without meeting sexual and medical teaching as intrinsic to the life of faith, with its sorrows and joys. But social teaching, it seems, exists only in documents, not in sacraments or ordinary devotional life.

The appearance that medical and sexual ethics are more personal and more sacramental than social ethics is based on two mistakes. First, the distinction between the fields is artificial: medical and sexual issues are social issues, and vice versa. Medical ethics, like social ethics, is concerned with the distribution of goods and with human dignity. Poverty, workers' rights, and environmental issues all have medical significance. Catholic teaching on contraception exists in relation to discussions of a just wage: the justice of a wage hinges on the responsibility parents have to raise their children. A wage must be sufficient to permit people to fulfill that obligation. *Rerum Novarum* opposed women's participation in factory work because the demand that both parents work was seen as an infringement on the just wage. Population control is perhaps the clearest moment for connecting Catholic social teaching with matters sexual and medical: opposition to artificial means of birth control is a part of the church's option for the poor, not a contrast with it. What is needed, according to John Paul II, is not "anti-birth policies," but "serious family and social policies, programs of cultural development and of fair production and distribution of resources."[10] Population growth is not a problem located in the fertility of poor women. It is an economic problem, as impoverished parents see having more children as a way to increase their few assets; it is also a cultural problem, as women find themselves required to be sexually available to men on demand; and these matters are profoundly interrelated in Catholic teaching.[11] Sexual ethics and social ethics are not alien categories, and the extent to which U.S. Catholics tend to favor either one or the other indicates that they mirror Democrat versus Republican politics, instead of attending to their own coherent teaching.

Second, Catholic social teaching is embodied in liturgical practice, although this is often not recognized. What is the eucharistic celebration if not a gathering for reconciliation and sharing of goods, a site to confront and subvert the pain of our mutual isolation, enmity, and competition for survival by recalling us to God's plenty and peace, established in Christ's life, death, and resurrection? While documents that establish details of Catholic teaching are essential for the church's witness within a world of political and economic complexities, those documents should be understood as reflections on the eucharistic life of the church, just as sexual teaching is a reflection on the baptismal and marriage vows, and medical ethics are tied to anointing and Christian burial.

It is, in this light, very strange that parish life and liturgy are commonly assumed to be distinct from social teaching. This distinction presumes that the "society" referred to in social justice is never the church itself. This presumption is so strong that concerns about social justice within the church itself are quite the exception in social justice discussions. As power is assumed to lie in the government and business, so the government and business are the foci of social justice. But this presumption is historically only very recent. Through most of its history the church has understood itself and lived its life as a public fabric, as a society, not as a private

---

10. John Paul II, *Evangelium Vitae*, §16.

11. David M. McCarthy, "Procreation, the Development of Peoples, and the Final Destiny of Humanity," *Communio* 26 (Winter 1999): 698-721.

233

conviction of an individual who belongs to a secular public. In Augustine's *City of God,* the "city of man" institutions are pale shadows, existing for the time being, of the true and lasting society, the City of God. We don't have to claim perfect identification between the church and the City of God to draw the conclusion that as it gathers for public worship the church is the society par excellence, and so social justice should pertain more often, rather than less often, to the church.

In this regard, it is useful to recall that worship is an act of justice, as the creature renders what it owes to the Creator. In the Eucharist, the "source and summit" of Christian life, people gather in a peace created by God and make peace with each other, sharing material and spiritual goods. In baptism that community is built up, and in penance it is restored. In ordination leaders who will be servants obedient to God are appointed. In weddings the whole community commits to the couple as the couple commit to each other in a faithful, forbearing love that witnesses to God's love. In the anointing of the sick, the isolation of illness and death is broken. In fact, these ceremonies have at times had much richer practical social significance. Weddings have been occasions for peacemaking between the families of bride and groom; the choice of godparents establishes bonds of trust to build peace; and deathbed rituals, including the tolling of the bell that would let everyone in town know that the time was near, were an opportunity for reconciliation and reparations.[12] Guilds existed for business purposes as well as for devotional life, charitable work, and mutual aid. The church's own most characteristic acts are practices of social justice within its own society, for the sake of all societies.

The idea, then, that social justice is simply something to be achieved outside the life of the church is an impoverishment of sense of the church, as though we were in it as individuals whose "society" could only be found elsewhere. In fact, the life of the church, the witness of the saints, and the practices of devotion are sites of justice, necessary aids to other works of justice, and witnesses to the rest of the world of what God's peace looks like.

One of the most telling flaws in the way Catholics commonly use the category "social justice" is its apparent separation from mercy, charity, and grace. It is true that the church's social teaching condemns the false charity that consists in offering minuscule and unsystematic assistance as a way of distracting attention from large and systematic injustice. But it is not true

12. See John Bossy, *Christianity in the West, 1400-1700* (Oxford: Oxford University Press, 1985). In spite of the title, Bossy does discuss customs predating 1400, to demonstrate the changes that occur after that date.

that Christian accounts of social justice can exist removed from the commands to love God, to love one's neighbor, and to love one's enemy.

Our account of justice needs charity because our understanding of justice, rendering what is due, depends upon what we think is due to whom. Imagine a society of individuals competing on a level playing field — free from loyalties, complicated histories, spiritual destinies — simply getting what they earn. In such a world one could claim that mercy, charity, and grace are violations of justice. They give what is not earned. But this is not the way Catholicism sees the world. All things are created from nothing, sinners were redeemed by an innocent, and forgiveness is not only possible but also a continual necessity and a mutual obligation. If the world is to achieve its purpose, which is to say, if justice is to be served, then mercy is necessary. Justice exists within this larger narrative of grace. What is due to my neighbor? The love of Christ, which offers itself to each creature and for which each person is created. Social justice is premised on mercy, for as Christians well know, if justice were served without mercy, then we'd have to acknowledge with Clint Eastwood's character in *Unforgiven* that "We all have it coming." Justice is not always served by a strict accounting of earnings, but by actions that uphold, witness to, or restore the order God intends for creation. Thus the justice question regarding wages or the death penalty (or even the debt of impoverished nations) is not "Did the person earn this penalty or benefit?" but "How can this person's dignity as creature and potential friend of God be restored, attested, honored?"

The category "social justice" suggests to some devout Catholics a sphere of cold legal disputes, angry demonstrations, and calculated compromises. But it is also the work of mercy and charity, the creative work of self-sacrificial love, and hope in God's power to make new a world of sin. It is the sphere of Christian friendship. Far from denying the comfort of Christian hope for mercy and eternal bliss, a right understanding of Catholic teaching on the social order sees it as precisely the sphere in which we most need such hope and in which that hope gains its foothold, through the work of grace among us. Only such hope can prevent social justice from turning into the tyrannical and Pelagian effort to create a just society through violence.

This larger version of Catholic social teaching including ecclesial life, liturgy, and mercy means that social teaching is, like all Catholic teaching, about holiness. Those who know the lives of the saints know about social justice, whether they realize it or not. Dorothy Day, a pacifist and ardent critic of capitalism, claimed that Thérèse of Lisieux was the saint most needed by social activists, because Thérèse taught the "little way" of love: a

Christian can live a heroic life of sanctity and can change the world by doing small, hidden things with love. In an era of global crises that provoke apathy in some and violence in others, Thérèse shows Catholic activists the path of one who trusts in the power of the cross. It is the faithful, painstaking work of love that transforms the world.[13] This is not to say that Bono and John Paul II were mistaken to try to gain debt relief for the world's poorest nations. Far from it: each meeting, each hour of research, each letter was a work of love to be done with reverence and hope. In the midst of global crises, Thérèse reminds us that in every moment, in every work, we are to recall with joy that each person is Christ's beloved. As it turns out, then, an ailing pope striking a pose in rock star sunglasses may be a fine icon of Christian commitment to social justice.

Case Study in the Integration of Justice and Beauty

It may be useful to see all these themes working together in a particular case. For Catholics in the United States, a particularly pressing and complex matter is the question of immigration policy for Mexicans. The United States gives only a small number of these immigrants legal permission to work in the country each year, but because of political and economic pressures in their home countries, many enter the United States and join its workforce anyway. Some of these immigrants have false papers sufficiently convincing to gain them entry into jobs. Others work off the books or for employers who are quite willing to overlook the lack of valid documents. Because of their lack of documentation, these workers are particularly vulnerable to employer abuse — low wages or even refusal to pay for work done; unsafe or inhumane working conditions; mandatory long hours without overtime; and even physical abuse, sometimes inflicted on workers who attempt to walk away from a job, resulting in a kind of enslavement.

Mexican immigrants are often Catholic, and so the Catholic Church in the United States has found itself in a difficult situation: U.S. law names undocumented immigrants as illegal aliens, criminals subject to deportation, and Catholic teaching affirms the responsibility of the duly constituted public authority to make laws concerning the common welfare. But within Catholic parishes these same "illegals" are fellow members of the body of Christ, workers whose rights are proclaimed in Catholic teaching,

---

13. *Dorothy Day: Selected Writings*, ed. Robert Ellsberg (Maryknoll, N.Y.: Orbis, 2005), pp. 185-204.

and members of the class of the poor and vulnerable to whom the church is particularly committed.

In a move that proclaimed clearly the church's international identity, the U.S. and Mexican bishops published a joint letter on this issue in 2003. *Strangers No Longer* drew on basic principles of Catholic social teaching to claim both that workers have the right to seek employment where it could be found and also that governments have the right to set laws governing immigration, within reason and keeping in mind the moral imperative of a nation to act toward the common good of all, and not exclusively for its own citizens.[14] The letter examines the problems of refugees, temporary workers, and those seeking permanent residence, emphasizing the need for policies that protect them and allow for their legitimate participation in their new society. While the bishops recognize the need to protect the interests of natives, they insist that nations with more security and opportunity have a greater obligation to welcome those who flee violence and/or poverty at home.

In this basic position we can see the bishops' seven themes at work, particularly in the affirmation of human dignity and of workers' rights, concern for the common good, and the rights and responsibilities of government. We should not be surprised that the letter puts some emphasis on the challenges migration poses to families and communities, nor that the bishops' approach is characterized by a concern to protect those most vulnerable. While the bishops affirm that migration is both necessary and valuable, they see that it is often a result of social crises in the home country, for example, those springing from debt incurred in the petrodollar lending spree of the 1970s or trade agreements that have undermined local economies. In these examples the real issue is the failure of nations to understand their economic, political, environmental, and spiritual solidarity. Human dignity, workers' rights, and the integrity of families and cultures are better served by building up local economies so that each nation can be strong enough to provide for those who call it home. The letter is permeated with the notion of solidarity, as it works first to make clear the interdependence of all parties and second to advocate policies that embody and will increase the commitment to the well-being of all.

But to read the pastoral simply as an application of these principles is to miss much of its import. Were the bishops offering policy positions only to the two nations, the documents would be of mostly academic interest:

14. United States Conference of Catholic Bishops, *Strangers No Longer: Together on the Journey of Hope* (Washington, D.C.: USCCB, 2003).

neither Mexico nor the United States is bound by its laws or its philosophy to pay heed to Catholic teaching. But this pastoral letter also addresses the church and its own politics within which migration is occurring. It cites John Paul II's 1993 World Day of Migration speech, in which he claimed that "the families of migrants . . . should be able to find a homeland everywhere in the Church." The goal is communion, expressed in hospitality. The celebration of the liturgy, in particular, must be an event of peaceable communion for all the baptized, an occurrence where all are honored and feel at home, where the culture and language of the migrant is respected. Ministry to migrants, whether in farmworkers' camps or in jails or in urban parishes, is called for, both from the migrants themselves and from the U.S. citizens around them.

But the most systematically significant section is a long treatment of cross-border collaboration within the church. Such collaboration is needed to train more ministers to accompany migrants as they shift between cultures, to prepare catechetical materials, to improve legal and social services, to improve hospitality along the border, and to offer opportunities for prayer to those making the journey, and opportunities to remember the many who have died along the way.

The discussion of pastoral or ecclesial issues transforms this letter. Insofar as Catholic social teaching is about encouraging modern governments to respect workers' rights and human dignity, the arguments are abstract and general and the recommendations seem to underestimate the necessity in a democratic polity for politicians to be seen to protect the interests of their constituents against real or imaginary outsiders. But when the bishops speak to the church, it becomes clear that this community must address this issue and that it has the occasion, the expertise, the resources, and the international reach to practice an alternative politics in this matter.

Moreover, the teaching addresses immediate local and personal concerns, as communities begin to realize that the parish identity is changing as migrants claim their place. In the turn to the church as a society, the bishops' plea for the United States to protect the rights of refugees and migrants has its own constituency, a site of resistance and a leaven for the larger society. And this is not a theoretical constituency: in Mexico "more than four dozen church-sponsored migrant houses await [migrants traveling north], like way stations along a modern pilgrimage route."[15] Church

15. Barbara Fraser and Paul Jeffrey, "Perilous Journey," *National Catholic Reporter,* August 13, 2004.

groups provide water and medical care in the desert, where hundreds of migrants die each year; they visit and provide support for jailed migrants; they provide safe places for the migrants' culture and language to survive. With support from Catholic Relief Services, the archdiocese of Hermosillo in Mexico has partnered with the dioceses of Tucson and Phoenix in a "diocese without borders" program, aimed at helping Catholics on both sides of the border to see their unity in the church, to practice solidarity.

Migrants have brought with them their devotions, and the shared practice of honoring Mary as *la morenita* (the little brown one), the virgin of Guadalupe; reliving Mary and Joseph's search for shelter in Bethlehem in the *posadas;* and grieving together at the sorrows of life in this sinful world during the Good Friday procession have become occasions for Catholics in the United States to grow in their faith as they honor the dignity of Mexican customs. Similarly, the struggle of Catholics of all nationalities to worship together in the Eucharist is clearly both a liturgical issue and a matter of justice as we share limited resources of space and personnel and attempt to overcome prejudices. How we worship, with whom, and in what spirit — these are questions of social justice, as well as matters for growth in faith and love.

The work of justice *is* a matter of facing horrors and refusing to look away. It is also a work of attention to detail, study of systems and statistics, but for the church it is always also a work of friendship, beauty, and holiness, because it is the work of meeting Jesus' Spirit in our brothers and sisters. At a Mass I attended in Tennessee recently, a priest from Mexico introduced himself as the new assistant pastor to his mostly gringo congregation. His devotion and warmth were clear, though his English was not always. One member of the congregation noted afterward, "I like him, but it's unfortunate that his first Sunday here he preached on the text 'His "joke" is easy and his burden light.'" But perhaps, for those of us accustomed to seeing social teaching as grim, dry, and abstract, cross-border migration is precisely an invitation to see the emotion, beauty, and joy of justice in Christian life.

Concurrent Reading

Day, Dorothy. "Therese." In *Dorothy Day: Selected Writings,* edited by Robert Ellsberg, pp. 185-204. Maryknoll, N.Y.: Orbis, 2005. Saint Thérèse of Lisieux (1873-1897) was a Carmelite who lived a short and quiet life, but after her death quickly became known for her aspirations to be a saint by a "little way." In her piece on Thérèse, Day discusses the political implications of the little way.

Goizueta, Roberto. *Caminemos con Jesus: Toward a Hispanic/Latino Theology of Accompaniment.* Maryknoll, N.Y.: Orbis, 1995. Goizueta offers a refreshing look at the church and the way of following Jesus, and gives an insightful account of the role of community in our lives.

John Paul II. *Dives in Misericordia.* Vatican City: Libreria Editrice Vaticana, 1980. The pope reflects on human life in relationship to the incarnation, death, and resurrection. The document can be found on the Vatican Web site, http://www.vatican.va/holy_father/john_paul_ii/encyclicals/documents/hf_jp-ii_enc_30111980_dives-in-misericordia_en.html.

United States Conference of Catholic Bishops. *Sharing Catholic Social Teaching: Challenges and Directions.* Washington, D.C.: USCCB, 1988. The document outlines major themes in Catholic social teaching and offers directives for integrating these teachings into the life of the church. Find the document on the U.S. Bishops' Web site: http://www.usccb.org/sdwp/projects/socialteaching/socialteaching.htm.

Chapter 11

Consumer Culture

WILLIAM T. CAVANAUGH

In January 2005 a twenty-year-old Nebraska college student auctioned off advertising space on his forehead. The winning bid was over $37,000. For that princely sum, the man spent thirty days with a temporary tattoo on his forehead extolling the virtues of a snoring remedy. Although the actual forehead would be seen by a limited number of people, the manufacturer hoped to benefit by the worldwide publicity that the human ad campaign generated. The human billboard himself was quoted as saying, "The way I see it, I'm selling something I already own; after 30 days I get it back."[1]

It would be easy to approach this story — and consumerism in general — with some stern finger wagging about the greed of people these days. "People will do anything for money. Everybody wants more, and nobody wants to share with those who have less. The world would be a better place if we all shared." And so on. But what makes consumer culture worth talking about from the point of view of moral theology is not primarily greed. The Nebraska man pulled this stunt to pay for his college education, not apparently out of plain greed. What is interesting about this story for our purposes is the way it illustrates something more basic about a consumer culture: its ability to turn virtually anything into a commodity, that is, something to be bought and sold.

The Christian tradition has always condemned greed, also called avarice. Jesus denounces storing up treasures on earth (Matt. 6:19-21). Paul at-

---

1. "Man Auctions Ad Space on Forehead," *BBC News*, January 10, 2005, http://news.bbc.co.uk/1/hi/technology/4161413.stm. For information on the winning bid, see Ina Steiner, "No Snooze for This eBay Auction: Ad Space Wins $37,375 Bid," *AuctionBytes.com*, January 25, 2005, http://auctionbytes.com/cab/abn/y05/m01/i25/s07.

tacks greed as a form of idolatry (Col. 3:5). Pope Gregory the Great included avarice in his list of seven deadly sins that would serve over the centuries as a catalogue of perils for the soul to avoid.[2] Greed usually signifies an inordinate attachment to money and things. We picture the miser counting his money, storing it up in the bank, or we picture the person reveling in her possessions, obsessed with stuffing her big house or houses with more things. This view of greed does not really capture the spirit of our consumer economy, however. Most people are not overly attached to things. Most people are not obsessed with hoarding riches; indeed, the United States has one of the lowest savings rates of any wealthy country, and we are the most indebted society in history. What really characterizes consumer culture is not attachment to things, but detachment. People do not hoard money but spend it; people do not cling to things, but discard them and buy other things.

In a consumer society detachment occurs in both selling and buying. Anything can be sold: health care, space, human blood, names (Tostitos Fiesta Bowl), adoption rights, water, genetic codes, the rights to emit pollutants into the air, the use of one's own forehead. The Nebraska man describes himself as the "owner" of his forehead, which he can sell and get back. Consumerism is the remarkable ability to be detached even from those things — like our foreheads — to which we are most obviously attached. But the detachment of consumerism is not just the willingness to sell anything; it is also a detachment from the things we buy. Our relationships with products tend to be short-lived. Rather than hoarding treasured objects, consumerism is marked by a constant dissatisfaction with material goods. This dissatisfaction is what produces the restless pursuit of satisfaction in the form of something new. Consumerism is not so much about having *more* as it is about having *something else*. This is why not simply *buying* but *shopping* is the heart of consumerism. Buying brings a temporary halt to the restlessness that typifies consumerism. It is this restlessness — the moving on to shopping for something else, no matter what one has just purchased — that sets the spiritual tone for consumerism.

Consumerism is an important topic for moral theology because it is a spiritual disposition, a way of looking at the world around us that is deeply formative. In many ways consumerism has affinities with the traditional Christian view of how we should regard material things. We will need to explore where consumerism and Christianity converge and where

2. Henry Fairlie, *The Seven Deadly Sins Today* (Notre Dame, Ind.: University of Notre Dame Press, 1978), p. 12.

they part ways. In the first section of this chapter, we will examine some of the economic conditions that typify consumerism and its detachment from production, producers, and products. In the second section we will look at consumerism as moral formation, and compare it with some themes from Christian moral theology. In the final section we will explore the Eucharist as a Christian practice that offers an alternative way of practicing consumption.

Detachment

Some critiques of consumerism are content to complain about the greed and materialism of the present age: people have abandoned God and the higher, more spiritual, values of life for the base pleasures of material objects. There may be some truth to these complaints, but they miss the mark in at least two ways. First, they set up a false dichotomy between the spiritual and the material. In the Christian tradition, which believes that God became flesh (John 1:14), the material world is sanctified and charged with spiritual significance. The Christian is not meant to choose between God and the creation. All of creation sings of the glory of God. In the Catholic tradition especially, the sacraments show us how we encounter God in everyday material elements. The second problem with such critiques of people's values is that most people do not simply choose material goods over spiritual values. The person who deliberately decides to be a hedonist and materialist is rare. Even pop singer Madonna, the self-declared "Material Girl," is into spirituality, a de-Judaized version of the ancient Jewish mystical practice called Kabbalah. Consumerism is not simply people rejecting spirituality for materialism. For many people consumerism is a type of spirituality, even if they do not recognize it as such. It is a way of pursuing meaning and identity, and connecting with other people. Many others, finding themselves in relentless pursuit of the requisite material things of the American dream, sense that there is something awry. They read reports of Thai women being worked to death making the plastic toys and gadgets that litter our lives, and recoil. The problem is not people deliberately choosing their own comfort over the lives of others because of skewed values. The problem is a much larger one of changes in the economy and society that have detached us from material production, producers, and even the products we buy. I will take each of these in turn.

243

Production

Take a look around your home or room and note the things you and your family own. How many of these items did you make? If you are a typical American, the answer is "very few." Even meals are often prepackaged affairs to be microwaved and consumed. We take this situation for granted; the things we have are almost all bought. In most homes in most cultures for most of human history, however, the situation was radically different. Before the advent of industrialization, the typical home was a site of production, not merely consumption. Most people lived on farms, and made the majority of the goods they used. People had less, and life was often hard. There is no need to romanticize preindustrial society. But the difference in our attitudes toward material things can hardly be overemphasized. We used to make things; now we buy them.

The Industrial Revolution depended on people moving from subsistence farming and handcrafts to factory labor. This was accomplished in several ways. The forced enclosure of common lands in England and the Continent often made subsistence farming untenable. The enclosure movement privatized common lands, dividing them up among landowners, usually to the advantage of large landholders and the detriment of subsistence farmers.[3] Cottage industries were wiped out by the flood of cheap manufactured goods from the new factories, often forcing people to seek work in the same factories that put them out of business.[4] The movement from handcrafts to factory work was significant. Today, however, we are even further removed from the production of goods. Fewer and fewer Americans have any idea what factory work is like, since the process of globalization has sent many manufacturing jobs overseas, with more such transfers coming every day. Not only do we not make the things we use; more and more, we don't make any things at all.

Why should we care? Perhaps because these problems concerning production have something to do with widespread negative attitudes toward work in our society. "Thank God, it's Friday" is a common sentiment, and not only among blue-collar workers; the cartoon *Dilbert* expresses a deep discontent among cubicle-dwellers as well. Many people do not see their work as meaningful, but only as a means to a paycheck. One's labor itself

3. For a detailed account of this process in England, see J. L. Hammond and Barbara Hammond, *The Village Labourer, 1760-1832: A Study in the Government of England before the Reform Bill* (New York: Harper and Row, 1970).

4. Rodney Clapp, "Why the Devil Takes Visa: A Christian Response to the Triumph of Consumerism," *Christianity Today* 40, no. 11 (October 7, 1996): 18.

has become a commodity, a thing to be sold to the employer in exchange for money to buy things. Work for many has become deadening to the spirit.

Negative attitudes about work are common, but it was not meant to be so. Our work is meant to be an outlet for creativity, a vocation to make our impress on the material world. Work is the way we put our very selves into the world of material objects. As Pope John Paul II writes, "Work is a good thing for man — a good thing for his humanity — because through work man not only transforms nature, adapting it to his own needs, but he also achieves fulfillment as a human being and indeed, in a sense, becomes 'more a human being.'"[5] The pope says work is the key to the whole social question, because the question facing society is how to make life "more human."[6] Being more human means, at the same time, participating in the creative activity of God. "The word of God's revelation is profoundly marked by the fundamental truth that man, created in the image of God, shares by his work in the activity of the Creator."[7] This is the true meaning of the call in Genesis to "fill" and "subdue" the earth, and have "dominion" over it (Gen. 1:28).[8] This spiritual view of work has an evocative appeal to many people who feel alienated from their work and detached from creative engagement with the material world. But this spiritual view of work has not waned simply because people have bad attitudes and negative values. It is rather that our whole system of production has changed. The system has shown a tremendous capacity to increase the volume and variety of goods produced, while also detaching us from the creation of things.

Producers

If labor has become a commodity to be sold, it is also a commodity to be bought. The people who make our things are less often ourselves or our neighbors, people with names and faces and aspirations to self-realization, and more often an impersonal "workforce." In a reversal of Genesis, "Man is treated as an instrument of production, whereas he . . . ought to be treated as the effective subject of work and its true maker and creator."[9] The people who make our things are referred to as "labor costs" that need to be mini-

---

5. Pope John Paul II, *On Human Work* [*Laborem Exercens*] (Boston: St. Paul Editions, 1981), §9.

6. John Paul II, *On Human Work,* §3.

7. John Paul II, *On Human Work,* §25.

8. John Paul II, *On Human Work,* §4.

9. John Paul II, *On Human Work,* §7.

mized. And one of the key ways to reduce labor costs is to move production overseas, where wages are much lower and protections for workers much more lax.

Hip-hop star P. Diddy launched his Sean John line of designer clothing with the slogan "It's not just a label, it's a lifestyle." Of the forty dollars or more that consumers in the United States pay for a Sean John shirt, the women who actually make the shirts, from start to finish, get fifteen cents. Lydda Gonzalez is a young Honduran woman who worked at Southeast Textiles, a factory in Honduras, sewing clothes for Sean John, Old Navy, Polo Sport, and other popular brands. The factory is located in Honduras's San Miguel Free Trade Zone, a compound surrounded by tall metal fences and armed guards. Lydda began working in a bakery at age eleven, and came to Southeast Textiles at age seventeen, hoping to pull her family out of poverty. What she found instead were miserable wages, twelve-hour shifts six days a week, and mandatory unpaid overtime. She was subjected to random searches, sexual harassment, and compulsory pregnancy tests. Her supervisor was abusive, the air in the factory was filled with textile particles, and the drinking water was tainted with raw sewage. When Lydda and fourteen coworkers got together to demand better working conditions, they were all fired, and their names put on a blacklist to be shared with other factory owners. She has been subjected to death threats for speaking out.[10]

Many transnational companies are pulling out of Central America, but not out of concern for the Lydda Gonzalezes of the region. Companies are going to Asia because they can cut their labor costs in half. Instead of the sixty-five cents an hour Lydda received, factories in China pay only thirty-three cents an hour, with some documented cases of wages as low as twelve cents an hour.[11] Workers making Disney children's books at the Nord Race factories in Guangdong Province, for example, must work thirteen to fifteen hours a day, seven days a week, and earn only thirty-three cents per hour in abusive conditions.[12] Such conditions tend to be the norm, not the exception. The Chinese have even coined a word — *guolaosi* — for death from overwork. A *Washington Post* article highlighted the death of Li Chunmei, a nineteen-year-old woman who collapsed and died after work-

10. Sarah Stillman, "Made by Us: Young Women, Sweatshops, and the Ethics of Globalization," essay that won the 2005 Elie Wiesel Prize in Ethics, available at http://www.eliewieselfoundation.org/EthicsPrize/WinnersEssays/2005/Sarah_Stillman.pdf.

11. Philip P. Pan, "Worked Till They Drop: Few Protections for China's New Laborers," *Washington Post,* May 13, 2002, p. A01.

12. National Labor Committee, "Disney in China," available at http://www.nlcnet.org/news/china/pdfs/Nord_Race.pdf.

ing sixteen-hour shifts for sixty days straight in a toy factory making stuffed animals for American children.[13]

We shop. They drop. What is the connection? It's often difficult to find out. Young author Tom Beaudoin tells a story to which many middle-class Americans can relate. He had a vague sense that other people were suffering because of the way his things were made, but he was too busy to know what to do about it. So one day he took some of his favorite branded items from his closet and decided to call the companies directly to ask how they were made. He often found himself on hold fifteen or more times, as he was routed through various managers, public relations representatives, even mail room attendants. On the few occasions that he was allowed to talk to someone with knowledge about production, such managers refused to take responsibility for the well-being of workers, since most production workers were distanced from the branding company by means of "outsourcing" work to independent contractors.[14]

Naomi Klein argues that the goal of transnational corporations is a kind of transcendence of the material world.

> [Such a corporation] attempt[s] to free itself from the corporeal world of commodities, manufacturing and products to exist on another plane. Anyone can manufacture a product, they reason. . . . Such menial tasks, therefore, can and should be farmed out to contractors and sub-contractors whose only concern is filling the order on time and under budget. . . . Headquarters, meanwhile, is free to focus on the real business at hand — creating a corporate mythology powerful enough to infuse meaning into these raw objects just by signing its name.[15]

According to Klein: "After establishing the 'soul' of their corporations, the superbrand companies have gone on to rid themselves of their cumbersome bodies, and there is nothing that seems more cumbersome, more loath-somely corporeal, than the factories that produce their products."[16]

We are invited to participate in this transcendence of the material world of production and producers. We are invited to buy products that miraculously appear on store shelves without inquiring into their origins. And

13. Pan, "Worked Till They Drop."

14. Tom Beaudoin, *Consuming Faith: Integrating Who We Are with What We Buy* (Lanham, Md.: Sheed and Ward, 2003), pp. ix-xiv.

15. Naomi Klein, *No Logo* (New York: Picador, 1999), p. 22, quoted in Beaudoin, *Consuming Faith*, p. 69.

16. Klein, *No Logo*, p. 196, quoted in Beaudoin, *Consuming Faith*, p. 69.

yet Beaudoin's dilemma haunts us. I stop to look at the clothes I am wearing as I write this. My shirt was made in Indonesia. My jeans were made in Mexico. My shoes: China. My undershirt, whose label instructs me to "Have a nice day," was made in Haiti, where a nice day for most people is one on which there is enough food to eat. Most of us would never deliberately choose our own material comfort over the life of another person. Most of us do not consciously choose to work others to death for the sake of lower prices on the things we buy. But we participate in such an economy because we are detached from the producers — the people — who actually make our things. Not only are the people who make our things often a world away, but we are also prevented from learning about where our products come from by a host of roadblocks. And so we inhabit separate worlds, entirely different ways of looking at the material world. The Happy Meal toys we easily discard reveal nothing of the toil of the malnourished young women who make them. They work for two days to make what we spend on a cup of coffee — and we don't give it a second thought. We do this not necessarily because we are greedy and indifferent to the suffering of others, but largely because those others are invisible to us.

Products

On a road that passes close to the house I grew up in, shopping malls have replaced corn. On one particular stretch there is a McDonald's fast-food joint, built recently in a retro style to look like the original McDonald's from the 1950s. Next to it stands a restaurant with a medieval English castle theme, built with drawbridges and turrets. On the other side of the castle is a Mexican fast-food joint, with some features that are meant to suggest an eighteenth-century Spanish mission. It shares space with a seafood restaurant, decorated with a scattering of nets and lifesavers and piratey paraphernalia. All of this stands in the middle of an Illinois cornfield.

This type of scene is so common that it hardly strikes us as odd. Of course, it's all fake. What would "authentic" mean in this context? We take for granted that other times and places — 1950s America, medieval England, Mexico, the high seas — are all available for our consumption. The expansion of the global economy has brought the world to our fingertips. Music, food, products, and ideas from around the globe are commodities for our enjoyment. This applies not just to low-end products like fast food, but to high-culture products such as single-malt Scotch whisky and yoga accessories. Globalization has increased our awareness of, and sympathy for, other times and places. At the same time, however, it produces a detachment from all times and places. What is "authentic" suburban Illinois culture at the beginning of the twenty-first century? It is, I suppose, fragments of traditional rural Midwestern life and urban Chicago themes, mixed with a hodgepodge of other times and other places. We stand back from culture like a shopper in a supermarket and pick and choose our culture from the infinite variety of experiences marketed to us. Because our consumption can take us anywhere, we are nowhere in particular. The stretch of road I have described is the same as other stretches throughout the country and throughout the world. If you were dropped out of the sky and landed on this road, it would take some investigation to figure out if you were in Chicago or Dallas, Montreal or Sydney.

This detachment tends to characterize our attitudes to the products we buy. Far from an obsessive clinging to our stuff, we tend to buy and discard products easily. We don't make them ourselves or have any connections to the people that make them; increasingly we have no connection to the people that sell them either, as small local businesses are replaced by gigantic chain retailers. Under these conditions our connections to products become very tenuous and fleeting as well. The products we buy are mute as to their origins, and the people we buy them from can tell us little. Products say nothing about where they come from and how they are produced, and we scarcely bother to wonder. We take for granted that one can buy fresh bananas in Minnesota in the dead of winter. Meat comes not from cows and pigs, but from little Styrofoam trays wrapped in clear plastic. We simply dump them in our carts and keep on shopping.

This does not mean that we have become indifferent to the products we buy. To the contrary, as human relationships fall away from the products we buy, relationships become more direct between ourselves and our things. The relationship of consumption has largely been reduced to the bare encounter at the store (or on the computer screen) between consumer and thing. Marketers know, however, that consumption could never keep pace with production if encounters with products were encounters with inert things. The product must be made to sing and dance and create a new kind of relationship between itself and the consumer. Over the course of the twentieth century, marketing moved from primarily offering information about a product to associating certain feelings with a product. Soft drink commercials say little about the actual fizzy liquid that you get when you buy a can, but rather try to associate the product with positive images like swimsuit-clad youth frolicking on a beach. "Branding" — that is, getting people to identify with a particular corporate brand — is about creating relationships between people and things. Branding consumers, as one marketer says, is about "creating mythologies about their brands by humanizing them and giving them distinct personalities and cultural sensibilities."[17] Another says, "Products are made in the factory, but brands are made in the mind."[18] Associating in one's mind with certain brands gives a sense of identity: one identifies oneself with certain images and values that are associated with the brand. Branding offers opportunities to take on a new self, to perform an "extreme makeover" and become a new person. Some people deal with depression by going shopping, because it offers the chance to start anew, to bring something new into one's life. At the same time, branding can also provide a sense of community with all the other people who associate with a particular brand.[19]

Why, then, speak about detachment from products when much of consumer culture is about creating relationships with products? Because such relationships are not made to last. There would not be a market for all the goods produced in an industrialized economy if consumers were content with the things they bought. Consumer desire must be constantly on the move. We must continually desire new things in order for consumption to keep pace with production. The "extreme makeover" is an ongoing process of the search for novelty, for bigger and better, for new and improved and different experiences. The shaving razor with one blade must be surpassed by the double-bladed razor, which was bested by three blades, then four, and now an absurd five blades on one razor. This is more than just a continuing attempt to make a product better. It is what the research division of General Motors once called — in a reference to changing car models every year — "the organized creation of dissatisfaction."[20] How can we be content with a mere two blades when the current standard is five? How can we be content with an iPod that downloads two hundred songs when someone else has one that downloads a thousand? The economy as currently structured would grind to a halt if we ever looked at our stuff and simply declared, "It is enough. I am happy with what I have."

The truth is, however, that we do not tend to experience dissatisfaction as merely a negative. In consumer culture, dissatisfaction and satisfac-

---

17. Quoted in Michael Budde, *The (Magic) Kingdom of God: Christianity and Global Culture Industries* (Boulder, Colo.: Westview, 1997), p. 38.

18. Quoted in Beaudoin, *Consuming Faith*, p. 76.

19. Beaudoin, *Consuming Faith*, pp. 53-58.

20. Quoted in Erik Larson, *The Naked Consumer: How Our Private Lives Become Public Commodities* (New York: Henry Holt, 1992), p. 20.

tion cease to be opposites, for pleasure is not so much in the possession of things as in their pursuit. There is pleasure in the pursuit of novelty. The pleasure resides not so much in having as in wanting. Once an item is obtained, it brings desire to a temporary halt, and it loses some of its appeal. Possession kills desire; familiarity breeds contempt. This is why shopping, not buying itself, is the heart of consumerism. The consumerist spirit is a restless spirit. It is typified by detachment, because desire must be constantly kept on the move.

Moral Formation and the Material World

What do changes in the economy have to do with moral theology? Isn't moral theology about moral issues such as abortion, premarital sex, and the death penalty?

Moral theology properly deals with such issues. As earlier chapters in this book have tried to show, however, moral theology begins with reflection on how persons are formed to see the world in a certain way. And consumer culture is one of the most powerful systems of formation in the contemporary world, arguably more powerful than Christianity. While a Christian may spend an hour per week in church, she may spend twenty-five hours per week watching television, to say nothing of the hours spent on the Internet, listening to the radio, shopping, looking at junk mail and other advertisements. Nearly everywhere we lay our eyes — gas pump handles, T-shirts, public restroom walls, bank receipts, church bulletins, sports uniforms, etc. — we are confronted by advertising. As one observer comments, "What the record reveals is an almost total takeover of the domestic informational system for the purpose of selling goods and services."[21]

Such a powerful formative system is not morally neutral. It trains us to see the world in certain ways. As all the great faiths of the world have attested, how we relate to the material world is a spiritual discipline. As one corporate manager frankly put it, "Corporate branding is really about worldwide beliefs management."[22] This does not mean that the moral effects of consumer culture are always negative. The global economy that has arisen with consumer culture has the potential to broaden our horizons and make us more aware of other peoples and other cultures in the world. Nevertheless, we need to be aware of the powerful formative effects of con-

21. Herbert Schiller, quoted in Budde, *(Magic) Kingdom of God,* p. 33.
22. Quoted in Beaudoin, *Consuming Faith,* p. 44.

sumer culture, and approach it with eyes wide open. Let's look at two ways that consumerism constitutes a spiritual discipline, and look at some Christian responses.

Transcendence

Consumerism has certain affinities with the great faith traditions of the world because, as we have seen, it trains us to transcend the material world. Not only do we seek to leave behind the bodily labor that goes into making things. Consumerism represents a constant dissatisfaction with particular material things themselves, a restlessness that constantly seeks to move beyond what is at hand. Although the consumer spirit delights in material things and sees them as good, the thing itself is never enough. Things and brands must be invested with mythologies, with spiritual aspirations. Things come to represent freedom, status, and love. Above all, they represent the aspiration to escape time and death by constantly seeking renewal in created things. Each new movement of desire promises the opportunity to start over.

The Christian tradition also recognizes the goodness of material things, and the necessity of transcending them. The basic Christian attitude toward material goods is established already in the opening chapters of Genesis. Because all things are created by God, they are good. "God saw that it was good" is a phrase repeated over and over in the creation account (Gen. 1:4, 10, 12, 18, 21, 25, 31). But precisely because all things are created by God, created things are not ultimate. Created things, though good, are never ends in themselves, but point outside themselves toward their Creator. As Saint Augustine says, all created things contain within themselves traces of the Creator. But precisely because of this, they are not ends, but means toward the enjoyment of God. According to Augustine, created things are to be *used*, but only God is to be *enjoyed*.

So the restlessness and dissatisfaction of consumerism are already found in a different form in Christianity. According to Augustine, as creatures in time we are passionate, desiring creatures, and this is good. The constant renewal of desire is what gets us out of bed in the morning. We desire because we are alive. Created things, however, though essentially good, always fail fully to satisfy because they are not ultimate. They are time-bound, not infinite. Created things fall apart. We lose interest in them over time. They die. *We* die. Only God is eternal. Only God stops the decay of time. As Augustine famously wrote in a prayer to God, "you have made us for yourself, and our heart is restless until it rests in you."[23] The restlessness of consumerism causes us constantly to seek new material objects. For Augustine, on the other hand, the solution to our dissatisfaction is not the continuous search for new things, but the turn to the only One who can truly satisfy our desires. This does not require the rejection of all earthly things, but rather an ability to see that all things point to God. People and things are united in one great web of being, flowing from and returning to their Creator. The Christian view elevates the dignity of things by seeing them as participating in the being of God, but simultaneously causes us to look through and beyond things to their Creator.

Community

Consumerism is a spiritual discipline that, like other spiritual practices, lends itself to a certain practice of community. In identifying with the images and values associated with certain brands, we also identify ourselves with all the other people who make such an identification. Consumerism also allows us to identify with other places and other cultures through our purchases. White kids in Illinois can listen to reggae and feel themselves in solidarity with the struggles of poor blacks in Jamaica. As Vincent Miller points out, however, such types of "virtual" community tend to reduce community to disembodied acts of consumption.[24] Miller cites the example of Moby's album *Play*, which sold ten million copies in 1999. On the album Moby combines samples of African American spirituals, gospel, and blues with techno-beat dance music. The song "Natural Blues" begins with a sample from a 1959 recording of Vera Hall singing, "Oh, Lordy, trouble so hard." The sample is chopped and mixed with dance music. Although such samples allow the listener to enter into imaginative sympathy with the struggles of the African American community in its long hard history, the samples are taken out of context and offered for consumption. Although Vera Hall and the other artists were not even thanked in Moby's liner notes, *every* song on the album was eventually licensed for use in a commercial, for such companies as Calvin Klein and American Express. Concrete suffering is abstracted from its context and offered as a commodity. No matter how much

23. Augustine, *Confessions*, trans. Henry Chadwick (Oxford: Oxford University Press, 1991), I.I (p. 3).

24. Vincent J. Miller, *Consuming Religion: Christian Faith and Practice in a Consumer Culture* (New York: Continuum, 2004), pp. 73-77.

the listener feels in solidarity with others, virtual solidarity offers no concrete results. As Miller notes, "This abstraction impedes the translation of ethical concerns into action, reducing ethics to sentiment. The virtual becomes a substitute for concrete political solidarity, or to put it another way, a fundamentally different act — consumption — is substituted for political action."[25]

In the Christian tradition, by contrast, one's attitude toward material goods is closely tied to an imperative of concrete solidarity with others. When the rich young man approaches Jesus and asks what he must do to attain eternal life, Jesus tells him to "go, sell your possessions, and give the money to the poor, and you will have treasure in heaven; then come, follow me" (Matt. 19:21). For Jesus, detachment from material goods went hand in hand with attachment to Jesus himself — "follow me" — and to his community of followers. Saint Antony of Egypt (251-356) took Jesus' command quite literally. Upon hearing this passage from Matthew's Gospel read in church at age eighteen, he gave away most of his possessions, and sold the rest and gave the money to the poor. He went off to follow Jesus without the distractions of material possessions, eventually gathering a community of monks around him.[26] Saint Clement of Alexandria (150-215) did not interpret Matthew 19 as meaning that Christians need to renounce all material possessions, but only those that are injurious to the soul.[27] Nevertheless, Clement also encouraged an attitude of detachment from material things that accompanied a concrete attachment to God and to other people. Clement treated material possessions instrumentally, that is, as a means to be used toward other ends, namely, the service of God and others.[28] Things are to be used "more for the sake of the brethren"[29] than for oneself, for "The nature of wealth is to be subservient, not to rule."[30]

Saint Thomas Aquinas (1225-74) derives this attitude of detachment from material things from the fact that God is the proper "owner" of all things. This is a common Old Testament theme: "The earth is the LORD's and all that is in it" (Ps. 24:1).[31] According to Aquinas, humans have domin-

25. Miller, *Consuming Religion*, p. 76.

26. Athanasius, *The Life of Antony*, trans. Robert C. Gregg (New York: Paulist, 1980), pp. 30-32.

27. Clement of Alexandria, "Who Is the Rich Man That Shall Be Saved?" §1, 15, available at http://www.earlychristianwritings.com/text/clement-richman.html.

28. Clement, "Rich Man," §14.

29. Clement, "Rich Man," §16.

30. Clement, "Rich Man," §14.

31. See also Exod. 19:5, "The whole earth is mine," says the Lord.

ion over material things only "as regards their use."[32] In other words, this is God's world, and we are just using it for the time being. Any dominion we have over creation is given to human beings in common by God. It follows that, with regard to the power to "procure and dispense" property, an individual has the right to possess property. However, with regard to its use, a person "ought to possess external things, not as his own, but as common, so that, to wit, he is ready to communicate them to others in their need."[33] We may possess property, but use it only for the common good, especially for the sake of the neediest among us.

In the Christian tradition, detachment from material goods means using them as a means to a greater end, and the greater end is greater attachment to God and to our fellow human beings. In consumerism, detachment means standing back from all people, times, and places, and appropriating our choices for private use. Consumerism supports an essentially individualistic view of the human person, in which each consumer is a sovereign chooser. In Christian tradition the use of material things is meant to be a common use, for the sake of a larger body of people. We do not help each other as individuals, but as members of one another. According to Paul's famous image (1 Cor. 12), we are all members of the same body, the body of Christ. There is pluralism in the body; some are eyes, some are hands, some are feet. And yet precisely because of such differentiation, all are needed. No member can say to another, "I have no need of you" (1 Cor. 12:21). Furthermore, Paul says, the members of the body that seem to be weakest are the most indispensable (1 Cor. 12:22-24). The poor and the needy are not just objects for individual charity. They are rather indispensable because they are part of our very body. "If one member suffers, all suffer together with it; if one member is honored, all rejoice together with it" (1 Cor. 12:26). The reason we do not cling to material things is precisely because of our attachment to others. We must constantly be ready to relinquish our claim to ownership, and use our goods for the common good of the whole body.

Being Consumed

There is no question about whether or not to be a consumer. Everyone must consume to live. The question is about what types of practices of consump-

---

32. Thomas Aquinas, *Summa Theologiae*, trans. Fathers of the English Dominican Province (Westminster, Md.: Christian Classics, 1981), II-II.66.1.

33. Aquinas, *Summa Theologiae* II-II.66.2.

tion are conducive to an abundant life for all. In the Catholic tradition, the Eucharist is a particularly important locus for the Christian practice of consumption. Let's conclude by considering this sacramental practice and how it might affect our daily practices of consumption.

In the Eucharist Jesus offers his body and blood to be consumed. "Jesus said to them, 'I am the bread of life. Whoever comes to me will never be hungry'" (John 6:35). The insatiability of human desire is absorbed by the abundance of God's grace in the consumption of Jesus' body and blood. "Those who eat my flesh and drink my blood have eternal life" (John 6:54), that is, they are raised above mere temporal pursuit of novelty. "Do not work for the food that perishes, but for the food that endures for eternal life" (John 6:27).

It would be easy enough to assimilate the consumption of the Eucharist into a consumerist kind of spirituality. The presence of Jesus could become another type of commodity to be appropriated for the benefit of the individual user. Indeed, much of what passes for Christianity in our culture today is addressed to fulfilling the spiritual needs of individual consumers of religion. Many types of religion — or more commonly, "spirituality" — are largely about self-help, using God to cope with the stresses of modern life. The practice of the Eucharist is resistant to such appropriation, however, because the consumer of the Eucharist is taken up into a larger body, the body of Christ. The individual consumer of the Eucharist does not simply take Christ into herself, but is taken up into Christ. Jesus says, "Those who eat my flesh and drink my blood abide in me, and I in them" (John 6:56). Paul writes to the Corinthians, "The cup of blessing that we bless, is it not a sharing in the blood of Christ? The bread that we break, is it not a sharing in the body of Christ? Because there is one bread, we who are many are one body, for we all partake of the one bread" (1 Cor. 10:16-17).

The act of consumption is thereby turned inside out; instead of simply consuming the body of Christ, we are consumed by it. Saint Augustine hears God say, "I am the food of the fully grown; grow and you will feed on me. And you will not change me into you like the food your flesh eats, but you will be changed into me."[34] In the Christian view, we do not simply stand apart from the rest of creation, as individuals, appropriating, consuming, and discarding. In the Eucharist we are absorbed into a larger body. The small individual self is decentered, and put in the context of a much wider community of participation with others in the divine life. At the same time, we do not lose our identities as unique persons, for as Paul says, each

34. Augustine, *Confessions* 7.16 (p. 124).

different member of the body is valued and needed for the body to function (1 Cor. 12:12-27).

If we remain satisfied with the unity of our own communities, however, we have not fully grasped the nature of the Eucharist. For becoming the body of Christ also entails that we must become food for others. And this often involves moving beyond our own communities and comfort. Jesus teaches this lesson in a dramatic way in his depiction of the last judgment in Matthew 25:31-46. When the Son of Man comes in glory, he will gather all the nations before him and separate those who will inherit the kingdom from those who will be sent into eternal punishment. To the former group he will say, "Come, you that are blessed by my Father . . . for I was hungry and you gave me food, I was thirsty and you gave me something to drink, I was a stranger and you welcomed me, I was naked and you gave me clothing, I was sick and you took care of me, I was in prison and you visited me" (Matt. 25:34-36). When the blessed cannot remember ever attending to Jesus hungry or thirsty, a stranger or naked, sick or in prison, Jesus tells them that whenever they did it to the least of his brothers or sisters, they did it to him (Matt. 25:40). Here "brothers and sisters" refers not just to Christians, for the Son of Man is judging "all the nations" (Matt. 25:32).[35] All the downtrodden are Christ's brothers and sisters. To those condemned for not attending to Jesus, he says, "Just as you did not do it to one of the least of these, you did not do it to me" (Matt. 25:45).

What is truly radical about this passage is not that God rewards those who help the poor. What is truly radical is that Jesus *identifies himself* with the poor. The pain of the hungry person is the pain of Christ. It is therefore also the pain of anyone who is a member of the body of Christ. If we are identified with Christ, who identifies himself with the suffering of all, then more than just charity is called for. The very distinction between what is mine and what is yours breaks down in the body of Christ. We are not to consider ourselves as absolute owners of our stuff, who then occasionally graciously bestow charity on the less fortunate. In the body of Christ, your pain is my pain, and my stuff is available to be communicated to you in your need, as Aquinas says. In the consumption of the Eucharist, we cease to be merely other to one another. In the Eucharist

---

35. *The New Jerome Biblical Commentary* notes that the term *adelphos* (brother) in Matthew sometimes refers to a member of the Christian community and sometimes to "any human being as the object of ethical duty"; the commentator concludes that Matt. 25:40 should be taken in the latter sense, noting that the word is dropped in Matt. 25:45. See Raymond E. Brown, Joseph A. Fitzmyer, and Roland E. Murphy, eds., *The New Jerome Biblical Commentary* (Englewood Cliffs, N.J.: Prentice-Hall, 1990), p. 669.

Christ is gift, giver, and recipient. We are simultaneously fed and become food for others.

Our temptation is to spiritualize all this talk of union, to make our connection to the hungry a sentimental act of imaginative sympathy. We could then imagine that we are already in communion with those who lack food, whether or not we actually meet their physical needs. We might even wish to tell ourselves that our purchases of consumer goods do in fact feed others, by creating jobs. But we have no way of knowing if such jobs create dignity or merely take advantage of others' desperation unless we find concrete ways to overcome our detachment from production, producers, and products.

The first step toward overcoming our detachment is to turn our homes into sites of production, not just consumption. Few of us have the means to make most of what we consume, but simple acts like making our own bread or our own music can be significant ways to reshape the way we approach the material world. Making things gives the maker an appreciation for the labor involved in producing what we consume. It also increases our sense that we are not merely spectators of life — for example, hours spent passively watching and listening to entertainment that others make — but active and creative participants in the material world. We can appreciate, as Pope John Paul II said, our true vocation as sharers in the creative activity of God.

Overcoming our detachment from producers is a daunting task when so much of what we need to know is hidden from our view. Nevertheless, there are ways to foster life-giving connections with the resources available to us. One way is to donate time and money to those in need. Another way is to try to ensure that our purchases contribute to a sustainable life for those who make what we buy. Buying things that are locally produced, at stores that are locally owned, generally increases the chances of relationship and accountability. There is also a growing fair trade movement that ensures fair wages and equitable treatment to producers around the world. The U.S. Conference of Catholic Bishops, through Catholic Relief Services (CRS), sponsors a program of fair trade in coffee, chocolate, and many other handmade items. The goal of the program, according to CRS, is to produce "a new model of international trade built on right relationships between us and the people overseas who create the items we consume — relationships that respect human dignity, promote economic justice, and cultivate global solidarity."[36] Rather than leave coffee growers to the mercy of "market forces" middlemen who try to pay them as little as possible, fair trade orga-

---

36. Catholic Relief Services, Fair Trade, http://www.crsfairtrade.org/index_flash.cfm.

nizations such as CRS ensure a sustainable wage for growers. They also educate American consumers, putting names and faces on those who produce what they consume.[37]

Finally, overcoming detachment from the products we buy is not a matter of developing a fierce attachment to material things. Things are not ends in themselves, but means to greater attachment to others. We are not to cling to our things, but to use them for the sake of the common good. But to have a good relationship with others, it is necessary to have a proper relationship with things. We must understand where our things come from and how our things are produced. Things do not have personalities and lives of their own, but are embedded in relationships of production and distribution that bring us into contact, for better or for worse, with other people's lives. A sacramental view of the world sees all things as part of God's good creation, potential signs of the glory of God. Things become less disposable, more filled with meaning. At the same time, a sacramental view sees things only as signs, whose meaning is only completely fulfilled if they promote the good of communion with God and with other people.

Concurrent Readings

Budde, Michael. *The (Magic) Kingdom of God: Christianity and Global Culture Industries.* Boulder, Colo.: Westview, 1997. Budde puts questions of discipleship and the church in the middle of his analysis of contemporary developments in capitalism and global culture industries.

Gertner, Jon. "The Futile Pursuit of Happiness." *New York Times Magazine*, September 7, 2003. Gertner reports on recent studies by psychologists at Harvard, the University of Virginia, and Princeton University on the promises, misjudgments, and frustrations of consumerism.

Miller, Vincent J. *Consuming Religion: Christian Faith and Practice in a Consumer Culture.* New York: Continuum, 2004. Miller charts how members of modern culture have been socialized by consumerism and how our religious beliefs have been affected by that socialization.

Schlosser, Eric. *Fast Food Nation.* New York: HarperCollins, 2002. Schlosser describes how fast food is produced and how the industry is managed. He gives clear evidence of the power of the industry and its harmful effects on the American diet, economy, countryside, and workforce.

---

37. You can take a virtual tour of coffee production in Matagalpa, Nicaragua, at http://www.crsfairtrade.org/coffee_project/index.htm.

Chapter 12

A Christian Ethic of Child Rearing:
Homeschooling as Case Study

JULIE HANLON RUBIO

When Christian parents gather over dinner or coffee, discussion often centers less on the most controversial moral issues of the day than on the daily struggles to raise children well. These discussions may not even be considered "moral" by the participants, but there should be no doubt that questions of how much time mothers and fathers ought to spend at work, what kind of substitute care (if any) is best for children, whether or not physical punishment is just, what sort of school children should attend, what kinds of neighborhoods families should live in, how much "screen time" children ought to have, and so many others are both mundane and moral. They are matters of ordinary, daily life, and they call forth reflection on what it means to be a good Christian parent.

Yet these ordinary issues have not merited much reflection in Christian ethics until recently. In Catholic theology marriage and family issues began to receive more attention around the time of Vatican II.[1] When the bishops of the Second Vatican Council called marriage "an intimate partnership of life and love," many theologians and laypeople rejoiced in the church's willingness to read "the signs of the times" and move from juridical definitions of marriage to theological discussions in which marriage relationships played a central role.[2] Although this is probably the most noted develop-

---

1. Concern about marriage rose in the American Catholic Church in the period 1930-1960, but responses to the perceived crisis came, for the most part, at the institutional level, in the rise of popular groups, and in the work of Catholic sociologists, rather than from theologians. See Jeffrey Burns, *American Catholics and the Family Crisis, 1930-1962* (New York: Garland, 1988).

2. *Gaudium et Spes*, in *Vatican Council II: The Conciliar and Post Conciliar Documents*, ed. Austin P. Flannery, O.P., vol. 1 (Northport, N.Y.: Costello, 1975), §48.

ment in the theology of marriage to emerge from Vatican II, it is not the only one. *Gaudium et Spes* also represents a shift from more abstract discussions of marriage to more grounded discourse on marriage in its real-life context: family.[3] The Council Fathers' willingness to speak not only of the marriage covenant that bears fruit in children, but also of the family itself as "a school for human enrichment"[4] in which parents and children help each other grow in virtue, was a significant move toward a theology that can speak to the challenges facing ordinary families in the modern world.

In the 1980s new signs of the times — most significantly, the changing roles of men and women — reshaped the theological discussion. Women theologians brought their own experience to bear on the theology of marriage and responded to secular feminist writing on the family. Relying both on the feminist insight that many women need more than mothering to feel fulfilled and on the Christian idea that followers of Christ are obligated to serve the needy and the stranger as well as their own kin, they claimed that the vocation of Christian women is not limited to mothering.[5] From their work came a broadly accepted understanding that Christian parents — mothers and fathers — have a dual vocation: a domestic calling to nurture their own children and a civic vocation to make a contribution to the common good.[6]

This dual vocation model fits nicely with contemporary Catholic theology on the family. In his *Familiaris Consortio,* John Paul II calls families to three distinct tasks: forming a community of love, serving life, and being the church in their home. After discussing the deep communion to which married couples are called, and their responsibility to serve life by welcoming children and recognizing the dignity of life in all its forms, the pope re-

---

3. Theodore Mackin, *The Marriage Sacrament* (New York: Paulist, 1989), pp. 539-44. Mackin claims that in this document "[t]he family is the sacrament grown to fullness" (p. 542).

4. *Gaudium et Spes,* §52.

5. Bonnie Miller-McLemore, in *Also a Mother: Work and Family as Theological Dilemma* (Nashville: Abingdon, 1994), tells the story of how she came to write her book by looking at her bookshelves filled with theological books and feminist books but none that spoke to both Christianity and motherhood. Neither her bookshelves nor her desire for integration is atypical. See also Lisa Sowle Cahill, *Sex, Gender, and Christian Ethics* (Cambridge: Cambridge University Press, 1996); Anne Carr and Mary Stewart Van Leeuwen, eds., *Religion, Feminism, and the Family* (Louisville: Westminster, 1996); Charles E. Curran, Margaret A. Farley, and Richard A. McCormick, eds., *Feminist Ethics and the Catholic Moral Tradition* (New York: Paulist, 1996).

6. Julie Hanlon Rubio, "The Dual Vocation of Christian Parents," *Theological Studies* 63, no. 4 (2002): 786-812.

minds his readers that "far from being closed in on itself, the family is by nature and vocation open to other families and society."[7] In contemporary Catholic teaching, then, families have both internal and external callings.

How are parents to live out this dual vocation? The open nature of the family implies that Christian parents must go beyond raising their children and make a contribution to the common good.[8] Usually this means parents will spend time away from their own children as they work at jobs that contribute to the good of society or volunteer substantial amounts of their time in the local community. A dual vocation for parents usually necessitates at least some day care and traditional schooling, or a reliance on others outside the small communion of the family to assist in the raising of children. If women and men engage in public work, they rely on "the support of a community of others standing by."[9] With this support, modern theologians claim that families can live a more balanced life that includes some work for both parents and some outside care so that children's real needs are met and parents are not left trying to do everything alone. Most theologians writing about family believe that men and women can rely on social institutions like school and day care while still rearing their children well, thus living out their dual vocation.

Recently, however, this idea has been challenged by a new sign of the times: the fragmentation of family life. There is widespread dissatisfaction with the hurrying and overscheduling that mark contemporary families, and with the constant fatigue experienced by men and women in dual-career marriages. Contemporary feminists are questioning the traditional male work model and beginning to articulate a new vision of work and family.[10] Movements advocating voluntary simplicity, attachment parenting, and homeschooling are spreading.[11] These alternative movements emphasize parental responsibility to spend time with children, build strong rela-

7. John Paul II, *Familiaris Consortio: On the Role of the Christian Family in the Modern World* (1981), §42.

8. See Florence Caffrey Bourg, *Where Two or Three Are Gathered: Christian Families as Domestic Churches* (Notre Dame, Ind.: University of Notre Dame Press, 2003); and Bridget Burke Ravizza and Karen Peterson Iyer, "Motherhood and Tenure: Can Catholic Universities Support Both?" *Catholic Education: A Journal of Inquiry and Practice* 8, no. 3 (March 2005): 305-25.

9. Miller-McLemore, *Also a Mother*, p. 123.

10. See Betty Friedan, *The Second Stage* (New York: Dell, 1981); and Joan Williams, *Unbending Gender: Why Family and Work Conflict and What to Do about It* (New York: Oxford University Press, 2000).

11. Homeschooling will be addressed in depth below. Voluntary simplicity is addressed in brief below. On attachment parenting see Gregory K. Popcak and Lisa Popcak, *Parenting with Grace* (Huntington, Ind.: Our Sunday Visitor, 2000).

tionships, and nurture values without advocating a particular family structure. All of this is leading modern theologians to wonder if the dual career/vocation model is optimal.[12]

In this chapter I want to begin to develop a specifically Christian ethic of parenting or child rearing that responds to the newest signs of our times. According to the dual vocation ideal, child rearing is a domestic vocation to which all parents are called, just as they are called to a civic vocation they might fulfill through paid or unpaid work in their community. A majority of married couples today are dual-career couples, that is, couples who combine child rearing with paid work. Modern theology would seem to support families like these who seek to embrace their dual vocation to family and world. However, the growing popularity of homeschooling provides an interesting test case for the new ideal, as homeschooling advocates dispute the claim that working parents who rely on social institutions to assist with child rearing can adequately meet the demands of the domestic side of their dual vocation.

In this chapter, then, I will begin by examining the homeschooling movement as a practice that challenges current family theology. Next I will turn to Christian theology on children to retrieve a deeper sense of what the tradition asks of parents. I will argue that though homeschooling in some form is a practice that should occur in all families, it need not be the only schooling children receive, nor the only vocation parents pursue.

The Challenge of Alternative Parenting Ethics: Homeschooling as Case Study

The homeschooling movement is of a piece with many contemporary alternative movements that respond to the problems of everyday life in a bureaucratized, busy, efficiency-driven world. Just as the voluntary simplicity movement offers an alternative to an overly structured life for adults, the homeschooling movement provides an alternative to an overly structured life for children.[13] In both cases, individuals want time to pursue what they

---

12. See Julie Hanlon Rubio, "Living the Dual Vocation of Christian Parenthood," in *Marriage in the Catholic Tradition: Scripture, Tradition, and Experience*, ed. Todd A. Salzman, Thomas M. Kelly, and John J. O'Keefe (New York: Crossroad, 2004), pp. 193-200.

13. On voluntary simplicity, see Duane Elgin, *Voluntary Simplicity: Toward a Way of Life That Is Outwardly Simple, Inwardly Rich*, rev. ed. (New York: Quill, 1993); Elaine St. James, *Living the Simple Life* (New York: Hyperion, 1996); Amy Dacyzn, *The Complete Tightwad Gazette: Promoting Thrift as a Viable Alternative Lifestyle* (New York: Viking Press, 1997); Joe Dominguez and Vicki Robbins, *Your Money or Your Life* (New York: Penguin Books, 1992); Linda Breen

see as important in life and more freedom to reject problematic cultural values. Both movements question the dominant model of the dual-career household because many have experienced the hectic pace of the new family and found it lacking. Homeschoolers, then, "may be one of the most recent social vanguards willing to take significant steps to protect their children from the effects of modernization and secularization on the American family."[14] Like many others, parents who homeschool are seeking a better way of life that involves more time with their loved ones and more attention to living out their own values. Moreover, they believe that homeschooling will give them the time and space they need to parent well.

Why are homeschooling parents willing to sacrifice so much to avoid the public schools? Many claim not to desire the very thing most Americans say they value about schooling: socialization. To avoid the influence of a culture they see as morally deficient, they seize the opportunity to form their children themselves. While most Christian homeschoolers want to avoid what they see as the secular humanistic agenda of the public schools (as well as sex education, drugs, and drinking), many are also distressed about consumerism, materialism, and the pressure to conform.[15] Of course, public schools do not teach these values explicitly, but the moral pluralism or fragmentation within the school environment does not give students a strong moral standpoint from which to resist the formative powers of the dominant culture. Rightly, many parents worry that if their children spend most of their days in school, they will be influenced by that culture in subtle but still powerful ways. While students might protest that they value the opportunity to express their individuality, often they are not fully aware that they are mimicking the fashions and attitudes of the entertainers, athletes, and movie stars who define the culture.

Thus, "[h]ome education appears to be a vehicle for some parents to protect certain religious beliefs and 'ways of life' by allowing them to regain control over the primary area of socialization — the education of children."[16]

Pierce, *Choosing Simplicity: Real People Finding Peace and Fulfillment in a Complex World* (Carmel, Calif.: Gallagher Press, 2000).

14. Maralee Mayberry, "Why Home Schooling? A Profile of Four Categories of Home Schoolers," *Home School Researcher* 4, no. 3 (1988): 12.

15. See Kathleen McCurdy, "Why Homeschool?" in *The Homeschool Reader* (Tonasket, Wash.: Home Education Press, 1997), pp. 15-16, who emphasizes the freedom for individual growth.

16. Maralee Mayberry, Brian D. Ray, and J. Gary Knowles, "Political and Religious Characteristics of Home School Parents: Results of an Ongoing Study in Four Western States," *Home School Researcher* 8, no. 1 (1992): 6.

Homeschooling parents welcome the chance "to teach their own values and beliefs to their children . . . in an environment where they [can] 'be' themselves."[17] Seeking a way to pass on a coherent set of countercultural ideas, they turn away from a school system that makes their jobs more difficult.

Most parents who have moral concerns also seek an alternative to the educational methods found in public schools. Their pedagogical concerns sometimes outweigh their ideological concerns and become more important over time.[18] Many parents speak of a desire to allow their children to learn at their own speed and to be directed by their own interests, rather than following a rigid plan of studies dictated by someone else.[19] While some homeschoolers rely on schedules and formal at-home learning programs, other parents cherish the flexibility of homeschooling and use life itself as a vehicle for learning. Most parents who homeschool want "to provide for their children an atmosphere in which to live, learn, and grow all at once, in a unified, carefully (though not always formally) organized way."[20] They want to allow children to go at their own pace instead of being forced to live and learn within the constructs of adult lives.

Homeschooling parents want to give their children the gift of time. They hope that along with time will come the freedom for individual development, without pressure from peers or teachers.[21] However, they also want to direct and shape their children's journey into maturity themselves. The two concerns are very difficult to separate, because these parents believe that time and freedom from social pressure are essential for development of strong individuals. Granted, they want to be the ones who shape their chil-

---

17. Kathie Carwile Johnson, "Socialization Practices of Christian Home School Educators in the State of Virginia," *Home School Researcher* 7, no. 1 (1991): 11

18. Mark Resetar, "An Exploratory Study of the Rationales Parents Have for Home Schooling," *Home School Researcher* 6, no. 2 (1990): 5. Resetar found that while 34.2 percent of parents in his study cited educational motivations for beginning homeschooling, 53.9 percent cited it as a motivation for continuing (p. 3).

19. Jon Wartes, "The Washington Home School Project: Quantitative Measures for Informing Policy Decisions," *Education and Urban Society* 21, no. 1 (November 1988): 45, notes that second to religion, parents desire "a smaller and more personal environment" for their children; Mayberry claims that pedagogy is a motivator for 22 percent of parents, in "Characteristics and Attitudes of Families Who Home School," *Education and Urban Society* 21, no. 1 (November 1988): 37.

20. Sonia Gustafson, "A Study of Home Schooling: Parental Motivation and Goals," *Home School Researcher* 4, no. 2 (1988): 12.

21. Gary Knowles claims that families that homeschool are characterized by "lifestyles [that] revolved around the welfare of the children," in "Understanding Parents Who Teach Children at Home," *Home School Researcher* 4, no. 1 (1988): 13.

dren's experience and they view schooling as a way of yielding their responsibility to someone else. They strongly believe that parents, who are closest to children, are "the optimal co-creators of the life experience."[22] However, while some might see their choice as an attempt to control children, they see it as a way to free them for authentic human development within the family rather than trusting in a morally deficient culture.

Of utmost importance is passing on religious and moral beliefs. Surveys of homeschooling parents show that the great majority are most concerned about the moral and religious development of their children.[23] They choose homeschooling because they believe it is an effective way of passing on their faith to their children. Kimberly Hahn, one of the minority of Catholic homeschooling parents, speaks about the Catholic idea that families are called to be domestic churches and argues that homeschooling gives her family the flexibility to live out this mission, because they can schedule academics around the religious life instead of the other way around.[24] With time comes a consistent focus on the spiritual that makes Hahn feel better able to offer a rich faith to her children, and more confident sending them into the world to influence others.[25]

While most parents feel comfortable sharing moral rearing with teachers, ministers, and other adults, homeschooling parents believe that the task of moral/religious formation is given to them by God, and cannot be delegated to anyone else. Typically citing Ephesians 6:4 ("Fathers, do not provoke your children to anger, but bring them up in the discipline and instruction of the Lord") and Deuteronomy 6:6-7 ("Keep these words that I am commanding you today in your heart. Recite them to your children and talk about them when you are at home and when you are away, when you lie down and when you rise"), they emphasize the parental duty to bring up a child in the faith.[26] If one takes seriously the responsibility to form one's children as Christians, these parents believe, it becomes difficult to give

---

22. Mayberry, "Why Home Schooling?" p. 10.

23. Mayberry, "Why Home Schooling?" pp. 7-10. See also Gustafson, "Study of Home Schooling," p. 10; Gregory J. Cizek, "Religious Education in Home Schools: Goals/Outcomes Mismatch?" *Religious Education* 89, no. 1 (Winter 1994): 44-46; Wartes, "Washington Home School Project," p. 45.

24. Kimberly Hahn and Mary Hasson, *Catholic Education: Homeward Bound* (San Francisco: Ignatius, 1996), p. 53.

25. Hahn and Hasson, *Catholic Education,* pp. 55-57.

26. Mayberry, "Why Home Schooling?" p. 8. One parent interviewed by Mayberry said that if she did not homeschool, she "would feel some sense of abandonment of my kid. I would be turning over their mind and spirit and their souls to a state institution" (p. 11).

over so many hours a day to others. Although Christian schools might be capable of religious instruction, according to homeschoolers, parents are really the ones who should be attending to the formation of their children's faith and character.

If the motivations of homeschooling parents are clear, their success is harder to gauge. On the one hand, many studies compare the academic skills of homeschooled and traditionally schooled children, and these studies consistently show that homeschool children are equal to or better than their peers.[27] Moreover, despite widespread concern regarding the socialization of homeschooled children, most studies show that schooling environment makes little difference in this area. Homeschooled children are just as likely, if not more likely, to have high self-esteem, and they are just as involved in activities outside the home.[28] Because homeschooled children typically have both a strong family environment and a wealth of experiences outside the home, they are at least as likely as other children to be strong community leaders. Worries about children emerging from homeschool environments lacking academic or social skills seem to be unfounded.

However, success in the realm of character development is considerably less clear. Ironically, while moral and religious formation is the most important reason parents give for homeschooling, there is little information about whether homeschooling actually works.[29] Yet it is important to know if the practice of homeschooling really does allow parents to shape their children in ways that typical dual-career families cannot.

There is only one comprehensive study on homeschooling that attempts to evaluate moral formation in a systematic way.[30] This study uses the DIT (Defining Issues Test) to compare the moral development of tradi-

---

27. Wartes, "Washington Home School Project," p. 46, found that Washington homeschoolers performed better than average (in the 65-68 percentile range) on standardized achievement tests. This is consistent with analysis in Oregon, Tennessee, Arkansas, and Alaska; see also Resetar, "An Exploratory Study," p. 4, who found that 90.9 percent of his subjects had standard achievement scores above the mean.

28. Norma S. Hedin, "Self-Concept of Baptist Children in Three Education Settings," *Home School Researcher* 7, no. 3 (1991): 3; John Wesley Taylor, "Self Concept in Home-Schooling Children," *Home School Researcher* 2, no. 2 (1986): 1; Paul Kitchen, "Socialization of Home School Children versus Conventional School Children," *Home School Researcher* 7, no. 3 (1991): 12; Vicki Tillman, "Home Schoolers, Self-Esteem, and Socialization," *Home School Researcher* 11, no. 3 (1995): 5; Larry Shyers, "A Comparison of Social Adjustment between Home and Traditionally Schooled Students," *Home School Researcher* 8, no. 3 (1992): 5-6.

29. Cizek, "Religious Education," p. 7.

30. Laura Manuel, "The Moral Development of Home Schooled and Public Schooled Adolescents" (Diss., University of Northern Colorado, 2000).

tional school and homeschool children.[31] Laura Manuel, the author, found that homeschooling parents scored significantly lower on the DIT than parents who did not homeschool. Both sets of children scored about average on the DIT, but the scores of public school children were higher.[32] Manuel suggests that the difference might be due to different experiences. She posits that the narrow range of experiences of homeschooled parents and children may limit their moral reasoning ability,[33] affirming Kohlberg's idea that "reasoning was stimulated by people being placed in conflict situations in their families, friendship groups, and societal institutions. The conflict itself was thought to be the key to development because the situation might require a child to consider issues from another's perspective."[34] Homeschooled children, who are often raised by authoritarian parents, may be "more likely to confuse conventional issues with moral issues and hence have lower moral judgment."[35]

But what does "conventional" mean? The reasoning model that Manuel uses is itself a conventional model that understands moral reasoning in terms of abstract consideration of conflictual situations. It may be that homeschooled children are more likely to engage in different methods of moral reasoning that are not well measured by the DIT. Manual herself acknowledges the limitations of her study. First, her definition of moral reasoning conflicts with the definitions held by her subjects.[36] Homeschooling parents typically report that their children make better moral choices than other children; they are quite sure that homeschooling has positive effects.[37] In addition, the study measures a certain kind of reasoning ability, not one's actual life choices, and thus can predict the use of that skill but cannot measure the quality of one's choices. In sum, it is likely that homeschooled children reason differently than public school children do, perhaps in ways that are not respected by the mainstream culture. Still, without hard comparisons of moral actions, it remains difficult

---

31. This is, according to Manuel, the most widely used measure of moral judgment in psychology today. It includes six dilemmas, with twelve items to be ranked as considerations. Higher scores are awarded for principled moral reasoning; "Moral Development," p. 86.

32. Manuel, "Moral Development," p. 106.

33. Manuel, "Moral Development," p. 9. Manuel seems to assume that homeschooling necessarily entails a narrow range of experiences. This assumption is questioned by homeschooling advocates.

34. Manuel, "Moral Development," p. 6.

35. Manuel, "Moral Development," p. 15.

36. Manuel, "Moral Development," p. 24.

37. E-mail communication with Laura Manuel, February 27, 2002.

to discern whether homeschooled children have a moral advantage over other children.

Even without these studies, it seems necessary to respond to the challenging critique of homeschooling parents, for their peaceful, child-focused homes where issues of faith and character are central stand in vivid contrast to the majority of middle-class families where the increasing demands of work, school, and activities make family time a rare commodity and moral teaching a luxury. Thus I ask, "What does the Christian tradition require of parents?" I will turn to Christian theology to retrieve an understanding of parenting as a vocation. This will set up the ethical question, "Are non-homeschooling families able to meet this obligation?"

Christian Theology and Parenting

The Significance of Children

One might think that even if contemporary theologians speak of a dual vocation of Christian parenting, historically the main emphasis would be on the importance of child rearing. However, despite the obvious centrality of children in the lives of ordinary Christians, children have not been a central concern of Christian theology.

However, the New Testament is an exception. The well-known story in which Jesus gets angry at his disciples for trying to keep the children away from him (Mark 10:13-16) is a challenge to those who privilege adult affairs over children's concerns.[38] A countercultural valuing of children is also evident in the blessing that follows Jesus' rebuke of his disciples, his warning to those who would lead children astray, and his insistence (in the context of a discussion on who will be the greatest) that those who welcome a child in his name will be great. As Judith Gundry-Wolf puts it, "Jesus thus redefines care for children as a mark of greatness."[39] In identifying himself with children, Jesus claims child care as important Christian work.

Few theologians in the Christian tradition assign to children a similar place of importance. However, many grant the significance of child rearing by the way they address children as moral and spiritual beings. For instance,

---

38. Judith M. Gundry-Volf, "The Least and the Greatest: Children in the New Testament," in *The Child in Christian Thought*, ed. Marcia Bunge (Grand Rapids: Eerdmans, 2001), pp. 41-42.

39. Gundry-Volf, "Least and the Greatest," p. 43.

Saint Augustine's belief that children have the status of noninnocence (they are not simply innocent or as capable of sin as adults) implies that children do have a moral life.[40] Jonathan Edwards's fire-and-brimstone sermons to children, though different in tone and emphasis, may be seen in much the same way.[41] More positively, the insistence that children are eligible for baptism and can legitimately profess the faith, found in authors as diverse as John Calvin, Menno Simons, and Martin Luther, also indicates that children are not simply instruments of their parents' wills.[42] They, too, are capable of experiencing God and deciding to devote their lives to the Christian faith. Recognition of children's importance can be seen in the acknowledgment that children sin and in the insistence that children can be in relationship with God. In both claims, the worth of children is evident and the significance of rearing them is implied.

The sense of children's importance continues to be a persistent theme around the edges of the contemporary theological tradition, and children have received a great deal more attention in the last decade.[43] However, the more pressing question across generations has been, "What obligations do parents have toward the children they bring into the world?"

The Connection between Parents and Children

A major emphasis of contemporary popular family theology is the importance of the parental role in caring for children. Christian parenting literature, along with self-styled religious experts on parenting like Dr. James Dobson and Dr. Laura Schlessinger, frequently focuses on the importance of direct parental care for children. The irreplaceability of parental nurture is assumed to be a Christian principle, though popular figures understand the limits of this nurture differently.[44]

40. Martha Ellen Stortz, "'Where or When Was Your Servant Innocent?': Augustine on Childhood," in *The Child in Christian Thought*, p. 100.

41. Catherine A. Brekus, "Children of Wrath, Children of Grace: Jonathan Edwards and the Puritan Culture of Child Rearing," in *The Child in Christian Thought*, p. 328.

42. Marcia Bunge, introduction to *The Child in Christian Thought*, pp. 16-17.

43. See Bonnie Miller-McLemore, *Let the Children Come: Reimagining Childhood from a Christian Perspective* (San Francisco: Jossey-Bass, 2003).

44. For instance, some are opposed to day care but not schools and say little about feeding or sleeping, while others shun both day care and schools and advocate attachment parenting practices such as long-term nursing, carrying babies and toddlers in a sling, co-sleeping, and physical bonding with older children. Others recommend Christian preschool and schooling.

Until very recently, official Catholic teaching was in agreement with this literature, as it asked women and men to give their whole selves to parenting, embracing it as a cross. The U.S. Bishops compare the earthly realities of parenting to the suffering and liberation of Christ: "The mix of joy and sorrow, of pain and pleasure, of anxiety and relief that generally accompanies childbearing and childrearing reflects the deepest pattern or rhythm of human existence. It is the paschal, Passover, Easter mystery being played out in the couple's lives; it is the death and resurrection of Christ being specifically reenacted within our times."[45] This serious work of the cross is not the sort of work one turns over to others.

Papal teaching clearly states that women will bear this cross most directly. In *On the Family,* John Paul II claims that women's work in the home ought to be celebrated and made more possible by society. If women must work outside the home, the pope asks that they make sure that their family life comes first.[46] In his later *Letter to Families,* he calls raising children "a genuine apostolate," but differentiates between the primary role of mother and the secondary role of father, who must "become willingly involved as a husband and father in the motherhood of his wife."[47] The home is presumed to be the ideal place for child care.

Recent writings have moved into new progressive territory by claiming that women have the right to work and bring distinctive gifts to public life. When women do work, John Paul II argues that employers and governments are obligated to see that they are able to fulfill their duties as mothers.[48] Benedict XVI continues this trajectory, saying that society needs the "genius of women."[49] Still, rhetoric celebrating traditional roles has not wholly disappeared.[50] Though there is growing recognition of the gifts women bring to the public sphere, the Catholic tradition still sees family in somewhat traditional terms. Ideally, mothers of young children have more responsibility for private life than fathers, who are more committed to public vocations. The

45. U.S. Bishops, *Parenthood* (Washington, D.C.: United States Catholic Conference, 1990), §8.

46. U.S. Bishops, *Parenthood,* §23.

47. U.S. Bishops, *Parenthood,* §16. The idea that a father's parenting is secondary to and derived from mothering is echoed in John Paul II, *On the Dignity and Vocation of Women* (1988), §18, as is the link between motherhood and suffering (§19).

48. John Paul II, *Letter to Women* (1995), §16.

49. Benedict XVI, *Letter to the Bishops of the Catholic Church on the Collaboration of Men and Women in the Church and in the World* (2004), §13.

50. *Equal Opportunity in the World of Work* (August 20, 1995), in *The Genius of Women* (Washington, D.C.: United States Catholic Conference, 1988), §19.

strong assumption (rarely made explicit) that parents should be primary caretakers of children drives this division of the dual vocation.

Despite this emphasis in contemporary Christian writing, few Christian theologians have devoted much time to this issue. Those who have root the parental duty to nurture in the special connection between parents and children. The fourth-century church father John Chrysostom sounds almost contemporary when he calls parents back to their primary duty to care for their children. Chrysostom puts the souls of children in parents' hands, and claims that "whether a child inherits the kingdom of heaven relies upon the care he or she receives from parents."[51] This strong sense of parents' ultimate responsibility comes from Chrysostom's belief that a child is intimately linked to her parents. He says in *On Marriage and Family:* "The child is a bridge connecting mother to father, so the three become one flesh. . . . And here the bridge is formed from the substance of each! Just as the head and the body are one, so it is with the child. That is why Scripture does not say, 'They shall be one flesh.' But they shall be joined together 'into one flesh,' namely the child."[52]

Chrysostom's belief that one-fleshness connects parents and children and links their lives and destinies together is echoed in the writings of the thirteenth-century theologian Thomas Aquinas, who uses natural law to link children and parents. He posits that because the child comes from the parents, they are best able to care for him. For Thomas, "the affective love of parent for child is appropriately among the most intense, intimate, long-lasting human attachments. No one is nearer to us than our children, whom we love 'as being part of' ourselves."[53] Given this assumption, Thomas's insistence that "[n]urture by the family — specifically the mother — is appropriate for children at this pre-rational stage" makes sense.[54]

Dual Vocation

Yet, in the writings of most Christian theologians, even when moral nurture is given the highest priority, it is not clear that parents are the only ones capable of nurture, or that parents have no other significant obligations.

51. Vigen Guroian, "The Ecclesial Family: John Chrysostom on Parenthood and Children," in *The Child in Christian Thought,* p. 69.

52. Guroian, "The Ecclesial Family," p. 67.

53. Cristina L. H. Traina, "A Person in the Making: Thomas Aquinas on Children and Childhood," in *The Child in Christian Thought,* p. 121.

54. Traina, "Person in the Making," p. 115.

From the beginning of the Christian tradition, it is clear that discipleship to Christ is the primary obligation of all Christians and cannot be overridden by the demands of parenthood. It is perhaps the Mennonites who make this point the most starkly, because their experience of persecution made the trade-off quite concrete at times. When it came time to choose between standing up for their faith and nurturing their children, many Mennonite parents reluctantly said good-bye to their children and went off to jail or death, leaving their children in the care of their community. They did not see themselves as failures as parents because they left their children with people to whom they could easily entrust the formation of their children in the faith.[55] This major emphasis on discipleship and formation in Christian thought, tragically exemplified in the ultimate sacrifice of the Mennonites, suggests that being a good Christian parent can sometimes mean entrusting children to others in order to fulfill a public vocation.[56]

However, most parents will take up the task of formation themselves, and in ordinary circumstances the tradition certainly obligates them to do so. For instance, in his "Address on Vainglory and the Right Way for Parents to Bring Up Their Children," Chrysostom criticizes his culture, mourning the emphasis parents put on giving a new child new clothes and wealth, when they could be focusing on teaching virginity, sobriety, discipline, and contempt of wealth and fame. Instead, he exhorts them, "Raise up an athlete for Christ."[57] Chrysostom seems to want parents to think of a child differently (as "a philosopher and athlete and citizen of heaven") in order that they might reconceive their own duties.[58] Parents are for him artists or sculptors, shaping their children's character.[59] Contemporary admirers of Chrysostom draw out the implications of this idea, noting that "[w]hen we teach our children to be good, to be gentle, to be forgiving . . . we instill virtue in their souls, and reveal the image of God within them."[60] The parent's role as a cocreator whose "work" is a reflection of God could not be clearer.

55. Keith Graber Miller, "Complex Innocence, Obligatory Nurturance, and Parental Vigilance," in *The Child in Christian Thought*, pp. 222-23. Miller relies on *Martyrs Mirror*, a collection of letters of 800 martyred Mennonite men and women.

56. Mothers who put their children up for adoption are another extreme example of this principle.

57. John Chrysostom, "Address on Vainglory and the Right Way for Parents to Bring Up Their Children," in *Christianity and Pagan Culture*, trans. M. L. W. Laistner (Ithaca, N.Y.: Cornell University Press, 1951), pp. 93-99.

58. Chrysostom, "Address on Vainglory," p. 102.

59. Chrysostom, "Address on Vainglory," p. 96.

60. John Chrysostom, *On Marriage and Family Life*, p. 44, quoted in Guroian, "The Ecclesial Family," p. 66.

Chrysostom's thoughts are echoed by many other Christian thinkers. In similarly significant language, Luther calls parents "apostles to children," and advocates the teaching of the catechism at home, church, and school.[61] John Calvin, too, emphasized instruction in piety, and stated that the primary duty of parents is to teach godliness and the submission of godly desires to the common good.[62] Although Menno Simons (along with the Mennonite martyrs) believed that faith could call parents to leave children in extreme circumstances, he also believed that when parents were able to remain with children, their most important task was to nurture their children's faith and character, and to help them work out their salvation.[63] Horace Bushnell, author of the popular nineteenth-century work *Christian Nurture*, counseled parents that nurture was a long process involving specific practices, and emphasized the importance of the parental role in faith formation, saying that "Religion never thoroughly penetrates life until it becomes domestic."[64] This strong sense that parents have a crucial role in faith formation is a consistent theme in the Christian tradition.

However, no historical Christian author gives parents full responsibility for moral or spiritual formation of their children. Rather, most theologians assume that parents share the task of rearing with churches, schools, and communities. One need not speak only of Calvin's Geneva to drive home this point, though his experiment is surely a primary example of corearing.[65] One might also refer to the Mennonites' sense of communal responsibility for children, in times of persecution, but also more generally,[66] or to Luther, who glorified the day-to-day duties of child rearing by parents while arguing that parents shared the responsibility to catechize with the

61. Jane E. Strohl, "The Child in Luther's Theology: 'For What Purpose Do We Older Folks Exist, Other Than to Care for . . . the Young?'" in *The Child in Christian Thought*, pp. 140, 146.

62. Barbara Pitkin, "'The Heritage of the Lord': Children in the Theology of John Calvin," in *The Child in Christian Thought*, p. 174.

63. Miller, "Complex Innocence," pp. 207-8.

64. Horace Bushnell, *Christian Nurture*, quoted in Margaret Bendroth, "Horace Bushnell's *Christian Nurture*," in *The Child in Christian Thought*, p. 356. Others who emphasize the family's role as domestic church include Chrysostom, Gregory of Nazianzus, and Augustine. See Florence Caffrey Bourg, "Domestic Church: A New Frontier in Ecclesiology," *Horizons* 29, no. 1 (Spring 2002): 42-63.

65. Pitkin, "Heritage of the Lord," p. 174. Pitkin claims, "In Calvin's view, it was society's duty to provide the right conditions for raising children to be godly."

66. Miller, "Complex Innocence," pp. 219-22. Miller offers a contemporary example of a Mennonite dedication service for infants that includes a congregation's promise "to share in your child's nurture and well-being" (p. 225).

schools and the church.[67] Even when Jesus tells his listeners not to lead a child astray, he speaks to his disciples, not specifically to parents.[68] Indeed, though Jesus strongly upholds the marriage bond, there is no record of his addressing parental responsibility for children. In short, moral formation is at the center of Christian discourse on children, and parents are seen as primary, but by no means exclusive, shapers of their children.

This seems to leave room for the pursuit of public work, if such work is a real obligation. Few in the historical tradition have focused on the problem of possible conflicting obligations of work and family. Clearly, until relatively recently women were responsible for most primary child care, though they shared the task of moral formation with men, whose work, until the Industrial Revolution, was centered in the home, allowing them a crucial role in shaping the character of their children. It was assumed that most men could provide for their families and instruct their children in Christian faith, just as it was assumed that most women would nurture and form their children. Single men and women were more able to take up more demanding public vocations, especially in the Catholic Church, which provided opportunities for women to enter religious life. Two shifts change all of this: the women's movement, which seeks public work for women, and the growing recognition of lay life as a vocation, equal in worth to religious life. Now both women and men have the opportunity to shape the world, and Catholic theology explicitly calls them to this task.[69]

In light of this, most contemporary lay theologians believe that the obligations of Christian parents are plural. Catholic ethicist Lisa Cahill, notably, brings to light the social responsibilities of the family, lending support to the idea of dual vocation. While acknowledging the Catholic tradition's emphasis on "permanent marriage and the two-parent family nurturing children," she insists that families become domestic churches by carrying out "the social mission of compassion and service in [the] spirit of Christian love."[70] She holds up African American families as role models for more privileged families, calling attention to their concern for each other across family lines.[71] According to Cahill, Christian families ought to be committed not only to internal nurture, but also to transforming society.[72]

---

67. Strohl, "Child in Luther's Theology," p. 146.

68. Gundry-Volf, "Least and the Greatest," p. 44.

69. *Gaudium et Spes,* §43.

70. Lisa Sowle Cahill, *Family: A Christian Social Perspective* (Minneapolis: Fortress, 2000), p. 129.

71. Cahill, *Family,* p. 129.

72. Cahill, *Family,* p. 81.

Cahill's relative lack of emphasis on the nuclear family's care for its own is rooted in part in her reading of Scripture. She claims that Jesus' hard sayings on family,[73] along with a historical record of early Christian families who began to live according to a new vision, support the idea that what is central to the early Christian tradition is not family per se, but "an ethos of mutuality, equality, and solidarity and in subsuming kin loyalty under compassion for the 'neighbor,' the 'stranger,' and the 'enemy,' as belonging to one's family in Christ."[74] Cahill places the social mission of the family at the center of its existence. While not dismissive of parental duties, Cahill seeks to open Christian families to the fullness of their mission. She claims that while care for one's own may be a universal family ethic, "the ultimate tests of a distinctively *Christian* ethics of family life go beyond the well-being of family members and the successful accomplishment of family roles. The Christian family defines *family values* as care for others, especially the poor."[75] Thus the primary mission of the Christian family is not care for children but care for others. The Christian tradition's strong emphasis on social concern calls families to reach outward. Cahill assumes that parenting is a dual vocation involving work and nurture for men and women.

Christian feminist theologians have made this theme of dual vocation more explicit. Methodist theologian Bonnie Miller-McLemore, for instance, argues that mature adult life involves both productivity in the world of work and nurture of children at home.[76] Contending that Genesis 1 gives to both men and women the responsibilities to fill the earth (have and care for children) and subdue it (work), she believes that living a fully human life means being creative in both ways.[77] Miller-McLemore carefully distinguishes herself from radical feminists who seem to diminish the work of parenting, though she clearly seeks to respond to their writings. Her own experience as a mother struggling to balance teaching and writing with caring for her family marks her work.[78] She argues quite powerfully that

73. For instance, "Who are my mother and my brothers? . . . Here are my mother and my brothers! Whoever does the will of God is my brother and sister and mother" (Mark 3:33-35), and "Whoever comes to me and does not hate father and mother, wife and children, brothers and sisters, yes, and even life itself, cannot be my disciple" (Luke 14:26).

74. Cahill, *Family,* p. 47.

75. Cahill, *Family,* p. 135.

76. Miller-McLemore, *Also a Mother,* p. 49.

77. Miller-McLemore, *Also a Mother,* pp. 36-37.

78. Miller-McLemore, *Also a Mother,* pp. 109-30.

women and men need assistance from the church and society as they strive to be "good enough" parents and workers.[79]

Christian theologians like Miller-McLemore and Cahill do not ignore the importance of parenting. In fact, they are among the strongest voices calling for a renewed attention to children. Yet they assume that children will spend at least some time in the care of others, followed by school, while parents juggle home and work responsibilities. With the rejection of sexist limitations on women's lives and the upholding of social responsibility comes the embrace of a dual-career traditional school model.

While this is not surprising, this is precisely what homeschooling parents find so problematic. In their view, it is difficult for mothers and fathers who are both away from home for much of the day to parent well. Specifically, they are concerned that parents may not be able to give adequate attention to the moral and religious rearing of their children. However, many parents believe that Christian schools are a viable alternative to homeschooling, as they can be communities where alternative beliefs and lifestyles are nurtured and supported. Others choose to supplement public or religious education with distinctive home-based rituals, discussions, and practices. Can Christian parents who embrace civic vocations also meet the demands of their vocation to parenting by employing options like these?

Conclusion: Toward a Christian Ethic of Child Rearing

Christian emphasis on the parental responsibility to shape children's moral and religious development invites a real consideration of the homeschool movement. The alternative vision of parenting held by homeschoolers calls into question the wisdom of the pervasive norm of the dual-career/traditional school family. The challenge of homeschooling ought to influence Christian theology of children in three important ways.

First, it should direct attention to what is, in terms of the Christian tradition, the central task of parenting — the moral and religious formation of children. Homeschooling parents make significant sacrifices to take up this task because they believe they are the best ones to do it. While it is not yet clear that they succeed more so than most other parents, they certainly commit more of their time and energy to rearing than most and seem convinced that they are making a difference in their children's lives. Contemporary Christian teaching calls families to become domestic churches and rec-

79. Miller-McLemore, *Also a Mother,* pp. 185-95.

ognizes the importance of this work of the home. Thus Christian parents ought to consider how they can truly become church if they are seldom at home with their children.[80]

Second, homeschooling advocates call Christian families to slow down and refuse to accept the structure of contemporary family life; they insist that time and formation are connected. The frenetic pace of this life and the resulting fatigue are persistent themes in recent sociological literature on the family and are facts of life for most women and men in dual-career families. Homeschooling parents are notable for their refusal to give in to this structure and for their claim to have more than enough time to accomplish their goals. While there are no definitive studies linking homeschooling and better moral formation, it seems intuitive that there is a relationship between the claiming of time and the formation of character. The refusal to give in to society's structures and the freedom to construct or reinforce an alternative ethic are intimately related. This insight of homeschooling parents should not be ignored because it seems impossible to escape modernization. Clearly, some are successfully resisting harmful aspects of modern life.

However, the Christian tradition also values the witness of other adults in the lives of children. Most people of faith would agree that friends and relatives, as well as those who teach, lead, coach, and counsel children, share some responsibility for their children's religious and moral development. Even those in the community who differ in their beliefs may play a significant role in the shaping of children. As many theologians rightly claim, "the village" (diverse as it is) can be a positive influence on children by confirming and questioning what is taught at home.[81] To severely limit such an influence seems to dismiss the gifts the Christian tradition affirms in the community.

Furthermore, the dual vocation to which the contemporary tradition rightly calls both men and women remains a significant obligation. The demands of keeping a home and forming children are serious, and they require a significant amount of time, but the Christian faith seems to ask more of its adherents, even those who are parents. The public call of the tradition can be heard in the hard sayings of Jesus, the sacrifices of the Mennonites, the affirmation of the role of society in Luther and Calvin, the contemporary understanding of lay life supported by the Second Vatican Council, John Paul II's theology of the family, Benedict XVI's affirmation

---

80. See Bourg, *Where Two or Three Are Gathered*.

81. See, for instance, Herbert Anderson and Susan B. W. Johnson, *Regarding Children: A New Respect for Childhood and Families* (Louisville: Westminster, 1994), pp. 91-110.

that the world needs the gifts of women, and parent theologians' embrace of work and family. Christian parents must look beyond their children to the world, and ask what the world needs from them.

Thus, while homeschooling may be the right choice for some families and a challenge to all the rest, it does not seem to be the only possible choice for Christian families. While homeschooling poses important challenges to current ideas about child rearing, it does not render them useless. Marks of a Christian ethic of child rearing might be a commitment to the moral and religious formation of children, a commitment to share the gifts of all family members with the community, and an openness to receiving the gifts of that community. Within this ethic, homeschooling, religious schooling, and public schooling would be acceptable choices, as long as parents fulfilled their responsibility to pass on their faith and morals, as well their responsibilities to the larger community. It is worth noting that at present, many religious schools do not provide a true alternative to mainstream culture. If Christian schools are to be places where children learn different ways of thinking and living, they will need faculty and administrators committed to this mission, and supportive communities of parents who are willing to invest in this mission and reinforce it. Public school families may need to make common cause with families of many different faiths who share their values, and will need to work hard to make religious identity central to their children's lives.

The key lesson of the homeschooling movement is that it is difficult to fulfill the internal responsibilities of parenthood without a lot of time. In Christian families, the ways adults structure children's lives at home and outside home must respect the need of children for time with parents and without structure. This will probably mean restructuring job responsibilities so that more contact among parents and children is possible. If most Christian families will not necessarily homeschool full-time, they ought to homeschool at least some of the time so that the home will truly be both a resting place and a school for virtue in a busy, overly scheduled world. The signs of our times demand nothing less.

Concurrent Readings

Bunge, Marcia, ed. *The Child in Christian Thought*. Grand Rapids: Eerdmans, 2001. The book offers a diversity of writers. It begins with a chapter on children in the New Testament and treats major figures in the history of Christian theology, from John Chrysostom to Karl Rahner.

John Paul II. *Letter to Families*. Rome: Libreria Editrice Vaticana, 1994. In this letter John Paul II sets forth an understanding of family as the "genealogy of persons" (i.e., where persons are "created") and family as a pattern of what he (following Pope Paul VI) calls a culture or "civilization" of love.

Salzman, Todd A., Thomas M. Kelly, and John J. O'Keefe, eds. *Marriage in the Catholic Tradition: Scripture, Tradition, and Experience*. New York: Crossroad, 2004. The volume provides chapters on marriage in Scripture and the early church. It accounts for shifts in the theology and practice of marriage in the modern era, and it deals with issues such as cohabitation and interreligious marriages.

Chapter 13

Gather Us In and Make Us Channels of Your Peace: Evaluating War with an Entirely New Attitude

Tobias Winright

Pass It On

"The peace of the Lord be with you." When I say this in class to my students, they initially are caught off guard and are not sure whether, or perhaps how, to respond. Usually, after a few seconds of silence, some hesitatingly reply, "And also with you." For these brave students, something inside nudges them to respond in such a way, so that it seems almost automatic or second nature to express in return their wish for peace to me. And yet, outside of the context of worship, this greeting and response appear out of place for most Christians, including those of us who feel compelled, even if falteringly, to respond accordingly.

In contrast, many Jewish persons, whether in the synagogue or at the corner coffee shop, greet others (and say good-bye to them) with *"Shalom aleikem"* ("Peace be with you"). Similarly, whether at the mosque or on the street, Muslims say to one another and to others, *"Assalam wa alaykum"* ("Peace be with you"). While a simple "Hi" or "Hello" tends to flow from the lips of Christians today in their everyday encounters with others (and sometimes even during the passing of the peace during worship!), early Christians apparently had more in common with our Jewish and Muslim brothers and sisters. In the New Testament, the apostle Paul instructed Christians, "Greet one another with a holy kiss" (Rom. 16:16; 1 Cor. 16:20; 2 Cor. 13:12). Indeed, at that time and place (the ancient Mediterranean world), people greeted one another with a kiss (they still do in parts of Europe and the Middle East) rather than a handshake, and this was a sign of peace. Paul therefore encouraged Christians to exchange this sign of peace, just as the risen Jesus Christ repeatedly greeted his disciples with "Peace be with you" (Luke 24:36; John 20:19, 21, 26). Although this ancient act of peace became incorporated into Christian worship, it has apparently fallen out of practice today outside of the context of worship.

This disconnect between how we pass the peace during Mass and how we greet one another in our daily lives pales in comparison to the stark contrast between the peace we pass and the rivalries, animosities, and interpersonal conflicts we encounter in our everyday lives at home, school, work, and on the highway (road rage!). Watch just a few episodes of MTV's *The Real World* and the frequently quarrelsome interpersonal dynamics between the roommates, and you will quickly see what I mean. Much more seriously, though, in recent years the graphic images of persons suffering horrible deaths in the terrorist attacks on 9/11 and of hundreds of thousands of dead or starving refugees in the Darfur region of Sudan have become indelibly impressed into our mind's eye, making especially pronounced this contrast between the peace we pass at worship and what unfortunately happens in the world.

Yet, when we go forth from worship and attempt to pass Christ's peace on to a planet where peace is often absent, the question of *how* to do so comes to the fore. When conflict erupts, how should Christians respond in a way that is congruent with Christ's call for love, mercy, and reconciliation? May Christians ever resort to the use of force, including killing, to restore or establish a just peace? If, for example, an enemy, whom we are called to love, threatens an innocent neighbor, whom we are also commanded to love, what should we Christians do?

My firsthand experience working in law enforcement — in corrections while I was a young person in college and in policing some years later after I became a college professor — served as a portal for me in asking these difficult questions. As a Christian who had regularly attended Mass, parochial school, and youth group Bible studies while growing up, I found that I struggled with whether I could use lethal force in performing my duties. I hoped to serve others and protect them from harm, but the conflicts and violence I encountered in the line of duty — and the use of force that might be required to prevent or stop such violence — seemed in tension with the peace of Christ I experienced at church and was called to pass along to the world.

To be sure, neither the tension between Christ's peace and its absence in much of the world, nor the difficult questions about how to pass along Christ's peace in the world, is denied or glossed over by the church. On the one hand, a few months after the terrorist attacks of 9/11, Pope John Paul II proclaimed in his Angelus message for Sunday, January 27, 2002: "Violence never again! War never again! Terrorism never again! In the name of God, may every religion bring upon the earth justice and peace, forgiveness and life, love!"[1] This echoed Pope Paul VI's plea in 1965 to the United Nations General Assembly: "No more war, war never again."[2] Soon after this speech the bishops of Vatican II emphasized for Catholics our *obligation* to work for the abolition of war: "It is our clear duty, then, to strain every muscle as we work for the time when all war can be completely outlawed by international consent."[3] Likewise, in their influential pastoral letter issued in 1983 on war and peace, the Catholic bishops of the United States posited, "Peacemaking is not an optional commitment. It is a requirement of our faith."[4] Indeed, the bishops defend and approve of those Christians who renounce the use of violent force and who instead employ methods of active nonviolent resistance to protect the innocent from aggression. "We believe work to develop non-violent means of fending off aggression and resolving conflict best reflect the call of Jesus both to love and to justice."[5]

On the other hand, in the face of genocide and humanitarian crises where civilians suffer at the hands of their own governments, Pope John Paul II claimed that other nations "no longer have a 'right to indifference' [and it] seems clear that their duty is to disarm this aggressor if all other means have proven ineffective."[6] In this way he linked the duty to defend others' lives with what the Second Vatican Council said about the right of nations to defend their own populations from aggression: "Certainly, war has not been rooted out of human affairs. As long as the danger of war re-

---

1. Available at http://www.vatican.va/holy_father/john_paul_ii/angelus/2002/documents/hf_jp-ii_ang_20020127_en.html.

2. Quoted in Eileen Egan, *Peace Be with You: Justified Warfare or the Way of Nonviolence* (Maryknoll, N.Y.: Orbis, 1999), p. 166.

3. Second Vatican Council, *Pastoral Constitution on the Church in the Modern World (Gaudium et Spes),* in *The Documents of Vatican II,* ed. Walter M. Abbot, S.J. (Piscataway, N.J.: New Century Publishers, 1966), §82. More universally, according to the *Catechism of the Catholic Church,* "*All citizens and all governments* are obliged to work for the avoidance of war" (New York: Image/Doubleday, 1995), §2308, emphasis added.

4. National Conference of Catholic Bishops (NCCB), *The Challenge of Peace: God's Promise and Our Response* (Washington, D.C.: United States Catholic Conference, 1983), §333. For a similar statement from another Christian church that is fairly representative of documents by other mainline denominations in recent years on war and peace, see the United Methodist Council of Bishops, *In Defense of Creation: The Nuclear Crisis and a Just Peace* (Nashville: Graded Press, 1986).

5. NCCB, *The Challenge of Peace,* §78. See also Second Vatican Council, *Pastoral Constitution on the Church in the Modern World,* §78.

6. John Paul II, "Principles Underlying a Stance toward Unjust Aggressors," *Origins* 22, no. 34 (January 28, 1993): 587.

mains and there is no competent and sufficiently powerful authority at the international level, governments cannot be denied the right to legitimate defense once every means of peaceful settlement has been exhausted."[7] Likewise, the U.S. Catholic bishops acknowledged in their pastoral letter in 1983 that "the fact of aggression, oppression and injustice in our world also serves to legitimate the resort to weapons and armed force" in defense of the innocent.[8] More recently, both the *Catechism of the Catholic Church* and the *Compendium of the Social Doctrine of the Church* underscore the right and the duty of nations to use force of arms to protect, under the rubric of "legitimate defense," their own citizens and innocent victims in other countries who are unable to defend themselves.[9]

As these statements from official church sources in recent decades show, the tension I felt and the questions I asked about promoting and protecting peace in the world were not mine alone but were also shared by the wider Christian community to which I belonged by baptism. While all Catholics are called and obligated to work for peace, it is "the *how* of defending peace which offers moral options."[10] That is, the Catholic Church allows for both nonviolence and legitimate defense through the use of armed force to promote and protect peace in the world. Although these are two different approaches to defending the innocent, they both share, according to the U.S. Catholic bishops, a "strong presumption against war" and for peace.[11]

---

7. Second Vatican Council, *Pastoral Constitution on the Church in the Modern World,* §79.

8. NCCB, *The Challenge of Peace,* §78.

9. *Catechism,* §2309; Pontifical Council for Justice and Peace, *Compendium of the Social Doctrine of the Church* (Washington, D.C.: United States Conference of Catholic Bishops, 2004), §500 and 504. For a helpful treatment of this shift from using the traditional phrase "just war" to "legitimate defense," see William L. Portier, "Are We Really Serious When We Ask God to Deliver Us from War? The Catechism and the Challenge of Pope John Paul II," *Communio* 23 (Spring 1996): 47-63. Similarly, Kenneth Himes suggests that this may point to the "need to develop a general theory of armed intervention." See Kenneth R. Himes, O.F.M., "Intervention, Just War, and U.S. National Security," *Theological Studies* 65 (2004): 149.

10. NCCB, *The Challenge of Peace,* §73. For helpful insights on this seeming "paradox where a tradition which gives clear priority to the imperatives of peace, at the same time, does not repudiate the 'just war' doctrine," see Brian V. Johnstone, C.SS.R., "Pope John Paul II and the War in Iraq," *Studia Moralia* 41, no. 2 (December 2003): 322; and Brian V. Johnstone, C.SS.R., "The War on Terrorism: A Just War?" *Studia Moralia* 40, no. 1 (June 2002): 39. Also, Drew Christiansen, S.J., views official Catholic teaching on war today as "a composite of nonviolent and just war elements" in "Whither the 'Just War'?" *America,* no. 10, March 24, 2003, p. 8.

11. NCCB, *The Challenge of Peace,* §70, 80, 83, and 120.

A few Catholic thinkers, however, have criticized this way of understanding nonviolence and legitimate defense, or, in other words, pacifism and just war theory. Specifically, they do not believe that just war begins with a presumption against war; they believe it begins with a presumption against injustice. Indeed, one of these critics, George Weigel, accuses church leaders of abandoning the traditional Catholic understanding of politics, war, and peace, thereby rendering the current "default position" of the church a "functional or *de facto* pacifism."[12] In his judgment the "classic" just war tradition, which he espouses, is "an extension of politics," and as such is "a tradition of statecraft," with a beginning point concerned with "defining the moral responsibilities of governments."[13] According to this version of just war theory, violence between nations is inevitable, and the use of force is the essence of the state's raison d'être. Thus the just war tradition "exists to serve statesmen [*sic*]" to make "responsible" decisions concerning war.[14] In addition, proponents of this perspective on just war regard pacifism and nonviolence as unrealistic and irresponsible with regard to foreign affairs.[15] This understanding of just war theory and pacifism, however, strikes me as far removed from one that took as its starting point what we experience during Mass and are to pass on to others in the world.

Put differently, when these critics appeal to some classic just war tradition, I wonder *which* tradition they have in mind. For, as Brian V. Johnstone, C.SS.R., points out: "To what does 'tradition' refer here? Does it mean the secular tradition which emerged and separated from the Christian tradition, with a view to providing a generally acceptable, rational code governing the initiating and conduct of war, which is now, at least in part, embodied in international law? . . . Or does it mean the just war doctrine as it developed and is maintained within the Christian, or specifically within the Catholic tradition? The answer can make a considerable difference to the way in which the doctrine is interpreted."[16] In Johnstone's view the Catholic critics of the current Catholic teaching on war and peace do not begin at the right place nor operate from a specifically Catholic perspective.

---

12. George Weigel, "The Just War Tradition and the World after September 11," *Logos* 5, no. 3 (Summer 2002): 15-16. See also George Weigel, "The Just War Case for the War," *America* 188, no. 11 (March 31, 2003): 7-10.

13. George Weigel, "Moral Clarity in a Time of War," *First Things* 129 (January 2003): 21-22.

14. Weigel, "Moral Clarity," p. 27.

15. See, for example, J. Daryl Charles, *Between Pacifism and Jihad: Just War and Christian Tradition* (Downers Grove, Ill.: InterVarsity, 2005), pp. 10-11, 88-106.

16. Johnstone, "The War on Terrorism," p. 43.

Because they regard just war theory more politically than theologically, they are in danger of becoming "apologists" for the foreign policies of a particular nation and therefore are less likely to use the just war tradition to evaluate any given war conducted by their nation as unjust.[17] In contrast to this approach, and drawing on the theological work of Saint Thomas Aquinas, who treated the topic of war in a section about the vices opposed to charity, Johnstone addresses war and peace in connection with a virtue ethic of charity, within "the wider teleological vision, such that the ethic itself must be integrated into a life of peace and friendship with God, and with one another, of which the causal power is the divine energy, the Spirit of Jesus risen . . . [and which] is to be embodied in the community of the faithful, and extended to the whole human community by the *opus* or work of peace."[18] In my view, this more theological, christological, and ecclesiological approach appears more consonant with the liturgical starting point of the present chapter.

I also think Patrick T. McCormick is correct in his observation that, contrary to what Weigel alleges, the real "default position" for most American Christians is to give the government a "blank check," which means that they support whatever their leaders say and do when it comes to war. According to McCormick, recourse to violence is deeply embedded in our culture, so that "the larger reality [is] that the vast majority of American Catholics and Christians approach the moral analysis of every call to arms with a strong presumption in favor of war."[19] Such a stance, to say the least, would seem inconsistent with what we experience during worship and are to pass on to the world. If this is indeed the case, Catholics and other Christians in the United States are in need of a major attitude adjustment.

Beginning with the liturgy may be a way for us Catholic Christians to "undertake an evaluation of war with an entirely new attitude," as the bishops of the Second Vatican Council called upon us to do.[20] In the remainder of this essay, therefore, I will maintain that the practice of Christian moral reasoning concerning nonviolence and the use of force is first and foremost embedded and embodied within the context of the liturgy, the wellspring of

---

17. Johnstone, "Pope John Paul II," p. 327. In contrast, Weigel thinks those who believe just war begins with a presumption against violence "begin at the wrong place. . . . And beginning at the wrong place almost always means arriving at the wrong destination" ("Moral Clarity," p. 23).

18. Johnstone, "The War on Terrorism," p. 51.

19. Patrick T. McCormick, "Violence: Religion, Terror, War," *Theological Studies* 67 (March 2006): 159.

20. *Pastoral Constitution on the Church in the Modern World*, §80.

our faith and the school where it is formed and shaped.[21] Indeed, the liturgy is the locus where recent Catholic teaching on nonviolence and just war, especially with regard to their presumption against war and for peace, has coherence. Moreover, this framework for reading Christian nonviolence and just use of force avoids either seeing pacifism as merely a deontological principle or reducing just war to a checklist of criteria for an algebraic "casuistry of means-tests."[22] Instead it understands them both as embedded in the Christian way of life and discipleship that is an outgrowth of the liturgy. This approach to viewing the ethics of war and peace is connected with the classic tradition in that it is anchored in one of the primary conveyers of the Christian theological tradition, namely, the liturgy. First, however, I shall turn to something that is read and proclaimed in the liturgy, namely, Scripture.

Scripture: From Scattering to Gathering

Probably one of the most uncontested claims anyone could make is that we live in a world often marred by conflict, hatred, and violence. These are symptoms of human sinfulness, whereby we put ourselves on a pedestal, making ourselves equal to God. In other words, human self-assertion leads to our alienation from God, one another, and indeed all of creation. Of course, this is not something new under the sun. The biblical story of Noah and the great flood reveals how ancient human conflict is: "Now the earth was corrupt in God's sight, and the earth was filled with violence" (Gen. 6:11). As this passage also notes, God did not view this as a good development. From the murder of Abel by his brother Cain (Gen. 4:8) to the boasting of Lamech that he would avenge himself seventy-sevenfold if anyone merely wounded him (Gen. 4:23-24), violence characterized the world following the primordial sin of Adam and Eve. Indeed, the story of the tower of Babel (Gen. 11) illustrates the effect of human self-assertion on a global

---

21. The approach taken here is not original to this chapter even though it has not been prominent in the Catholic literature. Indeed, I take my cue from a Benedictine monk from the early twentieth century by the name of Virgil Michel, who is remembered for his emphasis on the link between worship and ethics (he usually referred to this as the connection between liturgy and social justice). See Virgil Michel, O.S.B., *The Christian in the World* (Collegeville, Minn.: Liturgical Press, 1939), pp. 179-87.

22. Weigel accuses the presumption-against-war version of just war of reducing just war to simply a method of casuistry ("Moral Clarity," p. 22), but as this chapter hopefully demonstrates, perhaps the reverse is the case.

scale — the division and scattering of humankind. Still, this alienation be-tween humans and God, the boundaries between humans and other hu-mans, and the violence resulting from all of this were *not* God's original plan for creation. As William T. Cavanaugh writes earlier in this volume, "Sin and violence are a departure from the norm, not the way things are meant to be."[23]

The good news is that, contrary to Bette Midler's song, God did not just watch us "from a distance" and allow this state of affairs to continue. Instead, God attempted to work with and through a people, Israel, with whom God entered into covenant, calling them to be an example to all the nations by putting into practice God's ways of justice and peace. People who were alienated and scattered now were called and gathered by God. The starting, or focal, point for God's effort to restore the *shalom* — the harmony and just relationships, since real peace is not merely the absence of conflict — of all creation was the people of Israel. Indeed, God gathered this people into a community and called them to be a "light to the nations, / that [God's] salvation may reach to the end of the earth" (Isa. 49:6). The ultimate vision of the Hebrew scriptures was that someday peoples from "many na-tions shall come" to the "mountain of the LORD's house" in Jerusalem to re-ceive instruction in the just ways of God, and then

> they shall beat their swords into plowshares,
>   and their spears into pruning hooks;
> nation shall not lift up sword against nation,
>   neither shall they learn war any more.
>
> (Mic. 4:1-3)

Admittedly, numerous passages in the Hebrew scriptures are less clear on, or seemingly at odds with, God's invitation to be reconciled with one another and to transform our weapons of war into farming implements. For example, although many peace activists invoke the Decalogue's com-mandment "You shall not kill" (Exod. 20:13 and Deut. 5:17), some transla-tions of the Bible instead say "You shall not *murder*."[24] It is unclear whether this prohibits all killing or only the intentional killing of an innocent per-son. After all, the execution of a person found guilty of certain crimes — in-cluding murder, blasphemy, cursing one's parents, and failure to honor the Sabbath, just to name a few — appears to be sanctioned by God in the Mo-

---

23. See chapter 4 above, "Pilgrim People."

24. See Wilma Ann Bailey, *"You Shall Not Kill" or "You Shall Not Murder"? The Assault on a Biblical Text* (Collegeville, Minn.: Liturgical Press, 2005).

saic law. In addition, many supporters of the death penalty refer to the *lex talionis,* or "law of retaliation" (life for a life, eye for an eye, tooth for a tooth, etc.), which is found in (only) three places in the Torah (Exod. 21:24-27; Lev. 24:19-22; Deut. 19:19-21). However, most Bible scholars agree that this rule was not meant to call for vengeance, but to limit it. In other words, it was intended to ensure that the punishment would fit the crime. "Otherwise angry family members might take seven or more lives for a life, as Lamech boasted (Gen. 4:23), and as the Hatfields and the McCoys tried to do."[25] In addition to these references to capital punishment, though, there are other places in the Hebrew scriptures where God, who is portrayed as a warrior, calls for holy war and orders the Israelites to vanquish their enemies. Sometimes this involved the *herem,* which was a ban requiring the Israelites to take no prisoners, regardless of whether they were combatants or noncombatants, soldiers or women and children (Josh. 6:21; 8:24-26). Still, all this divinely sanctioned violence is sandwiched within the aforementioned overarching vision of God's desire to regather all nations in *shalom,* where, as poetically described,

> The wolf and the lamb shall feed together,
>   the lion shall eat straw like the ox. . . .
> They shall not hurt or destroy
>   on all my holy mountain,
>   says the LORD.
>
> (Isa. 65:25)

Indeed, this divine endeavor to gather together a reconciled people to be God's instruments of peace in the world carried over into the New Testament, with the life, death, and resurrection of Jesus Christ. He proclaimed, taught about, and made manifest in his own actions the kingdom of God, which, as noted by the popular hymn "Gather Us In," is not merely someplace "light years away."[26] Jesus announced that this kingdom "has come near" and is "at hand" (Mark 1:15; Matt. 4:17). While it is not yet completely in hand and fully present in our world, the kingdom of God is, as Jesus' teachings and deeds demonstrated, already in our midst and "among" us (Luke 17:21) wherever and whenever God's will is being done "on earth as it is in heaven" (Matt. 6:10). All that Jesus said or did "was evidence that the

---

25. Glen H. Stassen, "Biblical Teaching on Capital Punishment," in *Capital Punishment: A Reader,* ed. Glen H. Stassen (Cleveland: Pilgrim Press, 1998), p. 121.

26. This is from the fourth stanza of "Gather Us In," text and tune by Marty Haugen, in *Gather,* ed. Robert J. Batastini et al. (Chicago: GIA Publications, 1988).

kingdom was beginning to break into the world."[27] He put things in motion toward the peaceable kingdom.

One of the primary characteristics of this kingdom is *agape,* which is love that is indiscriminate, generous, giving, and forgiving — "a love that finds sheer delight in reconciliation."[28] Indeed, love of God and love for neighbor are central to Jesus' teachings and how he summed up the overall thrust of the Torah (Matt. 22:34-40; Mark 12:28-34). However, while Jesus instructed his followers to love God and their neighbors, in the parable of the Good Samaritan he included enemies within the category of neighbor (Luke 10:25-37). Moreover, he told his disciples, not only as individuals but also as a new community, "Love your enemies and pray for those who persecute you, so that you may be children of your Father in heaven" (Matt. 5:44-45). In the Beatitudes, at the beginning of the collection of sayings known as the Sermon on the Mount, Jesus announced, "Blessed are the peacemakers, for they shall be called children of God" (Matt. 5:9). Hence he explicitly linked active peacemaking and love for enemies with being sons and daughters of God. Elsewhere in this sermon he referred directly to the *lex talionis* and took it to a higher level: "You have heard that it was said, 'An eye for an eye and a tooth for a tooth.' But I say to you, Do not resist an evildoer. But if anyone strikes you on the right cheek, turn the other also" (Matt. 5:38-39). While some Christian pacifists have interpreted this literally to mean they must be passive in the face of attacks against them or against other innocent persons, others understand his words in the context of the other available options at that time, such as the one represented by the Zealots who took up violent arms against the Roman occupying forces. In this interpretation, Jesus perhaps meant "Do not resist as the Zealots do" or "Do not resist using violence."[29] Additional recent scholarship suggests that Jesus' nonviolence was in fact a form of resistance. For example, the counsel to "turn the other cheek" actually pulls the rug out from the oppressor's power to humiliate. The one who turns the other cheek in effect is saying, "Your first blow failed to achieve its intended effect. I deny you the power to humiliate me. I am a human being just like you. Your status does not alter that fact. You cannot demean me."[30] The person receiving the blow there-

27. Donald Senior, C.P., *Jesus: A Gospel Portrait,* rev. ed. (Mahwah, N.J.: Paulist, 1992), p. 50.

28. Senior, *Jesus,* p. 86.

29. Joseph J. Fahey, *War and the Christian Conscience: Where Do You Stand?* (Maryknoll, N.Y.: Orbis, 2005), p. 37.

30. Walter Wink, *Engaging the Powers: Discernment and Resistance in a World of Domination* (Minneapolis: Fortress, 1992), p. 176; Fahey, *War,* p. 38.

fore refused to allow the oppressor to have the last word on what was actually happening.

Not only did Jesus teach and proclaim the kingdom of God's way of love, mercy, and peace, he modeled it in his own actions. Indeed, we are offered a penetrating glimpse of the kingdom of God when we consider with whom Jesus spent much of his time. He sought out the downcast, the outcasts, the alienated, and the outsiders. He showed love for the poor, spoke with women, healed lepers, and ate with tax collectors. He even healed some Gentiles! Simply put, he was gathering those who had been scattered. In addition, when confronted by his enemies, he visibly demonstrated how God deals with evil, nonviolently laying down his life for others, including his executioners. Again, Jesus could have chosen the Zealot insurrectionist option of using violence to oust the Romans from the land and to reestablish an independent kingdom of Israel. However, even when one of his followers used a sword to come to Jesus' defense in the Garden of Gethsemane, Jesus healed the injured guard and admonished the worried disciple, "Put your sword back in its place; for all who take the sword will perish by the sword" (Matt. 26:52). With Jesus' death on the cross, which was considered one of the cruelest, most humiliating methods of capital punishment, reserved by the Romans for slaves who were thieves and for rebels who were not Roman citizens, it appeared that the violent ways of scattered humankind would continue on unopposed.

However, God's raising of Jesus from the dead on Easter does not let those who executed him on Good Friday have the last word about Jesus or the way things are, or *ought* to be, in the world. This most important of all Christian holy days vindicates Jesus and affirms that his life and teachings offer an alternative that is the *true way* that God wills for the world. And Jesus expected the people he had gathered to "follow me," even if it meant taking up a cross and losing their lives for the sake of the good news of the kingdom of God (Mark 8:34). Thus this loving, forgiving, healing way of life was supposed to be characteristic not only of Jesus, but also of this new people he had gathered. Indeed, when Jesus told his disciples at the Last Supper, "Do this in remembrance of me" (Luke 22:19; 1 Cor. 11:24-25), he was exhorting them not only to continue receiving the body and blood of Christ in the bread and the wine, but moreover *to be* the reconciling, broken, and bleeding body of Christ for others in the world. Because this community of Jesus' followers, the church, represented a concrete and visible alternative of reconciliation and peace, one of the earliest names for Christianity was "the Way" (Acts 9:2). Thus Jesus' teachings about love, mercy, and peace were not just ideals for individuals, but were embodied and put into practice by this community of believers upon whom the Holy Spirit of God descended on Pentecost (Acts 2). In this way the violent ways in the wake of Babel were reversed by the peaceable kingdom way of this new people, consisting of both Jews and Gentiles, following Pentecost. Finally, the ultimate vision of Revelation reconnects all of this with the Hebrew scriptures' overarching message of universal *shalom* that God intends:

> See, the home of God is among mortals.
> He will dwell with them;
> they will be his peoples,
> and God himself will be with them;
> he will wipe every tear from their eyes.
> Death will be no more;
> mourning and crying and pain will be no more,
> for the first things have passed away.
>
> (Rev. 21:3-4)

As with the Hebrew scriptures, in the New Testament there are some passages that seem to be at odds with this overall emphasis on love, mercy, and peace. For instance, Jesus said to his disciples, "Do you think I have come to bring peace to the earth? No, I tell you, but rather division!" (Luke 12:51). However, in its fuller context this passage is concerned with the division and opposition, even from one's own family members, that can be a consequence of being faithful to the ways of God.[31] In addition, Paul noted in his letter to the Roman church the divinely ordained role of the civil authorities, symbolized by "the sword," to maintain law and order (Rom. 13:1-7). However, the apostle never suggested that Christians may participate in such a capacity. These New Testament passages, therefore, should be interpreted through the lens of the overall biblical message of reconciliation and peace as ultimately made known in *the* Word of God, Jesus Christ.

Reading Scripture through the prism of Jesus' life, teachings, death, and resurrection makes sense, moreover, given that he is also the focus of Christian worship, which is the first and true home of Scripture. Indeed, Christians gathered to worship even before a final canon of authoritative writings was in place. Paul's account of the institution of the Lord's Supper, which was passed on to him, is evidence that early Christians celebrated the Eucharist even before they had the written Gospels (1 Cor. 11:23-26). In these

---

31. Fahey, *War*, pp. 78-79. Similar Scriptures that are addressed helpfully by Fahey include John 2:13-16, Mark 12:13-17, Luke 22:35-38, and a few others. See Fahey, pp. 75-83.

initial centuries of the church's history, the canon developed as the list of books that could be proclaimed in the liturgy (as David McCarthy noted in chapter 2). As such, Scripture should always be read and understood vis-à-vis what we proclaim and celebrate at Mass, where the overarching biblical narrative of God's endeavor to peaceably gather a scattered people is clearly discernible. I think it is fair to reiterate, therefore, that sin and violence are a departure from the norm, not the way things ought to be, and that the overall message of Scripture points toward a universal gathering characterized by peace, which would entail for us Christians a presumption against violence and war.

Liturgy: Gathered and Sent Forth, to Regather a Scattered People

The Catholic moral theologian Bernard Häring stated the good news in this way: "Once we are freed by Christ from slavery to sin, we have been set free for the kingdom of love and peace. This means, in particular, that we live in imitation of the nonviolent Servant of God, who is accessible to us on all levels, for healing, liberating, and reconciling love."[32] Indeed, access to Christ and his love may be found especially during worship. This new way of life in Christ is what we celebrate and thank God for when we gather on Sundays throughout the year. As the liturgical historian James F. White put it, "Each Sunday testifies to the resurrection. Every Sunday is a little Easter or rather every Easter is a yearly great Sunday."[33] Thus, as seen in the *Epistle of Barnabas,* early Christians regarded Sunday as "an eighth day, that is the beginning of another world."[34] The octagonal baptismal font found in many churches symbolizes this genesis of a new way of life in Christ. As Paul wrote, "So if anyone is in Christ, there is a new creation: everything old has passed away; see, everything has become new!" (2 Cor. 5:17). According to Geoffrey Wainwright, "This 'new creation' . . . means the service of God and of our fellow human beings, the love of God and of neighbour. Baptism is the sacrament of all this, gathering the whole process proleptically into a

---

32. Bernard Häring, C.SS.R., *My Hope for the Church: Critical Encouragement for the Twenty-First Century* (Liguori, Mo.: Liguori/Triumph, 1999), p. 27; see also p. 62 where this eminent moral theologian, writing toward the end of his life and career, advises, "These things would have to take a crucial position in any renewed moral theology."

33. James F. White, *Introduction to Christian Worship,* rev. ed. (Nashville: Abingdon, 1990), p. 57.

34. Quoted in White, *Introduction to Christian Worship,* p. 56.

single sign."[35] Hence, every time we Catholics dip our hand into the baptismal font or some holy water and make the sign of the cross upon entering the sanctuary, we are reminding ourselves of our baptismal identity and calling to be a sign of God's reconciling peace.

It is during worship that we Christians ought to experience already in the here and now the gift of God's forgiveness, restorative justice, and peace — between God and us, between us and others, and between us and the rest of creation. "Gather us in — all peoples together, Fire of love in our flesh and our bone," we sing in "Gather Us In," referring to the way God's inclusive and reconciling love should be incarnate in our lives together. After all, have you ever noticed how often peace is mentioned during the Mass? Indeed, for this reason, toward the end of their influential pastoral letter *The Challenge of Peace,* the U.S. Catholic bishops observe, "The Mass in particular is a unique means of seeking God's help to create the conditions essential for true peace in ourselves and in the world."[36] Similarly, toward the end of the chapter entitled "The Promotion of Peace," the recent *Compendium of the Social Doctrine of the Church,* issued by the Pontifical Council for Justice and Peace, says, "In particular, the Eucharistic celebration, 'the source and summit of the Christian life,' is a limitless wellspring for all authentic Christian commitment to peace."[37]

Soon after gathering together and beginning our worship of God, we often sing the Gloria, which proclaims, "Glory to God in the highest, and peace to God's people on earth." These words of praise and peace find their source in the birth narrative of the Gospel of Luke, where the angelic host appears to the shepherds in the fields, announcing "good news of great joy," rather than fear and terror, "for all the people," not only for one nation but also for all the world (Luke 2:10-14). In the anaphora, prayer is made for the peace and unity of the church, as well as for the promotion of peace and salvation in the world. Likewise, during the Communion Rite the priest prays, "Lord Jesus Christ, you said to your apostles: I leave you peace, my

---

35. Geoffrey Wainwright, *Doxology: The Praise of God in Worship, Doctrine, and Life* (New York: Oxford University Press, 1980), p. 412.

36. NCCB, *The Challenge of Peace,* §295. All subsequent quotes from the U.S. Catholic bishops are from this paragraph.

37. Pontifical Council for Justice and Peace, *Compendium,* §519. Moreover, on this page of the *Compendium,* the next-to-last footnote (#1102), which is by far the longest one in that chapter, highlights the emphasis on peace that runs throughout the Mass. The reference to the eucharistic liturgy as "the source and summit of the Christian life" is taken from Vatican II, *The Constitution on the Sacred Liturgy (Sacrosanctum Concilium),* §10, in *The Documents of Vatican II.*

peace I give you. Look not on our sins, but on the faith of your Church, and grant us the peace and unity of your kingdom." As the U.S. Catholic bishops write, "Nowhere is the Church's urgent plea for peace more evident in the liturgy than in the Communion Rite."

Then, after we together pray for God's kingdom to come and God's will to be done on earth as it is in heaven, and request that God forgive us our trespasses as we forgive those who trespass against us, the priest continues praying, "Deliver us, Lord, from every evil, and grant us peace in our day." Indeed, the U.S. Catholic bishops comment on this line by noting that we pray for God's peace for the here and now, "not just at some time in the distant future." At this point the priest says, "The peace of the Lord be with you always," and the congregation responds, "And also with you." This is followed with everyone exchanging with each other a sign of peace. Importantly, the bishops "encourage every Catholic to make the sign of peace at Mass an authentic sign of our reconciliation with God and with one another. This sign of peace is also a visible expression of our commitment to work for peace as a Christian community." So don't offer a wishy-washy, limp handshake or avoid eye contact while saying "Peace be with you" to one another! According to Sarah Mitchell, this is not meant to be a passive moment or simply a greeting: "Rather, it is a symbol and action of an urgent pursuit of relational encounter that will enable the Body of Christ to live out the life to which Jesus has called us."[38] In her view, moreover, the "potential outcome of this liturgical act is the true Shalom, the restoration of all relationships: between God and humanity, human beings with each other and with all of creation."[39] After this "gesture of peace"[40] and before receiving communion, the assembly sings the Agnus Dei, praying that the Lamb of God, who takes away the sins of the world, will "grant us peace."

Finally, we are not supposed to leave the peace we experience during worship inside the stained-glass windows of the church building. After all, at the conclusion of the Mass, during the dismissal, the priest blesses us

---

38. Sarah Mitchell, "Forum: Piecing Together: The Pax as Reconciling Sign for the New Church," *Worship* 77, no. 3 (May 2003): 244.

39. Mitchell, "Forum," p. 249. For similar commentary on the practice of exchanging the sign of peace during worship, see Hoyt L. Hickman, *A Primer for Church Worship* (Nashville: Abingdon, 1984), p. 65; and Kevin W. Irwin, *Responses to 101 Questions on the Mass* (Mahwah, N.J.: Paulist, 1999), pp. 120-23.

40. Pope John Paul II advocated "gestures of peace" that foster peace in people's hearts, in their lives in the community, and in the world. See John Paul II, "*Pacem in Terris:* A Permanent Commitment" (Message for the World Day of Peace), *America* 188, no. 4 (February 10, 2003): 18-23.

and usually says, "The Mass is ended, go in peace to love and serve the Lord." Rather than an exclamation of our gladness that the Mass has ended, it is to this call, or vocation, that we enthusiastically respond, "Thanks be to God." In other words, the peace we have just experienced and exchanged between God and us, and us and one another, is also supposed to be enacted and embodied in our lives through love and service in the world. This benediction is actually a sending forth commissioning us to *be* Christ's channels of peace by doing acts of love and service toward others. Simply put, we have been gathered and sent forth into a conflict-ridden world to regather a scattered humankind. Even if one attends worship only on Christmas and Easter (in other words, a "Chreaster," or as one church at which my wife worked put it, a "C & E-er"), this emphasis on the peace of Christ's kingdom should be obvious after only a bit of reflection about what is said and done during Mass.

Some years ago the liturgical scholar Robert Hovda referred to the liturgy as "kingdom play," in which worshipers gather and celebrate as if the kingdom of God that Christ represented has arrived.[41] This is not to deny that we live, as the U.S. Catholic bishops put it, in a "tension between the vision of the reign of God and its concrete realization in history."[42] That is to say, while we believe that Jesus embodied and inaugurated the kingdom way of life, and while we believe that we already have been graced to follow Jesus and continue his kingdom project, we also acknowledge that the kingdom of God is not yet fully present "on earth as it is in heaven." Nevertheless, during worship, more than anywhere else, we should experience and participate in the ways of the kingdom of God. Worship is thus a foretaste of the kingdom, sort of like an appetizer to the heavenly banquet. As the fourth stanza of "Gather Us In" says, "But here in this place the new light is shining, Now is the Kingdom, now is the day." The word "play" in Hovda's phrase may connote frolicking at the playground or pretending; however, it could also refer to a theatrical performance. Viewed in the second way, worship is a rehearsal of the kingdom of

---

41. Cited in James M. Schellman, "Initiation: Forming Disciples for Christ's Mission in the World," in *Liturgy and Justice: To Worship God in Spirit and Truth,* ed. Anne Y. Koester (Collegeville, Minn.: Liturgical Press, 2002), p. 134. William T. Cavanaugh similarly writes that the "task of the Christian is to live now as if that is in fact the case, to embody redemption by living a reconciled life, and thereby bring the Kingdom, however incompletely, into the present" (*Torture and Eucharist: Theology, Politics, and the Body of Christ* [Oxford and Malden, Mass.: Blackwell, 1998], p. 239).

42. NCCB, *The Challenge of Peace,* §58. Theological thought about the "already but not yet" of the kingdom of God is referred to as *eschatology.*

God, and an outgrowth of repeated rehearsals is hopefully the absorption of what we are rehearsing.

Thus, when we Christians gather together regularly and perform in our prayers, singing, and gestures concrete practices of love, mercy, and peace, we are nurturing the virtues of the kingdom in our lives. The songs we sing (such as "Gather Us In" or "The Prayer of St. Francis," where we ask, "Make me a channel of your peace") will come to *sing us;* the gestures we do (such as the passing of the peace) will come to *gesture us.*[43] Through worship we will come to embody and enact the peace of Christ. Moreover, not only are we formed and shaped by the words and gestures of the liturgy, we are also participating in an alternative way of being a community of people. Such worship ought to reveal in a concrete and visible way to the world the ways of God's kingdom that were intended to be true for all the world from the start. Christian liturgy is an icon that reveals, but also manifests among us, how the world is truly supposed to be, as God intended it all along. In this way worship is not only a source for a Christian ethic — providing us ethical principles and forming us in the virtues — but it also *is* an ethic.

It must be noted, however, that the liturgy does not automatically or magically transform worshipers and the way they live. Unfortunately, we often become "pew potatoes" at worship, simply going through the motions without comprehending or really meaning what we are saying and doing. If we do this, it is not God's fault, but ours. As Wainwright posits, "[T]he reception of God's grace requires, as I see it, an active engagement on the part of the recipient."[44] This is why the bishops of the Second Vatican Council, in the *Constitution on the Sacred Liturgy,* wrote, "The Church earnestly desires that all the faithful be led to that FULL, CONSCIOUS, and ACTIVE participation in liturgical celebrations called for by the very nature of the liturgy."[45] Therefore, educating Catholic Christians about what we say and do during worship should help us to be more intentional about and receptive to the grace of God that transforms us to be a peaceable people. Of course, the goal of genuine worship is to glorify God. Nev-

---

43. See E. Byron Anderson, "'O for a Heart to Praise My God': Hymning the Self before God," in *Liturgy and the Moral Self: Humanity at Full Stretch before God,* ed. E. Byron Anderson and Bruce T. Morrill, S.J. (Collegeville, Minn.: Liturgical Press, 1998), pp. 111-25.

44. Wainwright, *Doxology,* p. 403. Of course, sometimes the liturgy may be the problem and in need of ethical critique. For example, if only males have an active role (altar servers, lectors, Eucharist ministers, etc.), this may contribute to the perpetuation of patriarchy and inequality in the church. See, for example, Frances B. O'Connor, C.S.C., "The Injustice of the Lack of Justice for Women in Liturgy," in *Liturgy and Justice,* pp. 87-98.

45. Second Vatican Council, *Constitution on the Sacred Liturgy,* §14, emphasis in original.

ertheless, an outgrowth of it should be to make the adorers more into the image of the One they adore.

Unfortunately, we cannot just seclude ourselves and stay 24/7 in the liturgy. We are sent forth into the world. Hopefully, however, even if we cannot stay in the liturgy, the liturgy will stay in us as we go forth to love and serve the Lord. Thus we should come to embody and enact the peace of Christ during worship, but also go to embody and enact the peace of Christ in the world. Yet, the question lingers about *how*, especially when, for instance, an innocent neighbor's life is attacked or when an entire people is threatened with genocide. The Catholic Church currently allows for two approaches for how to embody and enact Christ's peace in the face of such violence: nonviolence (pacifism) and legitimate armed defense (just war). Drawing on a wonderful and, I think, fitting image from basketball, Megan McKenna writes, "We live with one foot in the world and one in the church. The difference lies, perhaps, in which foot takes the weight, which foot we pivot on as we move."[46] If we pivot with the foot that is planted in the church's worship, I believe it would be fair to say that both approaches should start with a presumption against war and violence, and this seems to be an appropriate way to understand the Second Vatican Council's call for evaluating war with an entirely new attitude.

Evaluating War with an Entirely New Attitude

At this point I think we have a promising basis for holding, as the U.S. bishops claim, that the two primary Christian responses to this question of how to be peacemakers — namely, pacifism and just war — begin with and share a presumption against violence and war. Given the repeated emphasis on receiving, being, and spreading Christ's peace during worship at Mass, we hopefully absorb a basic orientation toward reconciliation, restorative justice, and peace that then shapes the way we respond to conflict. While others might ground this presumption against violence in other ways, I do not think it can be denied that if we begin our consideration of war and peace with what we do and who we are in the liturgy, we will have a fundamental direction in our lives of discipleship whereby violence and war are regarded as evils to be eradicated someday. Therefore, in this final section of the chapter I will not provide a thorough historical survey of pacifism or the

46. Megan McKenna, *Rites of Justice: The Sacraments and Liturgy as Ethical Imperatives* (Maryknoll, N.Y.: Orbis, 1997), p. 38.

just war tradition. Instead, I shall highlight some of the ways these two approaches traditionally were linked with the liturgy, and then some of the implications of this connection for pacifist and just war Christians today. In short, neither approach will be reduced to a theoretical principle or a checklist of criteria abstracted from Christ, but both approaches will be seen as ways of Christian living and discipleship consonant with what we experience during worship.

John Howard Yoder has noted that there is "no such thing as a single position called 'pacifism,' to which one clear definition can be given and which is held by all 'pacifists.'"[47] Indeed, there are many types of nonreligious as well as religious pacifisms, non-Christian as well as Christian pacifisms. Generally speaking, Christian pacifists believe that the way of Jesus entails a strong presumption against violence. Accordingly, most Christian pacifists regard as unjustified all forms of killing and violence (e.g., war, capital punishment, self-defense, and the use of lethal force by police). Some Christian pacifists reject war and capital punishment but find humanitarian interventions and police actions acceptable and necessary at times. Again, there is variety even among Christian pacifisms. To be sure, the passive nonresistance pacifism of the Amish does not look exactly like the active nonviolent resistance pacifism of Martin Luther King, Jr., or Catholic Workers such as Dorothy Day. Nevertheless, running throughout these versions of Christian pacifism is a strong presumption against violence and war fundamentally based on following the way of Jesus.

But what would Christian pacifism look like if understood as an outgrowth of what we experience in the liturgy? First, it should be noted that this connection between worship and nonviolence was identified as far back as the early church. For early Christians, Jesus' nonviolent death on the cross out of love for others, including his enemies, witnessed to the way in which God resists and overcomes evil, thereby reconciling people with God and with one another. This was the primary reason for their pacifism, although there were related reasons as well, such as an abhorrence of idolatry.[48] Indeed, rituals were required of Roman officers, which soldiers had to attend and thereby give their indirect support of, including sacrifices to, and worship of, the Roman emperor, Caesar. Related to this, many military units often had their own cult, wherein a particular god was worshiped in

47. John Howard Yoder, *Nevertheless: The Varieties and Shortcomings of Religious Pacifism* (Scottdale, Pa.: Herald, 1971), p. 10.
48. See Tobias Winright, "Roman Catholicism, Pacifism In," in *The Encyclopedia of Religion and War*, ed. Gabriel Palmer-Fernandez (New York: Berkshire/Routledge, 2004).

return for that god's favor and assistance. Because for Christians "Jesus is Lord," they refused to join the Roman military with its idolatrous practices. Notice that their refusal to commit idolatry hinges on the question of whom to *worship*.

One prominent early Christian teacher, Origen (ca. 185-254), based Christian refusal to fight in the Roman military not only on the New Testament's portrayal of Jesus, who "nowhere teaches that it is right for His own disciples to offer violence to any one, however wicked," but also on the liturgical grounds that Christians "fight" for a peaceful and just order by "forming a special army — an army of piety — by offering our prayers to God."[49] This is not at all an example of passivity in the face of injustice and violence; rather, it is an active practice that these Christians truly believed was a form of resistance to evil. Much more recently, Wainwright makes a similar point when he writes, "Where Christians see fellow human beings suffering grave injustice, they have a primary duty to pray for them."[50] Origen also observed that just as the Romans permit their priests, who offer sacrifices to their gods, to "keep their hands free from blood" by not requiring them to fight in the military, so too should all Christians (not only the priests) be allowed to worship their God without being required to be a part of the military and getting blood on their hands.[51] Another early Christian writer, Saint John Chrysostom (ca. 347-407), even more explicitly pointed out how bloodshed is inconsistent with Christian worship. Indeed, he focused in particular on the Eucharist: "The Lord has fed us with his own sacred flesh. . . . What excuse shall we have, if eating of the lamb we become wolves? If, led like sheep into pasture, we behave as though we were ravening lions? This mystery [of the Eucharist] requires that we should be innocent not only of violence, but of all enmity, however slight, for it is the mystery of peace."[52] This viewpoint was also evident in the disciplinary and

---

49. Cited in Arthur F. Holmes, ed., *War and Christian Ethics: Classic Readings on the Morality of War* (Grand Rapids: Baker, 1975), pp. 48-49.

50. Wainwright, *Doxology,* p. 429. Similarly, the *Compendium of the Social Doctrine of the Church* says, "*It is through prayer that the Church engages in the battle for peace*" (§519, emphasis in original).

51. Cited in Egan, *Peace Be with You,* p. 28.

52. John Chrysostom, *Homilies,* in *Short Breviary,* ed. Monks of St. John's (Collegeville, Minn.: St. John's Abbey Press, 1975), pp. 220-21, sermon 33; see also Egan, *Peace Be with You,* pp. 38-39. Saint Thomas Aquinas (1225-1274) also noted that what is celebrated at the Eucharist is at odds with bloodshed in war, although this observation led him to exempt only priests and bishops, who preside over the Eucharist, from participating in the military. See Thomas Aquinas, *Summa Theologiae,* trans. Fathers of the English Dominican Province (Westminster, Md: Christian Classics; New York: Benziger Brothers, 1948), II-II.40.2.

catechetical rules of the church from the third century until around the fifth century. The *Canons of Hippolytus*, for example, said: "Of the magistrate and the soldier, let them not kill anyone, even if they receive the order to do so. . . . Anyone who has an authority and does not do the justice of the gospel, let him be cut off and not pray with the bishop. Let . . . a believer . . . if he desire to be a soldier, either cease from his intention or, if not, let him be rejected."[53] Indeed, many early Christian martyrs, such as Saint Maximilianus (d. 295) and Saint Marcellus (d. 298), decided to stay faithful to their baptismal vows to Christ and the church, and they were executed by the Roman authorities for their refusal to serve in the military. As Cavanaugh notes earlier in this volume, the early Christians lived no longer in fear of death: "Here were these people living as though it was possible to absorb violence with love, and not return the violence."[54]

Thus, it would be inaccurate to portray most Christian pacifists as adhering resolutely to a stance against violence as if it were some deontological, duty-bound principle. It would, moreover, be erroneous to assume that Christian pacifists are passive, irresponsible, completely separating themselves from the world, unrealistic, or not doing anything constructive to promote a just peace. Indeed, the word "pacifism" is derived from a combination of the Latin words *pax* and *facere*, which together mean "to make peace."[55] Accordingly, as the U.S. Catholic bishops put it, Christian pacifists "have from the earliest days of the Church committed themselves to *a non-violent lifestyle*."[56] Christian pacifism, especially in the light of the liturgy, is nothing other than a nonviolent lifestyle of peacemaking.

Hence, in recent times Christian pacifists have employed nonviolent methods, besides prayer and worship, as an expression of their nonviolent lifestyle for promoting and protecting a just peace. Indeed, much work is being done today on peace studies and conflict mediation, resolution, and transformation. In their 1994 statement that appeared in the wake of successful nonviolent revolutions in the Philippines and in eastern Europe, the American Catholic bishops observed that "recent history suggests that in some circumstances [nonviolence] can be an effective public undertaking as well."[57] That is, nonviolence as a method can be more effective than war, less costly in human lives than war, and can even lead to reconciliation. Such

53. Cited in Fahey, *War*, p. 44.
54. See above, Cavanaugh, "Pilgrim People."
55. Fahey, *War*, p. 29.
56. NCCB, *The Challenge of Peace*, §111, emphasis added.
57. NCCB, *The Harvest of Justice Is Sown in Peace* (Washington, D.C.: United States Catholic Conference, 1994), p. 5.

Christian pacifists also will seek to address the root causes of conflict. All of this is responsible and realistic, and it would seem consonant with the liturgy's sending us forth to be peacemakers by loving and serving others. Christian pacifists must actively contribute to a just peace; they cannot be passive while injustice happens. To neglect to work for peace and justice would be a sin of omission, to which the Penitential Rite at Mass refers: "I confess to almighty God, and to you, my brothers and sisters, that I have sinned through my own fault in my thoughts and words, in what I have done, and in *what I have failed to do*" (emphasis added).

At the same time, however, a Christian pacifism that is an outgrowth of the liturgy would not depend ultimately on the effectiveness of nonviolence. Christian pacifists are also realistic in that they can admit that nonviolence at times might not be effective. However, even when nonviolence seems ineffective, the more important thing for Christian pacifists is *faithfulness* to the way of the kingdom of God as Jesus proclaimed and embodied, and as Christians experience and celebrate at worship. To be sure, such pacifism is not passive. Nor is it withdrawal from the world. It is *for* the world, and it involves courage, hope, sacrifice, and taking risks for the world. This is the kind of Christian nonviolence that the Catholic Church in recent years has recognized as a valid calling or vocation for its members. As the U.S. Catholic bishops declared, "We believe work to develop non-violent means of fending off aggression and resolving conflict *best reflect* the call of Jesus both to love and to justice."[58]

Not all Catholics and other Christians, however, are pacifists. If, for example, an enemy, whom we are called to love, threatens to murder an innocent neighbor, whom we are also called to love, many Catholics and other Christians believe that the use of lethal force against the aggressor may be necessary and justified. In view of this possible scenario, Paul Ramsey, who based just war on the command to love our neighbor, argued, "Out of neighbor-regarding love for all one's fellow men, preferential decision among one's neighbors may and can and must be made."[59] At the same time, the love for enemy does not get shelved altogether; rather, it remains in force inasmuch as certain rules governing the use of force are followed out of respect for the dignity of the aggressor. Hence, over the centuries, beginning with Saint Ambrose (ca. 340-397), several criteria have been formu-

58. NCCB, *The Challenge of Peace*, §78, emphasis added.

59. Paul Ramsey, *War and the Christian Conscience: How Shall Modern War Be Conducted Justly?* (Durham, N.C.: Duke University Press, 1961), p. 305. Similarly, according to Johnstone, Pope John Paul II was opposed to war. "However, when violence is begun by another," legitimate defense of the innocent is a right and a duty ("Pope John Paul II," p. 324).

lated to circumscribe *when* and *how* such deadly force may be morally employed. These, taken together, have come to be known as the just war tradition, which became the primary approach in Christianity for ethically evaluating war from the fourth century to the present. Like pacifism, there are various versions of just war theory, secular as well as religious, and even within the Christian tradition somewhat different variants exist. According to one recent author, "The just war tradition has its roots both in natural law and Christian theology and has been developed through a continuing dialogue between secular and religious sources."[60]

This, then, brings us back to Johnstone's point made earlier, where he emphasized the importance for Catholics to be clear about which tradition of just war they are drawing from in discerning where they stand on the morality of any given war. Indeed, Johnstone persuasively shows that the *theological* grounds upon which to think morally about legitimate defense for Pope John Paul II echoed Aquinas's view that justice alone is insufficient, and it needs to be completed by forgiveness, which is a fruit of charity (love). Accordingly, just war for Catholic Christians must be "integrated into a context which includes justice, forgiveness and charity."[61] And, as I have attempted to argue, a primary context where Christians experience these virtues is the liturgy. Through repeated rehearsals of the kingdom ways during worship, these virtues will be "embodied in the community of the faithful, and extended to the whole human community by the *opus* or work of peace."[62] In this way, like nonviolence, perhaps just war can be understood more as a lifestyle than as simply a checklist of principles. If there is any space at all for Christians to justify deadly force or war, it can be only within this matrix.

Given what we proclaim and do during worship, and given what we are sent forth to embody and enact in the world, a presumption against war and in favor of peace should be evident in the Christian just war tradition. That is, violence and war are regarded as activities that require justification. There is a burden of proof placed on those who believe that the use of lethal force is sometimes necessary. "Charity would require," writes Johnstone, "the limitation of the use of violence to what is necessary to defend those persons under threat or attack."[63] Indeed, according to Duncan Forrester, a version of just war theory informed by a Christian predisposition against violence and

---

60. Charles Reed, *Just War?* (New York: Church Publishing, 2004), p. 32.
61. Johnstone, "Pope John Paul II," p. 313. See Aquinas, *Summa Theologiae* II-II.40.I.
62. Johnstone, "The War on Terrorism," p. 51.
63. Johnstone, "The War on Terrorism," p. 60.

an orientation toward reconciliation would seek to restrain and discipline the use of violence.[64] Thus the criteria of the just war tradition (just cause, legitimate authority, right intent, probability of success, last resort, proportionality, and noncombatant immunity) may be best understood as an outgrowth of this liturgical presumption against war and in favor of peace, and the restraint and discipline it entails for faithful Christian discipleship.[65]

As was the case with pacifism, the connection between worship and just war was also made earlier in the Christian tradition. Thus the approach I have been suggesting is not something altogether new, even though it may have gotten submerged in the tradition until recently. For example, the first Christian theologian who formulated some principles of the just war tradition, Ambrose, who was bishop of Milan, excommunicated Emperor Theodosius, who was a Christian, because of an incident that occurred in 389. After a group of angry citizens in Thessalonika rebelled against the demands of the Roman army and killed the commanding officer stationed there, Theodosius ordered a retaliatory strike whereby 7,000 Thessalonians were rounded up and slaughtered. This military action thereby violated right intent, in that it was done out of vengeance rather than justice, and it went against the principle of noncombatant immunity, in that it involved the killing of civilians. Thus, Ambrose wrote a letter to Theodosius informing him that he was to be excluded from the Eucharist until he publicly did penance. In this way Ambrose signaled that from the perspective of just war there continue to be actions in war that are contrary to what we experience in the Mass. When Theodosius submitted to Ambrose's invitation to do penance, during the Christmas celebration in 390, he was reconciled with the Christian community.[66]

The medieval *Penitentials* are another example of the ongoing way that the liturgy acted as a pivot foot for ethically evaluating war even after the just war tradition became the main accepted approach for the Catholic Church. From the sixth to the twelfth century, in the *Penitentials*, which were books containing guidelines for priests hearing confessions, penance continued to be assigned for killing in war.[67] Soldiers, even if they had

64. Duncan B. Forrester, "Violence and Non-Violence in Conflict Resolution: Some Theological Reflections," *Studies in Christian Ethics* 16, no. 2 (2003): 64-79.

65. For a description of each of the criteria of the just war tradition, see NCCB, *The Challenge of Peace*, §85-110. For a wonderful treatment of these criteria with an eye toward Christian discipleship and the virtues required for adhering to them, see Daniel M. Bell, Jr., *Just War as Christian Discipleship* (Eugene, Oreg.: Wipf and Stock, 2005).

66. See Cavanaugh, *Torture and Eucharist*, p. 244.

67. Fahey, *War*, pp. 91-92.

fought in a just war, still had to perform acts of penance for a time after returning home from the war. While doing so, they also were not supposed to receive the Eucharist. Again, this is evidence of the church's view that war, including just wars, involves evils, death, and destruction that are ultimately contrary to what God wills for the world. As such, this is evidence of a presumption against war and violence that is an outgrowth of what the church does in the liturgy.

Given that *The Challenge of Peace* and the relevant chapter of *The Compendium of the Social Doctrine of the Church* have reconnected the dots, even if only toward the end of each document, between worship and the question of armed intervention on behalf of the innocent, perhaps this is evidence of a retrieval of this earlier tradition that I have been describing. Although nonviolence and just war are two traditional approaches for ethically evaluating war, if we start with who we are and what we do in the liturgy, we will have a new attitude in that these are integrally connected with our life of discipleship. Because both approaches are part of the fabric of the Christian life as a whole, they each require discipline and virtues that will help us to be peacemakers in the world. While courage and conviction are necessary for pacifists to stand by their convictions and to take risks to promote and protect peace nonviolently, so too does the just war tradition, as an outgrowth of what we do in the liturgy, require "the courage and endurance to stand by our convictions, even when violating the criteria might lead to quicker or less costly victory. Just warriors only fight within the parameters of the tradition."[68] Nor will adherents of the just war way of discipleship give a "blank check" to any government. They will not accept Tennyson's refrain in his famous poem about the six hundred or so who took part in the suicidal Charge of the Light Brigade, "though they knew someone had blundered, someone had made a mistake, ours is not to reason why, ours is but to do and die." Rather, from a Christian liturgical-ethical standpoint, ours *is* to reason why, not just to do or die — or kill. To be sure, this might narrow the scope of justifiable armed interventions, but contrary to Weigel, it does not reduce just war in the Catholic Church today to a functional pacifism. Instead, as Kenneth Himes, O.F.M., puts it, "the case for war should be difficult to make. Not impossible, but difficult."[69]

68. Bell, *Just War*, p. 5.
69. Himes, "Intervention," p. 152.

Concurrent Readings

Bell, Daniel M., Jr. *Just War as Christian Discipleship*. Renewing Radical Discipleship series of Ekklesia Pamphlets, no. 14. Edited by Dan Bell and Joel Shuman. Eugene, Oreg.: Wipf and Stock, 2005. Available at http://www.ekklesiaproject.org. In this brief, accessible piece, Bell delves into each of the criteria of the just war tradition and clearly spells out what they entail with regard to the way of life associated with Christian discipleship.

Egan, Eileen. *Peace Be with You: Justified Warfare or the Way of Nonviolence*. Maryknoll, N.Y.: Orbis, 1999. One of the leading figures in Pax Christi USA, the late Egan provides a historical and theological reading of the pacifist and just war traditions, with a passionate defense of the way of nonviolence for Christians today.

Fahey, Joseph J. *War and the Christian Conscience: Where Do You Stand?* Maryknoll, N.Y.: Orbis, 2005. In this slim volume, Fahey lays out the various Christian ethical options concerning the ethics of war and peace, and he allows the reader to inform his or her own conscience with regard to articulating a moral position on issues related to violence today.

Holmes, Arthur F., ed. *War and Christian Ethics: Classic and Contemporary Readings on the Morality of War*. 2nd ed. Grand Rapids: Baker Academic, 2005. This is the new edition of a classic anthology containing short excerpts from primary texts on war and peace by Christian writers from early Christianity to today.

Schlabach, Gerald W. "Breaking Bread: Peace and War." In *The Blackwell Companion to Christian Ethics,* edited by Stanley Hauerwas and Samuel Wells. Malden, Mass., and Oxford: Blackwell, 2004. In a volume containing chapters that address numerous ethical questions from the perspective of the liturgy, this particular essay uses worship as a springboard for exploring the presumption against violence, international just policing, and the problems associated with the arms race.

Chapter 14

Love Your Enemies:
Toward a Christoform Bioethic

M. THERESE LYSAUGHT

On March 31, 2005, Terri Schiavo died. For the two months prior to her death, the United States watched the debacle of the fight over her life play out in the media. One could not pick up a newspaper, turn on the television, or surf a news Web site without encountering daily developments in her case. Photographs, cartoons, and images soon became iconic; one glance would tell what version of the story was leading the headlines. Like many of the "classic cases" in medical ethics, the case of Terri Schiavo gripped public consciousness in a powerful way.

Two years later the repercussions from her death and the public struggle that preceded it have certainly not died down.[1] Her name continues to incite passion. The case has caused distress within the health care system and for Catholics trying faithfully to navigate end-of-life decisions. The number of people seeking to complete living wills remains up, while many patients and families are worried that they can no longer be morally justified in refusing or withdrawing medically assisted nutrition and hydration. On the American political scene, competing political action committees have been formed to continue to lobby both sides of her case. Her husband has formed one called TerriPAC, to enact legislation to prevent the kinds of challenges her parents presented to his decisional authority. Another, Terri's List, has been formed to help elect politicians who supported or would support her parents' bid.

---

1. In the interest of space, I will not include a description of the case here. It was long and complicated, and how the story was to be told was a central part of the conflict. A quick Internet search will supply any interested reader with a surfeit of stories and Web sites on the case.

In the United States it is difficult to find a person not acquainted with the case. Almost everyone has an opinion. Yet the specifics of the case are elusive. What *were* the facts? Terri Schiavo suffered an event leading to anoxia and severe brain damage in 1990; there was a financial settlement in the case; soon after that her husband began a bid to disconnect her surgically implanted feeding tube, a bid to which her parents objected; legal suit and countersuit continued for the next twelve years; with the result that 2005 witnessed both a flurry of problematic legislative moves as well as a public vigil by primarily supporters of Terri's parents during her final three months; her feeding tube was disconnected on March 18, and it took her thirteen days to die. These seem to be the agreed-upon facts.

The rest is controverted, or perhaps it is more correct to say that the two sides of the case give radically different accounts in terms of: the cause of the anoxia; her proper diagnosis; her prognosis; the motives on each side; and so on. Each side told radically different stories. In fact, on the one-year anniversary of her death, her parents and former husband both released their "tell-all" books, each offering their own narration of the long and tortured history that constitutes *Terri's Story*.[2]

In this chapter I will use the Schiavo case as a place from which to examine that field we now call "bioethics." For while the Schiavo case provides a tidy focus for this particular chapter, I would argue that much that I will say here — at least the outlines — could be transposed to the analysis of other cases and issues in bioethics.

Medical quandaries, in our secularized medical culture, are usually cast as being about particular, highly charged treatment decisions. Ought someone be allowed to "pull the plug" or not? Generally, this question is answered by bringing forward one specific principle, for example, autonomy, the inviolability of life, or utility. The principle is applied to the case in a formulaic fashion and produces an answer; the answers emerging from the various principles are then seen as incommensurable. The question is: Which principle will trump?

I would like to suggest, however, that health-care ethics is not primarily about quandaries; it is not primarily about particular, highly charged treatment decisions. Do decisions need to be made? Certainly. But treatment decisions — and their execution — constitute a small percentage of the actions and interactions that occur in health-care settings, that surround the realities of being ill, suffering, and dying. Those truly concerned with

2. This is the title of one of the already many books on Terri Schiavo (by Diana Lynne, WND Books, 2005).

what Christian discipleship looks like in the face of illness, suffering, dying, and medicine — what we call health-care ethics — must attend at least as assiduously to the shape of their actions and interactions the bulk of the time. Christian health-care ethics, in other words, is not about isolated, rare, occasional treatment decisions; it is about the shape of the entire Christian life as lived within and around the context of medicine.

Secondly, quandaries in bioethics are often presented as opportunities for us (the viewers, or voyeurs) to weigh in on what in particular *other* people ought or ought not to decide or do in their specific crises. On the Schiavo case everyone, it seemed, had an opinion about whether or not her treatment should have been discontinued. I would suggest, however, that in this particular case especially, this was only one of the moral questions. In this case, because of the way the initial conflict was handled, because of the nature of bioethics, and because of the role of the media, an equally (if not more critical) moral issue arose.

This issue was the fomenting of enmity. I would argue that enmity became the centrally operative moral dynamic in the case. At its root, this case was not simply a conflict about treatment decisions. Rather, the case itself was fueled by a disastrous brokenness and enmity between members of Terri's family, between people she loved deeply. This was the engine that drove the case: a decade-long fracture within Terri's family, most likely with fault and conflict of interest on both sides.

What is more, the antagonism — rather than being modulated or defused by bioethics — was augmented by the discipline's inherently conflictual nature. It is not incidental that most of the "classic cases" that have shaped the field of medical ethics have been legal cases. As a result, medical ethics shares the weaknesses of the law, especially insofar as its model of decision making is essentially adversarial. Who gets to decide when those involved disagree? Whose rights trump rights or interests of others? Who *wins?* Certainly, conflict is what brings cases to the ethics committee or courtroom. But such a model fails truly to *resolve* conflict. It might move the question out of the hospital or the hospice room, thereby providing a tidy answer for the medical establishment, but rarely does it truly address or resolve the moral pain and alienation at the center of such cases.[3]

Then, familial antagonism augmented by a conflict-centered ethics was amplified by activists on both sides of the case. Media-saturated as we

---

3. For example, in the Schiavo case the decision was made over two years. The case came to an end. And yet, twelve months later, the hostility of the family members continues.

have become, the country seemed to take hold of the elements of the case that fit the mold of television drama, with its love for legal maneuvering (*Law and Order*) and medical theater (*ER*), both mixed with scandal. Through attempts to gain power through the media, as well as political and legal channels, activists used these avenues of discourse to shape the very *meaning* of the Schiavo case. While most Christians responded to the Schiavo case with regret and quiet dismay, sympathy and compassion — and of course, prayer — those who caught the spotlight of the media offered a response of a different sort: protest, tearful distress, outrage, civil disobedience, anger, hostility. Many a self-identified Christian was heard excoriating the opponents as agents of the culture of death, as "killers," as "murderers." One of the judges in the case, George Greer, was under the protection of armed guards and was ultimately asked to leave his Southern Baptist church.[4] Bioethicists played out the politics of the bedside vigil in print and private conversation, alternately referring to their opponents as either "scary" or "heretics." The actions of external activists, in other words, did not provide an alternative to the media drama, but reflected the dominant environment of fear and conflict. In the public sphere, secularists and Christians alike contributed to — even fomented — hostility and enmity.

Finally, wrapped up in these layered conflicts lurked the shadow of the ultimate enemy, death. Certainly a particular way of construing death — a theology of death — lies behind contemporary conflicts in bioethics. For those who have lost an eschatological horizon, those no longer shaped by the conviction that life transcends death, life becomes the ultimate and greatest good, an end in itself. Anything that threatens this end becomes the determinative enemy.

This, then, is what I believe to be an important reading of the Schiavo case — that it was not only a story about a particular treatment decision but it was equally a story of brokenness and hostility fomented into enmity by the actions of persons external to the case, some of whom even publicly identified themselves as Christians. To see this as a crucial reading of the Schiavo case shifts our attention away from immediate considerations of treatment decisions. It suggests that the case — and perhaps bioethics itself — needs to be approached in a radically different way than we are used to. It raises different questions. And those questions will require different sorts of answers. Here, I will argue, one of the overriding questions (though, ad-

---

4. "Judge in Schiavo Case Asked to Leave Church," *Christian Century*, April 19, 2005, p. 15.

mittedly, not the only question) is how one engages one's enemies, including, in the context of medicine, the enemy death.

Death as the Enemy, Medicine as War

In my description above, I suggested that activists in this case appeared to view death as the ultimate enemy. In staking out such a position, they merely embody the deep commitments of our culture. William F. May, onetime member of the President's Council on Bioethics and longtime member of the guild of theological ethicists, makes the case that contemporary medicine has both learned to and schools us to see death as the enemy.

In his book *The Physician's Covenant,* May describes at length how military metaphors and images, how the language of war itself, pervade the practice of medicine:

> The metaphor of war dominates the modern, popular understanding of disease and determines in countless ways the medical response. We see germs, viruses, bacteria, and cancers as invaders that break the territorial integrity of the body; they seize bridgeheads and, like an occupying army, threaten to spread, dominate, and destroy the whole. . . . Victims look for help to professionals, who, acquainted with the weapons of war, can take charge of the defense. The professional needs "intelligence." And so medicine has developed diagnostic procedures, scanning devices, and early warning systems more complex than the radar equipment of World War II, to let the professional know the enemy's location and the scale of the attack. . . . As in war, the very weapons used to fight the enemy can themselves endanger those on whose behalf one wields them. . . . The hospital becomes a military compound. . . . A kind of military discipline prevails there. . . . Modern medicine has tended to interpret itself not only through the prism of war but through the medium of its modern practice, that is, unlimited, unconditional war.[5]

This language of war is ubiquitous — found within medicine itself, but equally used by the media, in scientific journals, even by bioethicists. Take, for example, the realm of medical research. In 1971 Richard Nixon launched the "War on Cancer." Thirty-five years have passed, and this war is far from over — the same metaphor was employed and developed extensively in a

5. William F. May, *The Physician's Covenant: Images of the Healer in Medical Ethics* (Philadelphia: Westminster, 1983), pp. 64-66.

2002 report on cancer research in the major scientific journal *Nature*.[6] For many, and certainly for the media, clinical medicine via biotechnology is engaged in a war against disease, disability, suffering, and death. The tools of research and the clinic are the "medical armamentarium." Those who suffer from particular illnesses are "survivors." Cures are hailed as "magic bullets." And so on . . .

The metaphor of war is used most often when a new technology needs to be sold to political and public audiences in the United States. A recent example of this is the debate on human embryonic stem cell research. An article by two prominent bioethicists — Glenn McGee and Art Caplan — exemplifies this.[7] In their article "The Ethics and Politics of Small Sacrifices in Stem Cell Research," they use at least seven war-related images in seven pages. They characterize researchers who seek to develop therapies from human embryonic stem cells as fighting a "just war," a "war against suffering," caused by the whole gamut of diseases from Parkinson's to cancer to heart disease and more. They compare the annual mortality of cancer, which might potentially be alleviated through human embryonic stem cell research, to the number of people killed "in both the Kosovo and Vietnam conflicts." They suggest that advocates of human embryonic stem cell research plan to "sacrifice embryos for a revolutionary new kind of research." They characterize Parkinson's disease as an evil "dictator" dreaming up the most nefarious "chemical war campaign." Resonating with wartime rhetoric, they note that "adults and even children are sometimes forced to give [their lives], but only in the defense or at least interest of the community's highest ideals and most pressing interests."

But why war? How is it — to simply mention another example — that the race to map the human genome could become construed as an issue of national security (an analogy to war)?[8] How can one mount a war on something as amorphous as cancer? More importantly, what is required before someone can even start thinking about medical research and practice in terms of war?

To fight a war, as recent history reminds us all too well, requires an en-

6. Alison Abbott, "On the Offensive," *Nature* 416 (April 4, 2002): 470-74.

7. Glenn McGee and Arthur Caplan, "The Ethics and Politics of Small Sacrifices in Stem Cell Research," *Kennedy Institute of Ethics Journal* 9, no. 2 (1999): 151-57. The quotations in this paragraph are from this article.

8. John Beatty, "Origins of the U.S. Human Genome Project: Changing Relationships between Genetics and National Security," in *Controlling Our Destinies: Historical, Philosophical, Ethical, and Theological Perspectives on the Human Genome Project*, ed. Phillip R. Sloan (Notre Dame, Ind.: University of Notre Dame Press, 2000), p. 141.

emy, and for May, that enemy is death. As he notes: "death looms as supremely antihuman, the absolute, invincible enemy which, nonetheless, we must resist to affirm our humanity."[9] He argues that the vision of medicine as a practice of war and the understanding of death as the supreme enemy arise out of the broader religious consciousness of contemporary culture. In an increasingly secularized culture, people may no longer believe in God, but that does not mean that gods do not rule their lives. "The modern interpretation of disease as destructive power fits in with the religious preoccupations of our time. . . . However, the gods that enthrall modern men and women do not bless but threaten them."[10] For May, the god above all gods is death. Death and the related god of suffering are those we fear most, those that wield the most power over us.[11] Perceived as absolute evil, "the *summum malum* of violent death," he notes, "has replaced God as the effective center of religious consciousness in the modern world."[12]

These dark forces threaten us; before them we stand helpless, innocent yet powerless. Without a champion to intervene on our behalf and defend us, we have no hope. Medicine has become over the past four decades just such a champion — a redeemer. May notes that only recently has the image of physician as fighter replaced the image of physician as parent; "the goal of medicine [now] defines itself negatively and adversarially as being either to prevent suffering or to prevent death."[13] May describes the physician as "the titan who responds to the sacred by seizing power in his or her own right and doing battle with the enemy."[14] The physician is the one that wields "the retaliatory powers that modern biomedical research places at his or her disposal."[15] Medicine, in this way, becomes our savior.[16]

May highlights this language to demonstrate a larger point — that images and metaphors tell stories, compressed prototypical stories. Without

---

9. May, *The Physician's Covenant,* p. 63.
10. May, *The Physician's Covenant,* p. 31.
11. May, *The Physician's Covenant,* p. 34.
12. May, *The Physician's Covenant,* p. 67.
13. May, *The Physician's Covenant,* p. 69.
14. May, *The Physician's Covenant,* p. 33.
15. May, *The Physician's Covenant,* p. 34.

16. One might even say that "Christ the physician" (a traditional Christian image) becomes physician-as-Christ, the one who (with the help of biotechnology) fights relentlessly against the last enemy, death. As Michael West, founder of Geron, CEO of Advanced Cell Technology, and cloning advocate, notes: "We're trying *to save* the lives of our fellow human beings who have *no hope* today" (Faith Keenan, "Cloning: Huckster or Hero?" *Business Week,* July 1, 2002, pp. 86-87, emphasis added). Science has become hope for those who have no other hope. Insofar as hope is a theological virtue, this is a striking theological claim.

words, without arguments, they encapsulate narratives in which we become located, narratives that shape our social role, our identities, indeed, the choices we make, the actions we take, and the ways we live our lives. Who we understand ourselves to be is deeply implicated in what we do. As such, images and metaphors "do not simply describe the world, they partly create and re-create the world to conform to a [particular vision of reality]."[17]

What vision of reality is being presented where death is spoken of as "god," medicine as savior? If nothing else, we are being presented with a theological vision of reality. Indeed, a "religious consciousness" lies behind modern medicine and bioethics, one deeply at odds with Christianity. And it shapes us powerfully. For in the Schiavo case we found such faulty theological convictions wielded even by some Christians. Take, for example, this theology of salvation (known in the discipline of theology by the technical term "soteriology"). Medicine was implored as the agent of salvation — able either to "save" Terri from death or to "save" her from suffering the indignity inflicted on her in sustaining her life.[18] Equally, salvation seemed to rest in the hands of the judicial system — to Governor Jeb Bush, to judges, to congresspeople were offered from both sides laments and petitions not unlike one finds in the Psalms.

For Christians, of course, salvation rests not in the hands of Jeb Bush or medical technology, but in the hands of the triune God who has acted in

---

17. May, *The Physician's Covenant,* p. 20.

18. It is easy to slip into this account of medicine-as-savior because it is, in part, a parody of the account of salvation offered by the Christian tradition. For the Christian tradition, suffering, death, and the other forces that threaten us and fear of which dominates our lives are nothing other than what traditional theological language has referred to as "the principalities and powers." Within the Christian narrative, they are understood as enemies. For example, Saint Paul, in his impassioned exhortation on the essence of salvation, concludes: "Then comes the end, when [Christ] hands over the kingdom to God the Father, after he has destroyed every ruler and every authority and power. For he must reign until he has put all his enemies under his feet. The last enemy to be destroyed is death" (1 Cor. 15:24-26). Paul clearly regards death as the enemy. Even Christ, as portrayed here, saw death as an enemy, triumphed over it, and will ultimately *destroy* it. Here, and in the book of Revelation, we find language of a great war between Christ and the principalities and powers that rule the world, the last and greatest of which is death, an enemy that has ultimately been defeated by the cross and resurrection. The language here seems violent, even militaristic. As such, is it not appropriate to resist death, to war against it, to respond to it even with violent means if necessary? We need to take care in reading passages like 1 Cor. 15 too literally. For while Christ may well consider death an enemy, it would be out of character for the risen Christ to act violently, even toward this greatest of enemies. Christ, we believe, has triumphed over death. But as his initial victory was nonviolent, so also must be his final defeat of death.

Jesus Christ. Jesus was not necessarily absent from the rhetoric bandied about during early 2005. Ironically, Jesus took his place on some placards proclaiming this distorted soteriology. But this Jesus was more the Jesus of Mel Gibson than, perhaps, the Jesus of the Gospels — a bloody corpus abstracted from the rest of his story. Jesus became a rhetorical tool. Some mapped Terri onto Christ, rendering her a Christ figure, the Suffering Servant of Isaiah. Judges and politicians became her betrayers, "Judas Iscariots," in the words of Operation Rescue's Randall Terry.[19]

Though more could be said, I hope it is becoming clear how, in spite of the apparent rifts between some Christians and secularists in this case, when one presses behind the surface rhetoric, one finds a remarkable degree of overlap, of substantive agreement, of ideological and theological similarity in their positions. Insofar as this theology drives their actions, it calls for a theological response.

Holy Week

But where to begin? One of the most interesting editorial cartoons published in March 2005 subtly gives us a possibility. The cartoon depicts Terri lying in a hospital bed. Superimposed over her, though not immediately obvious, is the shadow of a cross mapping itself onto her body so that she becomes the corpus. Lying at the foot of her bed is a sponge and a bottle labeled vinegar. The cartoon, in other words, trades on the not inconsequential fact that Terri's final vigil began during Holy Week.

Holy Week stands as the most important week of the liturgical year, the week when the church celebrates in time and ritual the central claim of the gospel. Here, in other words, the church enacts the normative claims of the Christian faith. Certainly Christians are called to see Christ "in the least among us," as many of the placards of the protestors proclaimed; thus, to see Christ in Terri is a move that was certainly legitimate both theologically and according to most of Christian tradition. But while Terri was "read" as Christ, a *christological* reading of her dying and death was not at the forefront of the media hype. For as Christians, we are not called to save Christ from death but rather to follow him. We are to

---

19. Others described Terri using the language of martyrdom. Although I cannot explore it at length here, it would be equally interesting to analyze the martyrdom language used in this case, especially the differences between Christian public action in this case and the sort of Christian public action that surrounded the martyrdom of Christians in the early church or, for that matter, in the twentieth century.

follow him as he dies, understanding his death to mark God's victory over death. And we are called to follow him in the shape of his life. In other words, Christology is indeed normative for Christian ethics, but not as it played out in the public battles of the Schiavo case. What would public engagement in the Schiavo case have looked like had the Christians party to the vigil (although not them alone) understood Terri's death christologically or saw the primary christological agents to be *themselves* rather than Terri?

Let us briefly consider Holy Week: Beginning with Jesus' triumphal entry into Jerusalem on Passion Sunday, Christians follow him day by day, moment by moment, through his last meal with his friends; his great act of service to them as he washes their feet; his agonized decision on how to respond to the enemies he knows will soon accost him; his unjust arrest and the mockery of justice that followed; his betrayal by his friends; and his horrific walk up the road to Calvary. At the pinnacle of the story stands the crucifixion, the passion, Good Friday. Here Jesus accepts a clearly unjust death and utters the amazing words: "Father, forgive them; for they do not know what they are doing" (Luke 23:34). And through his entry into death, God vanquishes it.

As Christians follow Jesus to Calvary during Holy Week, we hold vigil, as did Terri's supporters. We watch as the one we proclaim to be God rejects hatred, violence, and even judicial resistance to the powers of the world as a way of saving his life. Jesus chastises those who suggest violence to protect him. He stands mute in the face of judicial proceedings, rather than seeking his rights or paying lawyers exorbitant amounts of money to find every last loophole to save him. He shows that his life (and therefore our lives) is not about winning against adversaries, asserting his rights, or triumphing over others. He takes the pain and brokenness, injustice and sin of the world onto his own body in order to reconcile it to God and to show us the path toward reconciliation with each other.

In contrast to our hyper-litigious outlook, Jesus understands faithfulness to God fundamentally to be about something else. It is not about saving his life, even his most innocent of lives. Because of Jesus' victory over death, life within the Christian tradition has never been understood as an end in itself. The passion stories speak first and foremost not about the inviolability of life — rather, they display Jesus' engagement with the principalities and powers that dominate the world and his commitment to loving his enemies, to praying for those who are persecuting him, to forgiving others as *the* exemplar of God's very character, God's very way of being in the world. And he indicates that *this* is the Way to be followed. *This* is the Christ to be imitated. This is the truth affirmed — against all expectation and "common sense" — by God in the resurrection.

The resurrection, Holy Week reminds us, is the center of the Christian story. Forgiveness and the commitment to concrete reconciliation between enemies in the here and now, even in the face of suffering and an unjust death — *this* is the story that the church retells and lives again each year at Holy Week. *This* is this story that Christians retell and live again each time we celebrate the Eucharist. *This,* the church affirms, in both its liturgical life and the shape of the liturgical year, is the overarching framework within which all other Christian convictions and principles must be ordered.

Thus, I would argue that the "public" engagement of Christians in the Schiavo case rooted in the liturgical practice of Holy Week would have looked very different. Even when life is at stake, even when an innocent life is at stake, even when a life may be taken unjustly, the eucharistic center of the church requires that Christian engagement with their enemies be shaped by love, normed by commitments to reconciliation.[20] In light of this, what might it have looked like had those who kept vigil for Terri Schiavo recognized that as they journeyed with her toward her death we journeyed as a church with Jesus to his passion, had they "read" her death not according to the conflictual story of bioethics and the U.S. legal system but through the lens of the central claims of the gospel?

Christian Practices and *The Gift of Peace*

There are no better answers to these questions than those exemplars in the Christian tradition. It is in the actual lives of people trying to live the Christian life that we can find the possibility of what we might call a christoform bioethic and learn what makes such a bioethic possible. One such exemplar that I would like to focus on here is Joseph Cardinal Bernardin and his autobiography entitled (not accidentally) *The Gift of Peace*. Bernardin is an important figure for at least two reasons. First, in his life and autobiography he explicitly embodies Christian engagement with medicine and the end of life; his story is in part the story of his terminal journey with pancreatic cancer. Moreover, for a number of years he was also head of the Office of

---

20. To be clear, I am not suggesting that the lens of Holy Week would lead us to a position that would simply "let go" or be passive in the face of threats to life or in the face of death. The question is rather of the shape of Christian engagement in the face of injustice and death.

Pro-Life Activities for the National Conference of Catholic Bishops, a position from which he launched into public consciousness the phrase "the consistent ethic of life."[21] Bernardin brings together in his life the church's deep commitment to life while reading it through the lens of the gospel.

The Gift of Peace is a deceptively simple book. On its face it seems a somewhat random series of autobiographical reflections — the story of how he was falsely accused of sexual abuse; his struggle with terminal pancreatic cancer; and a brief opening reflection on how he took up the practice of daily prayer. But he clearly includes these three stories between the covers of one book because he saw them as deeply interconnected. And it is these interconnections that are crucial to our consideration of the Schiavo case. Allow me to briefly unpack these pieces.

He begins the book — and frames the entire work — with his story of learning how to attend to prayer. He recounts that in the 1970s — then a forty-five-year-old archbishop — he was called to account by some friends for neglecting his own personal prayer life and attending too much to do the doing of "good works" and the business of being archbishop. At their urging he decided to devote the first hour of his day to prayer and meditation — to simply spending time with God.

One thing this experience taught him was how deeply he wished for control, how tightly we tend "to hold onto ourselves and everything and everybody familiar to us."[22] Learning to pray for him meant learning how to "let go," to release his hold on those things that hold him in bondage, and to open himself completely to God's presence in our lives. This was no quick or easy process, but it proved absolutely crucial to his ability to face what came later. As he notes:

> I have desperately wanted to open the door of my soul as Zacchaeus [the tax collector] opened the door of his house. Only in that way can the Lord take over my life completely. Yet many times in the past I have only let him come in part of the way. I talked with him but seemed afraid to

---

21. Importantly, immediately prior to becoming head of the Office of Pro-Life Activities, Bernardin chaired the bishops committee for the landmark document *The Challenge of Peace: God's Promise and Our Response*. As I have argued elsewhere, if one looks at Bernardin's life and writings as a whole, one can make an argument that the consistent ethic of life can be read as an ethic of peacemaking. See my "From the Challenge of Peace to the Gift of Peace: Re-reading the Consistent Ethic of Life as an Ethic of Peacemaking," in *Advancing the Legacy of the Consistent Ethic of Life*, ed. Tom Nairn (forthcoming).

22. Joseph Cardinal Bernardin, *The Gift of Peace* (Chicago: Loyola University Press, 1997), p. 7.

let him take over. Why was I afraid? Why did I open the door only so far and no more? . . . At times I think it was because I wanted to succeed and be acknowledged as a person who has succeeded. At other times I would become upset when I read or heard criticism about my decisions or actions. When these feelings prevailed, I wanted to control things, that is, I wanted to make them come out "right." . . . Have I feared that God's will may be different from mine and that if his will prevailed I would be criticized? . . . To come at this another way, I wonder if I refused to let the Lord enter all the way into my soul because I feared that he would insist that . . . I let go of certain things I was reluctant or unwilling to give up.[23]

This lengthy passage describes, I would guess, not only his life but also the dynamics of our lives. Equally, it captures an absolutely critical aspect of our exploration. Here we see the cardinal embark on a particular practice — the practice of prayer — a traditional Christian practice. It is through and only through this practice that he develops a particular disposition, attitude, skill, virtue — he names this "letting go," but we could equally call it "openness" to God and others, liberation from those things that possess us (pride, possessions, power, fear), trust in God, learning to understand God as the Lord of life, and so on. In his life he had long believed these things in theory, but he acknowledges that he had not really believed them in practice because he had not lived as if they were true.

These virtues, these dispositions prove critical for the last two major events of his life. The first of these is the false accusation of sexually abusing a seminarian. He introduces this chapter of his life with a meditation on "emptying oneself" — "emptying myself of everything — the plans I consider the largest as well as the distractions I judge the smallest — so that the Lord can really take over."[24] He quotes the Pauline hymn of the kenotic Christ ("Though he was in the form of God, / did not regard equality with God / as something to be exploited, / but emptied himself, / taking the form of a slave. . . . / he humbled himself / and became obedient to the point of death — / even death on a cross" [Phil. 2:6-8]) to convey what he means by "emptying oneself."

I will not rehearse the details of this part of the story here (I would encourage all to read it), but a few key elements are important. As with crisis situations in medicine, the accusation came out of nowhere and was devas-

---

23. Bernardin, *The Gift of Peace*, pp. 7-9.
24. Bernardin, *The Gift of Peace*, pp. 15-16.

tating. His world was, in many ways, turned upside down. The accusation struck at one of the key centers of his identity — his chastity. Because he was cardinal archbishop of Chicago and well known, when the news broke millions of people heard it and most likely believed it to be true. He was angry, bewildered at who could possibly launch such a false charge against him, and deeply humiliated. "As never before" he notes, "I felt the presence of evil."[25] Here a destructive power was at work, bearing down on him, threatening everything he held valuable — his life's work, his deepest convictions, his personal reputation, his position as cardinal of Chicago.

Yet at the same time he felt equally sustained by the conviction that "the truth will make you free" (John 8:32). He knew almost tangibly the presence of the God he had come increasingly to know in prayer. And the habit of prayer he had learned through ordinary days and years now becomes crucial. Before facing hordes of reporters the day after the accusation becomes public, he prays the rosary early in the morning, meditating on the Sorrowful Mysteries, and later spends an hour by himself in prayer and meditation. While he feels very much akin to Jesus' aloneness in the garden during his own agony, he equally knows that it is God's grace, strength, and presence that enable him to face the reporters, to stand calmly in the face of evil, and to speak the truth in love and peaceableness.

Moreover, from the beginning he finds himself overwhelmed with a sense of compassion for his accuser. A few days after the filing of the charges, he notes, "I felt a genuine impulse to pray with and comfort him."[26] He almost immediately writes a letter to the man, asking if he might visit him to pray with him. The man's lawyers never deliver the letter. The case eventually unravels on its own, and the charges are eventually dropped as the "evidence" proves to be fabricated. Bernardin could have simply rejoiced in his vindication, or he could have brought countercharges for defamation of character. But this is not the road he chooses. Rather, eleven months after the suit was dropped, he again tried to contact his accuser. This time he was successful. In the end, he met with him and — beyond what would be wildly unimaginable — was reconciled with him.[27] They became friends, such that six months later, when Bernardin was diagnosed with pancreatic cancer, one of the first letters he received was from his former accuser. It is a powerful story of forgiveness and reconciliation.

---

25. Bernardin, *The Gift of Peace,* p. 23.
26. Bernardin, *The Gift of Peace,* p. 25.
27. It is not unimportant that this reconciliation involves the sacraments of reconciliation and Eucharist.

Bernardin makes clear that only his openness to the presence and grace of God in his life, an openness given by God and cultivated through the practice of prayer, enabled this story to unfold as it did. Through the practice of prayer Bernardin learned to love God and to let go of the god of self-love. He developed the virtues necessary to be able to love one who was clearly his enemy, a person who he said inflicted upon him the most damage, in the most vicious manner, that he had ever experienced. What does such love look like? It is nonviolent — the cardinal made clear to his advisers and attorneys at the outset of the crisis that there would be no scorched-earth countersuit to beat the enemy down. It is compassionate — it feels the pain of the other, even of the enemy. It is reconciling — it seeks not to obliterate the enemy but to overcome the enmity between them through reconciliation. It reaches out to the enemy, to both create community with the enemy and to do the work of God's love in the world.

To this extent it is christoform — Bernardin makes clear that such is the nature of Christian love, rooted in the person of Jesus. Through his practice of prayer he has come to know Jesus as a fully human person, one who both experienced pain and suffering and yet "transformed human suffering into something greater: an ability to walk with the afflicted and to empty himself so that his loving Father could work more fully through him."[28] And it is this Jesus that he meets through his practice of prayer that increasingly becomes the One who shapes his life.

This experience becomes the prelude to the final chapter of his story, the story of his struggle with terminal pancreatic cancer complicated by painful spinal stenosis.[29] In his narrative, we watch as he uses the tools of medicine to resist the growth of cancer in his body. We watch as he wins a short-lived remission, and then as the cancer returns with renewed virulence. But importantly, the autobiography of his illness is not primarily about his illness — it is instead about how his illness leads him into a new world of ministry, meeting, being present to and praying for literally hundreds of others who struggle with cancer.

It is also about how his illness leads him to a new understanding of death. The final chapter in his story he entitles "Befriending Death." As the phrase suggests, he comes to regard "death not as an enemy or threat but as

28. Bernardin, *The Gift of Peace*, p. 46.

29. Clearly, Bernardin's medical situation differed from Terri Schiavo's medical situation. Nonetheless, he is a key exemplar insofar as the objective of this chapter is to shift attention to questions beyond those of treatment decisions — to attend to the question of the shape of Christian engagement with enmity and death in the myriad of ways they come together in the context of health care.

a friend."[30] The reorientation is first suggested to him by his friend Henri Nouwen, who learned it during his ministry among persons with disabilities in the Daybreak Community of L'Arche. As Bernardin notes: "It's very simple. If you have fear and anxiety and you talk to a friend, then those fears and anxieties are minimized and could even disappear. If you see them as an enemy, then you go into a state of denial and try to get as far away as possible from them. People of faith who believe that death is the transition from this life to eternal life, should see death as a friend."[31] Nouwen's insight resonates with Bernardin's life, shaped as it was by practices of "letting go" and giving God Lordship over his life; of practicing forgiveness; of ministering to others who were sick and dying. Liberation from the tyranny of suffering and death, reconciliation with death, and learning to love the enemy death to the point of calling it "friend" are for Bernardin the fruits of a worshipful life lived amidst the community of the broken. This he believes is "God's special gift to us all: the gift of peace. When we are at peace, we find the freedom to be most fully who we are, even in the worst of times. . . . We empty ourselves so that God may more fully work within us. And we become instruments in the hands of the Lord."[32]

Such peace, of course, is the peace of Christ. Even though the cardinal comes to refer to death as his friend, he continues to understand his journey as one that enters into Christ's passion. As he moves into the final phase of his illness, he notes, "the cross has become my constant companion."[33] As such, Bernardin's rereading of death is clearly christoform — shaped by a Christlike self-emptying, death, and resurrection. The love he gains for this enemy death is Christian love — *agape*, God's love for us — which is embodied most completely on the cross. Here and elsewhere, loving one's enemies means forgiveness of the real injuries, pain, and suffering they cause us. It means being reconciled to the presence and reality of the other. It means foregoing the fantasy that we "win" by eliminating or defeating them with violence. It might mean that we are rightly to "resist" their attempts to have power over us, to govern our lives with fear, to determine our actions.[34]

---

30. Bernardin, *The Gift of Peace*, p. 126.

31. Bernardin, *The Gift of Peace*, pp. 127-28. In learning to love our enemies, do they necessarily remain such, namely, *enemies*? The gospel does not promise that if we love our enemies, such enmity will disappear. In fact, it seems to promise that habits of loving one's enemies may well multiply them or lead to crucifixion or martyrdom.

32. Bernardin, *The Gift of Peace*, p. 153.

33. Bernardin, *The Gift of Peace*, p. 129.

34. In many ways, it ought not be surprising that Bernardin was able to embody such a counterintuitive approach to death. For importantly, he was also a first-order Franciscan

Toward a Christoform Bioethic

Here, then, we have what I am sure is a very different approach to the case of Terri Schiavo than most analyses offer. In addition, I hope it lays the groundwork for developing a new approach to Christian (and/or "Catholic") bioethics. In the interest of summing up, let me offer four points by way of conclusion.

First, the Schiavo case should highlight for us that quite often the central *moral* issue in end-of-life cases, or perhaps even within medicine and bioethics more broadly, is the need for reconciliation. Not only do families often come into the clinical setting "fractured," but there is also nothing like a medical crisis, especially one like this — where a sudden catastrophe in the life of a vibrant young woman then stretches on and on and on — to exacerbate or even create such fractures, bringing to the surface and magnifying all sorts of unresolved issues. And as is often the case, the one imperiled, about whom decisions have to be made, is the very one that helped mediate and foster the fragile family dynamic. Without her the family fragments.

---

oblate. This distinctive attitude of peace and reconciliation in the face of death finds a new form in the work of Saint Francis of Assisi. Saint Francis, that most popular saint of all times, is particularly noted for his deep devotion to Jesus and how closely his life conformed to that of Christ in the Gospels. Francis is often referred to as *alter Christi* — "another Christ." Two years before his death, Saint Francis retreated to a mountaintop hermitage in La Verna, Italy, where, in the course of months of intense prayer, he received the stigmata, the marks of Jesus' passion in his hands, feet, and sides. The pain of the stigmata was compounded over the next two years by additional painful conditions, including blindness. And yet he continued to be filled with joy, his enthusiasm bursting forth in one of his most classic prayers, *The Canticle of Brother Sun*. Here, as Francis praises the trinitarian God in each element of God's magnificent creation, he culminates with death: "Praised be you, my Lord, through our Sister Bodily Death, from whom no living man can escape." Francis greets death, in other words, not only as a friend but also as a sister, and what is more, as that through which God can be praised. Thus, via Francis and others, the Christian tradition acknowledges the reality of death — that it is, indeed, the greatest of human enemies — but at the same time, from the beginning and at many points thereafter, the tradition witnesses that the distinctive Christian response is to approach it by saying, "Peace be with you"; "Praise you, Lord, for our sister bodily death."

This Franciscan attitude pervaded Bernardin's life. It is reported that when Bernardin, as cardinal archbishop of Chicago, faced what he knew would be a particularly difficult or contentious meeting, he would open the meeting with Saint Francis's classic peace prayer that begins "Lord, make me an instrument of your peace. . . ." It is also not coincidental that the last initiative he started was the Catholic Common Ground Initiative designed to try to foster reconciliation among the increasingly polarized factions in the Catholic Church.

This, however, should not be unexpected. Families are fragile in all sorts of ways, and illness, disability, death can be extraordinary blows.

Yet this fact of brokenness and need for reconciliation are not treated as a dimension of "medical ethics" proper. Even Catholic moral theologians or Christian bioethicists — to whom the concept of "reconciliation" is more readily available than it is perhaps to secular bioethicists — proceed as if the sole question is finding the right decision maker or making the right decision. Reconciliation is portrayed as a long, messy, nonclinical process for the chaplain or the social worker; it's part of *sacramental* theology, not moral theology.

To this my response is: well, yes and no. As my analysis suggests, I do think the sacraments and the practices of the Christian life are the place to find the resources for addressing the pressing questions of theology and medicine. Consequently, I would argue that we ought to resist this too-clean distinction between sacramental and moral theology. Rather, moral theologians need to make much clearer the connection between Christian ethics and Christian worship and to demonstrate just how this connection might work.

Nor is reconciliation simply a "pastoral" rather than an "ethical" issue. It is important for more than our feelings of unity. The autonomy of choice and the sanctity of life have become the central (and often sole) moral questions in the realm of bioethics because they deal with what are considered critical human goods — freedom and life. These are considered essential components of who we are. But a truly theological anthropology, a vision of the human person rooted in the Trinity and the fullest embodiment of the image of God who was Jesus Christ, does not stop there. It does not relegate human relatedness and community to simply a "pastoral" dimension. To be in community is not simply nice but is necessary to who we are. And imperiled community is equally, if not perhaps more problematic than, imperiled autonomy. If morality and ethics are about the pursuit of central human goods under the aegis of faith, then the need for reconciliation is a central moral question.

Second, I would argue that, theologically, reconciliation must be the overarching context of all other moral and ethical analysis. Does this mean that freedom and the sanctity of life are irrelevant? Not at all. Rather, it is about the proper ordering of goods, as Augustine would say. Absent this proper ordering — this ordering of Christian commitments under the overarching context of reconciliation and forgiveness — we risk more than moral disorder; we risk — in Augustine's terms — real evil. Consequently, it is possible in the clinical setting to achieve a "legally" or "procedurally" correct decision that is a complete failure. Saint Paul reminds us that if we speak in tongues, have the gift of prophecy, give all we possess to the poor, and become martyrs, but have not love, we are nothing. Similarly, if we achieve a "procedurally correct" outcome according to the canons of bioethics — either discontinuing or continuing artificial nutrition and hydration in the Schiavo case — but have not reconciliation (which is, of course, love), what do we have?

In other words, as Bernardin's story makes clear, I do not mean to suggest that treatment decisions are completely irrelevant — when first diagnosed, he pursued treatment aggressively; when the cancer returned, he again initially chose treatment but then decided to withdraw treatment and to allow death to come. In this he embodied the long-standing wisdom of the Catholic tradition, that life is a gift to be valued but not to be pursued at all costs.

But the treatment decisions are not the focus of his account of the end of life. Instead, the focus is on how he lived in the face of death. These are the real theological-moral questions that every Christian will face. How do Catholics or Christians act in the face of death? How do we act when faced with this real evil that promises to tear apart the fabric of our lives? How do we act when faced with other people who, through their actions in end-of-life situations, become our enemies (even if they are members of our families)? On an institutional level, what would it mean to develop a decision-making process, algorithm, etc., that took the overarching goal of reconciliation seriously? What would it look like? What would the outcomes be? What would it look like for health-care institutions to name reconciliation as a "core value" and to make sure it informs their policies, practices, language, and ethos? What would it look like for Catholic moral theology or bioethics to be shaped around a commitment to reconciliation? Forty years ago the words "autonomy" and "informed consent" were foreign to the clinical setting. How different might clinical medicine look forty years hence if Christians conscientiously tried to introduce into medical ethics the language of forgiveness?

Thirdly, to be clear, forgiveness and reconciliation are not Pollyanna, touchy-feely, why-can't-we-all-just-get-along sorts of things. Rather they are concrete practices that require continual effort and a lifetime to learn. They are not the sort of thing one will wake up one morning to and say, "Aha! I'm a forgiving person!" As Bernardin makes clear in his own story, his ability to forgive his accuser and to face death not as the end but as the opportunity for a new ministry was a gift — a gift of God, sustained by God's gracious, creative, and life-giving presence — made possible by his two-decade-long practice of daily prayer. Practices like prayer help instill in us specific virtues so crucial in crises and as we die — virtues like patience and openness to the other. Equally, they habituate us to more readily see the world not under the descriptions our culture gives us as normative (e.g., fight a lawsuit with a lawsuit) but rather under the auspices of the Christian story.

Nor are forgiveness and reconciliation best left to the initiative of individuals. So counter to our nature is it to love our enemies, to forgive them, to be reconciled with them, that it's almost impossible to do alone (those people who figure out how to, we usually call "saints"). Christianity (as well as Judaism and Islam) has set aside special rites and special times to call us to account, knowing well that left to our own devices, we would never do it. It is too hard, especially when we are overwhelmed with the pain caused by alienation and brokenness. Forgiveness and reconciliation must be mediated by the community, by the institutions within which patients and families find themselves. These things must be intentional, they must be attended to, they must be practiced. And they must be practiced within the community of the church, both because without it they would never happen, and because without them the church itself could not be sustained, for they are its very essence.

Finally, I will grant you that love of enemy and forgiveness are far more difficult to legislate than the principle of sanctity of life or the right to autonomy. Nor are they easy to live out. But those who claim to be Christian — as did so many people in the Schiavo and other end-of-life cases — know that this is the ultimate context for all other commitments, even the Christian commitment to life. And it is our call as Christians to show that it is possible, to embody in our lives a politics not primarily of the state and federal court, not of health-care policies, nor of fear and enmity, but rather of redemption.

Action is the "test" of our belief. Do we face whatever threatens us calmly, truthfully, peaceably, as Bernardin did his accuser, relentlessly seeking reconciliation in the midst of it? Do we encounter the thing or person who threatens us as an opportunity to launch a new ministry, a new witness to Christ's presence in our lives, to create a network of prayer, friendship, and reconciliation, beyond what we ever could have imagined? Only by dwelling in the Christian story every day, in the Eucharist, and through feasts such as the triduum, can we begin to see life as a gift through which God can be glorified, enemies as those who need compassion, and death as the enemy transformed.

As we act, so we will witness. Many fear that speaking of bioethics in such resoundingly Christian terms cannot help but alienate those who do not share the Christian faith. But I disagree. The witness of Cardinal Bernardin has moved many who had little interest in faith or Christianity to see that there might be another way. Showing is always more powerful than saying. Christians, indeed, are called to minister to the brokenness of the world, but this ministry must necessarily resemble the lead of the one we claim to follow, namely, the witness of Jesus Christ, the trinitarian God incarnate. It is our call as Christians to show that it is possible, to attempt to embody this. And if we do, I bet we'd be amazed by how God's grace would heal the world.

Concurrent Readings

Albom, Mitch. *Tuesdays with Morrie*. Reprint, New York: Anchor Publishing, 2005. This is the story of one facing what is usually considered the worst-case scenario (or the best-case for assisted suicide or euthanasia), amyotrophic lateral sclerosis (ALS, Lou Gehrig's disease). In the face of this illness, Morrie Schwarz embodies an approach to the end of his life not unlike that found in Bernardin's *The Gift of Peace* — including the key emphases on new mission/ministry and reconciliation.

Ashley, Benedict, O.P., and Kevin O'Rourke, O.P. *Healthcare Ethics: A Theological Analysis*. Washington, D.C.: Georgetown University Press, 2006. Ashley and O'Rourke's tome (now in its fifth edition) represents the best vision of a traditional Catholic, deeply Thomistic approach to health-care ethics. Their work reflects critical engagement with the discipline of medical ethics as well as their personal experience working in the health-care context. It provides both theoretical chapters and chapters on "issues" that could be read alongside this chapter.

Bernardin, Joseph Cardinal. *The Gift of Peace*. Chicago: Loyola University Press, 1997. The significance of this book is outlined above. It is definitely a must-read.

Shuman, Joel James, and Brian Volck, M.D. *Reclaiming the Body: Christians and the Faithful Use of Modern Medicine*. Grand Rapids: Brazos, 2006. Coauthored by a physician and a theologian, this book uses literature, contemporary stories, and more to give a theological reading of medicine. Accessibly written, it integrates attention to our bodies and the gathered body of Christ in rethinking how medicine can be a practice of hospitality toward the suffering and helpless of the world.

U.S. Conference of Catholic Bishops. *The Ethical and Religious Directives for Catholic Health Care Services*. 2001. Available online at: http://www.usccb.

org/bishops/directives.shtml. This short pamphlet summarizes the Catholic Church's positions on questions in medicine. It pairs short theological reflections with the list of guidelines to be adhered to by Catholic health-care institutions. While relatively brief, it gives a good overview of a theological perspective on medicine — beginning, importantly, with "the social responsibility of healthcare institutions."

Chapter 15

Catholic Social Thought and Environmental Ethics in a Global Context

JEANNE HEFFERNAN SCHINDLER

In his provocative 1968 article "The Tragedy of the Commons," Garrett Hardin identified a set of issues he categorized as "no technical solution problems," defining a technical solution as "one that requires a change only in the techniques of the natural sciences, demanding little or nothing in the way of change in human values or ideas or morality."[1] Among these problems Hardin included environmental degradation, lamenting that the natural world is subject to the perverse "logic of the commons" whereby individuals and groups shortsightedly and ruinously overtax shared finite resources in pursuit of narrowly self-interested aims. Nearly forty years after Hardin's article, evidence of the "tragedy of the commons" is unmistakable, and with the rise of globalization it is ubiquitous. As Nicholas Boyle has noted, when we become aware of globalization we realize not only "the increasingly apparent economic integration of the whole world" but also "the ever more insistent constraints imposed by its physical limits."[2]

Evidence of our failure to heed those limits, that is, evidence of negative environmental effects wrought by various industrial practices and patterns of consumption, presents a stark picture. In the words of Pope John Paul II: "The gradual depletion of the ozone layer and the related 'greenhouse effect' has now reached crisis proportions as a consequence of industrial growth, massive urban concentrations and vastly increased energy needs. Industrial waste, the burning of fossil fuels, unrestricted deforestation, the use of certain types of herbicides, coolants and propellants: all of

---

1. Garrett Hardin, "The Tragedy of the Commons," *Science* 162 (1968): 1243.
2. Nicholas Boyle, *Who Are We Now? Christian Humanism and the Global Market from Hegel to Heaney* (Notre Dame, Ind.: University of Notre Dame Press, 1998), p. 152.

these are known to harm the atmosphere and environment. The resulting meteorological and atmospheric changes range from damage to health to the possible future submersion of low-lying lands."[3]

What can be done in response to this problem? As Aldo Leopold presciently observed in 1948, to avert a full-blown environmental crisis requires more than what Hardin would later call a "technical solution" and more than an appeal to enlightened self-interest. Too often, he noted, land-use directives derive from a simplistic formula of economic utility, which "defines no right or wrong, assigns no obligations, calls for no sacrifice, implies no change in the current philosophy of values."[4] Hence Leopold's plea for a more comprehensive "land ethic" is informed by what he calls an "ecological conscience."[5] It is my contention that Catholic theology yields vital — indeed indispensable — resources for the development of such a compre-

---

3. John Paul II, "The Ecological Crisis: A Common Responsibility," Message for the World Day of Peace, January 1, 1990, §6, reprinted in *"And God Saw That It Was Good": Catholic Theology and the Environment,* ed. Drew Christiansen, S.J., and Walter Grazer (Washington, D.C.: United States Catholic Conference, 1996), p. 217. Contemporary environmental research yields empirical support for John Paul II's claims. For instance, in an article documenting the deleterious atmospheric effects of industrialization, noted environmental scientist George Woodwell reports staggering statistics on the current levels of carbon dioxide emissions: "There is, today, 33 percent more carbon dioxide (CO_2) in the atmosphere than there was at the end of the nineteenth century. The burning of fossil fuels pumps 6.5 billion tons of CO_2 into the atmosphere annually; deforestation results in another 1.6 billion tons of CO_2 being released into the atmosphere" ("Fiddling While the World Burns," *Woods Hole Research Center Essays,* January 9, 2002). One of the cumulative effects of these emissions, global warming, will, he predicts, wreak special havoc with low-lying coastal regions subject to flooding. Woodwell's concerns find support in the work of the Intergovernmental Panel on Climate Change (IPCC), a joint venture of the United Nations Environmental Programme and the World Meteorological Organization. The IPCC's reports, "Climate Change 2001: The Scientific Basis" and "Climate Change 2001: Impacts, Adaptation and Vulnerability," document the scientific basis for anthropogenic global warming and its hazardous effects on human and biological systems, including greater weather extremes, from drought to heavy flooding, decreases in crop yields, water scarcity, higher rates of vector- and water-borne diseases, and a rise in heat-related mortality (www.ipcc.ch/index.htm). Various other forms of environmental degradation, such as the mismanagement of toxic waste, find documentation in the United Nations Commission on Human Rights report, "Adverse Effects of the Illicit Movement and Dumping of Toxic and Dangerous Products and Wastes on the Enjoyment of Human Rights," January 20, 1998, E/CN.4/1998/10. See also Calvin DeWitt's catalogue of environmental crisis points in *The Environment and the Christian* (Grand Rapids: Baker, 1991), pp. 13-23.

4. Aldo Leopold, *A Sand County Almanac and Sketches Here and There* (Oxford: Oxford University Press, 1949), pp. 207-8.

5. Leopold, *A Sand County Almanac,* p. 207.

hensive ethic and the formation of such a conscience.[6] In particular, the church's understanding of the sacramentality of creation, the requirements of a just social order, and the resources of the spiritual life are important elements in the theoretical and practical enterprise of conservation.

Sacramentality of Creation

In the first place, the conservation imperative as sketched by Aldo Leopold requires firm theoretical grounding. Quite simply, one must defend the premise that the natural world is valuable — even those parts of the natural world for which there is no apparent human utility.[7] One can find this grounding in the biblical account of creation, amplified by the Christian notion of sacramentality.

The creation account in Genesis offers an unequivocal affirmation of the intrinsic goodness of the natural world. Even before the creation of man and woman, God again and again declared his handiwork "good" (Gen. 1:1-25). As Bill McKibben poetically describes, nature is a veritable "museum of divine intent."[8] The church would add that the universe is sacramental, disclosing "the creator's presence by visible and tangible signs."[9] As the U.S. bishops affirm: "The diversity of life manifests God's glory. Every creature shares a bit of the divine beauty. Because the divine goodness could not be represented by one creature alone, Aquinas tells us: God 'produced many

6. There is some irony in this contention, given that Leopold lays much blame for environmental degradation at the feet of biblical religion. "Conservation," he laments, "is getting nowhere because it is incompatible with our Abrahamic concept of land. We abuse land because we regard it as a commodity belonging to us" (*A Sand County Almanac*, p. viii). His critique is far less pointed than historian Lynn White's, which contends that "Christianity bears a huge burden of guilt" for modern environmental problems stemming from "the Christian dogma of man's transcendence of, and rightful mastery over, nature" ("The Historical Roots of Our Ecological Crisis," in *Dynamo and Virgin Reconsidered* [Cambridge: MIT Press, 1968], pp. 89-90).

7. Leopold insists that we transcend a mere economic calculus of value: "One basic weakness in a conservation system based wholly on economic motives is that most members of the land community have no economic value. Wildflowers and songbirds are examples. . . . Yet these creatures are members of the biotic community, and if (as I believe) its stability depends on its integrity, they are entitled to continuance" (*A Sand County Almanac*, p. 210).

8. Bill McKibben, *The End of Nature* (New York: Random House, 1989), p. 72.

9. U.S. National Conference of Catholic Bishops (hereafter U.S. Bishops), "Renewing the Earth: An Invitation to Reflection and Action on the Environment in Light of Catholic Social Teaching," November 14, 1991, p. 6.

and diverse creatures, so that what was wanting to one in the representation of the divine goodness might be supplied by another . . . hence the whole universe together participates in the divine goodness more perfectly, and represents it better than any single creature whatever.'"[10] This sacramental vision of the wonderful, even whimsical, diversity of creation has inspired the Catholic poetic imagination, perhaps nowhere more vividly than in Gerard Manley Hopkins's "Pied Beauty." Reminiscent of the canticle of creation in Daniel, Hopkins virtually sings:

> Glory be to God for dappled things —
> For skies of couple-colour as a brinded cow;
> For rose-moles in all stipple upon trout that swim;
> Fresh-firecoal chestnut-falls; finches' wings;
> Landscape plotted and pieced — fold, fallow, and plough;
> And all trades, their gear and tackle and trim.
>
> All things counter, original, spare, strange;
> Whatever is fickle, freckled (who knows how?)
> With swift, slow; sweet, sour; adazzle, dim;
> He fathers-forth whose beauty is past change:
> Praise him.[11]

Nature has the power to inspire the praise of God, in the words of John Paul II, to prompt us to "contemplate the mystery of the greatness and love of God."[12] As the book of Wisdom affirms, "From the greatness and beauty of created things comes a corresponding perception of their Creator."[13]

But it is not only the contemplative power of the natural world that grounds the human duty to respect it; the very place of human beings in creation demands it. We are a part of what Aldo Leopold calls the "biotic community," living in intimate interdependence with the soil, water, plants, and animals, taken collectively as "the land."[14] Originally commissioned to exercise what John Paul II calls a "ministerial" dominion over creation, respectful of its integrity, harmony, and rhythms, sinful humanity arrogated

---

10. U.S. Bishops, "Renewing the Earth," p. 7.

11. Gerard Manley Hopkins, *Poems and Prose* (New York: Penguin Books, 1953), pp. 30-31.

12. U.S. Bishops, "Renewing the Earth," p. 6. Christine Firer Hinze eloquently adds, "Theologically, nature, as God's good creation shot through with *vestigia Dei*, is the occasion for profound, contemplative encounters that evoke both fear and reverence" ("Catholic Social Teaching and Ecological Ethics," in *"And God Saw That It Was Good,"* p. 170).

13. Wisd. of Sol. 13:5, cited in John Paul II's encyclical *Fides et Ratio* (§19).

14. Leopold, *A Sand County Almanac*, p. 204.

to itself an absolute dominion over creation, treating the earth not as a gift of God to be used with wisdom and care, but as a possession to be exploited in the service of greed and at the expense of justice to fellow creatures.[15] Indeed, so intimately intertwined is humanity with the natural world in the biblical vision that all of creation suffers from the effects of human sin. As Hosea vividly depicts: "There is no fidelity, no mercy, no knowledge of God in the land. False swearing, lying, murder, stealing and adultery! In their lawlessness, bloodshed follows bloodshed. Therefore, the land mourns, and everything that dwells in it languishes: The beasts of the field, the birds of the air, and even the fish of the sea perish" (Hos. 4:1b-3).[16]

Yet, despite the scourge of sin, God does not forsake his creatures. He mercifully covenanted with Noah, including not only humans but also the rest of creation in a new promise of fidelity to the whole earth, and in the mystery of salvation he promised to bring the entire creation to redemption in Christ, setting it "free from its bondage to decay" (Rom. 8:21).[17] God's creative and redemptive activities are thus closely aligned — the Creator who originally brought intelligible form out of chaos also rescues his creatures from the disorder of sin, re-creating the world. "The whole cosmos — all things on earth and in heaven — find reconciliation and peace in Jesus Christ."[18] In short, then, contrary to the interpretation of some environmental critics of Christianity, the exploitation of the earth perverts rather than fulfills the Genesis 1:26 mandate; likewise, the Christian narrative does not discard creation in favor of human redemption, but rather recognizes the interconnections between humanity and nature, creation and redemption.[19]

15. John Paul II, *The Gospel of Life (Evangelium Vitae),* 52; John Paul II's General Audience Address, January 17, 2001. As Calvin DeWitt points out, the Bible clearly warns against such acquisitiveness. "Woe to you who add house to house and join field to field, till no space is left and you live alone in the land" (Isa 5:8, cited in *Environment and the Christian,* p. 15).

16. Cited in U.S. Bishops, "Renewing the Earth," p. 4.

17. Saint Paul's fuller account of the comprehensive redemption of Christ merits attention: "For the creation waits with eager longing for the revealing of the sons of God; for the creation was subjected to futility, not of its own will but by the will of him who subjected it in hope; because the creation itself will be set free from its bondage to decay and obtain the glorious liberty of the children of God. We know that the whole creation has been groaning in travail together until now; and not only the creation, but we ourselves, who have the first fruits of the Spirit, groan inwardly as we wait for adoption as sons, the redemption of our bodies" (Rom. 8:19-23 RSV).

18. Anne M. Clifford, C.S.J., "Foundations for a Catholic Ecological Theology of God," in *"And God Saw That It Was Good,"* p. 36.

19. As Anne Clifford has argued, "The Bible does not legitimate human exploitation of nonhuman nature, nor is it inherently anthropocentric at the expense of the rest of cre-

Before the promise of redemption is fully realized, however, the temptation to degrade the environment will be perennial. As the empirical evidence attests, rather than using the Lord's creation as good stewards so that it "benefits people and enhances the land,"[20] sinful human beings have recklessly exploited the land, rejecting the biblical counsel to allow the land itself a Sabbath rest.[21] The consequent ecological crisis is, the church insists, a moral crisis, not simply a technical one. Sin has disordered our relationship to God, to one another, and to nature; not surprisingly, how we treat the natural world both reflects and affects our relationship to the Lord and our fellow men. In this regard, John Paul II and the U.S. bishops reserve particular criticism for the consumerism and materialism of advanced capitalist countries. The patterns of rampant acquisitiveness, excessive consumption (evidenced in the "disposable" culture), and reckless use of resources bespeak a failure of justice, a lack of due respect for nature, human life — especially among the poor — and the God of creation.[22]

---

ation" ("Foundations," p. 41). This, of course, is essential to an effective rejoinder to the criticism raised by Leopold and White noted in footnote 6.

20. U.S. Bishops, "Renewing the Earth," p. 9.

21. See DeWitt's reference to Lev. 25-26, in which the Lord declares, "When you enter the land I am going to give you, the land itself must observe a sabbath to the Lord. . . . But if you will not listen to me and carry out these commands . . . I will lay waste the land. . . . All the time that it lies desolate, the land will have the rest it did not have during the sabbaths you lived in it" (*Environment and the Christian*, p. 17).

22. Many have noted that the "developed" and affluent nations, especially of the West, consume a disproportionate amount of resources, creating a disproportionate amount of carbon dioxide emissions and toxic waste that in turn negatively affects poorer, developing nations. Internationally, developed countries "outsource" the dirtiest forms of industrial production to developing countries where environmental regulations are weak (and wage rates low). In 1995 the United Nations Commission on Human Rights appointed a special rapporteur to investigate the human rights implications of international transfers of toxic wastes. The following were among the findings: in 1989, 20 percent of the waste produced in developed countries was exported to developing countries; in spite of the 1992 Basel Convention, an agreement developed by the United Nations Environment Program to restrict transboundary movements of hazardous waste, no significant reduction in such trade has occurred; wealthy states (and corporations) have evaded international and domestic law restrictions on international transfers of toxic materials by "legally" shipping wastes to developed countries for recycling, often under circumstances in which no such recycling capability exists in the receiving state (ttp://www.hri.ca/fortherecord1998/documentation/commission/e-cn4-1998-10.htm (January 9, 2002).

Catholic Social Thought

Insofar as the environmental crisis is also a question of justice and social order, the resources of Catholic social thought helpfully bear upon it. The
term "Catholic social thought" often connotes the relatively recent corpus
of papal encyclicals from Leo XIII to John Paul II, but as Bryan Hehir has
noted, the term has a much wider referent. It encompasses a vast tradition
of theological and philosophical reflection on "the social question," from
the Hebrew scriptures and New Testament, to the patristics, to Aquinas and
the later Scholastics, up to the modern period. In proposing Catholic social
thought as a resource for our contemporary environmental conundrums, I
would add to Hehir's catalogue the contributions of twentieth-century
Thomists, such as Yves R. Simon. Moreover, I will argue that a Thomistic account of the virtues and the liturgy and prayer of the church are indispensable complements to the Catholic social thought in building a distinctively
Catholic environmental ethic.

Each of the above sources testifies to the ancient biblical insight that
"faith is essentially social."[23] As Bryan Hehir observes, "This truth means
that the dynamic of Christian faith, its doctrinal basis and its liturgical celebration, ineluctably seeks an expression in social charity and social justice."[24] There are two interrelated aspects to this expression. One is the concrete corporal and spiritual works of mercy undertaken by the church in the
service of a humane society, works such as providing food, clothing, and
shelter to those in need, denouncing injustice, and seeking the truth in social and political life; the other is the theoretical reflection undergirding
those practices, that is, sustained reflection upon the shape of a just social
order. The latter is the work of Catholic social thought.

As a political theorist, I find the "ontology of social and political
life"[25] elaborated in Catholic social thought to be a firm foundation upon
which to build a comprehensive environmental ethic. Two contributions in
particular merit attention here: solidarity and subsidiarity.

---

23. J. Bryan Hehir, "Catholic Social Teaching: Content, Character, and Challenges,"
in *Rerum Novarum: A Symposium Celebrating 100 Years of Catholic Social Thought* (Lewiston, N.Y.:
Edwin Mellen Press, 1991), p. 3.

24. Hehir, "Catholic Social Teaching," p. 3.

25. Kenneth L. Grasso, "Man, Society, and the State: A Catholic Perspective," in
Caesar's Coin Revisited: Christians and the Limits of Government, ed. Michael Cromartie (Grand
Rapids: Eerdmans, 1996), p. 79.

Solidarity and the Universal Common Good

Despite the fact that the popes from the pre-Leonine period (1740-1877) to the present consistently criticize liberal individualism, the dignity of the individual emerges in Catholic social thought as the central pillar upon which a just social order rests.[26] Papal encyclicals from the 1870s onward state this explicitly. Responding in particular to threats posed to the dignity of individuals both by industrial labor conditions and by collectivist social philosophies, Leo XIII, Pius XI, and Pius XII affirmed the prepolitical foundation of human dignity — "Man [sic] precedes the state," according to *Rerum Novarum* (1891)[27] — and the centrality of the individual in political life. As Pius XII insisted, "The human individual, far from being an object and, as it were, a merely passive element in the social order, is in fact, must be and must continue to be, its subject, its foundation, and its end."[28] Later papal encyclicals and Vatican II documents elaborate upon these convictions.

The ground of these convictions is theological, resting centrally upon twin facts attested by Scripture, namely, that the human person is singularly created in the image and likeness of God and that God himself became human to effect human salvation. The "essential coordinates" of a Catholic anthropology include human reason, uniqueness, freedom and morality, and our "dialogical personality" (we are conversation partners with God, "the one who hears the word," as Karl Rahner put it).[29] Based on these characteristics of human nature, various sources within Catholic social thought have further described the human person as a bearer of rights and obligations. As John XXIII insists in *Peace on Earth (Pacem in Terris)* (1963), "[E]very human being is a person. This means that they are gifted with the power of reasoning and free will. Therefore, they obviously have rights and duties that directly and simultaneously result from their own nature. They are therefore universal, inviolable, absolute, and inalienable."[30]

Of course, the fact that human persons intrinsically bear rights and

---

26. David A. Boileau, ed., *Principles of Catholic Social Teaching* (Milwaukee: Marquette University Press, 1994), p. 9.

27. Leo XIII, *On the Condition of the Labor (Rerum Novarum)*, §7, quoted in *Political Order and the Plural Structure of Society*, ed. James W. Skillen and Rockne M. McCarthy (Atlanta: Scholars, 1991), p. 149.

28. Quoted in Hehir, "Catholic Social Teaching," p. 4.

29. L. Roos, "The Human Person and Human Dignity as Basis of the Social Doctrine of the Church," in *Principles of Catholic Social Teaching*, p. 56.

30. John XXIII, *Peace on Earth (Pacem in Terris)*, §9, quoted in J. Verstraeten, "Solidarity and Subsidiarity," in *Principles of Catholic Social Teaching*, p. 137.

duties implies that we are intrinsically social. The person in a Catholic anthropology develops her or his capacities in relationship; moral and intellectual faculties grow within a network of social connections, ranging from the family to the church to institutions of civil society to the broader political community. These associations develop naturally in accordance with the order of creation. As Heinrich Pesch observed, human beings are "directed ontologically by their concrete nature to the community, as also the whole community by nature is directed to humans."[31] Such a social orientation yields social responsibility — often termed "solidarity" in Catholic social thought — that is incumbent upon the individual no less than on the community. The individual, the mediating institutions of civil society, and political authority should all be animated by this solidarity and should in their respective ways promote the common good, that is, in the words of Vatican II, "the sum total of all those conditions of social life which enable individuals, families, and organizations to achieve complete and efficacious fulfillment."[32]

In recent decades the concept of the common good in Catholic social teaching has expanded. As Drew Christiansen, S.J., points out, the church "has come to think of ecology as an essential component of the common good."[33] Moreover, the fact that globalization has made us increasingly

31. Verstraeten, "Solidarity and Subsidiarity," p. 134.

32. Vatican II's *Pastoral Constitution on the Church in the Modern World (Gaudium et Spes)*, quoted in *Political Order and the Plural Structure of Society*, p. 198. As Skillen and McCarthy relate, Jacques Maritain offers a more detailed, even extravagant, description of the common good: "[T]he public welfare and the general order of law," he maintains, "are essential parts of the common good of the body politic, but this common good has far larger and richer, more concretely human implications, for it is by nature the good human life of the multitude and is common to both the *whole* and the *parts*, the persons into whom it flows back and who must benefit from it. The common good is not only the collection of public commodities and services which the organization of common life presupposes: a sound fiscal condition, a strong military force; the body of just laws, good customs, and wise institutions which provides the political society with its structure; the heritage of its great historical remembrances, its symbols and its glories, its living traditions and cultural treasures. The common good also includes the sociological integration of all the civic conscience, political virtues and sense of law and freedom, of all the activity, material prosperity and spiritual riches, of unconsciously operating hereditary wisdom, of moral rectitude, justice, friendship, happiness, virtue and heroism in the individual lives of the members of the body politic. To the extent to which all these things are, in a certain measure, *communicable* and revert to each member, helping him to perfect his life and liberty as a person, they all constitute the good human life of the multitude" (pp. 185-86).

33. Drew Christiansen, S.J., "Ecology and the Common Good: Catholic Social Teaching and Environmental Responsibility," in *"And God Saw That It Was Good,"* p. 185.

aware of international interdependence, the potentially worldwide effects of national behaviors, and the needs of distant peoples has provided the impetus within Catholic social thought to expand the scope of human solidarity globally and temporally. Thus, John Paul II, following the lead of John XXIII and Paul VI, speaks of a "universal common good" that entails what Edith Weiss calls "intergenerational equity."[34]

This expansion of the concept of the common good has direct relevance for a Catholic environmental ethic. As John Paul II and the American bishops see it, it is incumbent upon human beings to take account of the ways their use of natural resources affects others, especially the poor, both domestically and internationally.[35] "The ecological crisis," in John Paul II's estimation, "reveals the urgent moral need for a new solidarity, especially in relations between the developing nations and those that are highly industrialized."[36] Developed nations must desist from those practices that directly or indirectly damage the land of developing countries to which they should extend financial and technical support to establish just and environmentally sustainable economies. In this connection John Paul II insists:

34. Though I will not discuss this at length here, John Paul II has clearly expanded the notion of the common good to include a concern for future generations (see, for example, John Paul II, "The Ecological Crisis: A Common Responsibility," §2, and "Ecological Conversion," General Audience Address, January 17, 2001, §4). A philosophical analysis of the concept of "intergenerational equity" usefully supplements John Paul II's remarks. In Edith Weiss's thoughtful discussion, she employs a notion of human community that dovetails well with Catholic social thought: "To define intergenerational equity, it is useful to view the human community as a partnership among all generations. In describing a state as a partnership, Edmund Burke observed that 'as the ends of such a partnership cannot be obtained in many generations, it becomes a partnership not only between those who are living but between those who are living, those who are dead, and those who are to be born.'" Thus, she insists, "The purpose of human society must be to realize and protect the welfare and well-being of every generation. This requires sustaining the life-support systems of the planet, the ecological processes and the environmental conditions necessary for a healthy and decent human environment." In short, "Intergenerational equity calls for equality among generations in the sense that each generation is entitled to inherit a robust planet that on balance is at least as good as that of previous generations." Edith Brown Weiss, *In Fairness to Future Generations: International Law, Common Patrimony, and Intergenerational Equity* (Dobbs Ferry, N.Y.: Transnational Publishers, 1989), pp. 199-200.

35. Degradation of the environment is almost always an offense against the poor. The rich consume the most resources (and consequently produce the most waste), and yet the rich rarely live near their own waste sites. As my Pepperdine University colleague, Robert Williams, wryly suggested, "The rich drive enormous SUVs and live in places like Malibu where ocean breezes push smog inland. The poor drive Geo Metros and Ford Escorts and live in those less desirable inland basins where smog collects."

36. Cited in U.S. Bishops, "Renewing the Earth," p. 7.

It must also be said that the proper ecological balance will not be found without *directly addressing the structural forms of poverty* that exist throughout the world. Rural poverty and unjust land distribution in many countries, for example, have led to subsistence farming and to the exhaustion of the soil. Once their land yields no more, many farmers move on to clear new land, thus accelerating uncontrolled deforestation, or they settle in urban centers which lack the infrastructure to receive them. Likewise, some heavily indebted countries are destroying their natural heritage, at the price of irreparable ecological imbalances, in order to develop new products for export. In the face of such situations it would be wrong to assign the responsibility to the poor alone for the negative environmental consequences of their actions. Rather, the poor, to whom the earth is entrusted no less than to others, must be enabled to find a way out of their poverty.[37]

Thus, in the language of Paul VI's *On the Development of Peoples (Populorum Progressio)* and John Paul II's *On Social Concern (Sollicitudo Rei Socialis)*, wealthy countries must advance the "authentic development" of poorer ones.[38] But the authentic development of poorer nations will not mimic the consumerist excesses or "superdevelopment" of the West and the environmental destruction it has incurred; rather, authentic development seeks sufficiency, that is, the securing of sufficient resources to live with dignity. Importantly, while these encyclicals affirm the right of peoples to social conditions that promote human development, they also warn against a narrowly economic calculus of value, arguing instead for a holistic conception of human flourishing — one that incorporates a variety of goods, including spiritual ones, beyond material acquisitions. Thus, in promoting the universal common good, the church is not suggesting that the lifestyle of advanced Western capitalist nations is the standard by which the achievement of the universal common good should be measured.[39]

---

37. John Paul II, "The Ecological Crisis," §11.

38. Christiansen, "Ecology," p. 185.

39. As Drew Christiansen has noted, the universal common good includes the basic conditions for social life. "A primary component, of course, would be the global commons: the air, water, and soil resources together with migratory stocks of fish and birds, which use vast ranges in their yearly life pattern or over an entire life-cycle. Likewise, the safe disposal of products, such as nuclear and toxic waste, which take collective action to secure, would be part of the common good" ("Ecology," p. 190).

Subsidiarity

But who is responsible for the universal common good, especially with reference to the environment? This is a difficult question, since the tradition of Catholic social thought has not reckoned with the new political-structural implications of globalization. Traditionally, Catholic social thought has charged the state, or political authority, with the task of willing the common good materially. According to Yves Simon, this means that political authority ("a public reason and a public will")[40] actually determines the requirements of the common good, communicates these requirements to the community, enforces them, and coordinates the activities of functional groupings and persons so as to effect the common good. Importantly, it should enjoy this distinctive area of competence without violating the autonomy of individuals or groups.[41] Simon is well aware, however, that in practice political actors often overreach the legitimate bounds of their office and impinge on the freedom of citizens. The state, civil society, and individuals should, in other words, relate according to the principle of

40. Yves R. Simon, *Philosophy of Democratic Government* (Notre Dame, Ind.: University of Notre Dame Press, 1993), p. 48. Simon illustrates his definition with an example. An army officer has been ordered to hold a certain position. This is the particular good entrusted to him. If he is a good officer, he wills the common good formally, that is to say, he desires the common good (in this case victory for the whole army) and stands ready to abide its requirements. He does not, however, will the common good materially. He is not in charge of the overall strategy of the campaign; he is not coordinating the various functional units involved in the war effort. He contributes to the common good precisely by attending to the particular good. His general, however, wills the common good formally and materially. Not only does he desire victory for the army and stand ready to abide its requirements, he actually determines the requirements of victory, informs his subordinates of their duties in light of the requirements, and coordinates the common action of all the functional units toward their common end.

41. Simon, *Philosophy of Democratic Government*, p. 71. Simon's subtle analysis of the different functions of political authority is relevant here. In brief, he argues that political authority in its most essential function, viz., willing the common good, arises not from deficiency but from plenitude; when there are plural means to achieve a common end, authority must choose the means. Insofar as political authority exercises this essential function, it in no way impinges upon the autonomy of individuals or groups. Indeed, Simon notes that according to Saint Thomas's speculations, this kind of authority would have been exercised in man's prelapsarian condition. Yet, in the fallen world there exist a multitude of deficiencies, which it is the proper function of political authority to correct; hence it exercises a paternal or substitutional function when it makes decisions for agents who cannot act well for themselves (e.g., criminals). Its use of coercion as an instrument is, Simon contends, accidental to its essential function, however necessary it might be outside of Eden.

subsidiarity. Pius XI accents the negative side of the principle, as he warns: "Just as it is gravely wrong to take from individuals what they can accomplish by their own initiative and industry and give it to the community, so also it is an injustice and at the same time a grave evil and disturbance of right order to assign to a greater and higher association what lesser and subordinate organizations can do. For every social activity ought of its very nature to furnish help to the members of the body social and never destroy and absorb them."[42] Simon accents the positive side of the principle, as he explains that it is good that the subjects in a community — whether individuals, families, townships, cities, or states within a nation — enjoy independence in attending to particular goods. Even if they perform the same function, it is better that the function be exercised by a multitude of self-ruling agents than by mere instruments of a centralized power (e.g., although all parents in a neighborhood exercise the same function, namely, child rearing, it is good that parents exercise autonomy in intending the particular good of their child, exhibiting particularly intense feelings and concern for his welfare). The differentiation of subjects invites plenitude, activity, initiative, and difference. Thus, the principle of subsidiarity for Simon entails that "whenever the welfare of a community requires a common action, the unity of that common action must be assured by the higher organs of that community," but at the same time, "wherever a task can be satisfactorily achieved by the initiative of the individual or that of small social units, the fulfillment of that task must be left to the initiative of the individual or to that of small social units."[43] Only in this way will the intellectual and moral capacities of such persons or groups develop most fully. Political authority, then, in its most basic function, does not impinge upon autonomy rightly understood, for it does not substitute for the judgment and decision of its citizens in areas within their competence.

How does this relate to the environmental question? This area needs development in Catholic social thought, but certain basic elements are already in place. As John Paul II and the U.S. bishops have expressed it, ac-

---

42. Pius XI, *On Reconstruction of the Social Order (Quadragesimo Anno)*, §79, quoted in *Political Order and the Plural Structure of Society*, pp. 166-67.

43. Yves Simon, *Nature and Functions of Authority* (Milwaukee: Marquette University Press, 1940), p. 47. In this connection Simon approvingly cites Leo XIII's *On the Condition of Labor (Rerum Novarum)*, which declared, "Let the State watch over these societies of citizens united together in the exercise of their right; but let it not thrust itself into their peculiar concerns and their organization, for things move and live by the soul within them, and they may be killed by the grasp of a hand from without" (Simon, *Philosophy of Democratic Government*, p. 130 n. 23).

cording to the principle of subsidiarity, every level of society has a role to play in environmental stewardship. For instance, John Paul II has stressed the need for a new education in ecological responsibility. From the state to the churches to the family, we must cultivate a new respect for — indeed a love of — nature that corresponds to a profound respect for human life. Beyond education he urges action — conservation by the individual, family, and nation.[44] And, since the effects of environmental degradation are transnational, the work of international bodies is essential to ensure the ecological common good. In John Paul II's words, we must have "a more internationally coordinated approach to the management of the earth's goods."[45]

This reveals the limits in Catholic social thought. It does not offer a developed account of the way such international bodies would act and what kind of authority they would exercise. They would not exercise the kind of authority traditionally given to the state in Catholic political thought, since this is a comprehensive authority for those under its care, but no such international body exists. Those international organizations that do exist, even among nation-states, exist by virtue of the voluntary agreement of members and have very limited authority, let alone effective sanction mechanisms. Absent an international political authority to superintend the common good, much environmental work will have to be done within the traditional nation-state structure, but it can be done with a vision that is international in scope. For instance, while sovereign states cannot be coerced to ratify an environmental treaty (such as Kyoto), groups within nations can promote the adoption of such a treaty using the ordinary political means at their disposal. Appealing to the principle of subsidiarity, it should be noted that, depending on the scale of the problem, much could be done at the national, state, and local levels in both the public and private sectors. Likewise, transnational nongovernmental organizations and institutions, like the church, have a unique opportunity to promote multilateral approaches to environmental health, which, given its nature, transcends juridical boundaries. As Marian Chertow and Daniel Esty have noted, a successful environmental strategy for the new century will entail "inclusive

44. "Not only should each state join with others in implementing internationally accepted standards, but it should also make or facilitate necessary socio-economic adjustments within its own borders, giving special attention to the most vulnerable sectors of society. The state should also actively endeavor within its own territory to prevent destruction of the atmosphere and biosphere, by carefully monitoring, among other things, the impact of new technological or scientific advances" (John Paul II, "The Ecological Crisis," p. 9).

45. John Paul II, "The Ecological Crisis," p. 9.

environmental decisionmaking"[46] among a variety of actors, including federal, state, and local officials, industrial organizations, environmental groups, civic associations, and individual citizens in public advisory groups. The combined work of such actors, coupled with the efforts of international bodies, has the potential to yield significant environmental improvement regionally and globally — a sine qua non of the universal common good.

Spiritual Life

The structural issues attending globalization extend our traditional understanding of concepts like subsidiarity and solidarity and point to the difficulty of achieving a truly universal common good. With respect to the focus of this essay, environmental responsibility, contributing to the universal common good through the means we already have, will be arduous. At the very least, as John Paul II and the American bishops have argued, it will require self-sacrifice by families, communities, parishes, and corporations, as well as by individuals and nations. From resisting instant gratification to developing "green" business practices to forgiving national debts, living humanely and ecologically will be painful. But it is imperative. As John Paul II insists: "The seriousness of the ecological issue lays bare the depth of man's moral crisis. If an appreciation of the value of the human person and of human life is lacking, we will also lose interest in others and in the earth itself. Simplicity, moderation and discipline, as well as a spirit of sacrifice, must become a part of everyday life, lest all suffer the negative consequences of the careless habits of a few."[47] To honor Catholic social teaching's principle of "the universal destination of goods," the wealthier inhabitants of the globe will have to sacrifice for the poorer, giving not just from their surplus but also from their substance.[48] "In the long term, this will demand readjustment and sacrifice on the part of the North, so that the global majority can enjoy a degree of development consistent with their human dignity and the sustainability of the ecosphere."[49] But this will not come easily. To em-

---

46. Marian R. Chertow and Daniel C. Esty, eds., *Thinking Ecologically: The Next Generation of Environmental Policy* (New Haven: Yale University Press, 1997), p. 234.

47. John Paul II, "The Ecological Crisis," p. 13.

48. See *Pastoral Constitution on the Church in the Modern World (Gaudium et Spes)*, §69; *On the Development of Peoples (Populorum Progressio)*, §47.

49. Christiansen, "Ecology," p. 188.

brace simplicity, moderation, discipline, and self-sacrifice, especially in a materialistic culture, requires conversion.

Here the church's resources are indispensable. Quite simply, it provides the spiritual wisdom and practices that foster the kind of character necessary to heed — and embrace — the conservation mandate. In Aldo Leopold's words, later echoed by John Paul II, the church can shape an "ecological conscience." Its proclamation of scriptural texts relating to the goodness of creation and human stewardship, for instance, reminds us that the earth and human life are gifts, not possessions. When the church at the Easter Vigil recalls the creation account in Genesis and when she prays the Psalms in the Liturgy of the Hours — "The earth is the LORD's and all that is in it" (Ps. 24) and "O LORD, how manifold are your works! / In wisdom you have made them all; / the earth is full of your creatures" (Ps. 104) — she reinforces fundamental presuppositions of environmental responsibility: the natural world is God's and it is good. As Hugh Feiss, O.S.B., describes, "We are pilgrims, guests, and workers in his world, not owners."[50] An attitude of faith fosters wonder and gratitude, which in turn inspire us along the way of discipleship.

Among the practices of discipleship is prayer. And the church's practice of contemplative prayer inspired by nature, fostered in the Franciscan tradition especially, elevates the spirit and encourages recognition of the connection between the immanent beauty of creation and the transcendent glory of the Creator. The ancient Christian teachings on the virtues, given systematic formulation by Aquinas, have direct practical bearing upon ecology. As a moral guide, the church habituates its members in the virtues of discipleship, including simplicity, temperance, and generosity — three virtues critical to environmental justice. Just as the church fosters these virtues, it also offers us the sacrament of reconciliation when we have failed to live them. Thus, it not only offers a theory of virtue relevant to ecology, it also provides the means for developing ecological virtues. Finally, the church's liturgical life reflects a "cosmic context," that is, the deep interconnectedness between human beings and the whole of creation: "The determination of times for celebration of the daily liturgy of the hours, the seasons of the church year, and some feast days derive from the rhythm of the cosmos."[51]

---

50. Hugh Feiss, O.S.B., "Watch the Crows: Environmental Responsibility and the Benedictine Tradition," in *"And God Saw That It Was Good,"* p. 149.

51. Kevin W. Irwin, "The Sacramentality of Creation and the Role of Creation in Liturgy and the Sacraments," in *Preserving the Creation: Environmental Theology and Ethics,* ed. Kevin W. Irwin and Edmund D. Pellegrino (Washington, D.C.: Georgetown University Press, 1994), p. 74.

Indeed, one of the purposes of liturgy and sacraments is "to give voice and expression to the inarticulate but real praise of God in creation."[52] Fittingly, then, the church makes use of the natural world in its most sacred acts. One of the constitutive elements of baptism, the sacrament of initiation into the body of Christ, is water. According to the church's rubrics, the water used in the sacrament should be pure and clean, symbolizing the purification of baptism. Pure and clean water, of course, depends upon a healthy ecosystem. Similarly, the church's central act of worship, the Eucharist, sublimely relates heaven and earth, reminding us of their intimate connection: the bread "which earth has given and human hands have made" and the wine, "fruit of the vine and work of human hands," become the very stuff of a miracle and a vehicle of grace. Productive crops and vineyards depend upon a healthy ecosystem, too.

The use of the goods of creation — water, oil, grains, and fruit — in the sacramental life of the church reveals "a harmony between creation theology and the paschal mystery."[53] We depend upon the good things of the earth for our highest praise of and most intimate communion with God; if creation is imperiled, "the very act of liturgy is imperiled."[54] One can hardly imagine a more powerful testimony to the interdependence of humanity — body, soul, and spirit — and nature.

Concurrent Readings

Berry, Wendell. *The Unsettling of America: Culture and Agriculture.* 3rd ed. Sierra Club Books, 1996. Though not written from a Catholic point of view, this work offers a profound reflection on the tight connection between culture and agriculture that complements a Catholic environmental ethic. Appealing to biblical, literary, and philosophical resources, Berry argues persuasively that the mechanistic presuppositions behind contemporary agricultural practices inevitably shape the way human beings treat each other. The technological reductionism at work in how we treat the land, he insists, manifests itself in how we treat one another. To remedy the problem of human injustice and the breakdown of communities will entail a profound reordering of our treatment of the land upon which we depend.

52. Irwin, "The Sacramentality of Creation," p. 74.
53. Irwin, "The Sacramentality of Creation," p. 86.
54. Irwin, "The Sacramentality of Creation," p. 87.

Christiansen, Drew, S.J., and Walter Grazer, eds. *"And God Saw That It Was Good": Catholic Theology and the Environment.* Washington, D.C.: United States Catholic Conference, 1996. The fruit of a consultation on the environment among American bishops and Catholic theologians and ethicists, this volume is a direct response to the challenge to develop a comprehensive Catholic environmental ethic posed by the U.S. Bishops' 1991 pastoral statement "Renewing the Earth." The volume includes essays from various theological fields, including systematic, sacramental, and moral theology, that draw upon an array of resources from the Catholic tradition in an attempt to provide the framework for a Catholic environmental ethic. An appendix includes a helpful selection of papal and episcopal primary sources on the question, including the pastoral statements of six national bishops conferences.

DeWitt, Calvin. *The Environment and the Christian.* Grand Rapids: Baker, 1991. In this work, written from a Protestant perspective, DeWitt provides helpful biblical references, especially from the New Testament, that illuminate the environmental crisis as to a considerable extent a result of sin. Failing to heed God's call to be good stewards of his creation and caretakers of one another, man has exploited both his fellows and the natural world as if both were his own possessions. The land itself bears the scars of human sinfulness. DeWitt insists that this situation is remediable, however, with the help of grace made possible through the redemptive work of Christ, the effects of which are not only felt in the human community, but also in the creation.

Graham, Mark E. *Sustainable Agriculture: A Christian Ethic of Gratitude.* Cleveland: Pilgrim Press, 2005. Graham examines the environmental, theological, and moral implications of what he considers the deeply flawed system of American agriculture. He then provides an alternative vision of the cultivation, production, and distribution of food rooted in Catholic theology and focused especially on the virtue of gratitude as fundamental to the proper reception of creation as a gift.

Irwin, Kevin W., and Edmund D. Pellegrino, eds. *Preserving the Creation: Environmental Theology and Ethics.* Washington, D.C.: Georgetown University Press, 1994. This collection of essays attempts to contribute to the development of a distinctively Catholic environmental ethics by appealing to distinctive sources within the Roman Catholic theological tradition, including its theology of creation, sacramental and moral theology, and social ethics.

John Paul II. "The Ecological Conversion." General Audience Address. January 17, 2001. One of John Paul II's more pastoral messages on the environment, this address observes that the environmental problems that are behaviorally induced are not mere technical problems solvable by a technological rationality; rather, they are symptoms of a moral and spiritual crisis that stems from a lack of respect for God's creation, for the material requirements of justice, especially for the poor, and a loss of a contemplative regard for the natural world. An adequate environmental ethics thus requires a spiritual and moral conversion at its center.

John Paul II. "The Ecological Crisis: A Common Responsibility." Message for World Day of Peace, no. 6. January 1, 1990. In this papal message John Paul II accents the transnational character of the environmental crisis, noting that it transcends juridical borders and requires international cooperation; the harmful practices of one region often impair the ecological health of another. He urges developed countries to cultivate a new solidarity with lesser developed ones that are often disproportionately affected by the shortsighted industrial policies of the former.

John Paul II. *Evangelium Vitae.* 1995. Section 42. While environmental concerns are not foremost in this papal encyclical, John Paul II does link a proper respect for and stewardship of God's gift of the natural world with a profound reverence for the gift of human life. Both are required by a comprehensive culture of life.

John Paul II and the Ecumenical Patriarch Bartholomew I. "Joint Statement on the Environment." Statement from the Fourth Symposium on Religion, Science and the Environment. Rome-Venice, June 10, 2002. A unique ecumenical effort, this statement bears the mark of the rich theological traditions of the Roman Catholic and Eastern Orthodox Churches. After calling the reader's attention to the grievous suffering of the poor, Pope John Paul II and Patriarch Bartholomew observe that all of humanity suffers from the degradation of the world's natural resources. They condemn the reckless exploitation of nature as a manifestation of the primordial sin of disobedience. As pride and greed motivate the sinful aspiration to a limitless technological mastery of nature, the pope and patriarch urge the faithful to live counterculturally, to practice humility, justice, solidarity, and prayerful discernment with respect to good environmental stewardship.

Northcott, Michael. *The Environment and Christian Ethics.* Cambridge: Cambridge University Press, 1996. This introductory treatment of Christianity and ecology draws upon biblical themes as well as a variety of Christian traditions in demonstrating that Christianity, unlike secular frameworks such as utilitarianism, "deep ecology," and animal rights theories, has distinctively valuable resources to apply to the environmental question. Christianity, Northcott contends, has the most solid foundation for affirming the objective and intrinsic value of the natural world, since it is God's handiwork and since Christ's redemptive purposes include all of creation.

U.S. Conference of Catholic Bishops. "Renewing the Earth: An Invitation to Reflection and Action on the Environment in Light of Catholic Social Teaching." Washington, D.C.: U.S. Conference of Catholic Bishops, 1991. This pastoral statement of the U.S. bishops interprets the empirical data of environmental degradation through a theological lens, stressing the religious mandate to be good stewards of God's creation and to promote just conditions of life for every human community. The document underscores the disproportionate suffering of the poor from the ill effects of environmental decay and urges Catholics to work toward the alleviation of this suffering as well as its underlying causes. Accenting the interdependence between "natural ecology and social ecology," the statement highlights the environmental dimension of the universal common good recognized in Catholic social thought.

Conclusion to Part 3

Immigration, consumer culture, homeschooling, war and peace, bioethics, the environment — these are but a few of the issues we could have included in a volume like this. Our treatment of contemporary issues is hardly comprehensive, but it is a beginning. Readers can take the chapters as models from which to consider any of the myriad of other issues that daily vie for our attention through the media or through our lives. How might we approach questions like the minimum wage, economic sanctions against "rogue" nations, stem cell research, or international economic policies?

We hope that through the chapters offered here, readers will begin to think differently about "the issues" traditionally treated in ethics and moral theology. We hope, on the one hand, that we have provided adequate "tools" for approaching standard questions, tools rooted in the richness of the Catholic tradition. Equally, we hope that these chapters complicate how readers will, going forward, approach standard questions. We hope we have demonstrated that some of the most important "issues" are those rarely addressed (e.g., "consumer culture" itself). We hope we have shown how problematical the usual categories and divisions are that make so many discussions predictable, intractable, and unfruitful. The point of these analyses is not simply to gain insights and perspective on issues. It is learn how to think theologically and to live the gospel.

Epilogue

Four Challenges

Michael Sherwin, O.P., in an essay titled "Four Challenges for Moral Theology in the New Century," outlines four objectives for contemporary moral theology.[1] The first is "to reintegrate moral theology back into the whole of theology" (p. 18). The second is to attend to a philosophy of nature, so that we can advance our "theological reflection on the effect of God's love on human nature" (p. 22). Third, Sherwin presents "the challenge to renew our understanding of the human person's growth in relationship with Christ" (p. 22). To meet this challenge, he proposes that we investigate the role of the infused cardinal virtues in enlivening our desire to acquire dispositions and habits of life that are directed to human fulfillment. Finally, he asks moral theologians to give deep consideration to their vocation as moral theologians, especially in relationship to the church.

Sherwin's four challenges offer an interesting way for us to reflect on our work in *Gathered for the Journey*. His first challenge is an explicit concern throughout the book. The first part of the volume deals with topics not usually covered in a text on moral theology, at least not covered in such detail. We hope that part 1 helps integrate moral theology into Christology, ecclesiology and considerations of Scripture, and worship. Sherwin's third challenge also has been taken up directly. We have attempted to give a rich account of life in Christ while keeping the basic struggles of the moral life in view. As Sherwin suggests, we include a chapter on the infused cardinal virtues, and we also take up the difficult problem of the relationship between grace and human

1. Michael S. Sherwin, O.P., "Four Challenges for Moral Theology in the New Century," *Logos* 6, no. 1 (Winter 2003): 13-26. The page numbers in the text refer to this work.

freedom. Our objective has been to give an account of openness to grace as active moral growth.

Sherwin's second challenge has not been considered directly. It fits with the topic, mainly, of the chapters on human fulfillment and natural law. In these chapters we have not engaged philosophers of science; however, our concern has been to create a context from which such a conversation can begin. Throughout the volume we have highlighted one of Sherwin's major concerns in relationship to the philosophy of science and moral philosophy, to show that "it is in and through human nature and from within a particular community and culture that we learn to be free and to acquire a universal concern for others" (p. 22).

In other words, our appeal to theological sources has not tried to transcend the historical and "embodied" character of human reasoning. On the contrary, our account of the Christian sources of moral reasoning has attempted to illuminate how human beings think through basic matters of life — in terms of "ends" and life's purposes and in the context of a tradition of thought and action. We hope our endeavor to understand life in the church will help non-Christians and non-Catholics understand better the connections between their convictions and way of life. Certainly, making these connections has been the task of the volume: to better live the life to which we Christians have been called.

This mention of our call brings us to Sherwin's last challenge: to attend to our vocation as moral theologians. Not all the contributors of the volume are moral theologians; however, there is a common concern among us about living a life of discipleship. As editors, we should take this closing paragraph to thank the contributors. A diverse set of authors has gathered to think and to write about the moral life, and we have been struck by their openness in stating their views, hearing criticisms, revising, and arguing back again. In a real sense, this volume has been an opportunity for thirteen Catholic scholars to recall that we have been gathered for a journey. We look forward to continuing this journey together, and we hope that as we continue, others will join in, helping us to advance the conversation, as we move together toward our common end.

Index

Ambrose, Saint, 302, 304
Aquinas, Saint Thomas: on children, 272; on conscience, 173-74; on creation, 27, 111, 331-32; on Eucharist, 300, 303; on God's relation to human beings, 30, 36, 135-36, 184-85; on human action, 156; on instrumental and secondary causes, 186; on law, 161; on property, 254-55; on sin, 169; on virtue, 177, 196, 207-8, 213
Aristotle, 136, 141, 199
Augustine, Saint: and *City of God*, 234; on desire, 252-53; on the Eucharist, 104, 256; on the love of God, 26-27; on the moral capacity of children, 270; on the ordering of goods, 324

Baptism, 35, 49, 53, 234, 293, 344; and common priesthood, 128-32
Beaudoin, Tom, 247, 250
Bell, Daniel M., 304, 305
Benedict XVI, 36-37, 216, 271
Bernardin, Joseph Cardinal, 317-22
Bible: authority of, 43-44; and ethics, 22, 61-66; and environmental ethics, 344; and forgiveness and reconciliation, 315-17; gathering of God's people in, 91-92, 97, 101, 103; God's call in, 117-18, 121-23; incarnational interpretation of, 44-46, 63-64; and law/

natural law, 154-55, 162-63; modern interpretation of, 63-64; peacemaking and violence in, 287-93; salvation history in, 46-49, 50, 89-96, 101, 103
Bioethics, 223, 307-15, 323-27
Birth control, 233
Bono, 225
Bourg, Florence Caffrey, 262, 274
Budde, Michael, 250

Cahill, Lisa Sowle, 275-76
Calling/vocation: of clergy and religious, 124-28; of discipleship, 121-23; from God, 117-20; of laity, 127-31, to proclaim the gospel, 130
Catherine of Siena, Saint, 28
Catholic Relief Services, 258
Catholic social teaching, 222, 225-39; and ecclesial life, 233-36, 238; and environment, 230-31, 329-45; and Eucharist, 233, 239; and holiness, 235, 335; and liturgical practice, 233, 238-39, 335; and mercy, charity, and grace, 234-35; principles of, 226-31
Charity. *See* Love
Children, 269-70
Christiansen, Drew, 337, 339
Chrysostom, Saint John, 272, 273, 300
Church: as body of Christ, 35-36, 96-99; as called by God, 31; and context of